Dieter Duhm

The Sacred Matrix

From the Matrix of Violence to the Matrix of Life

The Foundation for a New Civilization

About the book:

Is there a possibility left to put a stop to the global violence and to start a globalization of peace?

The answer offered in this book is: Yes, the dream of peace may become true. And that's serious:

Acting on the assumption of the most recent scientific realizations the author develops the concept of a global peace force that initially comes from a few points on earth, Healing Biotopes, and that is able to change the existing system in a future orientated way. „In the field building of evolution it is not the right of the fittest that counts, but the success of the most comprehensive", is one of his assumptions. The transition from the matrix of violence to the Sacred Matrix of peace does not act on the logic of a power struggle, but on a change of program that is possible to conduct in every moment.

Healing Biotopes are self-sufficient future communities, „greenhouses of trust", „acupuncture points of peace". They are centers in which post-capitalist technology is connected with ecology and social know-how. The author has been working with his team on the construction of the first prototype for more than 25 years.

ISBN: 978-3-927266-16-2
© 2007 Verlag Meiga
Printed by Lightning Source Ltd. UK/USA
Cover Design: Jana Mohaupt
Layout: Juliane Paul
Translated from the German: Sten Linnander and Kate Bunney
Original Title: Die Heilige Matrix. Von der Matrix der Gewalt zur Matrix des Lebens. Grundlagen einer neuen Zivilisation.

Translator's note:

Words in square brackets [ ] have been added to clarify certain concepts for the non-German audience. In some instances, I did not have access to the original of quotes from books that originally were written in English. I therefore had to translate these passages back to English from their German translation.

Foreword

A terrible injustice is taking place on earth right now. Many of those who resist it are sitting in torture chambers belonging to the military, police and intelligence services. Right at this moment there are hundreds of thousands of people there who are suffering the most unspeakable pain. And yet they continue. This is the standard that we must apply when speaking of global peace work today. Will the screams of the victims continue to go unheard – or will we create a world where there are no more victims?

Dieter Duhm, Tamera/Portugal, October 2000

Thanksgiving

To all friends and co-workers who persevere until today.

To all lovers who return to love despite deep disappointments.

To those afflicted all over the world who, despite everything, have not lost their humanity.

To the resistance fighters against worldwide injustice, to the incorruptible lone fighters, to the militant animal rights activists, to all who dared until they were broken, to all those who set the law of life higher than the written law.

To all who followed the truth and did not comply with the existing systems.

To all who have fallen in the great liberation struggle – from the revolution in Chile to today.

To women and mothers all around the world who have persevered in spite of fire and torture,

with deep respect and thanks.

The Movement continues.

For our children, for life, for love and for the liberation of all creatures.

Dieter Duhm

Contents

Chapter 4
The Issue of Sexuality

Chapter 5
The Concept of Healing

Chapter 10
Communities of the Future

Chapter 11
Political Theory

Chapter 12
Tamera and the Healing Biotopes Project

Introduction

I am sitting in a small café in Alentejo, the most rural area in Portugal. The Portuguese are conversing loudly at the counter, the waitress is friendly, and dogs are playing outside the open door. One drinks a sweet Bica, the Portuguese form of espresso. A small child is playing in a playpen. Above it the TV is roaring with the sound of machine gun fire, screams, burning houses: a war movie.

What will become of the child? What tracks do these impressions of horror leave in the soul of a small child? Every day TV sends out the information of violence into millions of huts in the most remote corners of the world. This information is reality. What will happen to children all over the world who will soon, in reality, experience what is shown here on TV? What about those who are experiencing it in reality right now, today, at this moment? In Chechnya or in Kosovo, in Sierra Leone or Rwanda, in Algeria or Colombia, in Guatemala or Tibet?

The rage of killing must end. The earth is the scene of a global killing rampage, which will continue to afflict more and more people unless we succeed in building a global power of peace that is stronger than the powers of destruction. It can no longer be accomplished through appeals for peace or through limited reforms. The destruction is carried out in the name of individual groups, banks, corporations, the arms industry, governments, the military, intelligence agencies, lodges, etc, who coordinate the global massacre. But these groups could not impose their will on the rest of the world unless human civilization itself were on the wrong track. Behind the global catastrophe we find a false matrix of life which encompasses us all, more or less. The massacre can only end when we find and realize the right matrix.

This book deals with the discovery of the new matrix and with the possibility of realizing it worldwide. In the course of this research we find certain principles in the structure of reality that enable a transfer from the old matrix of violence to the new matrix of life to take place. The logic of liberation that is thus revealed is convincing for all those who understand it. It follows a model of thinking that today suggests itself through a new combination of historic, scientific, and spiritual insights. The universe is not unambiguous, it is ambiguous. It contains – as a kind of super hologram and cyberspace – not only one, but many possible realities. Which of them are manifested and realized depends on our knowledge, our will, and our commitment. Today, at the end of the patriarchal historical era, we are facing a new type of encompassing revolution. The basic thoughts on which our way of life and culture are based must be exchanged for new ones. It is not a matter of an old-fashioned power struggle, but of redirecting the existing matrix of violence through suitable shifts into the matrix of universal life. This process holistically encompasses the ecological, social, sexual, and spiritual questions of our times and leads to the vision that in this book is described as the "universal state of being."

This book is the result of 25 years of research. 25 years ago I left my middle-class marriage and profession (university teacher) to create a research project in which a new foundation for human co-existence could be developed in theory and practice (see Chapter 6). This project resulted in perspectives that went far beyond the confines of the group and yet kept returning to it. A group of 40 people emerged who stayed together for many years, some up until today. The group is surrounded by a few hundred supporters, who are supporting the further development of the project. We felt that it was necessary to reexamine all questions about human healing and to formulate them not just for us, but for planetary life overall, for we began to understand what it means to be a part of the whole. This led to the development of the concept of healing biotopes, which are at the center of this book. The experiential reports and the theoretical explanations are based on very long and unusual community experiences. Using special methods of "life research" that we developed (Chapter 6), we learned more and more about the basic questions of life and survival of our times. This was basic research without limits, applied first of all to our own lives, then to life overall, and finally to the cooperation with all our fellow creatures in the bio-body of our earth and in the mental-spiritual body of the universe. It resulted in a growing peace project, which today has its center in Tamera in Portugal (see last Chapter). There the "Mirja Peace School" was established, wherein mankind's old knowledge of peace is combined with the insights of our times and developed further.

The book offers answers to many basic questions of our existence, our origins and history, our society, and our personal situations. It deals, for example, with how evil came into the world, the basic trauma in history, the source of our alienation, the roots of sexual fear, the possibilities of healing, our existence beyond birth and death, and the possibilities of creating a future world culture without fear and violence. While searching for valid answers, I had to discard or modify many existing theories and consistently develop others further. I am aware that all answers that are offered here are historical statements and therefore limited. We exist in a state of universal becoming and no insight is definitively finished and static. But the deeper and more essential the thoughts become, the more they approach the energy field of a new type of inexorable revolution and liberation. The vision of a new earth sometimes becomes so concrete that the goal seems to be lying tangible before us. The alienation has become global and all-encompassing, but the wall that separates us from the matrix of life and that has been constructed throughout history, has become thinner. It is as if we are standing right in front of it. Visions, thoughts, and reality all stem from the same source, and this source is obviously very near. The concrete vision and theory that is described in this book could not have been written if it were not already in the process of being realized. There is a deep truth behind Albert Einstein's words: "What can be thought, can also be done." I would like to expand the statement by stating: what can be perceived in terms of a new possible state of being, a new self-image, a new earth, and a new heaven, is in the process of being realized through the fact of its being perceived. The book offers answers to many basic questions of our existence, our origins and history, our society, and our personal situations. It deals, for example, with how evil came into the world, the basic trauma in history, the source of our alienation, the roots of sexual fear, the possibilities of healing, our existence beyond birth and death, and the possibilities of creating a future world culture without fear and violence. While searching for valid answers, I had to discard or modify many existing theories and consistently develop others further. I am aware that all answers that are offered here are historical statements and therefore limited. We exist in a state of universal becoming and no insight is definitively finished and static. But the deeper and more essential the thoughts become, the more they approach the energy field of a new type of inexorable revolution and liberation. The vision of a new earth sometimes becomes so concrete that the goal seems to be lying tangible before us. The alienation has become global and all-encompassing, but the wall that separates us from the matrix of life and that has been constructed throughout history, has become thinner. It is as if we are standing right in front of it. Visions, thoughts, and reality all stem from the same source, and this source is obviously very near. The concrete vision and theory that is described in this book could not have been written if it were not already in the process of being realized. There is a deep truth behind Albert Einstein's

15

words: "What can be thought, can also be done." I would like to expand the statement by stating: what can be perceived in terms of a new possible state of being, a new self-image, a new earth, and a new heaven, is in the process of being realized through the fact of its being perceived.

In certain places the book is very densely written. It is therefore advisable to take frequent breathers while reading it. I have tried to formulate the individual passages so that they can be read and understood by themselves. This made repetitions unavoidable in certain cases. May they contribute to amplify the basic statement that there is a realistic possibility for an overall healing and that the new thought patterns and solution models are available. They are developed step by step and finally summarized in Chapter 11. To the readers, who want to get as quick an overview as possible of the basic statements and goals of this book, I recommend that they read the final Chapter about Tamera and the Mirja School for Peace. Here, the current state of the project that is dealt with in this book is summarized in a concentrated form.

I would like to encourage all those who are seeking a new perspective and who agree with the thoughts in this book to participate in this project. To the young readership I would suggest that you do not spend too much time with the difficult parts that are hard for you to understand. They will become clearer as you continue to read. Read intensely the parts that stimulate and inspire you. Skip the parts that don't interest you so much at first. The book is dependent on my and your high energy and motivation. In established society it will make many enemies because it runs contrary to existing thinking at every corner. Help spread this book so that many people gain the courage to take part in the peace work that is presented here. The world needs your help.

Tamera, September 2000

P.S.: Most quotes in this book are made without precise references. I regret this, but most of my books and manuscripts fell victim to a large fire.

12 Basic Tenets

1. Today we are approaching the greatest revolution since the Neolithic era. It is the transition from the patriarchal era to a new form of human civilization.

2. The global structures of violence and fear, war between the sexes and male dominance, racism and genocide, exploitation of the Third World and exploitation of nature have historical origins and can therefore be changed historically.

3. The personal issues, for which today millions of people see a therapist, have historic origins and therefore require a societal and political answer, in addition to an individual one. .

4. The environmental crisis and the inner crisis are two aspects of the same overall disease. They can only be understood and overcome if they are seen in their totality

5. The love between the sexes has to a great degree been destroyed through the age-old war against Woman and the historical repression of sexuality. A new, non-violent culture is rooted in a new relationship between the sexes.

6. The healing of the love between the sexes is only possible through the re-integration of the human being into the sacred matrix and with the universal sources of his/her existence. Sexuality and spirituality do not exclude each other. They belong together, for they come from the same source.

7. The matriarchal and spiritual origins of human culture were lost through the imperialist expansion of male dominance through church, state, industry, and commerce. We must find them again at a new level to make a non-violent, global culture possible.

8. The human being and nature are originally connected to each other through **one** existence and **one** consciousness. Whenever the human being meets the beings in nature in a new spirit of love and cooperation, they answer with unconditional friendship.

9. For the realization of a new world based on cooperation and love there is a basic matrix, a plan of Creation, which is inherent in all beings. This matrix can be found in the cosmic data bank of our cell tissue. It can therefore be accessed and realized.

10. The new order cannot be established within existing life conditions. What is needed is the establishment of new life systems with sustainable communities that can survive and functioning healing biotopes as "greenhouses of trust".

11. The transition from the matrix of violence to the matrix of life follows a pattern of entelechy, just like the caterpillar transforms into a butterfly or ice turns to water. It does not follow the logic of a fight for power but that of a built-in change of programs.

12. The world is a web of frequencies and information. If the right code for the matrix of life is input, then (like radio waves) it reaches all beings and has an effect on all things. This is the basis for the concept of acting locally and having a global impact.

Chapter 1
A New Direction for Evolution

From the Matrix of Violence to the Matrix of Life

Are you searching for a newer world?
Don't search for it forever. See it.
Perceive it. Evoke it.
Create examples everywhere!

The evolution of violence has reached a boiling point. The existing systems will not last much longer on this basis. The Earth is dominated by a physical energy which leads to uncontrollable explosions and fires. The time is ripe for a mutation; for a transition similar to that of water into steam. The same medium - the same human material, but a completely new world. It is only a question of time. Either collective downfall and global holocaust, or a new global beginning on a new foundation. The blueprint for such a new beginning already exists: the universal matrix of life. We stand at a probably unprecedented historical point. Now everything depends on whether there will be a new concept available for meaningful evolutionary progress in a new direction. Into this historical and global situation we place the project of Healing Biotopes. This project is intended to trigger a change in the direction of global evolution:

- From the matrix of violence to the matrix of life.
- From the destruction of nature to cooperation with nature.
- From separation to reunion with Creation.
- From exploitation to sanctification of the Earth.
- From suppression of sexuality to its liberation.
- From male judgemental Gods to the female sources of life.
- From fear to trust.
- From a private way of life to a communitarian way of life.
- From private community to a planetary community.
- From the neediness of wanting to have, to the abundance of giving and serving.
- From global capitalism to self-organising self-sufficient systems.
- From the war between the genders to solidarity and love between the genders.
- From hard to soft power.

The Earth is dominated by a global chain of fear and violence. If we succeed in breaking this chain at some points and making the change from the old to the new matrix, this will have an effect on the whole chain, as the sacred matrix is always present, hidden behind all the violence, waiting to be accessed. The change does not happen through violence but by means of information, as all life is directed by information. The global code of violence has to be answered with a superior counter-code of peace. With this we have new possibilities for the liberation of the Earth.

The coming change will take place principally in three areas: our relationship to nature and Creation, our relationship to community, and our relationship to love and sexuality. The new information which we need for a non-violent world consists of new experiences and developments in these three areas. In all of these areas, a higher level of cooperation and reunion with the whole is needed. My book "The Sacred Matrix" therefore particularly focusses on these three areas.

The change from the old matrix to the new matrix is a transition to a higher-order system. We will continually meet the concept of higher orders in our deliberations. In all areas, solution of the existing conflicts requires a choice of a new higher-order system. Let us take the personal conflict between couplehood and free sexuality as an example. It cannot be solved on the private level of the individual. To be able to solve it, we must switch to a higher-order system, in this case a (functioning) community. Only in community is it possible to transform the torment of 'either/or' which arises on the individual level, into an organic 'as well as'. Chaos theory, system theory and mathematics give many hints about the transition to higher-order systems. These thoughts are part of a mental-spiritual holo-movement in which we live today, and we can therefore apply them to our issues as they are everywhere true. As a simple and striking example, imagine you receive the following task: Draw a small circle which encloses a very large area. The task seems to be absurd, as it cannot be solved in two dimensions. The solution is simple, however, if one enters the third dimension. We could form the large area which is meant to fit into the the circle, into a sphere! The smallest circle drawn on the surface of a large sphere is the boundary of a large surface. Therefore I could say, if I were an Eastern mystic: your boundaries and the boundaries of the Universe are the same! It is logical that on this level, new possibilities arise naturally. Those who think through this example and understand it fully, gain a clear idea of the kind of re-thinking that is now necessary if we want to change from the existing system structures to new system structures. The often quoted 'paradigm shift' is a leap of dimension; a holo-leap to new levels of our existence. These levels, however, are implicit in the blueprint of the world as an expression of the sacred matrix. It is our task to discover and apply them.

From the matrix of violence to the matrix of life. This formulation contains the statement that violence is not (necessarily) a part of life. The statement is deliberate. I am of course aware of the kind of objection which must immediately come from evolutionary science. Didn't life on Earth, the evolutionary ascent of the animal kingdom, give birth to an immense arsenal of lies, deceit, poison and violence, long before the 'fall' of Man? Two things can be said about this: First, from today's perspective it is difficult to say what the functions of the assumed instruments of death in the animal kingdom actually were. The second and main argument is that even if this all existed and still exists, there is no reason for things to remain as they are. The development of life follows, as we will see, certain basic information, encoded in the molecular chains of the genetic code and in the interconnections of the central nervous system. But this information is never final. Which powers of life which are accessed, whether violent or peaceful, depends on how the information is combined. Once we succeed in building peace-information which incorporates and unites the essential forces of life in a way that is free of contradiction, there will be no more reason for violence. Lies, deceit and violence will dissolve automatically when they no longer confer an evolutionary advantage. The peaceworkers of our time who have an overview of the historical situation therefore face the task of creating an overall information of life which forever erases the matrix of violence. This issue is solvable.

The Sacred Matrix

And forever the sacred stream flows forth
in subterranean darkness.
Sometimes its music sparkles from its depths.
He who hears it senses that a secret is near,
he sees it flee, and wants to grasp it,
he burns with a longing for home,
for he senses Beauty.

    Hermann Hesse

The Sacred Matrix is the matrix of life itself. It is present in the blossoming of a tree, in the scent of a flower, in the chirping of a bird, in the wallowing of a pig, and in the blowing of the wind. It is present in the depths of the oceans, in the folds of the mountains, in the river valleys, and on the mountaintops of eternal silence. It creates the structure of a crystal, a shell, or a dripstone cave. It brings forth the germination of grain, the division of cells, and the play of the galaxies. It sometimes peers out, pure and clear, through the eyes of a baby. Sometimes – in the most beautiful moments of love – it reaches our heart. It is then that we are transformed for a brief eternity and we know the goal of our journey.

We humans have a fine sense for the Sacred Matrix, and we feel it in many things. We let ourselves be touched by it in quiet spots, and we seek out certain places to be close to it. There are special sounds in the winds of the soul that touch us when we revisit the places of our childhood, when we sit at the shore of a lake that is as smooth as glass, when we watch the swells of the ocean as the sun is setting, or when we see the dewdrops sparkling in the morning. Here, very little has changed over the generations. People still climb to solitary heights to watch the sun rise from a mountain ledge, and they still look up at the stars at night and connect with eternity. It is in the connection itself that the sacred is revealed. People visit churches, breathe the sacred air, hear the tones of the organs, and enter into resonance with the Sacred Matrix.

Already as a child I sniffed at the apple blossoms and tried to find out what kind of bliss this scent reminded me of. I experienced the same thing again much later when I worked in an orange plantation in Corsica. There was something deeply familiar about this scent, and something infinitely beautiful. It was like the anticipation of a life that encompasses all of our longings, all fibers of our soul, and all our human desires. My soul knew of this life, and it tried to find it again from within. It tried to recognize it as precisely as possible and, wherever possible, to realize it. Many people have had such experiences, but only a few have had the opportunity to follow them. What is here both hidden and revealed is not only a dream or a yearning. It is a reality, the reality of the Sacred Matrix. We would not have this yearning, hear this sound of the sirens in our soul, or have this irrefutable feeling of a deep memory, if this reality did not exist.

The Sacred Matrix is the original, trans-historical, non-alienated, cosmic, and divine matrix of universal life. According to the plan of Creation for the human being, we are to realize it on earth. It appeared to us when we were children and when the candles were lit on the Christmas tree, it filled us with the bliss of first love, and it sometimes crossed our path at the edge of death. We can never leave it entirely, for we are born of it. We have gone through eons with it, and again and again we have seen it light up at the roadside and the fences of our territory. We met it in the beyond and we reconnected with it, so that we would never forget it again when we returned to Earth. Yet we always forgot it, and we have become so accustomed to forgetting that it now seems only a distant dream to us. But will not this earthly life that we are living here and now, and that seems so absolutely real, one day, when we return to the beyond, also seem like an unreal dream? Has not the game with the many different realities become so familiar to us that we can no longer see dreams as being only dreams? It is not a dream, but a deep, deep memory that wells up inside of us when we touch the Sacred, and this memory keeps re-creating our yearning. For the sake of truth we cannot but find and follow the content of this yearning in its entirety, for the yearning that is recognized and not suppressed or sentimentalized is the signpost that leads us to our sacred home.

What will the Sacred Matrix look like when it has been realized among humans? There are many images, fragments, and partial realizations that come from many different times and cultures. Among them are Minoan Crete, the advanced archaic cultures of pre-history, the era of the temples on Malta and the remains of the original cultures of peace in Australia, Tibet, Africa, and Latin America. It includes the Bishnoi and the Muria in India – especially the Muria with their facility called "Ghotuls", a house for children and youth with free, self-determined sexuality. Various research also points in this direction: Margaret Mead's possibly biased findings about the indigenous Samoan and Mountain Arapesh peoples, the reports by Jean Liedloff about the Yequana Indians in the jungle of Venezuela,

24

and the stories by Dhyani Ywahoo about her people, the Tsalagi Indians. Maybe it included the Queen of Sheba and the equally legendary empire of the Hyperboreans, supposedly spanning from Finland to Greenland (with the capital Thule) during the second millennium B.C. Tradition speaks of a "golden age", and today we can assume that it truly did exist.

The Sacred Matrix has already been realized on earth. We must find it again, but not by putting this mosaic back together stone by stone. Instead we must enter into a state of being in which it fulfills us, all by itself, and shows us a vision of future society. It is the state of connectedness; it is the universal state of being. The Sacred Matrix always assembles itself by itself, as soon as our consciousness resonates with the universal frequency. The more often we are in this state, the more we can see, and the more the world can reveal itself to us in the light of the Sacred Matrix. It is the self-revelation of a real possible life that is inherent in the human blueprint.

In this life there are no laws of fear, for there is no fear. There is also no violence, for there is no resistance to overcome. There is also no technology that is based on overcoming resistances, for in the Sacred Matrix we receive the necessary powers through resonance. There is no stealing and no conquering, no unfulfilled hunger, and no consuming needs, for we live on a planet of abundance. There is no humiliation and no cruelty, for we are all beings of the same Spirit and the same life. There are opposites, but no contradictions; there are conflicts, but no wars, there may at times be harshness, but not cruelty. There is no religious disguising or glorification of evil, for evil no longer exists. There are no longer any punishing male gods, but also no female deities such as the Indian Kali, the Greek Artemis or the Babylonian Inanna, wherein the union of good and evil is celebrated. These deities all arose during the patriarchal era, when the Sacred Matrix had long ago been distorted by the greatest mistake in the history of mankind. The icons of the Sacred Matrix, which were created during the prehistoric era, no longer exist or else they remain only as remnants. The deities from that time live latently in the present, waiting for new cooperation and resurrection.

While I am writing all this, the Sacred Matrix is operating like a coordinating program in my cells, as an operator in my thoughts, as a source of my vision. May it transfer to the reader, so that we together can find the passion and the power to bring it onto Earth.

The Matrix of Violence

This morning, August 11, 2000,
10,000 Indonesian soldiers
marched into Western Papua.
Thus begins the genocide
of one of the last indigenous cultures on earth.

The history of the patriarchal era was and is a history of violence: Kosovo and the history of the Balkans – Chechnya and the history of the Caucasus – the fate of the Kurds and the history of Turkey – the history of Greece – Roman history – the history of the Jews - the history of Christianity – the history of Islam – the history of the slave trade – the history of colonization – the history of capitalism – the history of the United States – the history of Africa – the history of Asia. If we take a normal encyclopedia of history, we mainly find the years and the names that are associated with the great conquests, wars, subjugations, expulsions, and annihilations. It is the same everywhere, whether in Troy or Carthage, in Samarkand or Nineveh, Jerusalem or Dresden, Hiroshima or Grosny. Jerusalem was destroyed by the Romans in the year 70 A.D. Do we know what lies behind such a succinct statement? Do we know what unspeakable misery, what horror, what absolute hell such a destruction of a city meant for its citizens? Those who do will soon close the history books again, for they find the same thing on every page, everywhere on earth. This history has been shaped by violence – and that obviously seems quite normal to the historians and to those describing it. What the great violent men of all times have brought about, what Pinochet, Mengistu, Saddam Hussein, or Russian or American intelligence services have done and are still doing today is, under these circumstances, not some kind of degeneration. It is a logical link in the matrix of violence. Those who do not speak up against Suharto or Putin should not curse Hitler. We must understand that the modern business policy of globalization, which is the basis for so-called democratic states and is protected by their governments, can be maintained only through the matrix of violence. The numbers that we read in a stock market report seem to be just as harmless and neutral as those we find in a dictionary of history. The fate of the living beings whose blood created these numbers is similarly horrifying. The numbers are the end product of a chain of actions with many intermediate links. If we follow this chain to its beginning, we find an abyss of brutality and state-sponsored criminality that is so deep we have to close our eyes in order to be able to keep on living. We can no longer say that we did not know about all this. Today, the so-called free market economy, with its globalization strategies, kills more people every day than a Stalin or a Hitler could ever have done. Germany is the third largest supplier of weapons on earth. Its economy would break down if it were no longer to supply every murderous regime with weapons. Helmut Kohl cooperated quite openly with the mass murderers from Beijing and Jakarta. He posed with his friend Suharto for photos in newspapers and on TV. This was the same Suharto who ordered the brutal murder of almost half a million people in East Timor. If we were to use the standards that were applied during the Nuremberg trials after the breakdown of the Third Reich, then many Western statesmen and business leaders would receive a clear death sentence. (This is not because they commit criminal acts, but because, through their policies, they contribute to the destruction of entire populations and peoples in the most destitute parts of the world.) True democrats should today do everything in their power to protect the worldwide victims of the systems that call themselves "democratic". This is not to say that the other systems are any better.

The [German] Greenpeace Magazine (No. 4/00) contained the following piece of news:
"International oil companies are co-responsible for atrocities committed in the Sudan. For companies such as Total, Fina, Elf, Shell, and Agip to be able to produce oil without interference, the Sudanese army has driven people away from their land on a large scale. According to Amnesty International this entailed massacres, rape, and sadistic torture. Among other things, government troops dropped bombs and shot at villages from the air, and people are said to have been nailed to trees. In addition, the soldiers destroyed the harvest and killed animals, so that those afflicted are in danger of dying of hunger. Oil production in Sudan did not get going fully until last summer, when a 1600 km [1000 miles] long pipeline was put into operation, (...) one third of which was built by the German company Mannesmann. Mercenaries from Afghanistan, among other countries, are said to have acted as guards during the construction work. The Sudanese regime is buying weapons with the oil income in order to continue the decades-old civil war against the rebels in the south of the country. And so, on the day when the first oil was to be pumped, a large delivery of Polish tanks arrived in the Sudan."
This piece of news illustrates, in the shortest form possible, the connection between business interests and worldwide cruelty and horror.

We find similar news coming from other areas of crisis on earth, and they can be found almost everywhere. In Sierra Leone we find the war around diamonds connected to – excuse me – the chopped off limbs of school children, in Chechnya we find the oil pipelines, in Australia the uranium, etc. Everywhere we look, we find the same connection between international corporations, national governments, the arms trade, and regional mass murder (sometimes disguised by religion). This is the worldwide practice that lies behind the numbers on the stock market. This practice is protected by the governments of the Western industrialized countries, who must prove their ability to govern by catering to the welfare of their own industry and their own people. This is how worldwide business imperialism, called "globalization", operates today. The system of violence is complete, and within that system there is no political way out. But there is another way out.

In order to fully understand what is meant by the matrix of violence, we must observe our own lives more closely. We will discover to what extent the way we lead our everyday lives in the West is coupled with real worldwide violence. The continuum of violence, which is ruling the planet today, is caused mainly by ourselves, our everyday consumer habits, and our silence. We are living in a state of acute complicity. Violence has been perpetrated to produce everything that we need for our daily lives, such as food, clothing, cosmetics, medicine, technology, automobiles, gasoline, culture, and entertainment. Violence against living beings - against the inhabitants of the forests, meadows, streams and oceans. Violence in animal laboratories, in animal husbandry, and in the slaughter-houses. Violence in the haciendas of the Third World, where we get our coffee, our sugar, our bananas, and much more. Violence against the indigenous farmers whose properties were stolen by the corporations, violence against the workers in countries with low wages who carry out the work of slaves for the profit of our economy. Merciless violence against all those who resist the global injustices and therefore end up in torture chambers. Never has so much torture and never have so many murders been carried out by western and other intelligence agencies as is the case today. Never before did consumerism flourish to the extent that it does today. Millions of people and billions of animals die for our prosperity every year. One glance into a filled refrigerator shows us the results of the world-wide imperialism that we are living within. Nobody could stand to look closely and see what we are actually doing to the animals. Instead of observing the creatures and their suffering, the terminology of profits is used. Hardly anybody has the courage to resist it. The soul's infrastructure hardens when softness can no longer bear to see things the way they are. A kind of collective scar tissue of the soul has enveloped our hearts and minds. The mechanization of life and the focus on the need for consumption and turnover require people to sacrifice their elementary need for contact, trust, love, and community. Elementary longings and life energies can no longer be translated into meaningful action. They break through violently, for example in hooliganism. Or else they eat their way inward resulting in the growing number of people whose lives have become unbearable due to loneliness, despair, and depression. Every 20 minutes a person commits suicide in Germany.

We, ourselves, are participating in this continuum of violence as long as we silently partake in a way of life whose hidden side is so soiled with blood. The fact that we still engage with each other as innocent people, that we try to counter all atrocities only by trying to create an intact private sphere, and that we watch and do nothing while a world goes to pieces is the result of a unique collective repression. The feats of repression of the highly armed consumer societies of our times greatly exceed the feats of repression of the Nazi era. Back then, one could still emigrate or resist. But where should one emigrate to today, and who should one resist? It is difficult to resist something that one is part of oneself. It is also difficult to fight an injustice that is no longer rooted in a single group or in single actions, but in the system as a whole – an injustice that is ultimately a prerequisite for its existence.

I am not describing all this in order to elicit moral nausea, but to show why the creation of a global power of peace is impossible while retaining our current ideas about life. We need a new matrix, a new concept for human culture and society. It will arise in any case, for the current system cannot hold up much longer. The question is only at what level we will then continue. Will a global holocaust throw us back to the level of cave dwellers? Or will we succeed in developing a new, realistic model of non-violent cooperation with all living beings? This concept must become visible at a few places on earth for it to become a field-creating global force. This is the purpose of the **Federation of Healing Biotopes**. The globalization of violence must be countered by a different type of globalization of peace. We need a new development on earth that helps us to fill the words "human being" with a positive content.

A New Plan for Culture on Earth

If all surgeons, all psychoanalysts, and all doctors
were to be taken away from whatever they are doing for a while,
and would congregate in the amphitheater of Epidauros,
where they, calmly and deliberately,
would discuss in detail the urgent needs of mankind,
then the answer would come very quickly,
and in one voice it would say: REVOLUTION!
A world revolution, from the top to the bottom,
in all countries, all classes,
at every level of consciousness.

   Henry Miller (in "The Colossus of Maroussi")

In order to end suffering on earth we need a new foundation for human civilization and a new concept for inhabiting our planet. Wherever we want to settle, we are entering into an already inhabited area, for the soil is full of animals and micro-organisms who have made this their home. They all have the right to be there, for just like us, they are a part of the organism of the whole. We will learn to communicate with them and maybe even to cooperate with them (see Chapter 8). Peace is no longer the renunciation of violence; true peace is the revolution of our entire way of existence. Those who do not like the word "revolution" can replace it with the word "transformation". With this we do not mean escapism from reality, we mean the real transformation of our life conditions.

   The direction for this transformation is clear. It is given, both theoretically and practically, by the unity of all life. We are all – humans, animals, plants, and microorganisms – organs of a large community of life, and we are all aspects of the same existence and the same consciousness. We therefore have a propensity toward cooperation, not toward mutual destruction. In order to understand the new possibilities, we need a new model of reality. The principle of violence must fundamentally and universally be replaced with the principle of cooperation: cooperation with matter, cooperation with nature, cooperation with all co-creatures, and cooperation with the beings and forces of the universe (see Chapter 8).

   Evolution must receive a new direction, for example as outlined in Riane Eisler's book "The Chalice and the Sword". We can no longer use power and violence against others. Instead, we must learn to use power and knowledge to deal with all beings from a place of solidarity. No longer using our power to kill, but to care for and to heal. We have experienced how beings in nature react to us humans if we approach them in a new spirit of love and cooperation. As soon as their initial mistrust has been overcome, they react with thankfulness and unconditional friendship. They positively offer us their services. What we know about dolphins is true for many animals: they seek contact and, if it occurs without fear, they exhibit unrestrained joy at the communication. There is hardly a person who can be as uninhibitedly happy as a young dog or a young pig that has learned to fully trust its contact with humans.

The power of the new peace work comes from being connected with the beings and forces of Creation. The power of universal life is greater than the power of the current destruction. If not, flowers would no longer blossom, birds would sing no more, and lovers would no longer embrace. The peace movement will learn what every natural female healer has always known: that it is divine forces that guide and support us in our work if we open up to them.

The superpower of the Sacred Matrix is constantly present. It is the power that moves the earth, that lets an embryo grow, and lets a blade of grass penetrate through a layer of asphalt. We can learn to connect with this power, understand how it functions, and use it in peace work. We can come to understand how it operates in our lives, in art, in prayer, in love, in sex, in healing, in community, and in the free movement of our bodies.

The coming cultural transformation will occur mainly in three areas: in our relationship to nature and Creation, in our relationship to community, and in our relationship to sensual love. The new overall information that we need for a non-violent earth is composed of new experiences and developments in these three areas. In all three it is a question of attaining a higher level of cooperation and re-connection with the whole. The book therefore focuses especially on these three areas.

A core area in which the power and the joy of life needs to be re-discovered and liberated is the area of love and sexuality. Here, where human evolution has gone wrong in the most drastic way, we find the deepest questions and the need for the most fundamental new beginnings. Could it be that one of the core reasons for our epochal disaster is that our species has never understood how to do what it actually likes to do most: to love – both physically and spiritually? Could it be that the tragedy of many generations consists of their not having been conceived in and born out of love – and that they now pass this original pain on to their fellow creatures? Could it be that Vladimir Putin in Moscow also acted out of such motives when he sent his army against the civilian population in Chechnya? Should one ask him or, for example, the Yugoslav dictator Milošević, the "Mignon question": "What have they done to you, poor child?"

We need a new concept of love, of universal, personal, and sexual love. We need a new freedom and a new order for our sexual relationships, as well as new courage that liberates us from the lies that our culture is based on. We also need an inner understanding about how to attain and retain joy. "It is your spiritual duty to be happy," said the Native American grandfather to his granddaughter Dhyani Ywahoo. Joy is a high value in the cosmic hierarchy. A new world that is worth living in will emerge from joy, not from fear. We are therefore called upon to create both internal and external life spaces where life can flow freely without being blocked by fear and distrust. One could say that we need "greenhouses of trust". This is one of the basic thoughts underlying the "Healing Biotopes" project that is described in such detail in this book. The therapy movement failed because it could not create spaces within our existing world where the results of therapy could gain permanence. What it tried to achieve can only succeed within spaces of trust and cooperation, in the communities and biotopes of the future. A healthy life on earth is connected to a healthy love life of the human being. Here we find the deepest of all revolutions. When there is no longer a secret war going on in love, then we will also have a whole new outer world.

If we leave the existing system, then we leave a sinking ship. The turbo-capitalism of today has obviously decided to self-destruct through the insanity of arming itself to its teeth, the insanity of the stock market, collapsing currencies, self-created natural catastrophes, and emerging civil wars. But we cannot leave the existing system without having developed a constructive concept for the future. If we step out of the system, we must know what we step into. What is the goal of our journey? Millions of people have seen through the deceit underlying the life that existing society expects them to lead. They are no longer prepared to undergo a meaningless education and they are not taken in by the false offers of happiness. Millions of people would have left the system a long time ago, if there had been anything better to enter into. The alternatives that we need today must be able to succeed where so many projects in history failed. They must have a convincing mental-spiritual concept that is clearly superior to the old concept of violence. Up until today, the peace movements have mostly been directed against existing injustices. They know what they are fighting against, but usually they know only vaguely what they are fighting for. What would happen if the fight would end in victory? Would a humane system really emerge? Have the revolutions in history led to more humane systems? Have they given people more beautiful faces, the children a better home, men and women more love, and life more joy? Were the revolutionaries and the peace fighters aware of how deep an inner transformation is needed for a peaceful human being to appear on earth? In Chapter 3, which deals with "the legacy of history", I will briefly describe the history of visionary social utopias. Why could these visions of an ideal human society not be realized? Because the mistake lay not only in the outer conditions, but especially in people's inner structures and ways of thinking. One cannot build a free society out of people who have been formed and shaped under authoritarian circumstances. One cannot create a humane form of free love out of repressed and dammed up sexuality. One cannot establish a non-violent society if the inner impulses of hatred and violence are simply suppressed and left unresolved. A revolution that has not occurred inside cannot succeed on the outside. This is one lesson of history.

The human being is not a random product of evolution on earth. There are no such coincidences in Creation. The human being and the earth belong together, both organically and mentally-spiritually. Together, they constitute a super-organism that in the long run can function only if the elementary powers and laws of life of both are united in harmony. We share the Gaia Hypothesis of a living earth and we take it further. With all its living beings and its landscapes, its metal core and its layers of rocks, its magnetic fields and its atmospheric layers, the earth is a unified, living organism in a unified, living, divine universe. This view does not necessarily have to be connected to the reawakening of old Goddess images. Nor is it a result of a special love of matriarchal mythologies. Nor will one understand very much if one tries to imagine the earth in this sense as an astronomically proportioned woman. Today we have access to entirely different intellectual and spiritual images that help us to understand the life form of unified super-organisms. We need a concept of human civilization that corresponds to the spiritual and biological conditions on earth. We need a new way of living that corresponds to the conditions of the super-organism that we are part of. Healing is no longer therapy; it is stepping over from one way of living to another.

The concept of healing must be taken from therapy into life itself. This is one of the basic thoughts of this entire book. It is not through therapy, and not through special methods and institutions, but through life itself that healing is to occur. Here, "life" means everything that belongs to life: eating and drinking, loving and celebrating, researching and working, ecology, technology, social structures, economy, division of labor, etc. There will not be a serious and believable perspective for healing on earth until we succeed in taking this step and until we have established the first concrete life models that function in this sense. When mankind's social and sexual foundation has been established, and when human energies can again flow in alignment with the Sacred Matrix and can unite with the whole, then entirely new types of solutions for the ecological and technological problems of our time will emerge. We will then find entirely new approaches to such issues as healing the ground water, the atmosphere and the soil, waste water cleaning, recycling, food, energy, information transfer, telecommunications, transportation, etc. During the last thirty years we have seen that life does not improve very much simply through ecology and technology. Human despair has increased and the human issue, for which we now must find a solution, has remained unsolved. The liberation of the foundation of human life not only changes the human being, it also changes the energy systems that surround him/her. For everything is one existence, one consciousness, one web of frequencies, light, and information, appearing in various states of density.

We humans have the intelligence to build computer-guided weapons and space stations. We are about to send tiny submarines through arteries and nano-canons containing information into sick tissue. All this is no longer science fiction. It shows us the great possibilities that arise when will and vision come together at such high levels. It is also a question of will and vision whether or not we will invest the same amount of intelligence and effort in the human area and in finding a new order for our life on earth that no longer collides with the original order of life and of the universe but resonates with it. We have the possibility of stepping out of our hardened cocoon of fear and armoring, choosing the Sacred Matrix for our further existence. This is not a never-ending task, for the Sacred Matrix already exists as a blueprint. We actualize it by seeing it, perceiving it, and accepting it. There is a deep connection between perception and actualization. Interestingly, the English word for this connection is "realize". It is through our perception that latent possibilities are realized or called into existence.

We are cosmic beings, journeying on earth, having access to the know-ledge of the world. We are organs of a living universe, and that is where we get our intelligence and our power from. We should not let this go to our heads, but neither should we identify with the small self-image which for thousands of years has been handed down from generation to generation in a culture of subjugation.

I close this section with words by Marianne Williamson:

We ask ourselves, who am I to be brilliant, gorgeous, talented, and fabulous?
Actually, who are you not to be?
You are a child of God.
There's nothing enlightened about shrinking
so that other people won't feel insecure around you.
We are born to shine, as children do.
We are born to make manifest the glory of God that is within us;
it is not just in some of us - it's in everyone!
And as we let our own light shine,
we unconsciously give other people permission to do the same
As we are liberated from our own fear,
our presence automatically liberates others!

A Different Model of Reality

If we turn to the divine order
all old thought patterns disappear of themselves.
We are then connected to other fields
in the cosmic data bank.

    Almut Kowalski

We need new models of thought in order to understand the world, including its darkest aspects, and in order to be able to take effective action against them. The more we understand, the more we distance ourselves from all dualistic models of thought. An example of such a thought model is the view that over there we have the evil ones, the fascists, the right wing radicals, the politicians, the corporations – and here are we, the positive ones, the peace workers. In reality we live in a continuum, in which each individual element contains everything that is present in the whole. The evil, which is present in our enemies, is present in us too, in a different form, for we are a part of the same continuum. This concept of the continuum – we could also say the whole or the holon – is an essential element of a new world view. It is a source of new possible solutions and answers (see Chapter 2 "Kosovo and Us" and Chapter 11). An example of the concept of the continuum is the fact that I do not end where my skin ends, but that I am connected with everything that exists on earth and in the universe. In this context, the philosophers who deal with holographic research have come up with a simple, hardly understandable, and yet meaningful statement: "The part is the whole". To understand what this might mean one can imagine a balloon with dots on it. Each dot seems to exist on its own, but they are all connected through the large balloon. We are all "dots" on the living body of the world.

Other laws operate in the whole, in the continuum, than in isolated parts. For everything is connected with each other, everything is energy in motion in waves that expand, criss-cross, reconnect, compress, and bring forth new events. Can a tornado be created if I turn a bug on its back and tickle its tummy, as Rolling Thunder is said to have done? Can I gain knowledge about what culture erected a stone circle without having read a history book? Can I communicate with plants or with mice? Can 2000 people change the world? Can a new peace movement change the world? Yes, we can. If we find the right frequency. We can have an entirely different effect in the world if we do not ask what the world **is**, but what it **does**; not what a thing **is**, but what the thing **does**. What we normally regard as the physical characteristics of a thing is in reality its frozen behavior habits that could change immediately if new conditions were to set in. We will see how everything in the world is in a constant state of "doing" and how this "doing" is controlled by information that we are constantly producing. **We can change the world by changing the information that we send into it.**

In addition to the innumerable individual topics, peace work on earth requires a global concept if it is to initiate a global change. There are many groups and committed individuals in all parts of the earth, who are engaged in peace work and healing work. What would happen if they were not fully absorbed by their work, but if they kept one eye focused on participating in an overall concept for mankind? What if the animal rights proponents, the youth groups from Greenpeace, the aid workers in Kosovo or in Guatemala, the representatives of Amnesty International, the resistance movement in Brazil, in Myanmar, or in Turkey, and the native American and Australian representatives of the last peace cultures on earth could see themselves as part of a worldwide peace movement? Is that unrealistic, only because it did not succeed at the large conferences that were held over the past two decades? Coordinating worldwide peace efforts is not a question of external organization and technology, it is a question of developing a concept that not only deals with local events, but also with the overall situation of life on and in our Gaia-Earth. "Nothing is more powerful than an idea, whose time has come" said Victor Hugo. But it has to be realistic. This means that it must correspond to one of the many latent possibilities in the building plan of Creation.

What is realistic? We can choose between two possibilities. Either we follow the example of the "realists" of the German Green Party and call a project realistic when it corresponds to the political and economic ideas of the existing systems – or else we call a project realistic when it corresponds to the needs of the earth, nature, and the laws of life and the universe. Today, there is hardly any connection between these two views. The concept of "reality", as it is used in society today, is too far removed from what reality means in a deeper and more encompassing sense. I will describe this polarity in the section about the "two world processes" (Chapter 7). Our lives, our love relationships, our society, and our entire era are currently foundering because our concept of reality is too small and does not allow for any healing. The generations that are currently controlling events on earth have largely lost their sense of reality. They speak of careers, return on investment, and old age pensions, and they call that reality. Already as a child one could become exasperated at the denseness of parents and teachers. We are not only dealing with the reality of supermarkets and stock market quotes, but of the reality of the encompassing life organism to which the human being as well as his victims belong.

What is reality? We must deal with this question in order to understand the possibilities that we have and to develop effective strategies for global peace in freedom. The issue of reality is also being addressed by "the other side", i.e. by the representatives of power today, and it is being explored at a breathtaking pace.

At the beginning of the 20th century, three great thinkers turned our mathematical and physical world view upside down: Albert Einstein (relativity theory), Nicola Tesla (systems for utilizing cosmic energy) and the mathematician David Hilbert (Hilbert spaces with multiple realities). Based on their equations and theories, many years of secret research resulted in the development of energy systems that led to the most mysterious and spectacular projects ever to be carried out in recent history. A series of American projects were carried out, from the Philadelphia Experiment in 1943 to the Montauk Project in 1983. According to reports by Preston Nichols and Peter Moon, they succeeded in technologically manifesting psi phenomena such as materialization and de-materialization, multiple existences, and space and time travel, all under bizarre circumstances. From 1943 to 1983 the American research projects managed to manipulate a different reality. Ever since these and other experiments were carried out, we can regard the existence of such a reality as scientifically proven. We are constantly surrounded by this "other reality". It exists behind, next to, and above our everyday lives, and it contains the possibility for real transformation. We do not live in a linear world of space and time with unambiguous patterns of cause and effect. Instead, we live in a multiple reality, where there are many realities in addition to the reality we have chosen at each moment. More and more researchers are focusing on the switch from one space of reality to another. This switch can be achieved technically through a change in frequencies and magnetic fields and mentally-spiritually through a "spinning" of consciousness. The theory of "parallel universes" and multiple holograms has become an integral part of our world view. It also underlies the thought that it should be relatively easy to step over from the old matrix of fear and violence to the Sacred Matrix, for this matrix already exists as a latent hologram in the building plan of the human being and of Creation.

Here we are following a new concept of reality, which - in addition to the already mentioned thinkers Einstein, Tesla, and Hilbert - has been prepared by the brilliant work of Walter Russell, Wilhelm Reich, Viktor Schauberger, David Bohm, and others. This revolution is only in its infancy, but already today it is showing us what new thought spaces it will take us into. A corresponding transformation is approaching in the social sciences and the arts, such as psychology, philosophy, theology, and history. We are arriving at an image of the human being that puts our perspectives and possibilities in an exciting new light. Throughout this book I would like to show how we can arrive at a new concept for peace work and healing on the basis of a new world view. This concept applies to the healing of the individual as well as to global healing and peace work.

We also need a deeper sense of the areas of reality that we have relegated to the world of dreams, religion, mythology, the drug culture, psychiatry, and criminology. What is experienced here are parts of our existence that have been split off from our daytime consciousness because they did not fit into the mechanized world of our time. The trimmed, one-dimensional human being is no longer able to undertake anything meaningful against the injustices. He screams, smiles, or suffers. He no longer knows where he is, and he ends up fighting those who are really his friends. We need a new mental-spiritual "flow" that unites us again. We need a new sense of the reality of overall human potential and of the forces that slumber within us. We need to understand and sense the ever-present possibilities that are inherent in Creation, the multiple structure of reality, the possibilities for development on earth, and the reality of a human evolution based on cooperation between all beings. We need to understand and sense how love functions and become aware of the real existence of a grandiose, sacred, limitless world.

What inevitably will bring an intelligent peace movement to success is its deeper connection with a larger view of life. It knows definitively why jealousy is not part of love, why fear is not part of life, and why subjugation is not part of religion. It knows of the projections and the world of movies that still make up our lives and it is able to set them aside. It has learned to differentiate between the matrix of violence and the matrix of universal life. It knows of the possibility of bringing about, in a controlled and conscious manner, a mutational leap in living systems and processes. It knows how to change the whole by undertaking subtle changes in the holographic web of the world. It is also beginning to understand that the universe is a unified living organism, which on its inside operates according to other principles than what conventional physics assumes. The universe is of a mental-spiritual origin, all things are manifestations of mental-spiritual energy, and they can therefore be influenced and changed by mental-spiritual means. This knowledge is the basis for a new type of political theory of global change (Chapter 11).

I have tried to present this encompassing peace knowledge, which could bring the world into a new state of being, in a systematic and easily understandable form. We need this mental-spiritual foundation in order to be able to concentrate our forces. The changeover from the old matrix to the new, however, does not occur at a desk and not at conferences, but in a life practice that especially touches mankind's core areas: the creation of functioning communities, love and sexuality, spirituality, and how we relate to our fellow creatures.

Chapter 2
The Earth's Cry for Help

The Earth's Cry for Help

The earth is a very resilient organism. It has access to great powers of regeneration and self-healing. Nature follows an inner image (entelechy) that reacts to all injuries by immediately activating a healing process, which is based on the feedback principle. Gravel pits are violent intrusions into nature. If a gravel pit is shut down, then it is immediately covered with an – at first sparse, then denser and denser – biotope of healing plants. More and more plants are added until the wound has closed and a new natural biotope has been created. But at some point a limit is reached. When the global strain becomes too much, the earth enters a critical condition that leads to unpredictable reactions. I suspect that, for some time now, we have been living in this condition. The global weather changes and the increasingly frequent natural catastrophes point in this direction.

The biosphere is a wonderful system in which the various parts mutually complement, depend on, and support each other. Nothing exists in isolation. Instead, everything lives in a highly developed fabric of visible and invisible communities. This fantastic interplay of evolution has been described in a very knowledgeable and empathic way by Jürgen Dahl in his book "Der unbegreifliche Garten und seine Verwüstung" ["The Unbelievable Garden and its Destruction"]. The bee and the sage plant together celebrate an incredibly fine way of co-existing. Here, we stand before true revelation. This is how the secrets of Creation operate. This is how cooperation, communication, and community work in nature if left undisturbed. The miracle is revealed at all levels – from the interplay of millions of molecules that constitute a single cell, to the interplay of living creatures in the tropical rain forest or in the world's oceans.

In life there is a desire for contact and communication that is probably inherent in all beings if they are not too fearful. The earth is fine as long as the contact between its living beings is fine. We – a research group of about 50 adults – have been living in Tamera [in Portugal] for a number of years on a 140 hectare (350 acre) property, where we as much as possible follow the principles of a non-violent co-habitation with all creatures. It took two to three years for the animals to get used to our non-violent behavior, and then they themselves began to seek us out. At first it was the cats and the dogs, then the pigs in the neighborhood, then the birds, the toads, and the smaller reptiles. Then – with a clear desire for communication – came the rats and, since last year, the snakes. A member of our group was standing quietly in water when something touched his right leg. It was a water snake, and it coiled itself around his right calf. Shortly thereafter a second water snake came and coiled itself around his left calf. Snakes began to lie around on or in front of our thresholds. One came to a building that was being built and lay in the newly cemented threshold, leaving behind its curved imprint. Once, when a woman lay on the terrace of our bodega, a snake came to her, crawled up onto her shoulder and slithered down her body. Immediately thereafter a cat came to her and lay down right above her crown charka at the top of her head. In a later chapter (Chapter 8) I will write more about unusual contacts with rats. There is a universal quest for communication in the universe, at least in the original plan of Creation.

The staff of Aesculapius, the symbol for medical doctors ever since antiquity, has a snake coiled around it. Snakes are a symbol for healing and wisdom, and of course also sexuality. Sexuality and wisdom used not to be separate concepts. In the biblical myth of Creation there was a snake in the Tree of Knowledge and in Hebrew the same word was used to denote both intercourse and knowledge. When the patriarchal systems began their attack on the female sources of power, they had to specifically curse and destroy the snakes. When the first Irish monks were sent to the island of Reichenau in Lake Constance to establish a monastery there, they were ordered to drive out the snakes from the island. It was with such methods that the human being drove a stake between himself and his fellow creatures. He abandoned the original rules of contact, exchanging them for the laws of violence and fear. Behind his exit from Creation we often find an unresolved aspect of sexuality, which male society wanted to eradicate with any and all means (see chapter 3).

Nature is disrupted in its ecological balance mainly because violence and fear disrupts the cooperation between its creatures. The interactions between the living beings result in the self-regulation of the size and density of a population, the birth rate, and the age of the first offspring. "If the human being does not get involved, a largely self-regulating and in no way violent feedback serves to maintain the size of the population." (Briggs and Peat in "The Development of Chaos".) If an entire species or a population is exterminated, then an organ is missing in the organism of the biosphere; if many species are exterminated, then many organs are missing. Assuming that about 4 billion species live on earth (as estimated by James Lovelock), some biologists see the earth as one enormous, single-celled organism, within which the species cooperate like the molecules in a cell. If this interplay is disturbed, then the feedback mechanisms that regulate the interconnected control circuits can produce chain reactions of false reports. From a certain critical point on, the result is a global breakdown. From this point of view, over-fishing the world's oceans, for example, carries with it an incalculable danger for the cellular structure of the earth.

When the earth's geomantic energy system, energy meridians, ley lines, and tellurian flows are cut off by wide highways or other breaks, then we find stunted growth and diseases in the vegetation. When the earth's water system - above or below earth – is polluted, then poisoning occurs, just as it does in the circulatory system of the blood in a human being. In addition, water is an important carrier of vital information. Information and energy are invisible, non-material systems that regulate the interplay of the beings that make up the biosphere. In Portugal, for example, the cork oak tree is dying out because the original "tribal cohesion", which existed between them, was lost due to erosion, an altered water system, and geomantic disturbances. The natural lines of connection, which consist of water, information, and energy and are supported by certain plants and animals, have been destroyed through human intervention. Today, this process of destruction is financed and promoted by money from the European Community. Planting enormous monocultures of eucalyptus trees and building a gigantic dammed lake (250 square kilometers or 100 square miles) also contributes to the destruction of the last biotopes that have remained intact. These interventions lead to regional weather changes, for they directly disturb the water and energy household of the biosphere. Environmental groups are fighting them in vain. The large-scale damage to the biosphere, which today is carried out and controlled by the centers of power and money, cannot be stopped through protests by small groups of people.

In the vital body of the earth, metals play a role that is so far little known. It is not a coincidence that certain high-grade metals, including uranium, can be found in large amounts in the sacred centers of the old peoples (the Colorado Plateau of the Hopis and Ayer's Rock in Australia, among others). Metals, too, are a form of energy and they have a special meaning in the energy system of the earth. When the human being began to mine tin and copper in the Bronze Age, in order to produce weapons, this was not only a step in the escalation of violence between people, it also constituted a new level of violence against the earth.

In the book "Tempel der Liebe" ["Temple of Love"] by the medially gifted author Sabine Lichtenfels, I see an authentic source of female world knowledge. I quote:

By now they had even forged powerful weapons from the sacred sources of Nammu, from different metals of this earth. This was a serious offence against the sacred laws of Nammu. These earth metals, in which important knowledge was stored, were not created in order to kill; instead they served to uphold the right flow of energies in the earth. One was only allowed to take them if Nammu said so in the dream, for example to make jewelry for the sacred dances during fertility feasts and feasts of love. Robbing the earth of these treasures thus resulted in increased earth catastrophes, which in certain areas destroyed the conditions necessary for the people to survive.

The earth's distress is not simply due to the direct damage to its natural circulatory systems: those of water, matter, information and energy. To an even greater degree it may well consist of the suffering that humans cause each other and their co-creatures. There is a close connection between human catastrophes and natural catastrophes. It is an energy connection, for the same universal life force energy Chi (or Ki, Orgone, Prana, or Mana) flows in humans as well as in nature. The movement of water and the creation of weather, the growth of plants and the communication between living beings are all controlled by the same energy as the emotional, sexual, and social life processes in humans. From a holistic view of life this is self-evident. It was well known in earlier cultures, and then it was increasingly suppressed through the mechanization of science. In our times, then, one of the great pioneers of modern life research, the psychoanalyst and orgone researcher Wilhelm Reich rediscovered these connections and described them in detail in his sexual economy and orgonomy. The suppression of elementary life energies in humans and animals leads to a negative form of energy, which Reich called "dor" (deadly orgone). It can be seen as a certain dulling of the atmosphere and it has a decisive influence on the weather. Inside the human organism the life-creating "PA biones" change into amoeba-like single-cell organisms, from which cancer cells can evolve. The inner processes in humans, as well as the creation of cancer and negative outer processes in the atmosphere are the result of suppressed life energies. That is the viewpoint, that we must open up to, in order to recognize the extent of the danger facing the earth today. The question here is not to what extent Reich's conceptual system can be adopted. To me the validity of his basic statements cannot be doubted. They are so critical of the conditions of our current civilization, that he was put in jail where he died under mysterious circumstances in 1957. He is not the only one whose pioneering discoveries have been suppressed or destroyed by established science. One year later another pioneer of modern life research died. His work could have contributed to restoring the health of the earth if it had not been mocked and suppressed. It was the Austrian Viktor Schauberger. Taken together, the discoveries of Reich and Schauberger constitute a theory of life, which will be become central to the schools of the new age. Based on the thinking of Wilhelm Reich, one can wonder how deserts came into being, for example the Sahara desert. Just ten thousand years ago there was lush vegetation there. Does this not suggest that the emergence of deserts may be connected to especially repressive forms of tribal and sexual practices that led to a collective bio-energetic disturbance in the population? The American Dr. James DeMeo has provided intriguing evidence of such correlations. We know of such connections from our gardens and house plants. Peter Tompkins and Christopher Bird describe them in their book "The Secret Life of Plants" and Cleve Backster, one of the researchers that they cooperated with, writes: "There are seldom sick plants in an active bedroom." It seems that we humans must re-learn to follow our own inner life processes if we want to understand and heal nature and the earth.

Instead, the opposite is occurring. Unlived life is not set free; instead, it is compensated through uninhibited consumerism and through economic, technical, and military measures that promote the global destruction of life on a whole new scale. This is especially true for the development of so-called "iono-weapons" (from "ionosphere"), which not only live up to, but clearly surpass the dimensions of deadly science fiction weapons. One of the projects, with which the earth is to be made controllable and destroyable, is the American HAARP Project in Alaska. With the help of targeted explosions in the ionosphere (the outermost layer of the atmosphere), radiation and frequencies are to be generated, that can cause earthquakes or change brain frequencies. With the help of suitable electromagnetic fields, the same effects can be elicited as with psychiatric drugs. (For further information about the HAARP Project, see the book "Angels Don't Play this Haarp" by Jeanne Manning and Nick Begich) The first stage of the HAARP device is already in operation; it is operating in an inconspicuous forest area in Alaska. It could be contributing to the creation of the constant frequency that we sometimes hear in the ether as a high chirping sound.

In 1979 the British biologist James Lovelock published the Gaia Hypothesis, according to which the entire earth may be a unified organism. He was on the right track of a fact that goes much further. Not only is the earth itself a living organism, it also spins around in a living universe. The universe is alive. Everything in the universe is imbued with Spirit, and everything is an expression of universal life. The earth itself is a living body, an acting living being with a soul and a consciousness of its own. Therefore, in principle, if we choose the right frequency, we can enter into direct communication with her. All beings in the biosphere are expressions of the soul of "Mother Earth" and all have been birthed by her energy, her temperament, and her joy of life. The earth is suffering in a real way from the destruction that humans inflict on it. Sometimes she quakes and shudders, resulting in earthquakes or volcanic eruptions. They are the results of energy movements that she carries out on her surface in order to heal herself or to ease the pain.

We need to fundamentally change our ideas and ways of thinking. We have learned to not think "animistically", i.e. not to project any mental/ spiritual beings into our environment, the way "early primitive cultures" did. We now begin to understand that our entire world – from the pebbles to the galaxies – is filled with a great, universal world soul. We have further learned that we shouldn't think "anthropomorphically"'" i.e. that we should not project life processes that we know from humans, onto other living beings and especially not onto "dead" matter. We now begin to understand that we ourselves are "cosmomorph", i.e. that the same movements of life occur in us in an analogous way as they do in all other things in the universe. We are – just like the oceans, the rocks, the plants, and the animals – a part of a "holo-movement" which encompasses and permeates everything that exists in an infinite ladder of scales and energy levels. We have learned that inorganic matter contains no life and that we can therefore use it for any purpose. We are now beginning to understand that it, too, is a condensed form of universal life and a state of universal energy, and that it takes part in the universal flow of the one life and the one consciousness. There will come a time when future generations cannot understand what their ancestors, i.e. we, today, did to the earth. May a new movement for a free earth see to it that this time comes very soon.

We cannot limit the healing work that lies before us to healing nature or healing the human being. We must unite both areas of healing, for in both cases it is the one life that is wounded: as outside, so within. The ecological outside of nature and the psychological inside of humans are two parts of the same whole. Outer destruction goes hand in hand with inner impoverishment and alienation. Ecological devastation and human devastation are two sides of the same global overall disease and it can only be correctly understood and overcome by being viewed as a whole. If the peace workers of the future become aware of these connections, then they know that they serve the earth when they create peace within themselves. They also know that they serve themselves when they see to it that the living creatures on earth can live and breathe freely again. We give thanks for these insights into the inner connections of a still shining and blessed world.

Kosovo and Us

"I, too, have a war criminal inside of me.

José Monteagudo

"Essentially, you are ALL the reason for the existing conditions
that, for example, awaken a desire in a thief
or that create the seeming necessity to steal.
You all have created the consciousness
that makes a rape possible.
When you see IN YOURSELVES
what has created the crime,
then you will finally begin
to heal the conditions in which it arose.

God (in "Conversations with God" by Neale D. Walsch)

Introductory Remark

Before I address the topic of Kosovo I must state that neither I, nor most people, know what really happened there. We did not know what happened during the Gulf War either. It was not until afterwards that information slowly trickled through, showing the events in an entirely different light than what was shown by our media. Relevant information hardly ever trickles through the news blockade of the large TV channels and the large newspapers. It is just like it was 30 years ago, during the Vietnam War, when it took years before the public learned to what extent they had been deliberately deceived by false reporting about the background and methods of the war of extermination against the Vietnamese people. There are many indications that we were equally deceived in the case of the Gulf War, the first Yugoslav war and the war in Kosovo. During the Vietnam War there was a liberal movement that succeeded in uncovering what was going on. Today, there are only a few courageous reporters and radio stations whose voices can be heard less and less often. In order to illustrate to what extent the truth can differ from public legend, I would like to recommend the (sometimes too one-sided, but very informed) book "Der Moloch" ["The Moloch"] that Karlheinz Deschner wrote about American imperialism.

49

The Continuum

A "holo-movement" of disastrous chain reactions has gripped humanity, ever since it fell from grace. Humanity is no longer connected to its sources and is therefore in a state of turbulence due to an inner short circuit. It is similar to the wave patterns that you can see on the surface of a pond. The turbulence is everywhere, but it is not visible everywhere. At certain points the waves extinguish each other, they balance each other out. There we have the zero points where the surface is calm, and where turbulence exists only latently. Elsewhere, the waves add up and create a visible disturbance. Together they form a continuum, within which both the calm and the disturbance are part of the overall turbulence. The same thing occurs on the surface of humanity – in small ways and large – and within us. Wherever the inner turbulence adds up or multiplies, we have accidents, derailments, emotionally charged acts, catastrophes, and wars. In part, it is triggered individually, but it all stems from the global turbulence that we are all co-creating, as long as we are playing along in the old resonant patterns. Global events, too, are a continuum. They affect all countries and all human beings, for the fabric of life is one unified whole. Perpetrators are a part of the continuum as are their victims, the police as well as the criminals, the good as well as the bad, the rulers as well as the ruled. Love conflicts, whaling, and orgies of violence and genocide are all phases of this continuum. Kosovo was a phase of that continuum.

Outer and Inner Violence

The accidents that occur on earth are eruptions that come from the whole. The whole of today's civilization carries this explosive substance within it. Our entire civilization has been suppressing elementary life impulses for thousands of years, thus causing the eruptions. Since the turbulence is in the whole, it is - latently or openly – also in each of us. We all come from a history where we have learned to suppress not only others but also ourselves. We have learned to take part in the great cultural fight against the elementary forces of life: against the elementary drive to be active, against the elementary sexual drive, and against the elementary drive toward knowledge (curiosity). This worldwide suppression created the explosive mixture that is seething in the belly of every society, waiting for a suitable trigger to break through the outer dykes. We cannot constantly fight the outer eruptions without putting out the smoldering fire within ourselves. We cannot permanently end outer violence as long as we use inner violence against ourselves or direct violent thoughts at others. We cannot create outer peace as long as there is war in our own love relationships. We cannot avoid applying the globally necessary corrections to ourselves. "Revolution without Emancipation is Counterrevolution" was the title of a political manifesto that I wrote almost 30 years ago and which at the time, at the beginning of the so-called "emancipation debate", was discussed in many groups of the New Left. At the time we did not really have an idea of what our own emancipation could look like, and we could therefore not translate the statement into a meaningful life practice. Yet the statement is still true today. In order to help ourselves and others we must find the points within ourselves and within the structure of society where the continuum of violence can be broken. The opposite is also true: We cannot stop our private wars as long as we do not change the structures of the continuum. There is no real self-liberation without political liberation. We need a new concept for our own life, but we also need a new concept for our overall life on our planet.

The Fiery Passion of Destruction and Destroyed Human Substance

Kosovo is only one part of a chain of collective eruptions of violence that are accelerating in frequency. After Kosovo we had East Timor and Chechnya, Iran and Iraq are again involved in an arms race, and they no longer even report on the atrocious civil wars in Africa – the Congo, Kenya, Rwanda, Sierra Leone, etc. Behind these wars, we usually find massive financial and political interests, but the methods and means with which the massacres are carried out are no longer characterized by political strategy, but by a wildfire of destructive passion. The parties involved thereby increasingly lose control. Why did it take so long for NATO to intervene in the first Yugoslav war? Why did so many civilians have to die, especially considering the "infallible" accuracy of American weapons technology? We obviously have turbulence here; something has gone out of control globally and violence has become an independent force of its own. What the Serbs did in Kosovo, what the young Russian soldiers did in Chechnya, what Islamic fundamentalists do in Algeria or in Afghanistan no longer has anything to do with rational political deliberations. The destroyed substance of humans themselves is today getting out of control. The same bloodbaths that have occurred between Albanians and Serbs could also take place between any other groups of people, for example between Prussians and Bavarians, if there were a suitable trigger and if the existing state order did not hold them

51

together. Violence is smoldering behind the façades. The new right-wing radicalism incorporates what latently exists in everyone: an unarticulated and yet deeply understandable cry of revenge, rage, and hatred. The indignation of the democrats against the right wing will have little effect, as long as the "democratic" society itself creates the reasons for the outbreak of violence.

Kosovo: the Result of a World Civilization Gone Wrong

Kosovo: this is no longer the violence of individual people or governments; it is the violence of a false human civilization, which covers the whole earth. Violence is erupting everywhere, where the thin layer of civilization no longer manages to stop it. It will also break out in the countries of the West – and they will try to protect themselves by establishing totalitarian violence. The democratic phase of our society is thus probably nearing its end and the technological methods needed to exert total control are standing ready. Satellite cameras can today photograph every square yard of the earth's surface. We live in an era of real globalization of violence. Our horror at the murder of the Jews perpetrated by the Nazis, the American intervention in Vietnam, the suppression of the Chilean revolution in September 1973 by the CIA and the military junta, the Chinese mass murders of the demonstrators at the "The Gate of Heavenly Peace," in Beijing, and the atrocities of the first Yugoslav war were similar to our horror at Kosovo. The only way to avoid the agony was by closing one's eyes. But in Kosovo the horror and the unspeakable terror came so close that it was difficult to close one's eyes.

The globalization of violence is not originally connected to any political system, culture, or race. It began 5000 years ago with the creation of the advanced male civilizations and reached a first high point through the triumph of Rome, already before Christ. The seed was there in the entire human species since the beginning of the patriarchal revolution about 7000 years ago during the Neolithic Era. It is an historic and spiritual result of the separation of the human being from his/her original sources. Violence is the result of an original separation. Long before the development of modern societies and long before the era of colonialism and imperialism, there were violent rituals, cruel mutilations, and violent tribal practices among many indigenous peoples, who also no longer lived in the original connection with their sources. The fact that the violence could escalate to the degree that we find today has to do with the globalization of capitalistic economic strategies, the globalization of markets, and the globalization of the killer mentality through a glorification of weapons and television. The highly organized weapon-producing corporations produce and disseminate napalm, poison gas, and many other killing agents all over the world. We should not be surprised when they are used, that is what they were produced for. What will Turkey do with 1000 Leopard tanks that our current [German] Social Democratic government will probably soon deliver? They will intensify their genocide of Kurds. And what do Social Democratic voters do, who know this? They vote for the Social Democrats. We live in a society in which the support or use of violence, if perpetrated by the state, no longer results in a collective revolt. The most recent example of this is the way that Western governments and business organizations courted Putin, who ordered the brutal shooting of civilians in Chechnya.

We ourselves are participating in the continuum of violence as long as we silently participate in a societal system that is based on worldwide exploitation. **Kosovo can only stop, when we ourselves put an end to a state of existence that is connected to global violence.**

The Inferno Approaches

The inferno is approaching inexorably. Violence no longer needs any rational reasons to break out at random. The critical threshold is sinking everywhere. A single football game can trigger a wildfire of violence. Every local war that is waged today carries the danger of becoming a growing wildfire that can no longer be controlled. We currently find especially dangerous potential sources of conflict in Palestine, Iraq, and Kashmir. Kosovo was dangerous for the whole of Europe, and the Europeans knew it. We all felt an undercurrent of fear. Milošević's threat to turn Europe into a second Vietnam was intuitively correct. Such wars no longer produce winners and losers, only destroyed villages, destroyed cities, destroyed landscapes, innumerable corpses, gruesome mutilations, and many orphaned children. Is the German Foreign Minister Joschka Fischer aware of this - he who once took to the streets to fight against injustice? Are the masterminds behind the scenes aware of this – all those who still today claim that war is a part of life? They should repeat their assertions while standing in front of all the burned children that today are lying on the battlefields on earth.

There is no longer a military solution to Kosovo, nor to all the violence that will come. Ultimately, there are also no diplomatic or political solutions, for the violence will keep on erupting. For eons now, we have introduced the information of violence into the world. We now need a new concept of life, through which we can gain the power and the wisdom to broadcast encompassing peace information into the ether of the world and create a corresponding network on earth. It no longer makes sense to demonstrate against established violence with peace doves and pacifist slogans. Neither does it makes sense to react to violence with counter-violence. The era of violent revolution has passed. For most people it also makes no sense to suddenly step out of the system, as long as there are no solid perspectives or visions. The right conclusion would be to prepare for this exit and to provide support wherever true alternatives are established. Today we have the knowledge and the expertise needed to create a global alternative, and I hope that I am describing the basic ideas and goals of this enterprise fairly correctly in this book. We need real places on earth, where committed people learn to develop a new planetary way of thinking and where they enter into cooperation with nature and all living creatures. We need places on earth, where our daughters and sons realize what is happening on earth, and where they get the opportunity to choose their profession not in the service of global destruction, but in the service of global peace work.

I, too, Carry a Yugoslav War within Me

I would like to continue and deepen the thoughts about the topic of this chapter from other points of view. The Spanish medical doctor and peace worker José Luis Gil Monteagudo has written an unpublished manuscript about the NATO intervention in the war in Kosovo, entitled: "I, too, carry a Yugoslav War within me." It is such a mature combination of political and human insights that I would like to quote some passages without comment.

I read the press, listen to the radio, and gather the thoughts that many experts and non-experts have had about this war, which is closer to us than other wars. I see a war scenario and I ask myself: "Does all this have anything to do with me?" "Could it be that my way of living and the decisions I make on a daily basis contribute to the continuation of this war?" "What can I personally learn from all this suffering?"

If I want to discover the true answers to these questions, I must allow the light of my consciousness to reach into the dark corners of my being. Some are more easily accessible: I see clearly the Serbian village and the Kosovo Albanians inside of me – the declared victims of this war. But to think that there is a part of me that is as hardened as the paramilitary groups, as tyrannical as a Miloševic or a NATO general, that is really hard for me. Are there corners in my soul that are bolted with a padlock and protected by guards 24 hours a day? Are they entirely inaccessible?

I do not like to associate myself with the military; after all, I declared that I was their opponent many years ago. I do not want to take up arms or contribute to others doing so. But ... in truth I always liked the war movies in which heroes go on a killing spree for a good cause. Is there any legitimate cause for killing a human being? Although it does not seem that way to me, a part of me says yes. There are situations in which violence, even bloodshed and corpses, seems to be justified for humanitarian reasons.

We all keep looking for the "guilty party", but life has shown me that I need to be extremely wary of this categorization. One can never end violence with violence.

I thus continue to explore the corners of my mind - the corners that are normally out of my reach. I think of Miloševic, but ... no, really, that's going too far. I refuse to think that this person lives in me every day. Well, maybe this evil one is not quite so evil, maybe he has his reasons, I could at least listen to him for once ... No, that is not possible! Something in me rebels. I *don't want to think that I, too, am Milošević. I could accept it as a theoretical mind game, as a daring stylistic venture, but to feel, to **feel** the tyrant in me and to observe how he acts, what injustices and crimes he commits every day, that seems to me to be asking too much. There are definite areas in my soul that want to remain shut. I ask Love and Courage to stand by me, and I hear the squeaking of some hinges on the heavy doors ...*

I imagine the face of the tyrant, the way it is depicted in the media. Something in me refuses to look at him directly. I judge him too much. I see the face of an arrogant, egoistic, cynical, inflexible man ... my God! If all this is also supposed to be part of me, then I think I will stop this game. I don't like the direction that this is taking ... I take a deep breath and continue to look at him. I try to relax my gaze. I begin to see something else. I see the deep sadness that is reflected in his eyes, I see the darkened face of someone who is suffering ... "Yes, but don't mistake him for a victim, now; we're dealing with a perpetrator here, don't forget that." ... I ignore the shrill voice in my head, and continue to observe this sad look.

Now I only want to see a human being, as if I knew nothing about him. I now - and I'm almost ashamed to say so – only want to understand my brother Milošević.

I remember facts from his biography: when he was still young, his parents committed suicide. God! I had forgotten that entirely. Nobody, who does not feel valued himself, is able to value others. Only someone desperate can commit atrocities.

Yes, now I see the eyes of a boy who is broken by these suicides. His father and mother have taken their lives ... I try to imagine the childhood of a boy whose parents are as sick as that ... Most probably a child who went through a terrible birth and grew up under terrible conditions. An abandoned being in a human catastrophe...

Is there such a great difference between slaps in the face and knife stabs? Are they not fed from the same source? Is there a difference between physical slaps in the face and the wounds that words, spoken by a sharp tongue, can inflict? These wounds of the soul often need much longer to heal than the bodily ones. They contain a concentrated poison, which was distilled in the dark side of the mind. Does it make any difference if the words are spoken or if the effect they have comes from the power of the mind? And in all this, is it really crucial if this process occurs consciously or unconsciously? Is there anybody who thinks that s/he is free of these poisons?

Yes, I announce decidedly: I, too, carry a war criminal inside of me. I can see it for the good of everyone. I do not want it to keep on working within me and be the last one to notice. [...]

Why did NATO not act in the area of the great lakes in Africa where, within the last five years, one and a half million innocent people died, where there were hundreds of thousands of refugees, and where still today tens of thousands are killed every month? The reason is simply that the government that caused this massacre is willing to buy the sheriff's silence with oil, uranium, diamonds, etc.

Why does NATO not act in Kurdistan, where more than one million Kurds had to flee, pursued by the Turkish military, and where thousands are being tortured in the jails? Because Turkey is part of the same NATO and is one of the main customers who buy weapons from the United States.

Yugoslavia is being destroyed [by NATO] with "intelligent" weapons; more than 1200 people, among them 400 children, had to die, and 5000 were seriously injured. They were bombed in their houses, traveling in trains, in hospitals, in radio and TV stations, in embassies and in jails. And, as if it were of no consequence, the civilian population is left without electricity, water, and bread.

In all this, the Serb military hardly suffered at all, and they were obviously the last to go without water or bread. One lets the civilian population suffer for humanitarian reasons and commits mistakes, which are described as "marginal effects".

The treaty of Rambouillet was a dictate with clauses that violate Article 52 of the Vienna Convention, which states: "A treaty is void if its conclusion has been procured by the threat or use of force ..." The Serbs did not sign, the bombing began, and, as usual, the truth about the war itself was its first victim.

Why did one not seriously try to find a diplomatic solution? Because there was no interest in this. The capitalistic globalization process, which is controlled by the economic power that the United States indirectly rules, wanted a war in Europe.

The panorama is alarming. On the one hand, we are more conscious and have a greater sense of solidarity than ever before, but on the other hand, we have never been more effectively manipulated. Truth is conspicuously absent and lies are conquering our planet.

I have finally found the creator of all this pain: this powerful unknown, the one who gives the orders that cause the suffering of millions of beings. I have the guilty one. I think that I am aligned with him and can hear his words: "Bravo, very good, you have finally found me. You are one of the few smart ones, who discover me through persistent seeking. Yes, I am one of the powerful eccentrics, who control the mental and physical movements on earth. It is too bad that I'm not the only one, but maybe one day I will be. The only purpose in this world is to have power and, in order to get it, one must fulfill one condition: one must be free of any and all scruples, remain focused on one's goals, and work for them regardless. Morals are for the weak. Why should I accept reprimands in the name of a highest being or a love that does not exist? Do you think that I am the real problem that must be eliminated for peace to reign on earth? How many people do you think would do what I am doing, if they were only in my position? I tell you: they are legion. How many do you think would like to be in my position? Millions and millions."

It is finally clear to me: there is nobody on this earth who does not believe that they are right, and I believe that the life of each individual, in its own way, expresses one aspect of the universal learning task. Every life path is thereby a suitable form in which to explore, among other things, the innumerable mistakes that the human mind is capable of committing.

I know that each mistake that I commit is potentially a step on the stairway that brings me closer to God. But I also know that I must realize, understand, and transform the mistake in order to turn it into such a step. I recognize that, in spite of all good intentions, there is a secret manipulator in me. I also recognize all doubts that my dark brother harbors: toward God, toward my higher self, toward human goodness, toward the existence of love, all the way to doubting my own existence.

I now need an honest anchor in this turmoil of war and peace; nothing and nobody really seems to be authentic, including myself, of course.

I therefore continue to seek points of reference in the publications about the war. I suddenly make a surprising discovery in statements made by two totally different personalities: a few days apart from each other, a former NATO general and the former Serb Vice President use two words that make me take notice: Jesus Christ. Both of them use him to support their contrary positions.

I ask myself how this great soul, who greeted every being by wishing him/her peace, would have acted in this war. He also lived in a time of gruesome wars and his behavior set an example for how to react to all conflicts.

Is it possible that a Jesus Christ lives in me, too? Absolutely, I am a potential Christ, just as we all are. This Christ is our true nature behind all other appearances. On the day when we can realize our Christ nature and fulfill the divine plan, all wars will disappear from this world and peace will surround us. With every step in this direction the true history of humanity begins, a history full of love, surprises, and adventures, a history of enthusiasm and creativity.

For this Christ to be realized, the sack must be turned inside out and Milošević, the paramilitary, the power in the dark shadows, NATO, and the victims all tumble out into the light. It is only in this way that we open the door to truth, for truth is the strongest source of power on the path of transformation.

Stop the Insanity of Normality

(A poem by a young woman after visiting with her parents and her relatives)

They speak of peace
and buy bananas from the hacienda, where they killed the farmers.
They hate me, when I say something about it.
They speak of freedom
and drink the coffee, that slave hands had to harvest.
They speak of health
and use a system of medicine that dissects laboratory animals.
They speak of beauty
and kill the beauty of the wild and sacred life.
They almost killed mine, too.

They speak of love
and ignore the blood that was lost for the things they buy.
They speak of tolerance
and judge those who don't play their games any more.
They speak of humanity
and take part in the deadly game
that they call "culture", "decency", or "morals".
They speak of justice
and no longer see the appalling injustices in the shops, the streets and the factories,
in the churches and the courts, in newspapers and television and in the Third World,
which has to pay for their affluence.

They preach at conferences
and no longer react to the misery on their own doorstep.
They no longer react to the torture chambers on earth.
They do not know what it means to die in fire.
They do not need to grieve any more, for they have stopped loving.
They ask us when we will come home,
if we have the right health insurance,
and they give careful thought to our pension.

Can Evil Disappear from Earth?

They came in the morning with their jet fighters
and dropped napalm on the sleeping villages,
then they made a sharp turn
and mowed down the fleeing villagers.
One of them said that it was better than sex,
better than anything before and after in his life.

> Donna Leon in "Latin Lover"

What have we done,
that these young men have no scruples any more?

> Ruth Pfau

Friedrich Nietzsche stated that a humanitarian God cannot be detected in history. We can hardly contradict him. But which history does this refer to? What entitles us to describe the history of the last five thousand years as "history" itself? This was not the entire history; it was the history of patriarchy. If we look at the whole, it was a very small excerpt from the overall history of humankind. Long before our historical era there were highly developed cultures that had access to much higher cosmic knowledge than we do today and that were connected to Creation in an entirely different way. Enigmatic pre-historic discoveries, spiritual archeology, and some attempts at writing a female history (Sabine Lichtenfels, Marija Gimbutas, Riane Eisler, Eluan Ghazal, among others) reveal an entirely different view of the origin, development, and sequence of human history, of different forms of human community-building, and of different possibilities for human technologies. Weapons and defense installations did not exist. One of the last of these highly developed cultures existed on the island of Malta some six thousand years ago. There they built the enigmatic temples, whose ruins one can still see (see Chapter 3, last section). Evil has not always existed.

I will abstain from making a definition of evil. When I see how the civilian population is bombed in Chechnya and how hand grenades are thrown into the last basements where the sick and the old still live, then I do not need a definition of evil. Philosophy is sometimes a method of distraction. When I see how the same man who ordered all this, Vladimir Putin, is courted by our Western politicians, then a rage grows in me that is so cold that I have to do my utmost to keep my sanity. It is exactly here that this sanity tells me: stop! You are working for peace. You are a part of the continuum of which Putin is a part. Do not give in to your rage. You have arrived at one of destiny's crossroads. If you follow your rage now, then you will create thoughts that feed evil instead of eliminating it. For this evil – forgive me for saying so – is latently in you too; it is in all of us. Some of this rage is in all of us – the rage that made somebody like Putin cultivate his cold destructive will, maybe already in his childhood. Maybe Alice Miller was right in her analysis of the lives of violent criminals when she referred to their desperate childhood. There are situations where you are so deeply hurt that you are left with only one thing: the vow of revenge. You could otherwise not go on living, you simply would not have any energy, and you would not be able to cope with what had happened. Such situations often occur in childhood and just as often in love. It is the drama of our current entire world. If little Vladimir could have stretched out fully in the warm arms of a big mama, and if this mama herself could have stretched out in the joy of life and love, then there would have been no Putin as we know him.

I have repeatedly found myself in a rage that almost robbed me of my senses. The things that were undertaken against us during the campaign accusing us of being a cult (see Chapter 6) made me lose my composure to the degree that I had to fight real murderous impulses. Most of us probably know the feeling of boiling rage, which makes us helpless, insane, or desperate, as long as we cannot channel it into directions that are more meaningful. Sometimes, when it becomes too overpowering, a new quality awakens in us: so-called "cold rage", which suddenly puts us into a state of unusual power. It is stronger than any fear. It feels good to take action or to meet a superior in a state of cold rage. One is invincible in this state, but is that the solution? Is Putin, who has so intensely cultivated cold rage, a solution? During the short period of the student revolt, I experienced situations in which my rage was stronger than any fear and where my opponents shrunk away from me because there was no fear in me. The question that revolutionaries for peace are faced with is what to do with this rage? We should not simply suppress it, for then it will consume and devour us. Nor should we simply follow it, for then we will simply become a further link in the eternal chain of fear and violence. We should not anaesthetize it, or else we will lie to ourselves and others. Our rage contains an incredible potential of power. We should not give up this potential thoughtlessly. Like a good chess player, we must check to see how and where we can put it to use or transform it into a higher energy.

Let me say right from the start that the energies that need to be liberated for the creation of a global force of peace are exactly the same energies that have done so much harm up to now. They are the energies of rage and the energies of sexuality. Profound peace work that not only pays lip service to the words has to do with these two areas, for they characterize – consciously or subconsciously – the lives of us all. Here, we find the reservoirs of power in ourselves that we must uncover, liberate, and integrate, in order to become powerful enough to build a free earth. This is the reason why we cannot simply follow our emotions in these two areas. Nor can we follow any moral or religious prejudices. Instead, once we have learned to become quiet, we must turn to a different frequency and begin to listen to a new, deeper, more intelligent, and more humane voice from within. We do not consist only of the ping-pong of action and reaction. We are cosmic beings and we have the possibility to "stop our inner dialogue" (Don Juan to Castaneda) and gain an overview of the situation from a higher level. We need to find entirely new concepts for dealing with the energies of rage and sexuality. These concepts must allow us to integrate the powers that have so far been paralyzed without becoming destructive. Here, in the area of rage as well as in the area of sexuality, we find ourselves at a deep point of bifurcation, at the crossroad that could determine the further course of our evolution. Here are the points where small exemplary shifts could change a world. But here, too, we obviously find the greatest difficulty, for both rage and sex are raging inside of us like natural forces in an ocean that may be calm today, but that can break through all dykes tomorrow. **This ocean is we, ourselves.**

During many regression trances (past life regressions) I could observe how, in a soul's karmic biography, i.e. in the series of sojourns in the incarnated and non-incarnated spaces, evil comes into existence, how it develops, and how it can be dismantled (see the story of a former priest in Chapter 4). In a person's individual development, evil appears as the result of traumatic experiences that could not be processed properly. These experiences often occur in the sexual or religious areas of life. Evil is often the result of a long but failed effort to lead a sacred life. It can be the result of incredible frustration, from which arises – at first secretly, then openly – an unspeakable aversion against everything that one had previously labeled "good", i.e. true hatred against all talk of humanity. One who is truly evil no longer wants to be good. Energetically, it would be unbearable. To be evil is not an original state of being; in most cases, it is a reaction to all the things one has experienced. Life itself becomes evil if it is mistreated long enough. Many of the people that I am cooperating with in friendship today had earlier incarnations as violent criminals. They sided with evil and committed atrocious acts. Some of them later chose incarnations as victims and experienced the other side of their actions. They then made a new decision and therefore find themselves in the circle of the most committed peace workers.

The atrocities in history have had the result that certain parts of our brain no longer seem to function. Just as the human mind has reacted analytically to the physical world, up to today it reacts equally un-analytically and naively to the questions of humanity. Evil has become so independent that it is regarded as an integral part of life or even of divine order – with no thought about what causes it. Evil has succeeded in acquiring unchallenged civil rights on earth. If, in the long fight between good and evil, a victory was achieved, then it was evil that won. Let us look at the earth as it is today. There is hardly a farming family in the Third World that still owns its own land, hardly a native people that still lives on a land where nature has not been devastated, hardly a population of animals or people that still lives in freedom. The theory of imperialism, once the basis for the anti-imperialistic fight, is not more interesting to the comrades of the past than a stock market report. Most of them make a profit themselves from the same conditions that they took to the streets to overcome. It is unbelievable to what extent the revolution of the Sixties could be intercepted and turned into its opposite.

Many people today have come to terms with evil to the point of stating with a serious, almost knowing expression, that it is simply a part of life, like suffering, death, or war. What are their arguments? The first argument is: "It was always like that." The second argument, which sounds dialectic, is: "Good could not exist without evil." The third one says: "War is the father of all things" and comes from Heraclitus (although he states it in a different context). All three arguments are stupid, but not only stupid. It truly always was that way, if one looks at history over the last few thousands of years. Take a historical dictionary and open it at random. One gets sick if one not only reads what it says, but actually imagines what it all meant in reality. A long time ago, I gave up reading history books, for it is really no fun to take in, over and over, this endless repetition of conquering, subjugation, mutilation, intrigue, revenge, genocide, and limitless sadism. I can well understand from what position Ulrich Horstmann wrote his book "Das Untier" ["The Monster"] and that he no longer wants to believe in any humanity. I include his wonderfully written book in the literature list, even if I disagree with him. What we read in our newspapers could just as well have been parts of reports coming from Rome, Alexandria, or Antiochia. In the historical development over the last two thousand years, there has been no visible improvement. Instead, evil seems to be a natural constant for humanity. If we accept this as a fact, then any serious commitment to peace, or even world peace, is meaningless.

There are assertions about the issue of evil, especially from esoteric circles and from within transcendental psychology, that are based on "holotropic" experiences (Stanislav Grof). They claim that evil is an independent, meaningful, and even necessary power within the building plan of the universe. It is true that in holotropic states, for example under the influence of drugs, one can enter into states of horror, from which one cannot escape on one's own. Evil then seems to have an objectivity of its own, against which one is powerless. But precisely here lies the mistake. These phenomena are not objective; instead, they are projections of the soul that stem from a deep inner fear. Aided by the drug, the fear enters into resonance with the world, transforming it into a threatening construct. If this fear were not to exist, there would also be no horror images. If, on top of it all, we believe in the projections and see them as real because we cannot distinguish between projection and reality, then we enter into full resonance with the images. Once this resonance is in place, then the situation becomes truly dangerous and we lose control. This mechanism is one of the reasons why strong psychedelic drugs are dangerous. But it is not proof of the cosmic existence of evil, only of our inability to differentiate between projection and reality in the deeper areas of our consciousness. As soon as we have learned to do this and not to identify with the horror images, they pass us by and disappear again. Other scenarios, with increasing light influences, take their place. When the inner fear disappears entirely, the deepest state, called "enlightenment" or "transcendental experience", begins. It is an unequivocal state of the most concrete and definite reality. One can also reach it without drugs. There has never been anything evil in any state of enlightenment. Wherever the forces of life and light are not blocked or resisted, evil does not result. Instead, we find the perfect bliss and revelation of life. It is only when they are blocked through inner and outer resistance that restriction arises and an inner collision occurs that is experienced as fear, insanity, and demonic hell. Hell is the blocking of the most elementary life energies and heaven is the liberation of the most elementary life energies. The old fight by the Persian Zarathustra, the fight between the two world forces of good and evil, Ormuzd and Ahriman, is not a basic law of Creation. It is the result of an historic process, in which the human being began to attack the sources of his own life.

The followers of the modern esoteric scene like to refer to the Swiss deep psychologist Carl Gustav Jung who, in his theory of archetypes, truly regarded the archetype of evil as a kind of natural constant of the human soul. He had access to unusually comprehensive material from the areas of mythology, ethnology, and dream symbolism. Without a doubt, we find evil symbols, images, and actions everywhere. But let us look at the time span that this material encompasses. The myths are usually less than three thousand years old. They thus come from a time after the patriarchal revolution, i.e. after the historical "fall". One cannot make any statements about natural constants of the soul and about structures that transcend time from such a short time span. All so-called natural constants and "eternal laws", even the physical laws, are only valid for a certain time span, during which the conditions are so stable and constant that deviations can be ignored. If entirely different conditions were to rule, whether human conditions or physical conditions, then the deviations would be so glaring that no one could speak of "constants" any more. This topic illustrates a weakness that characterizes most scientific discoveries: they suffer from a flagrant lack of historical reference. The raw material, from which C. G. Jung created his theory of archetypes, is historical and is therefore not eternally valid.

Today we find two basic reactions to the atrocities and cruelties of this world: revenge or indifference. Revenge arises in those who are directly affected and who have seen the horrors with their own eyes. Indifference arises in those not yet affected and who do not want to get involved, no matter what. Their arguments serve to repress, not to enlighten. They themselves were silenced with such arguments, when in their youth they wanted to protest against the falsehood of the world. Statements such as: "Well, that's the way life is" or "Where there is light, there is darkness" or "You will get your rough edges knocked off, too" have always been used as excuses by adults who have gotten tired of being confronted by their children's penetrating questions.

We now come to a related question: did evil exist already before the patriarchal revolution? We do not know. What we do know, with a degree of certainty, is that in prehistoric times there were highly developed cultures in which evil, in the forms that we know it, did not exist. We can even surmise that in such a late culture as that of Crete (before the invasion by the seafaring people around 1700 BC) it was practically nonexistent. There were real cultures of peace at the highest level, and there are still peoples in which an age-old knowledge of peace is still alive. This is true of very small groups in Venezuela and in the Brazilian rain forest, among the Australian aborigines, the Todas and the Bishnoi in India, the Hopi, and probably among some indigenous peoples in the Tibetan Plateau, the South Pacific, and at other places on earth. In her book "At the Fire of Wisdom" Dhyani Ywahoo, a Cherokee Indian, has given an encompassing description of a message of peace that stems from the ancient history of her people.

Where does evil reside and how does it arise? Origen of Alexandria, one of the first Church Fathers, presumed that it resides in sexuality and thus drew the heroic consequence of personally castrating himself. Plotinus, the last great Gnostic philosopher in the third century A.D., saw it in matter and was ashamed of having a body. Mani held similar attitudes (also the third century) as did the Manicheans that followed him, all the way to the Cathars, who were annihilated at the beginning of the 13th century during the so-called Albigensian Crusades. Here, too, we find a strict dualistic separation of Spirit and matter, whereby Spirit was assigned to the principle of good and matter to the principle of evil. We find this strange classification in almost all religious and esoteric literature of the last 3000 years. Matter here usually appears in the form of the human flesh, which, with its "base urges", stands in the way of the salvation of the human being. And thus, in spite of all distortions, we are shown where to find the roots of evil: in the body, in the urges of the body, in sexuality.

True enough, here we do find one root of evil, as long as the human being is not able to listen to and understand the voice of his/her body in a more positive way. During the patriarchal era, humanity created a mental-spiritual world, which right from the start was in stark contrast to the demands and needs of the body and of sensuality. The collision of body and Spirit was pre-programmed. It was not rooted in the nature of Creation, nor in a divine order, but in the power interests of patriarchal systems that had to break away from everything that was female, soft, physical, and sensual. The goal was to become invulnerable and produce subjects that could be controlled. The male fight against the flesh, against woman, and against sexuality went so far that the representatives of the church during the Middle Ages seriously considered exterminating the female sex. This is evidenced by the Inquisition and by the text "The Witch Hammer" (see Chapter 3), which was published at the end of the 15th century.

One must have understood how deep such historical processes were burned into the memory of the human flesh in order to understand why, still today, almost all moral views assign sexuality with its "base urges" to evil. There is, in a very convoluted way, some truth to it: as long as sexuality is suppressed because it is unclean, as long as it has to be repressed, hidden, and kept secret, it gives rise to subconscious perverse forces and fantasies. These, then, at some point break through as wild eruptions, and the subjects can once again see what they have always known: that nothing good can come from sex. Wilhelm Reich, the great sexologist and orgone researcher, has written the most essential things regarding this topic – his books should be taken down from the bookcases and dusted off. Evil does not lie in sexuality; it lies in its suppression. The cause of evil is not the human urges but the human beings themselves, who in the name of power, religion, and so-called decency suppress these driving forces.

(In my mind's eye I can see how some readers shake their heads and think that in our country sexuality has been liberated for a long time now. In truth, the youth of today has an easier start in their sexuality than before. But what happens later, when a relationship has solidified, what happens in marriage, in professions, in public life? The sexual revolution, which began at the end of the Sixties, did not get far. Like everything else, its impulses were integrated and marketed. I have described the overall sexual situation at length in the book "Der Unerlöste Eros" ["Eros Unredeemed"].)

Some readers probably know the mythological figure of Lilith, who is mentioned in the Old Testament. She supposedly embodies the evil female principle. In reality, she embodies the principle of female and sexual wildness, which does not let itself be subjugated by the rules of the male culture and religion. In her book, "Tempel der Liebe" ["Temple of Love"] Sabine Lichtenfels writes about this: "Lilith was the aspect of the female that could never be captured. She was the wild and female nature that could not be tamed through the millennia. **In spite of all attempts at taming it, this female aspect reigned in the background and inflicted damage wherever it was not granted its right to life.**" If they are not liberated in time, all life forces that are suppressed at some point transform into powers of evil. Even the deepest love, if humiliated for too long, transforms into feelings of hatred and revenge. That is a natural law, and humans have obeyed it diligently.

It is high time for us to free ourselves from the fairytales of evil that have been repeated from religion to religion, from culture to culture, and from generation to generation. The "base urges" are not the powers of evil; they are expressions of the movement of divine forces, as soon as they exist within the bodily organism of a human being. If we follow them in freedom, they are the prayer and celebration of the body. Sexual pleasure that can express itself freely is a manifestation and a revelation of the divine. Pleasure is a principle of Creation. One of the deepest aspects of Creation is that it unites the pleasure of organs with their functionality. Sacredness produces pleasure, when it fully encompasses the body. The goddess likes to reveal herself in a wallowing pig. For a long time now, she has wanted to reveal herself again in the pleasure of the sexes wallowing together. She wants to do so as freely, as joyfully, and as often as possible.

In our groups we have conducted deep trances in order to understand more about the source and nature of evil and about the possibilities of changing it. Today, summarizing our insights, we come to the following result: evil is the result of the human being splitting off from the order of Creation and from universal Love. Evil has no substance of its own but, given the conditions of a society that is hostile to life, it has the ability to spread and assert itself very quickly. This then gives rise to the image of its frightful superiority, as has been recorded throughout patriarchal history. Evil tends to materialize quickly in the form of weapons technologies, as systems of rule, and wars, and it thus suggests a natural existence, as if it were a part of a healthy society. In reality, however, it is dependent on our projections and on the metaphysical belief that it is an integral part of life. If we were able to withdraw all our projections from evil, then it would crack up and break down like a murderer, whose victims suddenly no longer exhibit any fear and no longer direct any projections toward him. Evil largely lives from being demonized and disguised ideologically. It thrives on being demonized by occult and superstitious people, and it grins when it is consecrated metaphysically. But even the most hardened devil breaks out in a sweat when it meets someone who can see through him and who responds to him with true amusement. Hell on earth would end if people took back the power that they have given away to the projections of evil. They will then have the power to build a world wherein evil no longer has an evolutionary advantage and thus dies out by itself.

Some questions remain open. There are things in Creation that make us ponder. Why did the animals throughout evolution need their murderous tools and their defense weapons? Why are there sweet-looking plants that have thorns as hard as steel? Why are there even barbs on some of these thorns? Did aspects of evil exist in evolution already before the appearance of the human being? Were parts of evil present even before the patriarchal revolution? Is there something in nature that is structurally based on violence – violence in terms of cruelty? Maybe here, finally, we should try to define evil more precisely. Is violence already evil? Are hyenas evil when they, beginning with the lower body, devour a gnu alive? Something rebels in us against calling this "evil". Maybe we should only speak of evil when there is free choice and when then cruelty (or lies, etc.) is chosen. It seems that only the human being is capable of this. But no matter how we define evil – it must disappear from the earth to the utmost extent possible. "Fear must disappear from the Earth" said Michail Gorbachev. We must see to it, that evil, too, disappears. If it were ever part of a divine plan of Creation, then we must see to it that the plan is corrected. In our holistic world, we are always a part of God; not out of arrogance, but because that is the way it is. We are not outside of Creation; instead, we will always be one of its guiding organs. Therefore, it is up to us whether evil continues to exist or if we can design a more intelligent concept for life on earth.

The Archimedean Fulcrum

The search for a key point of change

Where does the matrix of violence change over to the matrix of life? Where is the "hole" through which we can go? Where is the point whose change can change the entire matrix?

The matrix of violence has asserted itself historically. So far, all attempts at countering it with an equivalent on the side of peace and healing have failed. The revolutions and the peace movements have failed, the therapy movement has failed, and all attempts to improve human beings through morals or religion have failed. Is the human being brain damaged? I am afraid so. It is, however, not physiological but mental damage. We obviously live under the spell of an historical mental illness. Our question thus becomes: Is there a special point from which we can effectively and fully overcome our mental illness? At its core, the whole history of massacres and the parallel history of attempts at salvation could revolve around a few basic questions that must be solved in order for a new history to begin. Perhaps all great saints were engaged in this quest. Karl Marx also had this question. He found the key point in the liberation from private property and in the socialization of the means of production. Wilhelm Reich found it in the sexual revolution, Buddha found it in inner emptiness. All these answers were definitely not quite correct or not sufficient, but they circle around a topic that we cannot escape. Today – supported by the insights of mathematics, holography, and chaos research – we know that an entire system can change if one changes a single parameter in the system.

Increasingly, I think that there must be a surprising, elementary solution to the suffering on earth and for changing the old matrix in ourselves. Maybe one must introduce an idea, a set of information, or a factor into the world that is contagious and that, through self-amplification, gives the entire development a new direction. In chaos theory this process is called "bifurcation". Is there a point in the workings of humanity and in ourselves from which a non-violent development for all of us could be initiated?

During the third century B.C., Archimedes of Syracuse, the great mathematician and physicist of ancient Greece, discovered the law of leverage. His question was: How can I access unlimited power from a single point? In his enthusiasm about his new discovery of leverage he said, in essence: give me the right point and I will turn the world upside down. Here we find a technical principle of power increase, which up to today has led to more and more fantastic results. Beginning with a small force, the physical processes of multiplication, iteration (self-amplification), and resonance can result in a great final force. I once stood on the top platform of a 34-meter high observation tower and started to set it swinging back and forth. After a few motions the entire tower was swinging so much that, even if my arms had had a hundred times more power, I could not have stopped it. I kept on visiting this tower and was always amazed at this phenomenon. Who or what is multiplying the power? It is the resonance with the free vibration frequency of the tower. It is the resonance with the whole. It was mysterious, but it led me onto an interesting path: one "only" needs to enter into resonance with a part of a larger whole in order to multiply one's own power. This is also true for the spiritual law of resonance: you "only" need to enter into resonance with the higher frequencies and powers of the universe in order to access much higher energies and information than would otherwise be possible. This is the experiential fact that we are referring to when we speak about the solutions to the tasks that lie before us and say, "not with our own power". Resonance with the whole – this became a key concept for our work. Give the whole the impetus and it will take care of the rest by itself. This whole can be the universe, it can be mankind, it can be a community, or it can be oneself: the resonance with one's higher image and one's entelechy. Resonance gives the sprout of grass the power to break through a layer of concrete. The technology of the future will be a resonance technology. Here, we are very close to a core point. If, through suitable actions or a suitable thought, I enter into resonance with the Sacred Matrix, then I, too, come into resonance with the power of this matrix. It is through resonance that transformative powers come to my aid and cause things to occur that I could not have achieved on my own. We can rely on this spiritual natural law. It also applies when we seek answers to our questions about the key places involved in possible change. I must provide the whole with the right impetus by formulating my question as precisely and intensely as possible. Then I can be a receiving organ for the answer that comes. Let us thus continue on our way to the answer.

If we succeed in fully dissolving the global chain of violence and fear at a single place, then this new information about the solution exists in the entire chain. The chain is no longer as stable as before. It can now break more easily in other places, too. The suppressed impulses of joy, pleasure, and freedom can come forth and create new life in other places, too. That is the "field effect" of a single exemplary process when it realizes a possibility that is present also in the other links in the chain.

If the circle of information of violence and fear is disrupted at an important place, then this information can no longer flow as strongly and as coherently as before. If something more than just a break occurs there, if new information is input there, and if this information is powerful enough, then the entire system can begin to wobble and even "topple". Let us thus try to find such a place and introduce the corresponding information.

First a comment. We must always return to the holistic image of the world in order to see our place in it and be able to perceive the possibilities that we have. There is only one existence. We humans are a part of the whole. The human "holon" is a particle in the super-holon of the world. As such, it participates in the forces and the laws of the whole. Moreover, the whole repeats itself in all its parts; the macrocosm repeats itself in the microcosm; the superholon of the world repeats itself in the human holon. If we translate this to our topic, then the violence and fear we see in the world, is also inside of us. They are in each of us, since we are all a part of this holistic world. The healing power and the beauty of the whole are also in us (as a latent reality, as a matrix, as a power, and an inner image or entelechy). In order to make use of the outer healing power, we must make use of it in ourselves. In order to break the outer chain of violence and fear, we must also break it inside ourselves. If you find the Archimedean fulcrum in yourself, you also find it in the world. The outer Archimedean fulcrum is also the inner Archimedean fulcrum, and it is usually easier to deal with there. Under the conditions of today's worldview, the path toward political action begins with a path of insight into oneself.

Could it be that we are able to dissolve the entire circulatory system of fear and violence in ourselves, if we can deprive it of power at a decisive place in our lives? Could it be that we then will have found the point where the worldwide outer circulatory system of fear and violence can be deprived of power? From a holistic as well as a spiritual point of view the answer is – at least in theory – yes.

Where does this point lie? Where can we and must we intervene in our chain of actions in order to let a new chain of creativity and joy emerge from the old chain of fear? Where is the Archimedean fulcrum for the transformation of the old matrix of fear and violence into the new matrix of life? Where, inside of us, must we set a new course?

I would like to describe a nighttime experience of mine that illustrates the importance of our topic. While taking a walk at night in Oberteuringen, a village close to Lake Constance, I came upon a farmhouse. A German shepherd dog was lying in front of his kennel watching me, without barking. I have an intimate connection to dogs, and I immediately felt that he was just as tense as I was, and that everything now depended on me. As I was trying to keep him calm by focusing on friendly thoughts, I noticed that a latent fear arose in me that was hard to stop. Then the dog started barking. The vicious circle started on both sides. The potential friendship, which was possible in the beginning, turned into a world of danger. I sensed that he would wake up the whole valley if I did not leave quickly. A small irritation led to an unstoppable change from trust to fear. I witnessed a typically paranoid process that was happening inside of me, a process that occurs in a similar way all over the world. Joy and reconciliation could have developed, but instead the global structure of fear and (potential) violence asserted itself. A small shift can be enough to determine whether we have war or peace.

In this example, the issue was trust or fear between a dog and a human being. But are there not other places in us where a change can influence much, much more, maybe even our entire relationship to life, to ourselves, to love, and to the world? Or our relationship to a neighboring family, to another community, to a political movement, or to another people? Yearlong or lifelong enmities often arise because, at a certain point in the relationship, a small shift did not succeed. It could not succeed because those involved were stuck in their old structures and could not let go of them. We never had a true religion of peace that offered people concrete help in overcoming conflicts, and – except for the words of Jesus, Mani, and a few other teachers of peace – there was no ethic of peace anchored in real insight into the connections.

If we were able to consistently and reliably undertake this small shift, which leads from (latent) war to peace, everywhere – in our daily work, in dealing with political opponents, in the clinch within a love relationship, in dealing with the police and authorities, when facing a violent criminal, etc. – then we would be true masters of peace work. We would find ourselves firmly on the deep Tao of peace and healing. A group of ten committed people, who could cause this switch to occur anywhere, could move the world, for there is nothing more contagious than the true power of peace, when it is free of fear. Anyone, who remains within the Sacred Matrix in spite of danger, is protected from danger. Jesus knew this and it was also stated by Laotse in the Taoteking. We must thus learn to switch from one matrix to another. We have the switch in our hand more often than we think. For example, how do I act if I am subjected to public slander? Do I then have the will and the peace knowledge present not to react according to the old matrix of fear, hatred, or revenge? Much could depend on these things – and maybe we should not ask these questions morally, but scientifically. Let us take a mental-spiritual microscope and hold it over such decisive moments. We notice that they contain everything that can serve violence, but also everything that could end violence. We obviously find ourselves close to an Archimedean fulcrum.

But how do we achieve this shift? How do we achieve it permanently and without false morals? One answer might be by connecting stronger and more reliably with the Greater. The answer is not just a phrase, for in this book it is clearly described what is meant by the Greater. Yet it is not quite enough. We can continue the questions and answers ad infinitum. Apparently, the Archimedean fulcrum appears anew every time we change levels. It is not a point at all, it is more a line, which goes through all areas and which marks the same type of change within all areas. If we join all these marks together, we get the overall pattern of the Sacred Matrix. If we succeed in creating change in one essential area of life, then we actualize the overall matrix. If we retain the change, we will notice how the building blocks of our lives slowly re-assemble like a kaleidoscopic transformation in slow motion. It is the matrix itself that causes this transformation as soon as we have achieved the change at an essential point. As soon as we enter into resonance with the Sacred Matrix at an essential place in our lives, the transformational powers come to our aid, resulting in a changeover from the old to the new matrix. There is not just a backward pull, there is also a forward pull. The matrix is an autonomous, living, spiritual entity. It develops its own dynamics and has the inherent power to realize itself, for it contains the matrix of Creation. There is not just one Archimedean fulcrum point; instead there is a certain geometric line on which these points lie: the "Archimedean line". Everywhere on this line we find the same decision and the same possibility to step over into a life that is deeply connected with the whole. The healing biotopes are designed to change the overall situation of life in such a way that the changeover from the old matrix to the new can easily be found by the participants.

In this deep connection, we find the power to fully leave the old path of fear and to walk the new path of trust. Here we find our most decisive issue, determining if we will have a future with or without violence. The decisive question is: to what extent are we – also in situations of fear, resistance, rage, jealousy, enmity and war – able to remain connected to the Greater and thus to change the situation? To what extent are we able to see ourselves and the world, including our opponents, through the eyes of God, even when we are in emotional distress or despondency? To what extent are we able to react with our Great Soul instead of with our fearfulness, even in difficult situations? Have we learned to think that way and to switch our inner computer correspondingly? Have we learned to practice doing this? Do we have an image of peace, which is more beautiful and powerful than the reaction patterns of our old body of emotions? Do we have a will for peace and trust that is stronger than our fear, our rage, and our joy of revenge? Here is the Archimedean fulcrum. We begin to become bringers of peace when we learn to stop reacting with private emotions in situations where we have so far reacted with rage or fear, with feeling hurt and wanting revenge, with defiance or enmity, and instead retain our connection to the great matrix. When I see human beings the way God or Goddess see them, can I still be afraid of them, can I still curse them, can I still wish their downfall? When I no longer do all this, do I then lose my power over him or do I gain a power and an authority that comes from a different source.

Here, the book of power is re-written completely. Here, Machiavelli and his Prince Cesare Borgia no longer prevail; instead we find Jesus, Nelson Mandela, Jacques Lusseyran, Martin Luther King, Albert Schweitzer, Dhyani Ywahoo, Ruth Pfau and Sabine Lichtenfels. Whenever we succeed in leaving our personal reactions behind, we gain a spiritual power that lies beyond our private person, and that is therefore understood and accepted by every being. Even the wildest predator animal accepts this power and obeys its magic. We no longer project onto the representatives of the old matrix, and we thus deprive them of the old power that they had over us. It is through this process that they sense their own doubts. Their habitual patterns of behavior have lost their content and their energy. Jacques Lusseyran, the blind youth leader in the résistance (the French resistance against the Nazis during the Second World War), has written an unforgettable book about this entitled "And There Was Light".

He was stronger than his foes, for he could allow himself no fear and no hatred. He described it that way himself. Here, a true peace process has been initiated and it is needed all over the world. Those who have gone through this process within themselves understand the principle and may recognize the deepest point that is at stake when dealing with true peace work.

Chapter 3
The Legacy of History

Patriarchal History is not the Whole History

The human being, who is described in this chapter, is not simply the human being as such, but the human being of the patriarchal era, i.e. the human being after the great separation. This era covered a time period of approximately 5 – 7,000 years and is thus a relatively small part of the overall history of the human being. Before this era there existed several primitive cultures, but there were also entirely different and much higher developed cultures on earth. The reason why they are relatively unknown in current historical research and archeology is that they did not leave behind many material remnants. They had access to spiritual technologies that spared them the material efforts that we have to expend today. They lived in complete connection with the cosmic, divine world and therefore had access to powers and possibilities that later were lost and had to be replaced by complicated tools, machines, buildings, rules, laws, and technologies of communication. We should take care not to identify with the image of the human being from the patriarchal era. We should stop our habit of looking at the history of the past few centuries or millennia and say: see, the human being has always been this way! For what we see here is not the human being as such, but a very specific type of human being. **Of all the possibilities of human existence on earth, only those were realized that had the best evolutionary advantages, based on the conditions of violence.** One can immediately understand that this did not lead to the development of the best type of human being and human culture. But, in addition to all wounds and hurt that we suffered during this era, an inviolable divine soul and an entelechy are alive in us; this is the eternal matrix of the human being. We are cosmic beings and do not only live in this life. If we return to our cosmic connection, we have internal access to all the sources of knowledge and power that we had before the patriarchal era and that are now being rediscovered at a new level. Today, a few decades before the end of patriarchy, we can distance ourselves from this era and calmly observe what happened during this time and what happened to us during this time. We can speak the truth, and we no longer need to downplay the issues, for we are preparing ourselves for an entirely new age. We must speak clearly, for we are cosmic travelers, and we must learn to understand what happened in Kosovo, in Auschwitz, in Vietnam, in the Crusades, and in the witch trials and also why it happened. We need to understand it so that we can build a world in which such things can happen no more. We no longer need to defend the life that we have lived so far, for it is no longer about judgment. We have played along, we couldn't do anything else, and we carry the marks and the scars from this era in our bodies and souls. But we also have the God/dess in us who allows us to recognize and heal the scars.

The Great Separation

The author Walter Schubart disappeared in the year 1941 under national socialist rule [in Germany]. He wrote one of the most wonderful books about Eros, entitled "Eros and Religion". In it he describes, among other things, the connection between the pain of separation and the religion of redemption. According to Schubart, all pain of the soul is ultimately the pain of separation. In the beginning of the human history of suffering there is an original event of separation and abandonment. This original event occurred some 7000 years ago. It is connected to the separation of humanity from age-old religious and social orders through the emerging patriarchal revolution. Schubart summarizes this in one simple statement: "The undoing of humankind is man."

The separation deepened over the millennia. The result was that the human being broke away from his/her connection with Creation, the sexes broke away from their original love connection, and the individual broke away from his/her original tribal connection. The process that was later called the "fall of the human being from God" or the "human being falling out of Creation" during the "time of the great exile" (Weinreb) spread all over the earth. A new state of existence developed among humans. It was based on power and dominance over others, subjugation of other peoples, replacing the female priesthood, replacing the mother goddesses with male gods, establishing hard rules and laws, fighting any kind of resistance, destroying nature, and mercilessly exploiting its beings. Fear and distrust spread among all beings. They began to protect themselves against each other. The original trust in each other and in Creation was broken. The old knowledge that came from being connected with the whole was lost, often destroyed violently. In its place came new knowledge, weapons technologies, engineering, and power machines to break resistances. The cultural era of male dominance was created. The corresponding parameters of human and social life were created, and the human being of today has taken them on like a second skin. What many people today take for granted is in reality the result of this separation. The laws of our civil society, the ideas about love and marriage, the various forms of religion and art, even the paradigms of science and the ideas about the structure of the universe are rooted in this state of separation. These laws and ideas are not eternal natural constants. Instead, they are tied to a very specific phase of human history, during which human perception, human thinking, and human actions were a result of the separation. Today we are about to shed our skin again, for the second skin, which we grew during the time of separation, no longer fits over the forces that are growing within us. Nor can this skin be transformed, for it is too small, too constricted, and too false. Instead, we must shed it, so that the being that was hidden beneath it can step out into the light.

We must overcome the great separation, if we want to overcome the primal pain in love.

Lost Knowledge

The human being and nature were once connected in a different way. An animal or a tree was a cosmic being, whose soul one could feel and with which one could enter into contact. The earth was sacred to humans. We do not have any precise knowledge from this time, but we can sense the knowledge that was there. We can almost sense it like a memory. In the circle of time, is not all knowledge "memory", as Plato said?

There is age-old knowledge of peace in humanity. It stems from a time before humans used written language to take down and pass on their knowledge. The tribes and cultures, who kept this knowledge, have long since died out. A few traditions have remained as have the ruins of some monuments, for example the temple ruins on Malta and Gozo, the Hypogeum on Malta, the stone circle at Évora in Portugal and some other monuments from the Neolithic age. What has remained is especially the input into humanity's collective, mainly sub-conscious, memory and the possibility to remember, using inner, spiritual methods.

In early times the priestesses and their tribes were connected to the secrets of Creation, and they knew of the great web connecting all life on earth and in the universe. They knew themselves as being a part of an encompassing great life and one great consciousness. It was the state before the great separation, before the "exile", as Friedrich Weinreb called it.

Knowledge is power. This was known by the great patriarchal systems of power that solidified and spread on earth ever since the Egyptian pyramids were built. They therefore spared no effort to root out the original knowledge or to integrate it into their own systems. During regression trances that I carried out during seminars in Tamera, we received information about such a process in early Egypt. Priestesses from other cultures, for example from Malta and later from Crete, who were initiated into the original knowledge, were forced, under hypnosis, to reveal their knowledge. It was through this "betrayal of the mysteries" that the male cosmology could become so perfected that it was possible to develop entirely new types of power systems. Today, we can still see one result of this in the Egyptian pyramids. The new power blocks were built in a belt around the earth: in Mesopotamia (Sumeria), on the Nile, in Peru, in China, and at the river Indus in India. The earth's noosphere (the global mental-spiritual field) came under the dominance of a power-oriented male cosmology and finally – through the triumph of Rome – fully under the rule of purely imperial power interests.

The remaining cultures that were based on the old knowledge had to protect themselves from the new adversary by withdrawing into inaccessible, inhospitable, and hidden regions on earth in order to survive. Today, we still find small remaining groups or individuals spread over the entire earth. Events keep occurring somewhere in this world that bring new pieces of this original knowledge to light. The knowledge lies deep in the so-called Akashic Records (world memory) and in the deposits of our collective consciousness. We can gain medial access to it through trance and hypnosis, and we thus get an image of history which of course is radically different from what we are taught in school today. We clearly recognize that the evolution of mankind did not simply go from bottom up, like a genealogical tree, but that right from the beginning there were high spiritual beings who at the same time brought the culture of knowledge "from above to below". We do not have to agree with everything within the anthroposophical world view to recognize the basic validity of Rudolf Steiner's statements about the existence of history-generating spiritual beings. This means that the creation of cultures, including language, came about in part through spiritual means, as described by the anthroposophical philosopher of history Sigismund von Gleich in his book "Marksteine der Kulturgeschichte" ["Milestones of Cultural History"]. There is an evolution that goes from below to above, but there is also one that goes in the opposite direction. Today we obviously live in a time when there are many tears in the fabric of reality that make the old connections visible again.

Original knowledge was kept in secret locations and old sacred shrines far into historical times. In part it was incorporated and passed on by the old occult schools. This old knowledge was used by the church masons' guilds of the Middle Ages, which brought forth the miracle of the Gothic cathedrals. Still today, the cathedral of Chartres, this wonder of wonders, contains age-old secrets in its structure, its structural engineering, and its design. It stands on a hill and under the cathedral floor there are four historical layers, of which the oldest dates back to the early Stone Age. Here, early man had erected a sacred shrine, made of stone. This was presumably a source of prehistoric knowledge. Such shrines of stone were apparently placed over the entire earth according to a geomantic system of energy lines and intersections that were known at the time. They formed a spiritual force field of a global cosmology and culture that remained intact until the end of the Neolithic era.

The Romans feared the sacred sources of the peoples that they suppressed and therefore destroyed them. This work of destruction was continued by the Christian church. Immediately after taking power under emperor Constantine, the church set about to extinguish all remaining sacred fires of the old world, destroying the "heathen" cults and shrines and either converting or exterminating the believers in the old faith. To a large degree, the treasures of knowledge of Greek Antiquity also fell victim to this assault. Justin, the emperor of Constantinople, closed Plato's Academy in Athens in the year 529. In the year 772 Charlemagne, the leader of western Christianization, conquered the last Germanic people in Saxony and destroyed the "Irminsul", their sacred shrine, later forcing their leader Widukind to be baptized. Writings that did not fit into the canon of the church were destroyed. This included such central texts as Plato's "Timaios" and other evidence of an ancient knowledge that was vastly superior to that of the church. Due to the overall attack by the church against the mind of man, western civilization was robbed of the legacy of antiquity, as Nietzsche rightly points out. Already in 280 B.C., Aristarchos, a Greek astronomer, knew that the earth is a sphere that circles around the sun. When Copernicus and Galileo said the same thing 1800 years later, they were almost burned at the stake, for the Holy See in Rome had determined that the Ptolemaic world view, according to which the earth is a flat plate, was the right one and had labeled all other claims heresy. The church's ban against thinking had been enforced at all levels, and truth was punished by death. When the Italian physicist and astronomer Giordano Bruno, one of the greatest thinkers of all times, did not recant his teachings of an endless, living universe in which the suns are moving around each other in ever greater systems, he was burned alive on the Campo di Fiori in Rome on February 17th, 1600. This is how the heretic and his work were to be wiped off the face of the earth. Bruno was connected to the great knowledge of early times. Still today, with his teachings, he would be regarded as a heretic, at least in the area of science, for he believed in an infinite living universe with living celestial bodies that are imbued with souls.

In the Middle Ages there were women who were still connected to the old healing knowledge. They therefore had access to special healing powers that, according to the church, they were not entitled to have. They were called "witches" and were burned alive. This marked the beginning of the era of the Inquisition. For five hundred years everyone, including children, suspected of adhering to false teachings, of carrying out heathen rituals, and of being in league with the devil was burned. Millions of people, mainly women, fell victim to this bestial church movement. Here, once and for all, a memory was imprinted into the body. It was the intent of the church that nobody should ever again think thoughts of their own, seek paths of their own, and feel bound by their own ethics. It was the highest and most unscrupulous claim to power that up until then had been made by any human institution.

In this way the old knowledge was erased, and the ban on thinking is still in effect – of course in a different way. Today it is no longer the doctrines of the church but those of science that must be adhered to if one does not want to lose one's good reputation or endanger one's social standing. But today the ideological systems that can be summarized under the name of science are beginning to crumble, because almost all sciences have reached limits that they can no longer overcome by using their old axioms and assumptions. It is slowly becoming known that there is a higher principle that holds the world together at its core. It is slowly becoming known that psi phenomena and religious revelations not only stem from the fantasy world of sick minds. Slowly, but surely, more and more people experience that there are healing possibilities that lie entirely outside of conventional medicine and that the deeper connections in life lie beyond the physical laws. Slowly, a true renaissance, in the original meaning of the word, could begin: a rebirth of original, greater, more powerful knowledge. Maybe today we are witnessing the greatest paradigm shift that ever occurred in the history of the human mind.

(I would like to add, in parenthesis, that this paradigm shift occurs in all areas. We will, for example, gain entirely new ideas about the size of the universe, the time spaces in evolution, and the dating of historical eras and events. The methods that have been used so far do not hold true, for they are based on untenable premises. As an example, the C14 dating method is based on the premise that the half-life values of radioactive materials are the same during all times and in all circumstances. Since such and other similar assumptions are false, we will soon be facing entirely new world views. It is not least due to the surprising archeological findings that have been uncovered by Erich von Däniken and by the Swiss engineer Hans-Joachim Zillmer ("Darwin's Irrtum" ["Darwin's Mistake"]) that science will be forced to develop entirely new concepts of evolution and history, letting go of the concept of a linear development that occurs from the bottom up.)

The Holy War against Woman

All evil is small compared to the evil of woman.
A godless man
is better than an agreeable woman.

Synod of Tyrnau, 1611

Woman relates to man,
as the imperfect and the defect relates to perfection.

Thomas of Aquinus

Mulier non est facta ad imaginem Dei.
(Woman is not created in the image of God.)
Augustine

But, just as the congegration is subjected to Christ,
so are women subjected to men,
in all matters.

New Testament (Epheseans 5, 24)

Reichenau is a vegetable-producing island in Lake Constance [in Southern Germany]. During the 8th century A.D., Karl Martell, Charlemagne's grandfather, established an important monastic center there. Today, there are three Romanesque churches on the island stemming from this era, and they are among the oldest Romanesque churches in Germany. In his chronicle about the founding of the monastery, Hermann the Lame, an 11th century abbot from Reichenau, writes:

"Saint Pirmin, abbot and bishop, is taken to Karl (in the year 724) by Princes Berthold and Nebi and is given Reichenau. He **drove away the snakes there** and, during the three years he spent there, he established the monastic way of life."

So Saint Pirmin drove out the snakes before founding the monastery. This sentence seems to have a special meaning or else it would not be mentioned in such a short and simple chronicle. What does driving away the snakes mean? Were there exceptionally many snakes living on the island of Reichenau? That is not very probable. The real meaning becomes clear, when one knows what the word "snake" meant to a Christian monk at the time. It was the snake that seduced Eve to give the apple to Adam.

In plain English: the snake is to blame for the sexual sin of humankind; it is the seducer into evil per se, i.e. into breaking the sexual prohibitions. Later "snake" and "woman" came to mean the same thing. Woman, "this snake", was declared to be the incarnation of sin. There was, at the time, in addition to the many lesser sins, one single main sin: the "sin of the flesh", fornication. It was worse than treason or murder. The honorable church fathers, from Augustine to Thomas of Aquinas, all the way to modern popes, have made horrendous statements about this issue. An indescribable hatred against sexuality, against all things feminine, and against their own urges must have filled these men. The Christian church movement led to the cruel development that culminated in a planned partial extermination of the female gender during the Inquisition. During the 15th century two Dominican monks dared to speak these thoughts and published them in 1489 in the famous document entitled "The Witch Hammer". Next to the Bible, this book became the most read book in the Western world. As we know from church history, the thoughts that were developed there were translated into reality with such bestiality that there are no words to describe the unfathomable horrors that were committed.

Yes, it was unfathomable, and yet it was the logical consequence of a mental-spiritual development, which runs from the beginning of the story of Creation, through the Old Testament and all the writings that follow. The recommendations for how to deal with sinful peoples that can be found in the five books of Moses is horrendous. This is how Jehovah speaks to his people: "And ye shall overthrow their altars, and break their pillars, and burn their groves with fire; and ye shall hew down the graven images of their gods, and destroy the names of them out of that place." (Deuteronomy 12, 3) It was a barbaric structure of the soul that was projected onto the God Jehovah and then idolized. The sins of worshiping false gods and of fornication were to be burned away and destroyed once and for all. The cruel words that we find there are still today seen as constituting a sacred text, for they are a part of the Old Testament of the Christian Bible. How was the biblical admonition: "Thou shalt not kill" ever to be able to assert itself when, before that, the course had been set in such a different direction by command of the highest God? God himself had given the command to kill, and the believers did their best to obey.

It is difficult to speak about the history of the church and still retain a clear mind. Karlheinz Dreschner has done this in his book "Das Kreuz mit der Kirche" ["The Cross with the Church"]. Today we would prefer to skip over this barbarity, just like we would prefer to skip over the history of fascism or the current events in Chechnya. But we must take into consideration the entire spectrum of human history to date in order to be able to start a truly new one. The historical fight against woman must be seen in its entirety if we want to understand what is still happening today between the sexes. The fight was about the sexual driving forces, depicted in the form of a woman and a snake, and it was about attractive and intelligent women. During the 5th century AD in Alexandria there lived a beautiful and intelligent woman called Hypatia, who taught neo-platonic philosophy. She had an important influence on the cultural life of the city. But in that city also lived Cyril, the Christian bishop. When Hypatia refused to distance herself from her teachings, the bishop incited a band of monks against her. They pulled her into a church, tore her clothes from her body, and cut up her body with oyster shells and broken pieces of glass. Cyril was later canonized and is still today seen as one of the fathers of the Catholic Church. Anyone who believes that this story is exaggerated or that it constitutes an exception to the rule, should read Karlheinz Deschner's volumes entitled "Kriminalgeschichte des Christentums" ["Christianity's Criminal History"].

Many people know of one of the most moving love stories of the Middle Ages: the story of Abelard and Heloise. Their passionate sensuality was put to an end by the church: during a nighttime attack, Abelard was castrated in his bed and Heloise was put in a convent for the rest of her life, where she led a miserable existence in solitude and sexual despair.

In order to be able to gauge the depth of this fight, we need to know something about the meaning of the serpent. In early times it was the symbol for sexuality and healing. In the vibrating pattern of the universe, the serpent was at a point where sexual power and healing power came together. The serpent is the incarnation of a high healing knowledge. By studying wounded snakes we can learn much about the inner process of healing. If we watch how they coil up, how they rest and then change their position, we can sense how one can keep one's body energies at rest so that healing can take place without interference. Here, the Goddess is showing us a state of deep bodily meditation in the form of a snake. The sexual process, too, if it can occur peacefully, leads to a state of deep bodily meditation. The combination of sexuality and healing teaches us that sexual energy is a very special kind of healing energy. When the sexual energy can spread throughout the body through the Kundalini movement of a snake, then healing occurs in the entire body.

The snake is an assemblage – a condensed hologram – of the healing forces operating in Creation. In earlier cultures it was honored to the point of being seen as a Goddess, and in some cultures it was seen as the Great Goddess herself. One was, of course, fully aware of its sexual meaning. In the East it was Kundalini, the inner female soul of humans, which lies coiled in the pelvis and which, through correct yoga practices, can be made to uncoil and rise up through the "chakras" to one's head and bring enlightenment. What a connection between sexuality and insight, between Eros and religion! The snake inhabited the famous Khmer temple of Angkor Wat in Cambodia, where it embraced the king every night (see Barbara Walker's book: "Woman's Encyclopedia of Myths and Secrets"). The snake has something of the mysterious Lilith, as we will see later.

The fact that the biblical story of Creation associated the serpent with evil is by no means a matter of course. Long before the Jewish cult of Jehovah, there was a male serpent god in Palestine. Those belonging to the Jewish tribe of priests of the Levites called themselves the "Sons of the great serpent Leviathan". The Bible shows that Jehovah was a rival of the serpent Leviathan, for the two gods fought each other (Psalms 74:14, 89:10; Isaiah 51:9 – information by B. Walker). We need to be aware of this background in order to understand the ideological depth of the story of Creation in the Bible. From the beginning, in the myth of Adam, Eve and the serpent, we are dealing with two religious worlds that are engaged in a merciless fight against each other. The old world of Baal (which itself carried some signs of male degeneration), the world of sexual power, of serpent worship and of ecstatic cults was to be annihilated by the prophets of the new world of Israel. The revelation of Creation, which lies in the fruits from the "tree of knowledge" and is the revelation of sexuality, is to be prevented forever. The biblical story of Creation is an unparalleled example of man's fear of sexual truth and of woman. Thus began an unprecedented fight in human history, the fight by the (male) mind against the flesh. It continued in the tradition of the Christian church and today it finds its expression in the slaughter-houses of the world. In the Bible it is written that during the Last Judgment the two divine opponents, Leviathan and Jehovah, would face each other in a last fight (Isaiah 27:1 and Revelations 12). If we remain in mythology, may we pray that this fight results in the great divine synthesis of the two: the synthesis of mind and body, of religion and Eros. But one thing is certain: this synthesis will only arise if Eve has a say.

Snakes are beings that do not attack humans unprovoked. If they live in a biotope in which they can again trust human beings, then they seek contact with us. On our property in Portugal, where the animals in our

91

surroundings never cease to surprise us, they come to us and bask in the sun on our thresholds. They have also been known to coil up around our legs or crawl up on the stomach of a woman who is lying naked in the sun on a verandah. We are no longer afraid of them. The animals of this place have so often offered us their friendship that we can no longer mistrust them. We, too, are building a kind of monastic and cultural center here. Just as the monks on the island of Reichenau, we, too, are serving a sacred power. But today we do not drive away snakes, we drive away superstition and the fear which, due to human ignorance, was associated with this divine being for so long. We are ending the historical animosity between human being and snake, for we are ending the war between the sexes. Man was not fighting perversion or pornography; he was fighting the elementary force of sexuality, for he could not deal with it. He fought it in woman by imprinting the most cruel punishments onto her body. Considering this background, we can appreciate what we mean when we today speak of "free sexuality". What was once hunted down, punished and exterminated is now to be liberated, accepted, welcomed and celebrated! There is no deeper reversal than this, and no revolution is more stirring than this one. We know the confusion that a soul experiences when it today comes to earth in the form of a woman and encounters the elementary sexual force that she has been punished for during millennia. Now, suddenly, she is supposed to no longer hide her sexual longings, but reveal them. She will only be able to accept this gift if she lives in a space of complete trust that protects and encourages her. Here, we find maybe the deepest issue of all healing biotopes and the deepest overcoming of patriarchal history and culture.

History, Inscribed into the Body

The human being is an historical being. We came from history, we are a part of history, and we carry history inside of us as information and memory. History is stored in all our cells. Knowing and using such stored information constitutes a part of our possibilities.

Many forms of existence have been experienced in human history. All of these forms of existence are present as possibilities within us. Also, many new forms of existence that have not yet been realized are present as possibilities. The various forms of existence throughout history have been deposited, layer by layer, in our inner information warehouse. We thus find history sedimented in our own souls, our consciousness and our subconscious. An event in the present suddenly resonates with an event from an entirely different time, one falls into a trance and re-experiences that time. Elizabeth Haich, the author of the book "Initiation", is said to have arrived at the contents of her book in this way, i.e. by re-experiencing an initiation into a mystery school in old Egypt. We experience a similar re-experiencing in the regression trances. We have worked with specific topics throughout several incarnations until we solved them. If they have remained unsolved, they show up in our present lives in one way or another. There are many areas of pain and conflict that we could not solve under the given cultural conditions during the last three thousand years. They appear today – often already during childhood – and shake our souls until we become aware of the issue behind them and start to work on it consciously. From then on the issue becomes a life task. All of us, or almost all of us, have come to earth with such an issue. **Finding this issue behind our everyday matters is of itself a part of the healing work.** We then gain an entirely different attitude toward our so-called difficulties or problems. We are then no longer ashamed of them or see ourselves as neurotics or failures. We do not go to a therapist; instead, we recognize a part of our life task and finally give our lives a meaningful direction.

Earlier traumas and pains are often deeply engraved into our bodily organism. Hare-lips, birthmarks, liver spots, or subcutaneous scars, sometimes also deformed limbs, are signs of injuries that we have received in earlier incarnations. In one regression trance a woman experienced being fatally hit by lightning in the 12th century. On her body we found the entrance and exit places in the form of scars that could be seen quite clearly from a certain angle. Here, too, we need to re-learn, for we do not come to earth as clean slates, but rather as books full of experiences.

The history of the patriarchal era was characterized by a merciless war against the originally female, religious sources of human culture and against the organic needs and sensual joys of the body, especially in the area of sexuality. It was a war against the truth of emotions and against all authentic thoughts that diverged from proclaimed dogma. As Karlheinz Deschner wrote, history became "criminal history". Under these conditions there were few possibilities of experiencing history as a healing history. We all carry the scars of history in our souls and our bodies. A beautiful forty-year-old woman showed us an unusual deformation of her pelvis. Her pelvic bones seemed to have been pushed in on both sides. A regression showed her living in one of the earliest Christian communities in Tyros. Roman soldiers destroyed the community and she was tortured. They applied pelvic screws to her. Another woman showed us her deformed foot. In an earlier incarnation in India her foot was chopped off. Speech impediments such as lisping often have karmic origins. It was thus a tradition in many countries to cut out the tongues of those who were regarded as traitors or held other beliefs. A discoloring or waves on one's skull, such as Michail Gorbachev has, usually indicate karmic injuries. There is hardly a single part of our bodies that does not somehow have signs of our karmic history.

However, not only criminal history is stored in our cells. There, we also find the original matrix and the human entelechy that does not contain any violent suppression of life. In our cells, we have stored the entire history of the human race before the great separation. We carry the cultural experiences of a non-violent life and a non-violent sexuality as they were lived at the centers of highly developed ancient civilizations. There is, deep within us, the memory of a time when we were safe and secure in the world, when there was no persecution and violence between people, when the sexes lived in mutual trust, and when sensual and religious love were not yet separated from one another. As soon as a collective field has been created for these memories, many people will begin to remember.

The Fear Virus

The suppression of life and the methods used to accomplish this have given rise to a fear on earth with which we all, without exception, are infected. This is the fundamental fear behind the scenes that governs and characterizes our lives, from our physiological processes to our sexual behavior and our belief systems. It has so completely become second nature to us that we hardly recognize it any more. Since everybody else is infected with it, too, the resulting social behavior is regarded as normal. The fear that arose through the violence of history and that is constantly renewed by today's power systems has long ago become a part of our culture. A truly fearless person would constantly break the norms in our culture and would, therefore, soon fall victim to the psychiatric or judicial systems or become the target of an assassination. The inner system of fear prevents people from fulfilling their elementary desires in life, but at the same time, it protects them from being ostracized socially. Fear is necessary to maintain the high degree of conformity and opportunism required of the members of our modern society in order for the established injustices to be tolerated. The general structure of fear makes the human being governable and controllable to a degree that surpasses what Orwell described in his futuristic novel "1984". Aldous Huxley described it even more perfectly in his novel "Brave New World". In his vision of the future, we find a scenario that has already been surpassed. The power that can turn a human being into a sheep is the fear of punishment and social ostracism. It has been created through the system of punishment, which has domesticated the human being during five thousand years of history. Without this fundamental fear there would be no dictators and no subjects, no ruling class and no oppressed masses, no unnatural laws and no forced conformity. Nor would there be any disturbed children and students who follow meaningless study plans, no adults who hide behind the confines of their profession and their marriage, no Gods, and no Old Testament.

Fear has been branded into the human being through unspeakable methods. These methods were always used whenever one economic, political, religious or ethnic group wanted to impose its authority over another. Many of us were victims (or perpetrators) of these excesses in some earlier incarnation and have experienced in our own bodies what millions of people are experiencing today. At the heart of fear is usually a trauma so terrible that those who have experienced it will do anything in order to not come into contact with it again. This trauma often lies in the sexual area. That is why, in our texts, we so strongly emphasize that a new culture be rooted in a new relationship between the sexes.

In order to no longer come into contact with a trauma, our souls have erected an inner protective barrier around our central fears. It consists of such defense mechanisms as memory loss, blanking out and obscuring facts, as well as locks, screening devices, and defense weapons of all kinds. Often, when danger nears and when the old wounds could break open again, we instantly transform our defense into an attack. We protect ourselves by attacking our alleged aggressor – who may well be our love partner – in anticipation of his/her attack. In this context psychoanalysis speaks of the "identification with the original aggressor". These latent structures of aggression pervade our entire civilization and constitute a part of its protective system and its strategy for avoiding fear. The aggressiveness of ideological debates does not usually stem from rational commitments. Instead, it is the result of the desire to avoid, at all cost, the fear of the opponent that threatens to erupt. Political, religious and moral convictions usually serve to deal with unresolved conflicts in the area of love and sexuality. When then two different so-called convictions interact with each other there can rarely be a resolution, since both sides are concealing the real issue. This type of phony discussion and phony culture was one reason for the breakdown of the philosophical culture of our times. People have been burnt and they protect themselves from the re-opening of their wounds. When they look around they see how necessary these protective measures are. Especially men, but also many women, have grown a veritable ring of armoring around their heart chakra in order to no longer come into contact with the old pain of love. In our healing work in Tamera we speak of a "slab of concrete" across the chest. I call this entire protective system the "fear virus". It prevents meaningful communication and self-observation, but it also protects the soul from a recurrence of the unbearable. These systems of defense are neurotic, but they are necessary as long as society is based on violence. This constitutes the failure of psychotherapy. There is no point in wanting to rid people of their neuroses without providing them with a different society. All experience shows that they will defend their neuroses tooth and nail before they are prepared to truly change their lives. Even if they sense that they will never find fulfillment, they would rather hold on to their old images of love, their old beliefs about faithfulness, jealousy, and the fear of abandonment than to again fully open their hearts and bodies. They will calculate and take preventive measures rather than give themselves freely. It is precisely this that will prevent them from attaining what their souls most yearn for: devotion and self-abandonment. They – all of us – are caught in complicated vicious circles of fear and caution that allow little chance for a permanently fulfilled love life.

What I call the "fear virus" Wilhelm Reich called the "character armoring" and "body armoring". The character armoring consists of all the moral, religious, ideological, and emotional measures that a human being takes in order to protect him/herself from again exposing his/her wounds. The collective character armoring structure does not allow people to attain love and insights, but it does enable them to find certain conventional, more or less regulated forms of co-existence. At the same time they must take care that nobody steps out of line too much, since that could endanger their whole defense system. They therefore react to seekers of truth and outsiders with fear and anger. It is like in Plato's allegory of the cave where some of the people break out of the cave and discover the light of the sun: they are taken back and exterminated. Or in "Jonathan Livingstone Seagull", the famous book by Richard Bach, where the young seagull pays for his brilliant flights of discovery by being banned from his group of seagulls.

The character armoring is always connected to the body armoring. The body armoring is a result of the totality of the inner and outer counter-movements that the body automatically undertakes in order to block and ward off dangerous drives and impulses from within. In a culture, where the population has been forced to suppress their own elementary energy movements with the help of a stick and carrot, the body armoring becomes an integral part of the collective biology.

Due to the structure of the body armoring, the biological energy of the human being consists of two parts: a natural one that is connected to original, organic, and forceful movements, and an opposite one that suppresses these same movements. This has led to an absurd situation in human civilization, for these energy flows block each other mutually. People then complain of headaches, tiredness, and a lack of energy, whereas in reality they suffer from an excess of energy, which however blocks itself. The original energy has nowhere to go. Almost all our psychosomatic illnesses and chronic sufferings, our animosities and allergies, our dark moods and depressions stem from an original excess of energy, which cannot find any way out of the regulated system of a society hostile to life. This is an important consideration for the concept of healing and for developing a realistic vision of the healed human being. When the body armoring has been dissolved, we have access to powers that are several times greater than "normal", and we can apply them without tiring. It is good to know how much energy one has. People, who live without body armoring, are in a state of dynamic equilibrium in which an equal amount of energy flows into them from the cosmic energy reservoir as is spent. And, as we know, the cosmic energy reservoir is practically unlimited. Every good marathon runner knows this. The type of movements he carries out as he runs and breathes is such that new energy can constantly pour in. That is the secret behind all extreme physical feats.

Together, the character armoring and the body armoring constitute a defense system against fear, functioning automatically and keeping us separated from the central sources of power in life. It was mostly around these sources of power that the traumatic injuries occurred. It is especially the sexual source of power, which lies in the lower abdomen, that must not be touched deeply so that old yearnings and painful desires do not re-awaken. Sexuality must therefore – in spite of all the playacting and passionate moaning – be as shallow and superficial as possible, pur-chasable, manageable, calculable and capable of being integrated. The abdomen should be protected from deeper pulsations. This is achieved by the fashion of the pulled-in abdomen and the muscular armoring of the solar plexus, the abdominal wall and the pelvic floor. This armoring also interrupts the energy connection between the genitalia and the heart, i.e. the flow of energy between the sexual chakra and the heart chakra. Sexuality and love can then no longer truly come together. The result is that sex is reduced to the physiological process and that sensual love and religious love, Eros and religion are permanently separated from each other. This separation constitutes our most severe illness.

If we want to find healing we must get out of the ghetto of our armoring. If an entire healing culture is to be created, we must step out of history by dissolving its inner traumas and by starting to live in the service of an entirely new life. The peace work of our times thus presents two epochal issues: the dissolution of the historical knot of fear and the dissolution of the neurotic systems of defense that we have erected against each other in order not to be touched in the painful zones of our souls. As long as the structures in society remain unchanged, neither of these tasks can be solved by psychotherapy. They require the creation of spaces where new social and cultural experiences can occur, where fear is no longer fed, and where therefore the old systems of defense no longer make sense. The peace project, which is described in Chapter 6, was founded on these two thoughts.

The Closed Heart

The most central and maybe the most widespread form of defense against pain is the closed heart. One closes one's heart in order not to be hurt emotionally. Millions (or billions?) of people live their lives with closed hearts because at a time when their hearts were still open, they had to experience things that were too terrible. People with closed hearts do not allow any emotion, any love, any pity, or any messages of salvation to touch them. They are afraid of being deceived and of once again experiencing the terrible things that made them close their hearts. They keep their hearts bolted shut, even when the most beautiful and moving things occur. Once and for all, they no longer want to be cheated, deceived and disappointed, especially not in love. This decision is rooted so deeply in their cells that they would rather die than give it up. It is an absolute inner madness, but, if we look at the causes, it is fully understandable. This madness is destroying not only the human being but also nature, for a humanity that is caught in this madness has no understanding of the soul of nature and her creatures. At the heart of today's ecological catastrophe we find the closed hearts of humans. After everything that the loveless, antisexual human being has done to his heart, we cannot expect any permanent healing of the planet without a deep healing of the human heart. Here, healing means opening, especially opening in the area of love, but this time without the experience of pain.

During one of our regression trances, a 45 year old woman experienced a lifetime in 17th century Russia, where she lived a lonely and closed off life in a mansion. When she was young she had had a very loving way of dealing with children and animals. Then, as a young woman, she experienced terrible things in her city, fled to the mansion, and lead a lonely, overbearing and "correct" life with a closed heart. She developed an ice cold philosophy of life. In her house she established a strict order and cleanliness. Sexually, she loved perverse practices without any emotional relationships. She could no longer afford to open her heart. Even outside in nature, where the trees were blooming, the grass smelled sweetly and memories from her childhood arose, she could not stay for long without feeling her great pain. Only toward animals could she still be warm.

This woman fought everything that she had once loved. She needed to do this to protect her soul. She acted as so many others have. They fight what they have once loved: they fight love, they fight sexuality, they fight an easygoing way of life. They also fight religion, Jesus or God, their yearning for home, their memories, their own better judgment and conscience. They also fight against their emotions, their remorse, and their pity. Almost all people – some more, some less – live in this fundamental structure of resistance against everything that they truly love.

One can slowly begin to understand why, under these conditions, new projects that actually attempt to heal the human being and improve life on earth are so strongly resisted and slandered. The slanderers have to resist what would otherwise touch their hearts. They have to protect themselves from their own repressed desires that arise in them if they commit themselves to the goals of such projects. How should a person, who has experienced sexuality only in the form of degradation and maltreatment, react to the words "free sexuality"? How should a person, who has never experienced love, react when hearing that there are people who are working to spread love. What does someone, who in order to survive has gotten used to lying, do with a message that is so strongly focused on truth? We are no longer surprised that an old hatred arises in them when they hear of such things. Here, the existing system has won a macabre victory: the subjects are not only robbed of their most beautiful possibilities in life, they also fight those who mention these possibilities. The "liberators" are not fought by the oppressors, but by the oppressed. Wilhelm Reich described these connections in his book "The Murder of Christ", and Plato referred to them in his famous allegory of the cave. One can sense with what prudence global peace work must be carried out as soon as it touches people's inner issues. Overcoming the "character armoring" and the "body armoring" is today not only a topic of individual therapy, but especially a social and historical issue of our entire civilization. The Sacred Matrix can only take effect when people are able to open their hearts again, for love is the foundation for a new culture.

What Was the "Fall" of History?

What caused the great separation? What caused human beings to step out of the order of Creation, to separate themselves from the original Mother Goddesses and build violent systems of power? In her book "The Chalice and the Blade" Riane Eisler speaks of a dramatic shift of power. Earlier, the power of humans consisted of giving and caring for life; after the shift to patriarchy it consisted of destroying life. What caused this shift? How could a species on earth - the human being - act so intensely against its own members and against all fellow creatures? How did the war between the sexes arise? Was it, as some people assume, due to brain damage that arose through a collective mutation?

We know the answer that the Bible gives in its story of the Creation of Adam and Eve: it was Eve! She obeyed the serpent and seduced Adam to sexuality. That is the biblical story of the Fall of Man. It was written by men, and it is one of the clearest historical documents of the ongoing fight by the male world against woman and against sexuality and the wisdom with which it is associated. In the original Hebrew text the same word is used for "intercourse" as for "knowing". That Adam "knew" his woman indicates their bodily union. This union is a true revelation for both of them, as it is for all lovers. Adam and Eve then let themselves be driven out of paradise by the male God, and the human species was thereafter condemned to lead a harsh life, to experience "trials and tribulations," and to bear children under great suffering. This story of Creation is not an explanation of the historical "fall", it is in itself a "fall," for it labels woman as a devil and it writes this story, once and for all, into the sacred books. It was easy for the Dominican monks, who wrote the "Witch Hammer" toward the end of the 15th century, to refer to the biblical story of Creation when working to annihilate the female sex.

As cruel and underhanded as this biblical myth may be, it is still not entirely without depth and wisdom, for it clearly shows that the reason for the "fall" can definitely be sought in the sexual area. The old tribal fathers who invented the myth were at least somewhat acquainted with life, for they knew that only a power as great as sexuality could go against the commands of the Lord. They knew instinctively that humans would be controllable and could be ruled over only if one took this most beautiful power in their lives and declared it a sin. The biblical story of Creation is thus itself a part of the war of annihilation against the love between the sexes and a part of the death that the human being has wrought over humans. The respectable Genesis of the Old Testament is the genesis of barbarity and annihilation. Once the male Hebrew God had driven the first lovers out of Paradise, love was beyond saving. But how could such incredible distortions of life occur? Who could invent such fiendish things? And why?

Many reasons have been provided for the patriarchal revolution during the Neolithic Age. Friedrich Engels and other Marxist theorists make economic reasons responsible for it. Wilhelm Reich illustrates this view in his publication "Einbruch der Sexualmoral" ["Breakup of Sexual Morals"], in which he shows how a change in the economic structure led to a new repressive sexual order among the Trobriands in the South Pacific. In his book "Voices of the First Day", Robert Lawlor, specialist in the history of the Australian Aborigines, declares agriculture to be the culprit. Ernest Bornemann, in his book "Das Patriarchat" ["Patriarchy"], says the same thing about animal husbandry. Other deliberations see the cause in sudden climatic changes, for example through the impact of meteors hitting the earth. Others yet suspect that the male power of killing took on a life of its own during the Bronze Age because much more effective weapons could be forged using the new metal.

All these explanations seem meaningful and are probably all true. And yet they all seem inadequate. There must be something deeper, some event that occurred deep inside the human being that was able to turn the order of things upside down so completely and turn against life with such a passion for destruction. Considering the key role that sexuality plays in human and social life, it is safe to assume that this event had something to do with sexuality. This direction of thinking opens up a door through which we see a different panorama of human nature and human history. Human history is always also sexual history, and an essential part of the information that we need for the healing of life on earth comes from the sexual history of mankind. It was a transformation of sexuality itself, something new in the sexual sensation and the longing of the sexes that made humans gradually leave their old matriarchal tribal order and enter into new connections. At first it was probably not a violent process, but rather one that occurred gradually with increasing intensity and encompassed more and more regions on earth until, like a field, it led to the beginning of a new culture: the culture of male conquest. It began with the conquest of woman by man. Man, who during the matriarchal culture had been a servant of the Goddess and a love servant of the women, now became their conqueror. Those women, who at first resisted it, later allowed this game to be played, because it corresponded to a secret longing from within. The women had outgrown the historic phase wherein their longing could be fulfilled by love servants or by immature men. In them, too, a longing had arisen for a partner, for an equal and strong man, for a feeling of security with a man, and for personal love. These are processes within the human soul that gradually grow over the millennia and only then lead to external changes in life. The matriarchal era that had existed for thousands of years had, in fact, run its course. There truly was a need for a new religious structure and a new social structure between the sexes in order to accommodate the new productive forces of the soul. Here, too, we find that Marx's theory of revolution is valid, according to which radical societal change occurs if the development of the productive forces no longer fits the current conditions of production. Marx was only thinking of the material productive forces and the material conditions of production. But we can effortlessly expand his theory to encompass non-material, sexual productive forces of the soul. There are incredibly energetic productive forces in the area of the love between the sexes, for it is the source of the entire human species. There is not a single individual, a single tribe or a single people that did not come from sexuality. A change in the psychosexual relationship between the sexes must – even if no other external change occurs – sooner or later lead to a change in the social structure. The question of whether power is in the hands of women or men and how it is distributed between the two sexes is at heart a sexual question. It is also ultimately a sexual question whether humans have a male or a female God. It is most definitely a sexual question whether or not one treats the living world in terms of care or in terms of violence. Of course women did not, at the end of the matriarchal era, want violence; they simply wanted a new type of sexual relationship to man, who was becoming an adult. The fact that this resulted in violence was due to man's inner development, triggered by his new sexual lust and ability to conquer.

In her book "Traumsteine" ["Dream Stones"], Sabine Lichtenfels has reconstructed this process with such sensitivity and vividness that there is nothing more to add. It was a new sexual longing that led first to a sexual revolution, then to a social revolution. Man, who had not yet truly matured to the point of becoming a personal partner, had gained the power to conquer women sexually. He had thus dissociated himself from Nammu, the great Goddess. He no longer had to follow her laws in everything. He could fetch his brides from other tribes if his powers and his weapons allowed it. He was now filled and guided by a high and joyous feeling of strength and power. Now he could slowly make use of the advances in weapons technology. Bronze swords could be forged from tin and copper, and they were far superior to the old arrows and weapons of stone. Male power grew in proportion to the power of the weapons. The smiths became a revolutionary group. Their art determined the power of their people. Thus began the era in the history of humankind, when power was measured by how many lives one could kill, and when the man no longer had to ask for the consent of the woman that he desired. This was the patriarchal revolution, with which the great separation began. Thus began the history of a global catastrophe that could not have been more gruesome. It probably began with the invasion of the Kurgan people from Central Asia into the river valleys to the south. These invasions, occurring at different time intervals beginning in the 6th millennia B.C., destroyed the existing cultures and established the great power blocks at the Nile, the Euphrates and Tigris, the Indus, the Yangtze Kiang (China) and in Peru. It is currently experiencing its last phase in the excesses of Islamic fundamentalism and global capitalism. Thereafter, this history will end and a new one will begin. And yet we must realize that this was not the history, rather it was a dead-end street of history from which our planet will be healed if we succeed in ending the insanity quickly.

A History of Salvation and Social Utopias

Tomorrow lives today,
and it is always sought after.
The faces that turn to utopia
were different at different times,
and so were the details that they thought they saw.
But the direction always remained the same,
and the hidden goal was shared;
it seems to be the only constant in history:
happiness, freedom, non-alienation – a golden age.

    Ernst Bloch

During the time of the student revolts at the end of the Sixties, we had a great dream: a free world without exploitation and oppression, without class rule and false authorities, without force and heteronomy. The dream did not come true. That is clearly one of the reasons for the deep process of de-politicization that began during the Seventies and has reached its apex today. The societal goals were reduced to personal goals, the revolution transformed itself into therapy, and class consciousness turned into a general desire for consumption. The comrades from back then today carry the same ties as their opponents used to carry. It is dangerous when a great dream is not fulfilled, for one tends not to want to have dreams any more. Life is then sealed off as it is. Someone who no longer has a dream or a vision has stopped believing in change and in making a commitment to something new. But this is exactly what the groups that are in power on earth want, so that they can play their game to its conclusion.

Humanity has dreamed many great dreams and has often believed in an approaching salvation that then did not occur. The entire issue of the "second coming of the Lord" (parousia) and the corresponding chiliastic movement that envisaged a thousand year reign of Christ was characterized by a great enthusiasm, followed by an even greater sense of hopelessness. Today, we can only relate to such emotions by comparing them to situations in which we fall acutely in love, followed by total abandonment. Here, we had a life force that cannot be outdone. The despair that followed was correspondingly great when, instead of the expected salvation, pure hell broke loose, as it did in the early Christian community in Tyros. The community lived in anticipation of the Kingdom of God on Earth, as promised by Jesus. There are accounts of the beauty and joy of the lives they led in anticipation of salvation, for they were the perfect example of an early Christian community. But instead of the promised Kingdom of God, the Romans, who had been notified by St. Paul, came and annihilated them. The Cathars experienced a similar fate. After a great time of growth, they were attacked and annihilated by the Catholic Church during the Albigensian crusades. Their idea of purity could not stand up to the power of evil, since they knew so little about the source and existence of evil within themselves. The Anabaptists in Münster [Germany] also had similar experiences. In 1536, after initially creating a community of God in the city, they were exterminated by the imperial and episcopal army. Here, too, God's kingdom on earth was to be established. Their young leader, Johann van Leiden, had already let himself be declared the "King of Zion", for their goal seemed to be so close at hand. Throughout the middle ages the conviction kept surfacing that the Kingdom of God was near. The people had committed themselves so strongly to hope that their belief in God was maintained until the bitter end. When, during the battle at Frankenhausen in 1525, Thomas Münzer realized that he and his badly armed peasant warriors were surrounded by the enemy, he pointed to an approaching storm and saw it as a sign of the salvation that now would come through God. He was then captured and slowly put to death under unspeakable torture.

The history of the patriarchal era is not only a story of suffering, but also - and this was almost worse - a story of often hoping for salvation, yet never experiencing it. What happens within the human soul when, again and again, great hopes are disappointed, great promises are not fulfilled, and great dreams are lost? It gives up. When it comes to the great hopes and goals of humanity, we are today living in a time of global resignation.

But the soul only gives up for a while. It cannot give up forever, for forever is defined in the context of eternal life and not eternal death. Eternal life is consciously or unconsciously written into the human heart. After every pain a new hope grows, for something inside of us knows that life cannot be like that. Somewhere in us there is a connection to the sacred core of the world that whispers to us to keep on going, to try new ways, and to keep on seeking until the goal has been found. What this goal looks like and how it is described and handed down depends on the circumstances of the times and the culture. Since Greek antiquity a considerable number of social utopias have been described in writing, providing images of a healed world and a desired society as it was seen at the time. From Plato's philosopher's state (Politeia) to Marx's classless society, the male mind has tried to describe in writing a realistic dream of a more beautiful, free, and just world. These dreams usually had their roots in an illusory world of lofty ideas rather than in the inner reality of the people, which is why they did not have an impact on reality. Sometimes, as with Jesus, Robert Owen or the anarchist Kropotkin, their time had not yet come. Maybe it has now.

Ernst Bloch is the most eloquent philosopher of social utopias and their mental-spiritual background. If we still had time to read great literature, I would thoroughly recommend his Opus Magnum: "Das Prinzip Hoffnung" ["The Hope Principle"]. He created a special word to denote the true, yet veiled goal of history: "nondum" (Latin for "not yet"), the "not-yet-fulfilled", an image of the desired content and goal that underlie all utopias. This is a trans-historical matrix that constitutes the foundation of our historical existence. In our research group in Tamera we call it the "original historical utopia".

This historical human utopia can seldom be seen as clearly as in the founder of Christianity, Jesus of Nazareth. Jesus had a grand vision. He spoke of the coming "Kingdom of God on Earth". Through the power of his personal closeness to God, he was filled with a love that he thought would soon touch all of mankind. He felt that the time was right for a fundamental transformation of the human community in terms of an encompassing, forgiving love. Even on the cross he is supposed to have said: "Father, forgive them, for they know not what they do." Jesus was – in spite of some scholars' skepticism – a historical figure. He, alone, could not liberate humanity, but through his life he has shown us a new possibility of existence that still has an effect on many people. It is amazing how many people, from revolutionaries to atheists, truly love Jesus today. Wolf Biermann has written a song about Che Guevara in which he describes the Cuban revolutionary as "Jesus with a gun". Jesus' message was not heeded. Instead, the Church turned it into its most extreme opposite. But the Christ impulse that he embodied continues to be active in the souls of many people. A new image of the human being has arisen through him. The expression "God's Kingdom on Earth" is still valid today, although we would translate it in a different way. This concept brought about a change in the direction that religion has taken: happiness, love and salvation are to be celebrated here on earth, not in the hereafter. Heaven should come down to earth and life on earth should again fully connect with the divine. The cosmic and the social orders should come together again.

That is still today our highest goal. (I will keep coming back to these ideas in the next chapters.)

In connection with these ideas that Jesus spoke of, the dream of the "heavenly Jerusalem" was developed during early Christian times. In his text "Civitas Dei" from the year 425, the church father Augustine turned this idea into the utopia of the "Thousand Year Reign" in a "city of God", which was to be created by the church. Here, the typical Christian idea of a connection between power and asceticism had been changed so radically that there was not much left of the original thought. A similar thought, but a much gentler and more loving one, was developed eight hundred years later by Joachim di Fiore, an abbot from Florence. Based on the Bible, he developed a vision of history consisting of three successive states or eras of the world. The third state was the "societas amicorum" (society of friends), a state of monks living in brotherly love, also toward Jews and heathens. Here, Christ is fervently viewed as the Messiah of a new earth. It was a deep vision, but unfortunately the women were missing. Joachim's document triggered a wildfire of anticipation, for he had calculated that God's Kingdom would begin in the year 1260. First, the Antichrist was to be defeated. The Antichrist was the emperor Frederick II. It is difficult to determine what excited the Italian masses more: the expected last battle against the Antichrist or the imminence of the coming Kingdom of God. But the Stauffen emperor thwarted the plans of the believers: with no further ado he died in the year 1250 and could therefore no longer be fought. The hope for the coming paradise was lost in a tremendous turmoil of disappointment, hope, and anger, and the Joachites began to fight each other. It was a typical process resulting from betrayed hopes.

During the renaissance we find further great social utopias. This was the confused era in Western civilization, when the darkest Middle Ages fought the humanistic enlightenment and when a "rebirth" of Greek antiquity was celebrated, while at the same time the excesses of the Inquisition had a stranglehold on life. In the middle of this chaos three great utopian documents were published. The first was "Utopia" by Thomas More (1516), describing a communist democracy without private ownership. It contained deep, authentic, humane thoughts. Humans become evil only through distress, so why should they be so severely punished? Pleasure and the joy of life were seen as justified goals of human actions, and humaneness had fully taken on an earthly form. But adulterers should be severely punished! The time was not yet ripe for the freedom of sexual happiness to be incorporated into the utopian scenario. This thought could not be expressed publicly until 270 years later, by the early socialists.

One century after Thomas More, two other visions of the future were published: "Nova Atlantis" by Francis Bacon (1623) and the "City of the Sun " by Campanella (also 1623). Francis Bacon invented an island that was patterned on the legend of Atlantis and included the technical knowledge of the old Atlanteans. The citizens had telephones and steam engines, submarines and airplanes, they had psi powers, and they could create rain artificially. All this in a vision from 1623! In Campanellas City of the Sun there was a strict astrological order, so that everything occurred in cosmic precision at the right place at the right time. People lived in a communist way and with a relatively tolerant sexuality, but they were constricted by a dictatorship of the stars that did not allow them much freedom. One is reminded of the strange state that the Jesuits, in a spate of extreme missionary zeal, founded in Paraguay during the 17th century. Campanella lived for 27 years in Spanish prisons, but he never gave up his convictions. He welcomed the birth of the French king Louis XIV, who was not by chance called the "Sun King".

A great name among the humane visionaries is Robert Owen, an English industrialist during the time of the early socialists (around 1800). He worked with an unusual commitment for a humanization of the life conditions of the English working class. He suspected that there was a connection between a communist life form and sexual liberation, and he founded the "New Harmony" community in Indiana, USA. Robert Owen was a noble man in the deepest sense. He was correspondingly honored by a man who was similar to him in many ways: Friedrich Engels, the friend and patron of Karl Marx. Before Friedrich Engels wrote the Communist Manifesto together with Karl Marx, he wrote some statements at the age of 22 that I would like to quote in order to illustrate the effusive spirit of the times:

The self-consciousness of humanity, the new Grail, around whose throne the peoples are gathering and rejoicing (...) That is our profession, that we (...) tie our sword around our waist and joyfully lay down our lives for the last sacred war, after which shall follow the Thousand Years Reign of Freedom.

That is how deep the anticipation and the belief in the coming reign were in the minds of the young revolutionaries. That is how deep the chiliastic movement was, and all through the darkness its hopes had remained in the hearts of the people. In the "Paris Manuscripts" and even later in the Communist Manifesto, the young Karl Marx also wrote with the same passion about the final liberation of the human being from a thousand years of slavery. One can sense the meaning that hope once used to have. They truly wanted to improve the world. And today? Today, if you want to improve the world, you are regarded as a starry-eyed nutcase.

It is a tragic aspect of the historical utopias that the different lines of thought developed by the pioneers could not come together. The social issue and the sexual issue, for example, never truly came together. Marx and Engels could not subscribe to the ideas of the one man who had worked more than anyone else for the liberation of sexuality: Charles Fourier. He developed the "Phalanstères" project, a vision of free love, embedded in agriculture, crafts and Christian love of one's neighbor. Every day, from noon until 1 pm, he waited for the patron who would help him to finance the project. But the patron never came. We may smile, today, when we read about how schematically Fourier imagined sexual liberation. But Fourier had arrived at the center of the issue. He did not have empirical success, but his name will forever be connected to the idea of sexual liberation.

If Marx had understood Fourier's ideas, and if he had included them in his concept, then a different kind of communism would have arisen. One of the fundamental thoughts of communism was the abolition of private property. This resulted in a new economic model, but there was not yet a new model for the inner relationship between people, especially no model for the areas of love and sexuality. Men were still allowed to see and treat their wives as private property, and the same was true for family heads toward their families and for parents toward their children. A tight fence was still built around every love relationship, the love partner was privatized, and sexuality was banned from public life. After the October Revolution in 1917, there were some tendencies toward an anti-authoritarian way of raising children and – for example under the auspices of Alexandra Kollontai – for the liberation from the old ideas around love and sexuality. But these tendencies were soon reversed in the name of party discipline. Sexually, a proper Soviet citizen was to behave like a proper bureaucrat during the Czar era. The emotional structures of a communist functionary hardly differed from those in other authoritarian, capitalist, and fascist systems. It was the type of structure that [the German philosopher Theodor] Adorno described as an "authoritarian personality" with its sexual repression, its belief in authority and its fight against dissenters. The economic system was revolutionized, but the sexual system remained feudalistic, Christian, middle-class, and capitalist, as it did everywhere. Here lay the central inner inconsistency of Marxism and of the communist movement that it gave rise to. Marxism saw one area as being separate from the other, thus ignoring the inner unity that connects the different areas of life in human society. Whoever wants to create a new economic system must establish a new sexual order. For, as Marx rightly said, the societal existence of the human being determines his consciousness and his sexual existence is fundamentally a part of his societal existence. One main reason for the worldwide failure of communism was that the liberation from the class society did not go hand in hand with liberation from its historically developed sexual ideas. The communist dream was not taken to its conclusion. It could therefore not be realized. It will reappear in an entirely different form, when people have learned to lead a communitarian life where they no longer need to lie about love. The communist dream is the original dream of the human community.

A dream does not have reality-creating power until it is dreamt realistically, i.e. when what is dreamt corresponds to a real possibility in life. The New Left movement, which was created in Germany during the Sixties, soon took notice of the texts by Wilhelm Reich, describing his sexual theories, and pirated editions of these texts were spread in large numbers. It was sensed instinctively that there can be no free society without free sexuality. In groups and communes one tried to understand the essence of free sexuality, but no progress was made. We did not yet have a concrete vision of a new life. One did not know what free sexuality meant in terms of content, and one could not yet see it with one's heart. The sexual issue could not be solved overnight, for it was connected to too many misunderstandings, human collisions, claims of ownership and power struggles, competition, fear of abandonment, and pains of jealousy. As usual, the first failure resulted in a reversal to its opposite, and in large numbers the comrades began to marry and create their own private lives. That was the end of the movement. But what is five years of a movement compared to five thousand years of oppression? Historically speaking, the students' movement's first attempts at taking its first steps were a small, almost childish beginning of an overall movement that had just begun. This movement cannot be held back forever by today's counter-propaganda. **A future worth living requires a different model of sensual love or it will not come about at all.** Countless people would agree with this statement if they knew what this new model could look like and if they had the courage to speak of it openly. It is difficult to speak the truth about sexual matters without endangering one's own love relationship, marriage, or social position.

I could not give up the dream. After the failure of the New Left, I sought out other possibilities to continue to work with these new thoughts. Again, I spent a few years learning and traveling, I visited over a hundred communes, and was amazed at my political friends who by now had settled down in the country to seek the meaning of life by milking sheep every morning. One no longer read Karl Marx's Political Economy, but the Tibetan Book of the Dead, the Bhagavad-Gita and old books about herbs. The political vision had broken down. Could a new, different vision arise so soon thereafter? Could political thinking so quickly be exchanged for a new spiritual and ecological thinking? Had it really been true political thinking? Or were the ideologies really so interchangeable? The goals of the fight against imperialism, which shortly before had been proclaimed by millions of young people all over the world, suddenly no longer existed, and there was hardly a trace left of the sexual liberation movement. The more the old dream broke down, the longer became the psychological conversations at breakfast, at lunch, at dinner and at the evening meetings. It was in this situation that I – the first time in October 1975 – visited [the community of] "Friedrichshof" in the Austrian province of Burgenland. It was created and led by the Austrian painter and action artist Otto Mühl.

Friedrichshof was a revolutionary experiment. The plan was to create a community with free sexuality and authentic, honest human relationships. Here, there was a concept and a vision: bioenergetics, translated into group life and into social design. No project up until then had so radically attempted to translate the idea of sexual liberation into reality as this one did. The project had a bad reputation, I disliked many of its views and methods, and yet it was the only project that had a relatively truthful way of dealing with the "number one" topic. That alone was enough for me to get over my personal aversions and to enthusiastically study the conditions there. Sixty people lived there under the leadership of an impressive artist, in a totally unfamiliar system of free sexuality, a total lack of private property, and a grotesque lack of comfort. There were no radios, TV's or newspapers. There were no sofas or recliners. There was no alcohol or other drugs and practically no cigarettes. It was the harshest living environment that I had ever been in. It was only tolerable because of the emotional vitality, the creativity, and the sexual contacts. In front of the guests' quarters, which consisted of a slightly modified grain silo with a pigsty, there were a few puny acacias, otherwise there were only open fields. There were no diversions, not even through nature. Everything had to be created by humans. If there was anywhere anything fundamental to learn about the creation of community, then it was here. For almost all other communities had already failed and no new perspectives were visible anywhere.

What was being established here was one of the most radical social utopias that had ever been dreamed of in the history of the community movement, from its beginning with the American Hutterites up until today. And yet this experiment, too, failed because of the usual conflicts around sex, power and money. They did not know all that had to be done in a community in order to be able to solve such problems. They knew something about the importance of sexuality, but they knew nothing about the universal and spiritual conditions of our existence. These conditions must be considered and integrated if we want to create a community with truly free sexuality, without hypocrisy and the misuse of power. The emotionality that was developed there was not free or else they would not a few years later have experienced the eruptions of hatred and public denunciations that divided the community and finally destroyed it. This project failed, as did the communist one before it, due to dogmatic narrow-mindedness. But we are not here to judge, but to learn from the mistakes of others.

We cannot end this brief history of social utopias without at least taking a brief look at the Sannyas movement that was founded by Osho (Shree Rajneesh Bhagwan). For a short while it succeeded in creating one of the 20th century's most amazing experiments: Rajneeshpuram, a New Age city of a few thousand inhabitants in the US state of Oregon. The project created an astonishing synthesis of sexuality, spirituality, and emotional liberation, which for a while was connected with a definite global vision for the future of mankind. Altogether, there were almost half a million Sannyasins on earth. Their red clothes testified to their willingness to act on their beliefs. And yet they did not have mature enough concepts to guide this collective willingness. Bhagwan's encompassing mind knew much about the background of religions and of the history of ideas, but he did not know much about the work that must be done in order to dismantle the inner structures of power, dominion, competition, and fear. Here, he relied on Western therapists who offered many groups and seminars in Poona, where they were originally stationed, and yet they did not quite deal with the heart of the matter. And so, in spite of all outer

113

successes, the old conflicts around power, sex and love could continue to grow under the surface until they created the disaster in Oregon that resulted in a media frenzy. To me, this movement was as interesting and important as the one created by Otto Mühl. Here, too, a new direction was being explored that we today can integrate and develop further on a more solid foundation. When we today look for authentic texts around spiritual and sexual issues, then some of the writings of Osho, the Indian revolutionary and philosopher, are still among the best.

When trying to judge the historical and philosophical importance of peace work today, it is not important if one is for or against the representatives or the statements of a given social utopia or movement. What is important is to look beyond the shortcomings and mistakes of a movement and to recognize and see its inner gestalt or entelechy. It is important to see to what extent this image is aligned with the larger process of human evolution that keeps reconnecting us with the powers of Creation and with the trans-historical matrix of a non-violent, universal life. We hold this process inside of us as an inner signpost, we can recognize it, and we are definitely faced with the decision whether to follow it or to perish.

Paradise Lost.
Memories of an Ancient Civilization

Knowest thou where the lemon blossom grows,
In foliage dark the orange golden glows,
A gentle breeze blows from the azure sky,
Dost know it well?
'Tis there! 'Tis there
Would I with thee, oh my beloved, fare.

　　Goethe: Mignon's Song of Longing

There are fairytales that are truer than the facts of today because they illuminate a deeper core of truth. They contain a memory of something that already was or shall be. They cast a light on a real possibility in Creation of a deeper human life. One of these stories is the one of the lost paradise. It is an unusually profound story that we can follow if we allow ourselves to resonate with it and enter into a state of deep dreaming while awake. In the past, visions came about through this type of dreaming. From here, the priestesses and their apprentices became seers and on their mental-spiritual horizon they saw the things that sank down into the past and those that arose in the future. They could let them come closer and look through them, and they could see what always exists, beyond the past and the future. They saw the connection between humans and the divine; they saw the mirror of Creation in the order of the tribe, in the love between the sexes, and in their joint caring for life. They saw the connections between the various centers of the earth like the lines of light in a crystal. "Dreaming seeing" was their method of accessing knowledge. They built their own spaces for this to occur. One of these spaces was the subterranean Hypogeum on the island of Malta.

　　Paradise lost is life before and after the great separation. It is the vision of a human society that is aligned with Creation. It manifests on earth what we used to think of as "heaven". What did we, as children, mean when we spoke of "heaven"? Heaven was the epitome of everything that was good. It was paradise. If such a vision of paradise remains intact during thousands of years, then there must be something true about it. No child would believe in such a heaven if it had not experienced this heaven in some form before. These are not just images that comfort us in a difficult reality; they are images of reality itself that reside in us in a latent form – either as memories or as dreams –and are waiting to be realized.

115

We know the lost paradise. Humans were free of fear. They could therefore contact and communicate with all beings. They could stay in a deep state of perception for a long time without the risk of their stream of perception being interrupted by fear or fright. With growing curiosity they could follow the tracks of an animal and understand what it was doing, and they could grasp and connect with its soul. They constantly lived in the present and they let themselves be guided by what the present presented to them. Through their presence they achieved a high, almost extra-sensory level of sensual perception. By smelling the landscape they could sense the changes in the weather. They could go into caves and into water and gain profound insights into the origin of life. Because of their openness to the elements, they knew why all life came from water. It was an adventure and a joy to discover and come to know all this. They were close to the divine world and they discovered it in everything; it was the medium that they moved around in. They retained full memory from the other world that they came from. When they focused on the flow of things they could develop powers that are incomprehensible to us today. They thus built their temples and erected their dolmen and their stone circles. This was not based on physical effort, as it would be for us; instead it was based on the full connection with a flowing energy. They knew the secret of effortless work. In extrasensory sensuality they could listen to the tones of nature for a long time and sing along with it. They noticed how an entire world vibrated in these tones, and they knew the music of the spheres long before Pythagoras and Johannes Kepler did. They received images of the stars and they saw what they meant. This was how they developed an astronomy that came from an innermost connection to the universe.

In her books about the stone circle at Évora in Portugal ("Traumsteine" ["Dream Stones"]) and about the temples on Malta ("Tempel der Liebe" ["Temple of Love"]) Sabine Lichtenfels has described an historical journey of discovery. Through archaeological studies on location, combined with an unusual path of spiritual guidance, through trances and a mediumistic perspective, she encounters an ancient civilization that had the characteristics of a highly developed paradise. In 1994 the author travels to Portugal and visits the stone circle close to the city of Évora in the Alentejo region. This stone circle is one of the best preserved documents of the Stone Age. It is considerably older than Stonehenge and other mystery places of the megalith culture. While inside the stone circle, the author enters into a network of information through mediumistic inspirations and receives messages and images of the tribal culture that created the stone circle. It contains unusual insights into the world memory bank, the so-called Akashic Chronicle of human evolution and history. A voyage of discovery begins that goes far beyond the local importance of the stone circle. A long chain of "coincidences" and good fortune, of clues, dreams, trances, and encounters leads to an almost complete picture of an ancient civilization, which must have existed for at least 2000 years, probably longer, in different parts of the world. It ended during the fifth millennium B.C. through the invasion by the so-called Kurgan people, a much less developed male culture that was more violent than anything to date.

In the peace cultures of Évora and Malta there seems to have been no fear of wild animals, cold, storms, stronger tribes or neighboring enemies. From the beginning, the tribal order guided the children and youth into a deep connection with all fellow creatures. Communication with animals and plants was as natural as their vegetarian diet, clairvoyance, free love, self-healing and self-sufficiency in all things, for Nammu, the Mother of the Earth and the Sky, provided for everyone. The female priests and the tribal elders were her natural servants and representatives on earth. They had a natural authority, not by domination, but through their knowledge. Together with Nammu, their highly developed knowledge about astronomy and geomancy, sacred places and sacred shrines, and other peoples and continents helped them to realize a dream on earth, which had been lying dormant in humanity for a long time.

It is a great discovery. If such a model of a non-violent human culture has truly existed and if it functioned during several thousand years on earth, then we know that the vision of a non-violent society is more than just wishful thinking. The atrocities that the human being has committed everywhere on earth during the last five thousand years are then not the result of an eternally valid law. War and violence are then historically developed deformations and no longer universal constants of human existence. The possibility for a non-violent world becomes a real tangible possibility. The discovery of matriarchal peace cultures, as described in the books by Marija Gimbutas, Riane Eisler, Heide Göttner-Abendroth and others, is then filled with such realism and presence that we look at our own era with completely new eyes and wonder how such cruel alienation and forgetting could ever occur. The deepest impression we are left with is that we are seeing a real source for our own lives, a source that has been constantly flowing because it is a part of the universal nature of the human being. Here, we find the matrix of a trans-historical, universal order of human society. The author speaks of a "prehistoric utopia". This utopia is latently present as a reality in all things. It is the real, but not yet realized, possibility within the process of human history. It is the essential utopian content that Ernst Bloch was seeking when he spoke of the "nondum of history" in his great work "Das Prinzip Hoffnung" ["The Principle of Hope"].

If we follow the journey of discovery that Sabine Lichtenfels describes, we know that it cannot be invented. We sense that it was more than the private will of one person that was interested in transmitting and awakening a comprehensive truth about our history. We now know of yet another source for the creation of new living spaces, and we have yet another essential argument for our belief in a non-violent future. This legacy of history, too, resides in us. I give thanks to the universe for this message. It has again opened our eyes to the importance of sexual love in the destiny of human history. The processes of sexual desire that are described in the book about the stone circle ("Traumsteine" ["Dream Stones"]) and that ultimately lead to violence cannot be invented, for one can feel the logic and the consistency of the inner processes. It was the power of the sexual desire on the part of both sexes that led them to breach the boundaries of the old religious tribal order and break the sacred laws of the Mother Goddess. The human being thus began to fall out of Creation. If we pay close attention to the story of this "original fall" then we feel such empathy and understanding – if not sympathy - towards those involved, that we can hardly blame them personally. There was no evil or cruel intent involved, and yet we spontaneously understand the inner logic, which resulted in the chain of violence and fear that evolved out of this event and put its stamp on our history for thousands of years. The sexual war that raged during the entire patriarchal era and that brought many women to the edge of physical annihilation during the Inquisition can only be overcome once we return to the historic and mythological source of this war and reintroduce the sexual issue into the universal order of our existence. The "prehistoric utopia," which we here encounter in the form of a highly developed tribal civilization from the Neolithic Age, shows us a vision and a direction for this liberation. It represents the liberation of both sexes so that we can fully overcome the patriarchal dead end street.

I quote a morning prayer from the book "Quellen der Liebe und des Friedens" ["Sources of Love and Peace"]:

Imagine that you are standing in front of a time portal.
This portal is the opening into paradise.
You walk through it and look into a new world.
It is truly the Garden of Eden.
It exists already now as a latent reality.
Live in the consciousness of this higher presence.
Hear the call of the birds, the plants, the animals and the angel beings.
They are waiting for the human being.
An entire world wants to reveal itself to you – in you and around you.
Recognize within yourself your own higher image.
It exists already now at this moment.

Chapter 4
The Issue of Sexuality

A future worth living does not come from computers,
but from a new relationship between the sexes.

Global insanity can only be overcome
once sensual love is no longer connected
with degradation.

Night Thoughts about a New Friendship between the Sexes.

My thoughts are dedicated to all those who love. They come from the hearts of many women and men, when they are in the state of love. Together, we must find a solution for this topic, an opening whereby none of the partners suffers anymore. We need a solution that comes from love, not from retaliation. We have suffered for too long where we wanted to love. There are too many people who once loved and today are living lives with closed hearts because they were betrayed. Up until today they have not understood or gotten over this betrayal.

The fight about morals between the representatives of the old morality and those of sexual liberation must be overcome at a new level, where the true longings of both can come together, based on human understanding and reconciliation. For this fight goes on in all of us, for example as a conflict between faithfulness to one person and the natural attraction to others. We can no longer define faithfulness in the old way, for that definition did not measure up to life, it was too narrow. We cannot ignore the developmental history of mankind. What is trying to break through in the area of sexual liberation is only the beginning of a new history. Whether dealing with pornography or personal ads, open marriage or group sex, exchanging partners or free sexuality: the historical development of the human being in the erotic area tends toward a dissolution of the old forms and of the old sexual morals. The human being no longer feels comfortable in the old structure and is instinctively seeking new possibilities. Let us see to it that it does not just lead to a dissolution of the old forms, but that this process leads to a new substance of love and the realization of the dream that so many are dreaming.

We dream of partnership, and maybe we live in a partnership. Has our dream really been fulfilled? Do I not secretly dream of another, larger, freer form of partnership? Can I really, from deep within my own core, join in with the choir of indignation when it comes to so-called affairs, to nighttime fantasies, and "indecent thoughts"? Do not I myself dream of such or similar things? If I am a woman, do I not sometimes have sexual fantasies that go against all morality and all so-called human dignity? Do I not fully understand why Erica Jong traveled the world to find the anonymous "spontaneous fuck"? And are men any different? Are these dreams really only dreams? Are they not very real longings that I have to keep to myself because they are seen as immoral? But who has invented these morals and why? Is it possible that the representatives of decency and human dignity, who have always surrounded our lives, had to create morals as an inner bastion against the immoral thoughts that they themselves are thinking, against the sexual fantasies that they themselves indulge in, and against the dreams that they themselves secretly dream?

Now that I am embedded into this society and live in a couple relationship or a marriage, where maybe I have children, do I really have to play along in this game of deception? I do not want to betray what was beautiful and sacred about the original ideal of marriage. But I do want to change what is too constricted about it, too small and too untruthful. The truth is that I love him or her. But it is also true that specifically due to this love, I have the ability and feel the desire to love others. In reality if I, as a woman, have begun to love a man, I love the male sex, and as a man, if I have begun to really see and love a woman, I love the entire female sex – unless I am carrying around too many fears. If, in this growing freedom, I could love without judgment and without losing my partner, then I could begin to think about everything in freedom and I could express entirely different thoughts. I want a partner who understands all this and who helps to make it happen. S/he would be my anchor, my faithfulness. With her or with him I would have a partnership forever. I would warmly invite everybody who wants to join us in this joy. Who or what is really stopping us from saying and doing this? In the most beautiful moments I have the feeling that love is the model for all human relationships, not just for those between two lovers. I want to carry out into the world what I experience in this one relationship in terms of a feeling of security, solidarity and sensual as well as mental and spiritual joy, and I want to be able to share it with others. And then I want to come back and tell her/him everything about it. I believe that true partnership between man and woman is the source of a general spiritual and sensual humaneness. If I could truly trust someone, then I could neither hate nor be jealous if s/he would love or desire my wo/man as much as I do. I would expect it, and I would be surprised if it were not so. Why does one have to fence off one's lover from the rest of the world?

Pornography, brothels, or indiscriminate sexuality are of course no solution. They are only the other side of the coin of the too narrow image of love that was connected to the old forms of marriage, faithfulness, and partnership. Because these forms were too narrow, distrust and habitual swindling have become the norm. Under these circumstances, permanent love and faithfulness could not arise. The old forms that were supposed to protect love have ruined it instead. Or does someone believe that those, who today live in the old forms, tend to have happy faces?

And what about us? Have we not become masters of deception? Do we not know the thoughts that so many are thinking: If my fellow human beings only knew what I really think and feel! I break the law in every sexual fantasy that I have. I have to "normalize" myself every morning anew. Must it forever be necessary for people to get used to this double life? Does one have to settle for this so-called normal way of life forever? Do not all the others feel the way I do? Whom are we really obeying, and whom do we bow to? Are they our own laws? Have we ever even thought about it? When will the human being begin to take his life in his own hands? When will he have the courage to take a stand for his own desires and longings and begin to take action? Doing what we love. I once read a powerful statement: "When I love, then I love, and no external law may step in front of the altar of my love." Since I am a woman or a man, when I speak of love, I always also mean the sensual and physical union with all those whom I love and desire.

Partnership is one of the most beautiful things I know. I have always dreamed of it. But is it really an irrevocable law that I can only have it with one person? Does not this love for one person create the joy, of which Jesus said: "Go ye into all the world…"? Is there not, when our world has again been put in order, a closeness of the heart and a love between people, in small but growing groups, where more and more people join in, and yet where intimacy is retained? I would like to go out again and again, but I would also like to return again and again. I want this most intimate and familiar sense of home, which gives me the courage to go out, to open up for me when I return. I am like a child who has found the joy of discovery, but who still needs security. Are we maybe all such children? If we are, then we should agree on this common humane foundation and we should stop pretending. Since we already have become adults, whether recently or long ago, we should use our experience and our intelligence to ensure that these matters of the heart finally see the light of day and help us build a new, humane, joyful society of women, men, and children. We need a new vision for our lives together and the courage to make it real. We need an idea that helps me if I, as a woman, love two men and an idea that helps me when I, as a man, desire several women. We need a new idea for sensual love in its entirety. I am ready and willing to do what it takes. The foundation for a new future is truth between people, especially between lovers and, as [the German singer] Nina Hagen once said, this truth is the new form of our religion.

What is Sexuality?

Man:
Sexual life was given to the human being
in order to distract him from his true path.

   Albert Camus

Woman:
A woman's identity is always sexual,
there is none other

   Cathérine Breillat

Sexuality is the source of human life. Rarely has a human being been found who was not created through sexuality. Sexuality is the basic "mana" power of the human body. Every psychosomatic illness is based, either directly or indirectly, on a disturbance in the sexual energy household. Sexual energy is a life energy, which flows through all body parts, not just the genitalia, supplying them with health. Sexuality is the conceiving power in the universe, which, when it flows through the soul and the body of a human being, elicits deep feelings of longing, desire, and passion. Pure sexuality is sexuality that is not clouded by fear, degradation, or bad thoughts. It is lusty nakedness without the farce of false emotions. Pure sexuality is one of the strongest forces in human life and one of the strongest creative forces in human culture and history. Sexuality is the basis for all areas of human existence, and it therefore runs through society as an invisible web of attraction and repulsion.

Sexuality is "topic number one", for like nothing else it characterizes people's longings, addictions, and secret fantasies. If Albert Camus had known true sexuality, he would not have written the statement above. Sexuality contains the sweetest of grapes, but they were often declared to be sour because they were out of reach. Sexuality is not limited to the heterosexual relationship between man and woman, but that is where it has its roots and its goal. Sexuality is the love gift of the sexes that was given to us by nature at birth. The world emerged "from an original wedding night" (Walter Schubart). Without sexuality we can neither understand the world, nor the history of human beings, nor ourselves. Sexual knowledge is true mystery knowledge. If we knew everything about sexuality, there would be much that we would not need to know, and yet we would know much more than we have ever known. If we had a fully satisfied sexual life, then there is much that we would not need to have, and yet we would have more than we have ever had. If we were to see the divine in sexuality, then we could do without many religions. If a human society were to access the full healing power of sexuality, then it would hardly need any hospitals or prisons. If we were to love sexuality, then we would love all bodily things and would no longer destroy them. Sexuality is the power of the soul in our world that keeps all bodily things together. Sexuality is pure lust, it is pure. The filth was invented and added by humans. Sexuality is the deepest pleasure of the flesh, the passion of the flesh. But it is also the deepest bliss of the soul, the spiritual joy at what one can mutually give each other, and the joy at having "arrived". Pure sexuality is the biological form of love. It is love. But it is not necessarily personal love. Sexual love is sometimes quite animalistic, sometimes it is a cosmic, almost sacred love, and sometimes it is these things together. Right sexuality is the right joining of the two halves of human beings: man and woman. Free and pure sexuality is the mutual bodily re-cognition of the sexes. It is deep communication, deep union, and deep recognition at the physical level. Sexual knowledge is body knowledge. But the body is always of the soul and therefore sexual knowledge is always deep knowledge of the soul. Not knowledge of traditional psychology, but knowledge of life. If our medicine were to consist of sexual knowledge, we would need less therapy and fewer instruments. One single park for free sexuality would replace ten hospitals. Sexuality is a world power. Mata Hari, the first public naked dancer, confused entire nations and armies at the beginning of the last century, until she was shot dead by the French military during the First World War. Sexuality has always played a role in politics. It almost caused the fall of Willy Brandt and of Franz Josef Strauß. If Bill Clinton had not been such a coward, he would not have given in after his affair with Monika Lewinsky. Rather, he would have taken a stand for his joy at this woman and protected her from the public.

Sexuality is the area in life in which most lies are told today. Sexuality is the power that so far had to be excluded in order for human co-existence to function. But that, specifically, was the reason why it could not function. Sexuality is the area of human life of which 90 percent occurs in fantasies and only 10 percent in reality. Everybody has an allergic reaction to sexuality, because everybody wants it and hardly anybody has it. Sexuality is the aspect of life that people are most touchy about. If we hear that someone has won the lottery or has bought a beautiful car, then we may feel a bit envious, but if we hear that he has succeeded in seducing our neighbor, then we catch our breath. If our love partner says that he or she loves someone, then this may worry us, but if we hear that s/he desires someone and has gone to bed with him/her and that it was incredible, then we go pale.

Sexuality is the call of humanity, it is its shudder of panic, and its great promise. Pure sexuality is the ultimate bodily encounter of the sexes in freedom and joy, in natural equality and solidarity. Loving sexuality is the binding power of parents that makes their children flourish. Sexuality is the basic force in our lives and without its full recognition, liberation, and fulfillment we can never have true emancipation, neither of men nor of women. Ernst Bloch sought the great "nondum", the unredeemed goal of history. We can at least provide him with an essential part of the answer: sexual fulfillment. That he was so far from this thought is understandable, for a human society that makes it possible for its members to experience sexual fulfillment still lay beyond all utopian horizons. Sexuality is as deep as religion and both come together at its source. Sexuality is the power of the Goddess.

Who is Lilith?

Let me start out by saying that she has long since caught up with me and cast her spell over me. I got to know her when I was twenty and since then I cannot break loose from her. She has plagued me, tormented me, and kept me awake, so that I would remain faithful to her. She is my great female soul, my sexual seductress, almost my twin sister. Everyone, who has known Lilith, is forever marked by her. They curse her or become addicted to her. She is seen as the embodiment of evil, for she represents the power of sexuality.

Lilith is a mythological figure. She is a woman, who symbolizes both the good and the bad demonic nature of the sexual driving forces, and at night she haunts both men and women in their dreams. Lilith is older than Eve. She appears already in the Babylonian myths and wanders like a ghost in the realm of the gods that is still not quite controlled by man. Sabine Lichtenfels had the following to say about Lilith (in her book about Malta entitled "Temple of Love"):

Lilith? Why did I dream of this name? Was that not the aspect of the feminine, that in the Bible was condemned as being evil itself?

Eve was the one who wedded Adam and was finally driven from Paradise. But Lilith was the aspect of the feminine that could never be caught. It was the wild female nature, which even through the centuries could not be tamed. This female aspect reigned in the underground in spite of all attempts to tame it and it wreaked havoc whenever it was not given the right to live.

Before the Hebrews invaded the "promised land" of Canaan three thousand years ago and destroyed the existing culture there, both the women and the men there saw Lilith as the "sacred mistress." Then began - first in old Israel and then in Christianity – the merciless fight against Lilith and against all those who worshiped her. Lilith and her daughters, the "lilim", continued to haunt the men. Abstinent monks tried to ward her off by crossing their hands, which held on to a crucifix, over their genitals. It was said, that Lilith laughed every time a pious Christian had a wet dream (pollution). When a boy laughed in his dream, people said that Lilith was caressing him.

During the Middle Ages she was regarded as the Devil's sister. The Christians called Lilith's daughters the "whores of hell" or the "witches of the night". They appeared in people's dreams and were supposedly very beautiful. Just like their brothers, the so-called "incubi", they were believed to be so knowledgeable in the art of love that a man who had had an experience with a night witch could no longer be satisfied by the love of a mortal woman. Lilith was the power and the figure who was to be erased from the universe, once and for all, during the witch trials of the Middle Ages. She was the power of pure sexuality, unbound by a partner, place, or law. She is the power that keeps intruding into the life of humans and causes true havoc, as long as humans hold on to their medieval prohibitions and do not create a new erotic culture with enough place for Lilith's free and wild joy - the joy of personal as well as anonymous sexuality. Lilith is the eternal admonition to create a new sexual order for humanity, so that the woman who has been displaced can return in her fullness.

Lilith and the Confused Spouses

It is difficult to reconcile Lilith with the traditional concepts of marriage and faithfulness. Again I quote from the book "Temple of Love" by Sabine Lichtenfels:

I thought of the legend of Lilith and how she visits men at night in order to celebrate the feast of the anonymous encounter with them. The jealous married women guarded their men so that they would not be sought out by Lilith, for they suspected that the longing awakened through Lilith would sweep them away to the longing for other women. Aroused by Lilith's appearance, a man would be driven by his restless desire, and his longing would again and again drive him to distant shores, out into the world, to other women. The married women suspected that now that they lived in a golden cage with their desired prince their own desire could not be satisfied. Although on a glorious day, in the intoxication of the first joy of love, they had promised each other eternal love and faithfulness, although they had believed that they had arrived at the goal of their greatest wishes and desires, everything had now changed. Her unfulfilled desire and her worries caused her to have many a restless night. Every seductive smile by a beautiful woman, every tight bottom, and every well-rounded bosom became a threat. The thorn of envy and resentment suddenly poisoned her originally pure, loving heart. This also drove away her best women friends and she found herself again in isolated loneliness together with her husband, whom she had so strongly desired before, but who now often seemed like a stranger to her. She felt that her own body would remain behind in unfulfilled hunger. Their love nights no longer led to the fulfillment that she longed for. The originally euphoric, deep, and sensual embraces had become flat and mundane. The first lines of frustration and disappointment could be seen in her face. And so, as the years went by, her original wildness and beauty slowly transformed into the features of a frustrated house monster. As she thus watched over her husband in jealousy, so did he watch over her. Although he kept seeking signs of Lilith in the distance, in the bars, on business trips, in the darkened light of expensive brothels, he did this secretly, in hiding. This life was not allowed to see the light of day and become a part of his public life. There he was the well functioning husband who watched over his wife. She was his security, she was the Mama that he had bought. The adventure that was afforded him was not by a long shot afforded to her. He was happy that she was jealous, for that gave him the certainty that he could rule over her. Once in a while they still performed the duties of marriage, but otherwise their lives were centered around cars, television, money, travel, children, and good food. They plastered their lives full so that they would not be reminded of the pain of their unfulfilled love and of the great promise that they had once made to each other.

While all this was going on, Lilith kept on visiting millions of bedrooms. Millions and millions of couples experienced the same destiny in love. They thought that their unhappiness was their own very personal, private misery, and they did not suspect that the same drama was played out behind all their neighbors' walls. They all covered their dark fate with the veil of silence. While they sat in front of the window or went about their everyday lives, covering their frustration with consumption, they secretly dreamed of another, greater and more fulfilling love. They no longer noticed that all around them a whole world was being destroyed and that their own silence and growing need for vicarious satisfaction in the form of money and consumption essentially contributed to this destruction. They had blocked out the world and its issues from their lives.

At night Lilith visited not only the husbands. She also came to the wives. She gave them the wildest sexual dreams that usually were so far beyond what was seen as legitimate in this society that they were shocked and hid these dreams from themselves and especially from their friends. Only sometimes was the veil lifted and at the breakfast table one could read in the newspaper: "Jealous woman jumped to her death" or "Jealous husband shot wife and children. The reason for his deed was the young neighbor with whom she had an affair."

In this account, which every woman and every man can understand, one can see the entire reason for the necessity of creating a different model of sensual love, a model that gives us back the erotic freedom that we have given away to the judging eyes of others and liberates us from the need to constantly lie. Truth in sexual love is one of the great key concepts for healing the human being and the earth. Here, we are no longer dealing with therapy. Instead, as one can sense, we are dealing with the creation of a new erotic culture in a new human society.

Lilith's Words.
The Healing Message in Sexuality

It is the very source of the Goddess
that hits us in the passing glance of a stranger.
It is the memory of the source of Creation,
from which we all came.

The Earth will not rest,
and the sky will not pause,
until this longing has found its true fulfillment.

    Lilith

Lilith is an aspect of Nammu, the Goddess of Life, and thus an aspect of all women. All men are attracted by this aspect, even if they feel that they have to resist it with all their power. It is the aspect of the Lorelei that impacts the male sex with inescapable power until the day comes when both sexes recognize each other and unite. Then, as the initiates know, woman will be a revelation for man and vice versa. Goethe, our German prince of poets, is one of the main authorities on this female power. He experienced it so strongly physically during his own nights, and he described it so intensely in "Werther" and in "Faust" that the literary world, out of pure reverence, hardly noticed what most intimate of male issues was dealt with here. He encountered Lilith, the "eternally female", he craved for her and suffered under her, he left his office in Weimar in the dead of night to seek her sources in Italy. He "sought Helena in every woman" and in spite of his personal defeat, he took a stand for his deepest desire in life: "The eternally female draws us upwards." And he lets Faust, who remained totally unredeemed, groan:

In depths of sensual pleasure drowned
Let us our fiery passions still;
Enwrapped in magic's veil profound
Let wondrous charm our senses thrill...

In Hagar Qim, an ancient temple ruin on Malta, Sabine Lichtenfels fell into a trance-like state and encountered Lilith. In her book she writes of this encounter and gives a rendering of Lilith's words that touched me so deeply and urgently that I must include it in this book, especially since it contains the deepest of healing messages. Sabine Lichtenfels posed some basic questions to Lilith about the issue of Eros: What can be done so that the full intensity of Eros can be lived? How can this be combined with the great longing for partnership? How can women learn to overcome their jealousy when they love and desire the same man? What can be said about the powerful desire that is triggered in the area of anonymous Eros, for example, when one sees a well-built dark-skinned man? How can one here remain centered and connected to one's own power? Why is the fear so great in this area, and how can it be overcome?

This was Lilith's great answer:

During our first encounter on Malta, I already gave you many answers to your questions. I will try to do so again. The longing for the unknown in love, the intense desire that a glance by a stranger or the form of a body can elicit and the longing for a couple relationship and a partnership both share the same core. Two beings want to love and recognize each other in their beauty and freedom. They would like to give themselves. They want to arrive at the deepest foundation of communication in elementary body presence. **It is the very basis of the Goddess that we encounter when the gaze of a stranger, of a man or a woman, hits us full force. And it is the longing for the eternal presence of the Goddess and of coming home to her that touches us in our longing for permanent intimacy and partnership. It is the memory of the source of Creation, from which we all have come.** *It is a reminder of the fact that at the deepest level we are all connected in one existence. We want to find this again. All our cells want to be suffused and lit up by this insight. Nothing strange should separate us any more. The light of mutual recognition should shine onto that which is strange, just as it should shine onto the presence and familiarity of everyday life.* **The one cannot be understood, and especially not fulfilled, without the other. Neither can find fulfillment or peace without understanding the sacred aspect of sexuality. It is the longing for transformation, for the permanent presence of the divine that seeks fulfillment in the longing of the sexes. In both cases it is the Goddess who the man has briefly seen in woman and that he is now trying to encounter.** *In her male lover, the woman seeks the manifestation of male divine power. Behind all her longings we find the sensual Messiah. The longing of Creation is reflected in the longing of humans. The earth will not rest and the sky will not pause until this longing has found its true fulfillment. Every fulfillment gives birth to a new longing. That is the game of Creation that guides all becoming.*

There is nothing that seeks a balance in its own center, and nothing that seeks certainty in its own center as much as the fulfillment of longing in love. The rituals and the rules of life that our ancestors abided by served to find the balance in one's own middle and the power of calm and centering in oneself. ... There is ultimately only one answer to all of your questions. **The issue of love can only find its solution from the connection with the whole. In this connection lies the healing for jealousy, fear, violence, and the pain of the fear of being abandoned.** *Practice being connected with Creation and you will be taken safely to the goal of your longing. Follow the energy, but be awake and present as you do so. The divine voice lives within you. Only those who know this will also be able to meet it on the outside. No man and no woman will be able to satisfy your longing unless you have found this connection from within again. If impatience or fear arises in you, then that, too, is a sign of the presence of the Goddess. They are already the signs of a great blocked energy. ... Get to the bottom of your fear and you will find the answer. Follow your impatience and try to understand it spiritually; then you will find a new direction for your actions. Get to the bottom of your anger and you will find a mighty source of power for authentic action.*

By thinking that one wants to conquer what one loves for oneself, against the will of the whole, one at the same time begins to kill what one originally loved about the other. No Goddess will ever let herself be conquered and no freedom in love will ever let itself be locked up in a cage. The mutual penetration, which is aligned with Creation, lies very close to the desire to be conquered, and this results in misunderstandings. At a somewhat lower and less connected level, a woman's desire to fully belong to one man is the same thought as the desire, coming from the connection with the whole, to fully love and recognize a person. Since these desires are so alike that they could be mistaken for each other, the confusion is especially intense, once the power of Eros has thrown our cells into turmoil.

Only those who truly love will really recognize each other. The healing of the future will arise through the community of those who truly love. No matter what path the individual may choose, there is only healing in the connection with the one existence. *By connecting with the certainty of success that comes from complete trust and from a connection to Creation you will find the wealth of the world in yourself and in your surroundings. You will then encounter every lover, every unknown woman, or unknown man with the necessary alertness. You will see to it that all encounters have the space and freedom needed, so that what has not yet been seen and recognized in Creation can shine in. (...)*

If you reconnect with the divine source in yourself, it is quite possible that you sometimes have to take a stand against the rules and rituals of your community. All rules and habits need the creative spirit of renewal once and again. Creation might want you to take a stand for what you love, against the spirit of the entire group, yes sometimes against your entire country, because something entirely new is budding from within, something the others have not yet seen. From a trusting place you will hear and honor the voices of the others, you will not simply rise above them, and yet you will remain true to what you love. This will initiate processes of transformation. Those who truly love will see to it that others recognize it and can also love it. This path always leads to the community.

It is possible that you will rebel even against the laws of Creation. If you here, too, remain connected and let the eyes of Creation see through your eyes, then this can be an essential contribution to the processes of transformation in Creation itself. Here, too, one should not forget that it is the Goddess herself who wishes to transform through you and your understanding. This process does not yet contain the pain of separation. It only comes into play when you elevate yourself above others. It is only when you have become deaf toward the voice of the world and that of your heart, when you have gotten lost in the process of oppositions, when you no longer honor the laws of Creation from where you came, and when your longing wants to tear you away from yourself, it is only then that the true tragedy of forgetting sets in. That is why one says that love makes you blind. You are seeking externally what you have forgotten or betrayed within. You will treat a stranger or a lover differently if you trust that through him an answer will come from the world and from the Goddess, rather than if you follow your despair and the belief that your longing cannot be fulfilled. Based on this belief, you will run after the men and women, yet you will always return to the same point of pain in your own soul. Based on your trust, you will dare to do more courageous things. When you are connected with the Goddess you act from the conviction of your path, as if fulfillment were already with you. Even when your body is caught in desire and trembles with excitement, you will then still not abandon your inner center. You invite the Goddess to see with your eyes and to feel with your heart. Already this decision gives you the protection that you need. You will listen to the voice of your heart and know if to act or not.

Do not believe that this will always be rosy and easy. Nobody has said that it is always easy to find inner fulfillment. If we do not learn to act from this connectedness, also in the most difficult situations, we will destroy ourselves and the earth. (...)

*Too many people have fallen into these traps. Now we are facing a time of awakening for everybody. (...) She who gains insight will unfold all her gifts for the good of all; from this source comes her true wealth. Neither moral appeals nor the warnings of others will be able to bring you back to this connection. They can be an impetus for one's own development, but in the final analysis it is always one's own decision. Many people must go through a long process of experience until they return to this insight. Fulfillment in sexuality and in love will not be found in any other way. **Only those who recognize that the energy that flows when one is in a state of connection is more encompassing, more healing, and more powerful, will take this path again.***

A high level of presence is needed for this process to occur. The divine source can always be found in the present. Fear always enters into our lives from a past that one could not cope with and from a projected future. I am protected from fear when I am fully in the present. That is a great secret, but actually it is a very open secret. You can feel you are connected to the source, for then the messages that you receive, once you have taken them in fully, elicit joy, a sense of security, and presence. A deep opening occurs in our cellular system once the thought arises that we can feel totally safe in this world. This thought will turn you into a revolutionary in love, wherever you are. This is how deep the divine voice resides in you. This is the great revelation that keeps recurring; it is the great decision and the great freedom. It is up to you to allow it to occur or not.

*You will ask, again and again: how can we leave fear behind? And how do we get the power that can create peace on earth, in love, and in sexuality? And always the answer is that it is a decision to walk the path of trust and to make it possible for others to do so, too. Leave fear behind. Fear must disappear from the earth. Stay with fearlessness, day by day, hour by hour. **By studying what makes this possible, deeper and deeper, you will understand the laws of the universe deeper and deeper.** The answers will come to you through encompassing and existential study. In this way, you will find fulfillment in community, in partnership, and in anonymous encounters. You will discover that they all belong together and cannot be lived separately from each other. They all appear in a totally different light if you are in a state of connection.*

*If at some point one honestly does not know what to do, then the only answer from the Universe is: hold still until the power has formed itself to an answer within you. Do not waste energy on the spaces in-between. Wait until you know what needs to be done. Ultimately, it is all an energy secret about the right way to handle energy. **You can listen to every detail in the*** *world and you will always find the whole in it, and there will always be an answer.* Concentration is an important element for this. It is one of the first lessons in the universal school. Acquire the power of calm for your long journey. An immense healing power comes from calm. Calm itself has a high level of power and magic. Learn to see, to walk, to ask, and to gain realization at your own speed. *It is from this process that the universe sends you encounters that carry the power of insight and healing.* When you are in this state, everything is simple and clear. You know when you have the right speed, for then you are on the path of inner resonance.

Sexuality and Violence

A river becomes violent
if it is forced into a narrow and straight bed.
Violence is the eruption of blocked life energies.

Sexuality and violence are a basic theme of the entire patriarchal era, one could almost say: its core. One may understand that I want to keep this as short as possible, for it is too true and too horrible for us to focus on this topic for long. The topic of violence pervades the topic of sexuality, either consciously or unconsciously, in action or in fantasies, actively or passively, sadistically or masochistically. I do not know if there is a single adult person on earth, who is not somehow, in fantasies or suppressed thoughts, connected with this field. Behind the rejection of sexuality we often unconsciously find the historical connection with cruelty and violence. Nobody, no man and no woman, would otherwise have the idea of rejecting this source of joy in life. There is no aspect of life where we are all as injured, as disturbed, and as misdirected as here. **It must be definitively clear that a new, humane society of human beings can survive only if it embraces a totally new view of sexuality and realizes a corresponding new ethical order, which is no longer based on lies and suppression.** This is the topic of my book "Der unerlöste Eros" ["Eros Unredeemed"] and it was also one of the main thoughts when our project was founded 25 years ago.

The historical suppression of sexuality was and is connected with violence against women. There are no adequate words to describe the extent of this violence. We cannot imagine it, for we would break down if we were to experience it with our own eyes. But I must at least hint at it briefly.

China: For centuries girls' feet are tied up because small, crippled feet are more sexually enticing for men. Afghanistan: the persecution of women by the Taliban. Fingers with red fingernails are chopped off. Bangladesh: beautiful women who refuse male courtship get sulfuric acid thrown in their faces and the perpetrators remain unpunished. Yugoslavia: mass rape in war, as in all wars. Africa: every day 6,000 girls or young women get their genitalia mutilated without anesthesia. Anyone who has heard the cries of such girls, even only on TV, knows what I am talking about. "Circumcision" is the terse word that is used to describe this everyday insanity. One could go on for a long time: violence in the trade with girls and in prostitution, violence in marriages and families, a more subtle kind of violence in the media, violence in the sexual fantasies of both sexes. Even the cruelest sexual acts can elicit sexual lust. This is how deep the connection between sexuality and violence has entered into our cells as a historical legacy. The French philosopher Georges Bataille has described it in his book "The Tears of Eros". The – conscious or unconscious – connection between sexuality and violence is a part of the "social character" (Erich Fromm) of our society. It makes little sense to punish individual perpetrators for actions that arise from a collective structure. The only way they could be healed would be by protecting them from the influences of existing society, providing them with a totally different social framework in which sexuality is not connected with violence but with trust. But where are there such places in our world? As long as we do not change the collective structure, these deeds will always occur. Human society needs a new sexual foundation.

Violence is the eruption of blocked life energies. This is especially true in the sexual area, since it is here that most energies are blocked. There would be no war criminals, no sadists, no mass murderers, and no hooligans if we were to live in a society that is connected to the life energies of humans. Is it not idiotic to rave against hooligans and so-called right wing radicals and yet continue to actively maintain the societal corset that produces this violence daily? From psychology and history we know that it is often those calling most loudly for punishment who themselves secretly take part in sexual excesses and orgies of violence. Beware if someone demands harsh punishments! The moral apostles always had a sharp tongue, but one was not allowed to look behind their façades. The perverse atrocities that the Italian film producer and writer Pier Paolo Pasolini depicted in his movie "The 120 days of Sodom" were not invented; this truly did occur at Lake Garda [in Italy] toward the end of the Second World War. The strange events (crimes) around the girl murderer Marc Dutroux in Belgium had connections all the way up into high government circles. It seems that government officials, police authorities, and regional politicians were involved in an international ring of child smuggling with the goal of attaining sadistic satisfaction. And this in our times, in the middle of our society!

The lust for violence is ever-present. It is almost always a question of men who cannot handle their sexual energies. But then, who can? I refuse to accept any major moral differences as long as society is the way it is. A terrible ulcer of sex and violence is growing in its belly. If it breaks open, we have Sodom and Gomorra – today, just as we always have. A society that is inhumanely organized in the sexual area cannot be improved through religion, morals, spiritual welfare work, or psychotherapy. A whole different foundation for the sexual co-existence of the sexes is required. Recently, a book was published with a fine title: "We've Had A Hundred Years of Psychotherapy, and the World is Doing Worse". In spite of the genius of Sigmund Freud and Wilhelm Reich, psychotherapy could not solve the issue of sexuality and violence because it is not an individual, but a social and historical issue.

Past-Life Trance with a Former Priest

At this point I would like to repeat some basic thoughts underlying our work. The world is a continuum. The forces that characterize our times influence – in either a hidden way or openly – all parts of the continuum. The structure of violence and twisted sexuality exists as an inner turbulence, not only in individuals but also in our entire civilization today. It constitutes a latent pattern, which under suitable conditions comes up to the surface and wreaks havoc. We need this scientific image from holography and chaos research to arrive at a realistic assessment and to develop realistic strategies. Through its contorted matrix, society today produces the chains that are then violently shattered in the explosions of energies that have been held back for so long. This often occurs simultaneously in one and the same person. To illustrate this, I would like to provide an example of a man with whom I carried out a regression trance during one of our seminars. He was an imposing man, in his forties, well-liked by women, and he was the head of an interior design company. He came because of sexual impotence. The regression trance led to an incarnation in the 15th century. At that time he was a high church dignitary, wearing a cassock. Before carrying out his official duties, he and some other colleagues used to go down a steep set of stairs that led to several cellar rooms under the church. Down there were the women who were subjected to violence. I will spare the reader the details. These bestial activities occurred regularly, like a ritual. He thereafter walked up the stairs to begin his official duties. He said: "I need it in order to cleanse myself." Do we really understand what is being said here? He needed the sadistic excesses in order to purify his spirit and liberate himself, at least for a while, from the obsession of his sexual fantasies. He was cruel because he was dominated by a power stronger than he was. This was the power of sexus, and the attempt to suppress it morally had made it grow to become immense and demonic. He thus became both perpetrator and victim simultaneously. He was in no way an individual case, for he added something like: This was common for us, and ultimately we did it for a good cause. Karlheinz Deschner has written a chronicle of the Christian church ("Das Kreuz mit der Kirche" [The Cross with the Church] and "Kriminalgeschichte des Christentums" ["The Criminal History of Christianity"]), in which these diabolical connections between church morals and sexual excesses has been exhaustively documented. Wherever urges in life are suppressed instead of integrated, they come back to us as uncontrollable violence. In our long karmic biographies, many of us have experienced both the side of the victim and that of the perpetrator. Those who are victims today may have been perpetrators before and vice versa. Our friends of today may once have been our enemies, and vice versa. There is no point in judging, as long as the continuum and the matrix remain unchanged. The interior designer, who at the time, as a man of the church, maltreated women, is today a committed peace worker. His impotence is not only an illness, for it has (as is usually the case) a deeper meaning: it forces him to develop a new relationship to women. He is thereby following such a careful path of solidarity that one has the feeling that something like the "new man" is emerging here. He was thankful for his new insights in the regression trance and saw them as a confirmation of having gone astray in the past. Now he was able to understand and transform his issue of impotence in a much deeper way.

Millions of people have gone through such or similar experiences as victims and/or perpetrators and they are still doing so on earth today, right at this moment. But in many people it has given rise to reflection and new thoughts that they want to follow. More and more people, both men and women, are turning away from the dead end street that they are in and are looking in a new direction. May they all help to create a new era, when there is no more Dutroux and no more sadistic priests.

Impotence

Is it ultimately a question of cocks
and if they function?
Is it a question of their size?
The women say: no, no, no.
The men say no, but they mean yes,
for their entire behavior reveals
that for them it is all a matter
of how their cocks function.
I have never met a man
whose behavior was not dominated
by the size and stiffness of his cock.
That is the one thing that women never dare to say.
That is the one thing that we are determined to lie about.
And why? Because it is all too true.
A man, who likes his cock, likes himself.
And a man, who cannot trust his cock,
cannot trust himself. Nor can he trust any woman.
Or any other man.
Is it that simple?
I am afraid that the answer is yes.
Porno movies, baby oil, leather, black chains –
all these are compensations for cocks
that do not function or that function capriciously.
For when they function,
then all one needs is music and moonlight.

     Erica Jong in "Any Woman's Blues"

I regard impotence not only as a medical issue, but as every kind of inability to cope with erotic life. This includes the question: how do I even make contact with the opposite sex? There are a great number of people who have never succeeded in doing this. Many more youths than would admit to it are secretly plagued by this question. For many it is the main question of their lives. Many people visit supermarkets, conferences, movies, book fairs, discos, or therapy workshops with this question at the back of their minds. It is incredible how much gas is used, how many airplanes are flying around, how many vacation trips are taken, and how many bars, hotels and spas are built to make erotic contact easier or to replace them with consumerism. If we were to live in a society with fulfilled sexuality, we would experience an unprecedented financial breakdown. If humans were able to communicate their desires for sexual contact easily and nicely, then we would be spared the ecological catastrophe that is connected with tourism and with the various forms of entertainment in today's society.

In spite of drugs, parties and love parades, the sexual misery of the younger generation has hardly changed at all. The people who come to our centers naturally also come because of this topic. The success of the new centers will, to a large degree, depend on to what extent they are able to provide constructive answers to this problem. Can we, or can we not, provide an answer to the questions that today's youth has about love and sex, fear and impotence? Are we able to give them concrete help to have a more successful love life? Those who do not make progress in their own love lives will usually be limited in their role as peace workers, for they will secretly be occupied with entirely different fantasies and thoughts. The pointed boredom with which many youths today react to the political issues of our times is also connected to their unsolved life situation in the area of love. As long as they sense that the adults cannot help them with this question because they themselves are helpless, they have no interest in their conferences and seminars. Rainer Langhans, of Commune 1 in Berlin, once declared: "I'm not interested in Vietnam; I have difficulties having an orgasm." If one could offer a simple and effective way to overcome sexual fears and difficulties, then we would soon have the entire world on our side.

I now come to the topic of sexual impotence in the more narrow sense of the word. Every man knows it and has experienced it, and every fourth man is stuck in it. Viagra has shown what a sigh of relief would echo through the world of men if there were a real possibility to get rid of the painful problem of potency in a simple way. As Erica Jong pointed out, a man is identified with his penis to a high degree. His penis is his mark of quality, his trademark, his identity card. There is hardly a greater disgrace than to have an undependable, labile penis, and there is no worse insult for a man than when a woman calls him a "softie" in the literal sense of the word. Murders have been committed for such reasons. One of the main reasons why men are more afraid of free sexuality than women is their secret fear that, because their cocks are unreliable, they will not be able to hold their own on the free market. We would be spared so many intense discussions and philosophical debates if men were only able to make love physically without fear and complications! What would our philosophers and authors, Kant or Sartre have said about sexual love, if they had known it? What would have become of Nietzsche's "superman" if Friedrich Nietzsche, the man, would have been able to make loving contact with women. The "superman" in "Zarathustra" was his revenge against his own impotence. In the philosophical history of Western culture, sexual fears and impotence have almost always played the role of a secret navigator. It thus gave rise to much ingenious rubbish in the world. And that is why the painter Sonneberg, who spent most of his life in a psychiatric clinic, could truthfully say: "Once it is inside, life has meaning!"

Those who are impotent do not have an easy lot. They should, however, not choose to be worried, they should choose to be thankful, for if one learns to listen to the voice of one's body, impotence is a signpost toward potency. Those who take this path can turn into wonderful lovers. The issue of potency can teach us some things about the secret of erotic life that we may never have learned if our misery had not forced us to. In this context I would like to quote some humoristic, yet serious thoughts from the women's book entitled "Rettet den Sex" ["Save Sex"] (Editor: Sabine Kleinhammes). For some, who are engaged in research for themselves, this book could be of help:

First: Impotence literally means not being able to. But there is no sexuality in which one has to be able to do something. If somebody is impotent, then he thinks that he has to be able to do something that one actually doesn't need to be able to do – and that one can do naturally if one no longer thinks about being able to.

Second: In most cases the assumption that one must be able to do what one in reality does not have to be able to do - because one can do it naturally if one doesn't think about being able to – usually leads to disturbances in one's natural abilities. If someone then truly is not able to, then he feels confirmed in his false assumption that he has to be able to. This is how sex becomes a futile competitive sport!

Third: If someone truly is not able to and momentarily cannot see land, then he should not act as if he is able to. All those who are able to are at times not able to, and they simply accept their inability in a charming way, without much ado and without being ashamed.

Fourth: Sex occurs almost on its own, like breathing or speaking. Sex is the high art of sensual meditation, consisting of neither doing anything special, nor of leaving anything special out. Everyone, who possesses the corresponding organs, is aware of this art.

146

Fifth: With sex it is like with other sensitive things: one should not get too fixated on them. They resist and hinder life if one pursues them with too much determination. They need freedom, generosity, and sometimes almost our forgetfulness, so that they themselves can decide when they want to come. We know of the principle of casualness in art. It often applies to sex, too.

Sixth: Impotence is the inner fight between God and vanity. Vanity says that one must present oneself with certain abilities and certain knowledge. God, as usual, says nothing: neither what one should do, nor what one should not do, for s/he is the principle underlying the joy of existence that arises all on its own - a principle that lies beyond all personal merit.

Seventh: Every impotent man knows the experience of being incredibly potent in certain situations, for example when he is lying alone in bed, letting his fantasies run free while masturbating. He is thus not really impotent, but he believes that he has to be able to do something during real sexual contact which, when he is alone with himself, he does not believe that he must be able to do, because he is naturally able to. The proof: it is hard!

In younger years (below 60) impotence usually does not come from a sexual weakness, but from dammed up sexual energy that cannot find a way out, i.e. from an excess of energy. The energy remains stuck somewhere before it can really reach the genitalia. It often gets lost in the head, which then is not able to give the body consistent impulses. If central command is confused, then the body is also confused. If the head transmits inconsistent information, then the penis or the vagina cannot make any clear decisions. This, then, worries the head deeply, often triggering a vicious circle and resulting in a lower abdomen that goes on a total strike. The problem of impotence is usually solved on its own when an event or insight brings about a shift, which itself provides a solution.

Under the conditions of today's sexual practices, it is almost a sign of health when here and there people step away from the general competitive sport and the corresponding confusions that are labeled with the word "sexuality". Just as suddenly as he stepped out and could not perform any more, equally unnoticed will he step back in when the time is ripe. Maybe some of the passages in this book can be helpful when it comes to finding an inner foundation where the problem of potency or impotence no longer exists. Potency is not a medical issue; it is an issue of contact without fear. That is all that is needed for love to occur.

Women's Sexual Plight

Sire, remember me much, remember me often,
and remember me for long.
I call out to you with great greed:
I am burning brightly in hot memory of you.
Now I am a naked soul,
and you are a well-seen guest adorning my soul..

    Mechtchild von Magdeburg.

When I feel sexual desire,
I do not ask for love.
But when I desire,
without being anchored in love,
I cannot find fulfillment.

    Dolores Richter

The suppression of female sexuality was the main tool of domination during the patriarchal era. Men, immature as they were, could only handle the superior strength of the mothers by destroying the sexual power of women. Woman could only survive if she learned to suppress and hide her sexual nature. She had to practice and internalize this process of sexual disownment until nobody noticed it any more – including herself. She could thereby appear in new "innocence" and avoid the criminal court of male religions, male morals, male laws, male churches, and male gods. The result was a totally topsy-turvy world in which she began to hold as her own those male values that had once been burned into her with fire and sword: monogamy, extramarital abstinence, chastity, sexual obedience, and lifelong "faithfulness" to her master. These values, as well as the institution of marriage and the concepts of love and faithfulness, originated in the contorted mind of man. Monogamy was introduced in Europe (Greece) at the end of the 2nd millennium B.C. by King Kekrops as a method to ensure state dominance and order. For centuries women had to be forced into monogamy through the use of the most cruel methods before they started to accept this fate. We have reports from all cultures and religions of the patriarchal era about the methods that were used to get first the women, and then all subjects, "used to" monogamy. Indecency, extramarital sexuality, and "unfaithfulness" were severely punished through skinning, impaling, stoning to death, cutting out the genitalia, etc. Still today such methods are being used in many places on earth. Monogamy, which today seems to be almost totally natural and which for most people in the modern world is seen as an ideal of love, does not stem from a divine order, but from man's claim to power. (The rulers themselves did not observe this law.) The law of monogamy cut women off from their own sources and forced them to live a life that they themselves finally believed was right. But their Lilith nature, their other image, their unfulfilled longing, is still seething deep within. Man has not conquered woman, he has only trivialized her superficially. But he himself has lost a source of his own power by subjugating woman. He himself could not continue to grow, for a free man needs the sexual love of free women for his own inner growth. The result for both sexes was the situation that Barry Long has so clearly described: man can no longer reach woman sexually. And woman, whose sexual identity was taken away by male history, cannot tell the man this.

It is often not the words of men but of women that describe the pain of unfulfilled sexuality. Emma Goldmann, Erica Jong, Dalma Heyn, Sabine Lichtenfels, Leila Dregger, and Renate Daimler have all written about what goes on inside many women. Is there not in every woman an aspect of Josefine Mutzenbacher (if the story is authentic) who writes about herself: "I have experienced everything that a woman can experience in bed, on tables, chairs, and benches, leaning against bare walls, lying in the grass, in the dark corners of house entrances, in private rooms, in trains, in barracks, in brothels and in prison, and I do not regret any of it." She has said and done what others only feel and desire secretly. It is amazing what is felt and thought in female bodies, and what is felt and thought in male bodies! And what is kept secret! I have described this in my book "Eros Unredeemed". It took a long time before female readers dared to react to this book. Chapters such as "Healthy Nymphomania and the Hunger of our Cells" describe a - not only female - reality that it is risky to even mention. Not because it is pornographic, but because everybody knows that it is true. In spite of the media's obsession with sex, we still have a culture of silence regarding sexual matters. That is why one of Sabine Lichtenfels' books is called "Der Hunger hinter dem Schweigen" ["The Hunger behind the Silence"]. What is meant is sexual hunger. From this book comes the quote: "Sometimes I doubt that men and women only want the one thing. I believe that women want it infinitely much more."

What they need, what we all need, is contact, an opening of the soul, and trust. But that could not be provided under male rule.

It would be good if the male world were to be correctly informed about the extent of sexual energy in the female world. Men could then easier and without contempt connect with their own sources of life, for sexual energy is pure life energy, whether male or female. For man, woman is an embodiment of sexual energy, and the male longing for woman is connected to his constant longing to reunite with his own source of life. Woman wants this reunion; she desires it more than anything else. She often wants it to be more direct, juicier, more obscene, and more of the flesh than what decency allows. But she usually doesn't have the courage to admit it or to recognize it, for she is living under conditions that do not allow this desire, and history has taught her about the cruelty with which the male world reacts to her sexual desires. She has actually learned to react with horror to the sexual actions that she loves, because for centuries and millennia her original joy was so sadistically abused. Here we touch upon a tragedy that could make you cry forever. The sexes need a new repertoire of words and signs in order to be able to meet each other in the sexual area in a new and clear way. They also need real places on earth, where such meetings are possible. Healing biotopes are places for a gentle, clear, and honest liberation of sexuality.

Women's sexual misery stems from a history and society in which indecency and adultery were seen as deadly sins and they still often are. This is illustrated in the following quote from the book "Die Heimliche Lust. Der Mythos von der weiblichen Treue" ["The Secret Passion. The Myth of Female Faithfulness"] by Dalma Heyn:

"Depending on the culture, the adulteress is branded with a poker, her legs are impaled by a sword (...) or else she is killed, as is the case among the Senufos and Bambaras in West Africa. According to Moslem law, a man may, without further ado, murder a woman if he discovers that she is having extramarital intercourse. In today's Saudi Arabia she is stoned to death. In parts of Mexico she may get her nose and ears cut off before being stoned to death.

Female sexuality is so closely connected with punishment that the fate of women is always affected by it, whether or not she lives in the sacred institution of marriage. It is thus that Anna, the heroine of Sue Miller's "The Good Mother", who is divorced, is not allowed to have a new love relationship although her husband has remarried. The reason is that she is the mother of a child. Even the court psychologist, who regards her as a good mother because she has a good relationship to her daughter, does not succeed in invalidating the stigma of sexuality and thus to convince the court. In other words, a sexually active woman has a corrupting influence on her child and does not deserve to keep it. A sexually active woman is not a good mother."

How old must women become today in order to see through and admit to the circumstances around her own sexual repression? Renate Daimler has written a spectacular book entitled "Die verschwiegene Lust" ["The Secret Passion"]. The women who were interviewed in the book – all of them between the ages of 63 and 83 – confess openly to the pain of missed sexuality in their lives and to the desire to now make up for it as much as possible. Here, female emancipation is occurring in a new direction: emancipation from the old, false role of women, emancipation from the asexual kitsch image that the male world has imposed on women and that they reluctantly took on. Emancipation from the constant social obligation to appear different from what one really is; emancipation also from the one-sided feminist ideologies that are directed against men. The book by Dalma Heyn, from which the quote above was taken, continues in this direction. Here, too, we have powerful documents by women about the anti-female ethics of our culture and of the difficulty to truly be a woman in a world that is based on monogamy, double standards, and female submission.

There is only one reason why we do not find such women's books on the bedside tables of all young women: because they do not know how their female and male friends would react if they, too, made the same confession. As long as they do not see any possibility of changing their lives, they are all part of the same secret complicity of pretense. In so-called "real life", it is not possible to fulfill one's secret desires. That is the reason for the constant lie and for the moral double standards in the sexual area. It is the reason for the failure of the sexual revolution, which tentatively wanted to begin in the Sixties. Today, it is no longer "in" to follow one's sexual dreams, because word has gotten around that they cannot be fulfilled. The sexual misery is equally great on both sides. On the male side it has maybe been most impressively described in the book "Mars" by the young Swiss doctor Fritz Zorn, who died at an early age. Especially today, when truth is being suppressed, it is worthwhile to read and talk about such books. They help us on our path toward truth. There has seldom been a time when sexual propaganda and sexual reality

151

have been as divergent as they are today. This cannot be remedied by educational work or through accusations; here, concrete aid is needed. Healing biotopes must offer concrete aid for the sexual misery of our time.

The Heart of Sexual Misery

The cause of most of the unhappiness on earth
is that man and woman have actually forgotten
how to make physical love.
This is the greatest tragedy of all time.
The fundamental suffering of woman,
her constant dissatisfaction,
arises because man can no longer reach her physically.

    Barry Long

By now men, too, have accepted the importance of sexuality. Even the spiritual scene, which up to now was almost always against sex or at least wanted to play down its importance, has changed its tune. The clearest sign of this comes from the Australian Barry Long, who travels the world as a spiritual teacher. He has had sexual love experiences that were connected to encompassing revelations. I am sure he has said many strange things, and one may think what one wants about him. But what he says about sexual love are things that hardly anybody has dared to say as clearly as he does. I must quote some of his statements (I prefer using others' words for things that are especially important to me):

The cause of most of the unhappiness on earth is that man and woman have actually forgotten how to make physical love. This is the greatest tragedy of all time. The forgetfulness has been going on and slowly getting worse for so many thousands of years that it's now a tragedy for the whole of mankind.

Woman's basic unhappiness, her perennial discontent, is because man can no longer reach her physically. Her emotional excess, depressions, tearful frustrations, even premenstrual tension and the conditions leading to hysterectomy and other uterine problems, are due to man's sexual failure to gather or release in lovemaking her finest, fundamental, female energies. These extraordinarily beautiful divine energies are intense and exquisite and when left untapped in woman, as they are now, degenerate into psychic or emotional disturbances, and eventually crystallize into physical abnormalities. The womb gives birth to all things.

Man's basic unhappiness, his perennial restlessness, is because in forgetting how to make love he has abandoned his original divine authority and lost sexual control of himself. His emotional or psychic degeneracy manifests as sex obsession. All men, without exception, are sex obsessed. This means compulsive sexual fantasizing, chronic masturbation (even when living with a partner), sex repression leading to anger and violence, and the universal symptoms of chasing wealth and getting lost in work. Busyness and wealth-gathering compensate for being an inept lover and are cover-ups (in both sexes) for the inability or fear to love. Because of his neglect of love, neglect of woman, man suffers from premature ejaculation, guilt, anxiety, self-doubt, impotence, sexual atrophy masquerading as sexual disinterest, sexual abstinence due to repressed fear of failure, sexual bravado and lack of true wisdom - all of which he inflicts on woman, aggravating her basic discontent and his own restlessness.

To be a fully integrated male, a man has to assimilate in his body the divine female energies that woman can only release to him through right physical lovemaking. But the man has to be man enough. He has to be able to love her enough; that is, love her selflessly during the actual act of lovemaking. He has to be able to absorb and express sufficient love in his body to reach the highest part of her, and love enough to extract the divine energies from her deepest center. **To be able to love in this way is the authority man has lost - his only true authority over woman.** *This requires pure love. It does not depend on technique. A man may develop his sexual technique but he cannot use expertise to make divine love. Exciting sensations are gratifying and give him a form of authority, but they are not the love that woman craves. He may satisfy her, like a good meal. But soon she hungers again and eventually despises her appetite or herself, because she knows she is not being loved.*

To man, the fiendess of emotion in woman is hell on earth. This is the part of her he cannot handle or understand. The demon of his own failure to love comes to life to scorn, abuse and torment him. He is terrified of it. He bluffs and blusters his way through. Finally, as he grows old in the relationship and gives up for the sake of some peace, the fiendess will conquer him and force him to surrender the last vestige of his manliness and authority. Then they both grow old together, feeling safe, but half dead as they lean on each other in the awful world of compromise.

While the world continues as it is, the fiendess will not allow man to forget his failure to love woman rightly. Woman must be loved. The future of the human race depends on woman being loved because only when woman is truly loved can man be truly himself and regain his lost authority. Only then can peace return to earth. Yet woman as she is now cannot be loved for long (or for good) by man as he is now. Together they are trapped in a vicious cycle and if left to their own ideas of love, there is no way out for them.

154

These are true words. We also find statements that are this focused and far-reaching by Wilhelm Reich and, in a different way, by Sabine Lichtenfels. The groundwork was laid by Sigmund Freud but it was then dropped by psychotherapy because the consequences would have devastated the bourgeois ideas about life. Today, they can be integrated under new anthropological and spiritual points of view because we can now come to more adequate conclusions. It has become possible to create a real human society with real sexual fulfillment because the prerequisite, the reconnection of the human being with the Sacred Matrix of all life, is becoming visible. Peace work is always also work for sensual love. Without sensual love, every peace is fragile, for peace is – in the final analysis – always peace between the sexes. Again I repeat the statement: There can be no peace on earth as long as there is war in love. Since we are here, on our sensual, physical, round earth, peace always also means the sexual peace of our bodies.

Sexual Devotion – A Political Issue

I am wax in his hands,
when we are together in bed.

    Christine, 80 years old

The element of lust that is there,
on both the active and the passive side,
the element of lust and the element of absoluteness,
where there is no discussion,
these elements of fate must be seen.
Sexuality is waiting
for these elements to be integrated.
But what I am saying is only valid
on the basis of sensitive contact.

    Martina Gisler (in "Der Befehl" ["The Command"])

Devotion means to love something and to follow this love unconditionally. It is an opening without insurance. Devotion is a magnificent process. The female part of us, whether we are men or women, longs for devotion. The ability for devotion is a sign of health. Only those organisms, who have stored the information of mistrust deep in their cells, resist devotion.

I have conducted a little survey among more experienced women, asking them the question: What does devotion or surrender mean to you? The most common answer was: lust, gentleness, calm, presence, absolute passivity, bliss, "in any case something beautiful." All women, who have a positive relationship to sexual love, would have similar answers. Devotion is high up in the female spectrum of values.

What about men? Men usually play the more active role, but for them, too, devotion is an issue. Devotion and activity are not opposites, for I can fully devote or abandon myself to what I am doing. In the case of sexuality, this is also desired, for men who cannot abandon themselves to their own lust, are not exactly a special treat for women. For both genders it is a question of devotion. Sexuality is almost a synonym for bodily abandonment. But here we have the difficulty. If I am a powder keg full of repressed energy, and if my fantasies sometimes boil over, then how should I give myself with abandon? If at the first sign of attraction I am gripped by the turbulence of my sadistic or masochistic fantasies, or if my hunger for sex simply has become so great that it doesn't go in a healthy direction unless I control it, then to whom or to what can I surrender or abandon myself? If I do not know how you do "it" or if I'm doing it right, what the partner thinks of me, etc., how am I then supposed to abandon myself?

We are told that our head is in the way. That is true, but is it really only the head? What would we do if it were not there? Would not all the powder kegs explode all over? Would not, in this dammed up overall situation of life, the planet sink into a chaos of cries of lust and pain? Sometimes we should be thankful for our heads and for the fact that it is in the way and stops us from creating even more havoc. Sometimes we face each other and suddenly don't know what to do, losing our sexual joy for sheer awkwardness. Then the head starts to rage. The more it rages, the more our libido goes out the window, and the more it all becomes a question of success or failure. If only the phone would ring or someone would knock on the door, so that we could put an end to this hopeless situation! But usually we're not so lucky; no telephone rings, and we have to see how we can cope on our own. This is where the real problem of potency begins. There is no longer a trace of devotion or surrender. Maybe we can use our best masturbation fantasies to catch up sexually. Always hoping secretly that our partner doesn't notice what's going on inside of us.

If somebody is stuck in such a tough situation and experiences it repeatedly, then he (or she) has the displeasure of using his/her head again, but this time correctly, in order to ponder about sex and love from the beginning again, without taking on the clichés that our culture offers. I can only say that specifically in such situations it pays to take cosmic lessons and listen to the voice of life. Under the given life conditions and forms of communication and superficiality, it is not so unwise to be impotent once in a while. One is then forced to deal with the topic and one cannot just swim with the current. **Every experience of impotence could mark the beginning of a development toward a truly excellent lover.** Now one must find the path that leads from the stress of performance to devotion. Devotion is always a question of trust and contact. **True sexuality, both on the female and the male side, is always connected to trust and contact.** When they are present, the rest happens automatically. Impotence always vanishes when enough trust and contact are present. Trust and contact are also the only effective means for getting dammed up or slightly perverse sexual energies back onto a meaningful track. But that's just it: in sexuality we need trust and contact – after thousands of years of mistrust and violence. We need new ways for humans to live together to bring about a reconditioning based on trust. Devotion is therefore not a personal, but especially a societal and political problem, a question of our overall social structure.

During the cultural era from which we come, almost everything that we would have wanted to surrender to has become the subject of taboos, prohibition, and punishment. We know the tragic story of Héloise and Abelard, two of the most well-known lovers of the Middle Ages, whose mutual desire for total sexual surrender led to cruel punishments. Many of us have had such terrible experiences at some point in this or in a previous lifetime. We have all at one time or another learned to no longer openly show our desire for devotion but to hide behind an inner protective wall.

I am walking through Berlin and, as I watch the men, I imagine being a woman. I've been walking for two hours and have hardly found a single man whom I would trust with my devotion. There is no point in trying it again and again. I would really want to, but only if I can be fully certain that it doesn't result in any cruelty, contempt, or abandonment. But I can no longer see any reason to believe in something like that. This is the situation that many women are in, and it is one reason for the modern anti-sexual attitude that is so prevalent today. It is also the reason why projects for the liberation of sexuality are often labeled "sexist" by feminist groups.

Surrendering to sexual love? The goal of goals. But those who passionately surrender to each other often later face each other as enemies. Here our souls find themselves in a historic drama which must be dissolved in order for healing to be able to take place in our human and sexual relationships. We need devotion, for it is the natural process that overcomes dammed up energies and violence. Physically, it prevents inflammations that are caused by chronically dammed up energies. Devotion is our natural way of revealing ourselves to others. One cannot lie in devotion. We all love these states in which we do not have to lie. We all love the self-abandonment of cats and dogs when they stretch out in the sun. We are touched by the grunting of a wallowing pig. That is Marici, the Goddess in the form of a pig, who is enjoying sensual life. We sense the presence of pure, unadulterated life, and we would also like to grunt that way. Total surrender cleanses and heals our cells like tears of redemption, for the gifts of healing are built into the natural function of our souls and bodies. The entire universe of life is full of natural medicines. The entire universe of our cells is full of jubilation when surrender can occur fully and totally, without any remnants of fear and mistrust. Devotion is a basic process of the Sacred Matrix. If the church had understood that, then their priests would not have committed the sadistic crimes that I described earlier. We need social spaces wherein devotion becomes possible again. Since we don't have them, we must create them – in the name of warmth for us and our children.

Sexual Freedom – How Does That Work?

Monogamy is a lie.

Lotti Huber, 78 years old

We speak of love of our neighbor,
and when my friend is sexually loving
with someone else,
we speak of cheating.
Why do we free citizens of the earth
continue to follow this
stupid little catechism
in love?

Sabine Lichtenfels

He who binds to himself a joy
Doth the winged life destroy
But he who kisses the joy as it flies
Lives in Eternity's sun rise

William Blake

Free sexuality is a part of a free life. Free of fear and subjugation, free of duress and violence, but also free from the fixation on one person alone. As soon as people enter into a couple relationship, they can no longer imagine sexual freedom. They believe that their relationship would otherwise end. A young Portuguese woman, who visited Tamera with her friend, asked: "Sexual freedom – how does that work?" It doesn't make sense to answer that question with statements that are prepared in advance. The basic questions in life cannot be answered with ideologies or recipes. It is not a question of a theory or creed, but of an experience, and this experience is unambiguous. The answer is: free sexuality occurs of itself if we do not stop ourselves or our partner. In our projects we have never pushed a person toward free sexuality; without exception they did it all by themselves – for the simple reason that they were allowed to. The couples needed a while to get used to it and to come to an understanding with each other concerning the new situation, but then they did it. Letting go of inner pressure and duress is a part of free sexuality. You should only be together with someone if you really want to – not because of any ideology or group pressure. Even free sexuality, if misunderstood, can become a false dogma if one follows it at the wrong time, too quickly, and in a too demanding way. It should never be forced but it is alright to allow it. If one is open, one will notice that the requirement that one limit oneself sexually to a single person was a mistaken law. It was a law of the old matrix, and can no longer be upheld when sexual contact with others is allowed or even desired. A couple relationship that is based on sex alone and has no other common foundation, may break up as a result. But those who are in a couple relationship based on trust and love will use the chance to renew and beautify their own sexual relationship. Partnership and free sexuality do not exclude each other; they supplement each other. This is one of the most important insights resulting from free thought. There is no either-or between free love and love between a couple; it was the old fear that made us believe so. When two people truly love each other, they have no reason to close themselves off sexually to the outside, and they will not do this, because it would endanger their love. Whenever partnership is associated with the old kind of sexual faithfulness, both partners are in great danger, for at some point the sexual passion for the other grows cold, and at some point the desire for new erotic contacts awakens in both of them. Sooner or later they get a bad conscience, mistrust grows between them, they check up on each other, and they begin to lie. This scenario has been played out millions of times and is still being played out millions of times a day. It leads to the partners' giving up on love or to the cruel family tragedies that we read about in the newspaper. It lies like a great illness at the foundation of our entire society. If the partners are bored by each other, if they have nothing more to say to each other, and if their libido has been extinguished, then a common infirmity begins, that can only be camouflaged through the normal vicarious satisfactions of career, consumption and travel. The false ideas about sexuality are one of the reasons for the downfall of our civilization. The young Portuguese woman, who asked the question, should not force herself to have outside sexual contacts, but neither should she forever stop herself from having them. She will notice herself, when the desire is clear. Then she will tell her friend, provided they have a good relationship. He will swallow hard a few times and then maybe admit that he feels the same way. Both of them will be surprised that they react with true relief and maybe they will immediately disappear behind the bushes. They are both committed to working within the environmental movement, and they are working for a large Portuguese ecological magazine. They have a very honest relationship with each other and will not separate due to their enjoyment of "extramarital sex". The danger of separation is only there if they meet new partners who make them choose one over the other. This demand is cruel, stupid, and unnecessary. Here people are forced to make a decision that does not have anything to do with love, truth, or faithfulness. It is a part of the concept of love from the old matrix of violence. It is a reason for the never-ending suffering of the soul that occurs between the sexes.

Young people give each other vows of faithfulness out of love, but also because they are afraid to lose each other. When they are confronted with free sexuality, then fear and resistance are awakened. Can I hold my own in comparison to the other? Am I attractive enough? There are many who are more beautiful, more intelligent, and more able than I am. Will my partner not want to be with them? If I'm totally honest toward myself, don't I feel the same way?

These thoughts are understandable in a world in which most people have experienced the drama of separation. In order to reach true sexual freedom, we need a new world in which the structure of separation is overcome at its core: a world with functioning communities, functioning families, and solid relationships between people. Children must be able to rely on their relationships with their parents and with other adults, for then they will not become needy later. We need a deeper common basis for our relationships, we need to be embedded in the love of Creation, of Nature, and of the sacred forces of the world, and we need to jointly take responsibility for caring for life on earth. These are the basic values of the Sacred Matrix. If they are given, there is no more exclusion within love and sex. Sex means to use a divine energy for the mutual joy of those involved. No human being, who has found peace and quiet in him/herself, will suffer from a lack of sex. Nobody will ever think of comparing him/herself to others, for it is no longer the characteristics of their outer attractiveness that brings people together, but the mutual discovery of their souls. It is a personal attraction and a personal love, based on the special individuality of a human being. True individuality is not created through impressive external attributes, but through truth and an authentic life, embedded in the universal union with all beings. That is the basis for true sexual freedom and for personal love. It is the natural dowry of every woman and man, for we all come to earth with this great possibility. We are now facing the task of building a society in which we can realize this possibility. All those who love are very welcome to help with this.

No Sex with Children

When speaking about free sexuality, many people think of wildly living out suppressed fantasies. According to them this also entails sex with children, since children, as they say, are sexual beings. In reality sex with children, so-called "abuse", is a relatively common phenomenon in society. The Dutroux case in Belgium showed how a highly organized network of systematic child abuse, involving government circles throughout many European countries, was kept secret by the police and other authorities.

We have often intervened to protect children from sexual abuse and we often had to work hard to explain to the fanatics of free love why sex with children is not a part of sexual liberation. But we have also experienced how innocent men were accused of abuse and how the same accusations were directed at us when we defended these men. In "Emma" and other magazines fabricated reports were published that were so incredible that we were horrified at the inner lives of the female authors. The underlying facts are simple: we helped a man who was wrongly accused of abuse, and in this connection we learned how the authorities treated children in order to get them to make false statements. What opened up here was an abyss of war between the sexes, violence against the soul, slander, and moral decadence that made one's hair stand on end. The victims were the children. We spoke of the concept of "abusing the abuse". This was probably the reason why we ourselves were then accused of abuse. The "Stern" magazine also took part in this smear campaign. For us this whole story was another lesson in the overall drama of slander that we would have fallen victim to during the Eighties (see Chapter 6), had we not seen through the methods that are widely used today whenever "topic number one" is at stake.

In 1990 we published a small brochure entitled: "The Erotic Academy." It contained the following text concerning the issue of child sexuality:

The suppression of sexuality always leads to sexual addiction and to an inner dependence on the suppressed longings. But also the pure liberation of the elemental sexual force leads to addiction if it is not connected with a suitable mental-spiritual and ethical orientation. ...

A part of free love, in terms of sexual humanism, consists of carefully introducing the children to this topic, which for them – at their level – is hardly less interesting than for the adults. Free sexuality is incompatible with the sexual seduction of children. As with all other perversions, sexual abuse of children comes from the dammed up fantasies of repressed and therefore uncontrollable desire. It is not free sexuality, but un-free sexuality that has brought forth all sexual deviations.

Children are sexual beings, but not in the way that adults are sexual. Nelly Wolfheim's experiences ("Kindergarten und Psychoanalyse" ["Kindergarten and Psychoanalysis"]) and the reports of the sexual life of children and youths in the Ghotuls of the Muria, a small tribe in India, illustrate how children's sexual curiosity and joy of experience develops and organizes itself naturally if it is not disturbed by adults. It is good for adults not to express themselves too freely sexually when children are present. A child cannot yet understand the adult form of sexuality and often reacts to it with fears of castration, subconscious sexual fears, or simply with fear of Daddy. Children experience the best support for the development of a healthy sexuality and sensuousness if they see adults having sensuous and affectionate interactions that are full of joy and love. They then notice that what a man and a woman are doing together must be something beautiful.

I Love Being a Woman

Presentation by Sabine Lichtenfels at the Summer University in Tamera, 2000

If in the following I speak in the first person, then I am summarizing the voices of many of my fellow women throughout history. Here, I see female knowledge that has developed over the millennia and that has been under attack for many centuries. Today, in our current era, it is reforming and congealing into a field-creating power. I am trying to formulate something that I have found in many women - in their desires, fears, and needs, and in their deeper longings. What is said here is certainly not true for all women. I am trying to draw an image of a female archetype which, being connected to universal healing processes, today could generate a field to initiate a social healing process.

"I am a woman. I am thankful for that, for I like being a woman."
Already this statement, if spoken in full truth, requires a fundamental shift in the worldview of women, reconnecting them with their true and most beautiful sources. It requires me to liberate myself from the societal straitjacket, which for thousands of years has forced images upon me that do not correspond to my true universal source of life. In the history of religion, the historical break that robbed me of my female source of knowledge is expressed by the Fall. Since all women are the descendants of Eve, the entire female gender is to have sinned with her. Tertullian, an early Church Father, had the following to say about the female sex: "... your guilt must thus also continue to live. It is you who created the entrance for evil ... you first dismissed divine law, and it was you who beguiled the one whom the devil could not approach. This is how easily you brought down man, the image of God. Because of your guilt, i.e. for the sake of death, the Son of God also had to die." It was forgotten that there were much older myths of Creation relating to Eve. Eve originally meant "mother of all living beings." Many old peoples saw the goddess and the serpent as grandparents. Religious images show Eve as she gives life to man, while the serpent is coiled around the apple tree, symbolizing the tree of life. The human being was driven from Paradise through a historic cultural shift and, according to the Kabbalah, paradise on earth could only be restored through the reunion of the two sexes. Even God himself had to be reunited with his female counterpart, called "Sheshina", the divine Eve. Reconnecting with the original female sources seems to be an essential step on this path. I call what needs to happen historically the

"culture of partnership". This free thought carries within it an image of partnership that is no longer dependent on any conditions but that occurs naturally between two freely loving people, and which can include many other men and women on its journey of love. This kind of faithfulness arises from a free and empathizing perception and understanding of the world.

My biological longing for community

In early history the hearth was the social hub and sacred place of a community. The women were at the center, not only for a man and their children, but for the entire tribe. There is in me an archaic, original, and elementary longing that calls out for community. It calls out for life forms that are again embedded in a larger context. In my cells I seem to have an original memory, reminding me of an old form of matriarchal life together, where the hearth was the center of the community and thus also the social and religious focal point for the blossoming of the entire community. I want to live in a community of men and women, with children, animals and plants, in such a way that I do not have to hide my true image from the others. Perception and contact are elementary sources of life on a par with breathing. If this is given, then I love being a woman, for then I can be a woman fully. My fulfillment as a woman always occurred in the community. This basic biological longing still lives in my cells today. Under the conditions that we have in society today, I am forced to squeeze this longing for contact, permanence, and faithfulness into much too narrow forms. A larger community of love that is based on trust is needed for love and Eros to be able to unfold in a way that corresponds to my true femininity. The establishment of a human culture of peace depends on our ability to build functioning communities. It is strange that people can even live without community. In our western patriarchal culture they have all been torn away from their natural, universal, tribal connections. Today, communities always fail because of the topic of love. They always fail due to the unsolved problem of competition and jealousy.

I am a Sexual Being

In earlier cultures we were all connected to Mother Earth, in whose service we were. We called this connection with Creation love. We were all one large interconnected family, and all love relationships were connected with the greater whole. There were no private love relationships.

Here, I am approaching an essential aspect of my being a woman, an aspect that is usually suppressed and denied. It is the sexual aspect. "I am

166

a woman. Since I am a woman, I am a sexual being. And I like being a sexual being." Still today, in the 21st century, this statement, spoken by a woman, requires revolutionary courage. It is a type of courage that only few women have, although we are supposedly living in an era of so-called sexual liberation. It requires leaving shame and the fear of violence, suppression, and punishment behind. It requires leaving false morals, the fear of the envy of competitors, and the normative images of the beauty industry behind. It requires leaving the religious concepts of our patriarchal culture, the old concept of love, and helplessness toward men behind. And it requires leaving sexual comparison and the stress of performance behind. There is hardly anything that she does not have to leave behind in order to be able to make this statement freely and without secretly having a bad conscience.

A fundamental fear of sexuality is historically embedded into female cells ever since the establishment of patriarchy. The level of fear rises immediately if her sexual affirmation is no longer directed toward only one man. The images of violence, the annihilation and destruction of all female elements, and the sexual atrocities of a catastrophic history between man and woman, which are stored as sedimented fear in the cells of women, are awakened whenever they approach the topic of sexuality. The cruelty and the fear of it are, however, not a part of sexuality itself, but are a result of thousands of years of misguided and suppressed sexuality.

"I am a woman and I love being a woman. I am a woman and thus I am a sexual being, and as a sexual being I am a woman who relates to several men in loving sensuous connection and who wants to unite with them mentally, spiritually, and voluptuously." It is sometimes difficult to understand how much courage it takes to make such a statement in our times. It requires overcoming the fear of both women and men. It will result in the enmity of many emancipated women and the contempt of many men. Many women become furious because they see a positive commitment to heterosexuality as being a step backward to a renewed dependency on men. "Now she not only wants to be there for one of them, she wants to sacrifice herself for many. That just creates an even greater dependency." They see the statement as a boycott against the freedom and independence that they are seeking. Their disappointment in men and the resulting hatred of men has become so great that many women from the emancipation movement do not want to deal with the erotic or biological attraction between man and woman. For them, revenge against men has a greater power than the desire for peace between the sexes. They do not know that it is specifically fulfilled sexual

contact that transforms the images of subjugation or violent fantasies into images of true empathy and contact. Sexually fulfilled contact gives rise to truly free women.

My Idea of Partnership with a Man

There are only a few women, who can stand behind this in terms of a true emancipation of women. There are not many who can imagine that a woman wants a full erotic contact with a man on an independent and free basis. This is the free wish of a woman to enter into a partnership with a man, whereby she neither subjugates herself, nor turns away from him, nor places herself above him. Being a heterosexual woman, I say: I need men. But I do not need a man as a tyrant, a henpecked husband, or a ruler. Nor do I need a man in his old role as a teacher or instructor. I want him as a truly potent, sensual lover, as someone who knows sensual love well. I will neither subjugate myself to him nor will I stand above him and mother him, for neither role fulfills my true sensual longings. Nor will I bind him to me with tricks, for during the last several centuries I have experienced that blackmail in love destroys the very thing that we originally loved about each other. I will see to it that free and passionate encounters with men become possible in the way that I have wanted them for millennia. Eros is naturally free and will not let itself be confined to flow in artificial channels. The enlightenment that I am seeking does not occur in the beyond but in my cells, in an earthy and elementary way, and it is of a sexual nature, through and through. Here, I am referring to ancient female mystery knowledge that is slowly being remembered and is today eliciting a natural shift. But this shift can only occur if we sanctify our natural sexual source as a source of knowledge and universal love.

The friendships and the faithfulness that I want from men are the result of a different power than that of blackmail and false laws. Of course, I will support the men by showing them what I love and desire about them and what not. True devotion toward a man, which is also sexual, does not make me dependent; it makes me free. The fact that I subjugated myself outwardly for so long was only the result of my hopelessness when I felt that the erotic world of my longings might not exist. Because I resigned myself to this, I entered into constricted and exclusive relationships and put personal demands of love onto a man. But Eros demands an opening and a participation in the sensual world beyond all limitations of marriage. The laws of Eros itself have an anarchistic power that breaks all laws. The sensual recognition of the other gender and the recognition of the erotic reality give rise to a deeper love and permanence between man and woman, which is not based on prohibitions and limitations. By revealing oneself more and more fully to the other, it becomes possible to walk this path of insight that leads to a deeper faithfulness than was ever possible in marriage and in the exclusion of others.

Original Sexual Knowledge

There is an aspect of sexuality which in earlier cultures was characterized by our intimate connection to nature and to the Goddess. There were sexual fertility rituals in which we celebrated Eros itself. They were cosmic celebrations and, at the same time, a cosmic thank you to Mother Earth. Fertility rituals were practiced and carried out in public, whereby we women naturally were allowed to show and reveal our sensual lust. This was not the sensual revelation in front of a private man. It was a temple feast, during which we gave back our sensuality as a thank you to Mother Earth. The men, too, carried out the act of love not with us personally, but as an expression of service and gratitude toward the Goddess. A woman, who in a temple of love tried to bind a man to herself personally, had failed in her service to the Goddess.

This type of elementary, simple, and powerful sexual encounter between man and woman was banned in our culture. Love and sexuality were split. Historically this gave rise, on the one hand, to the romantic "minnesinger" and admirer of women, worshiping them and thus making them sacrosanct. On the other side it gave rise to the sexual offender who followed the elemental force of the forbidden Eros. The ban on both the sacred and the passionate aspects of sexuality led to various forms of sadism and masochism, all the way to real violence, resulting in a trail of blood and unspeakable violence that runs through the entire patriarchal history.

The desired realization of love in all its aspects requires that the sacred aspect of sexuality be integrated. We need natural forms of community in which this truth can be lived. A cultural historical shift would occur if we were to invest our power of caring into creating communities that are based on trust instead of pretense, so that we can live according to our erotic truth. Think of how much gasoline is burned up during the search for erotic contacts and how much vicarious consumption is needed to silence our erotic longing.

As truly as I am a woman, I have a sexual reality within me, just as I have a sacred reality. How could we for such a long time have allowed the sexual truth and reality to be driven out of religions? I would like to be able to honor the sacred quality of life itself with all the passionate devotion that lives within me. Of course I would also like to love and honor the male forces. What an image of fulfillment it would be if I were to fully surrender myself to a man because I know that this self-abandonment will not be misused! My female religious longing does not need any churches or altars. Patriarchal religions have come about through the suppression of our erotic and sexual reality. It was a tool of power that was used against the erotic authority of female cultures. The symbol for it was Eve and the serpent who were driven out of Paradise by the male God and condemned as being evil. But there is a sacred component of life itself which cannot be driven out and which has remained intact through millennia of destruction and suppression.

In the beginning of the 19th century a nun wrote:

"It suffices to raise one's spirit to God, and then no act is a sin, no matter what it may be (...) the love of God and the love of your neighbor are the highest commands. A man, who unites with God with the help of a woman, is following both commands. The same is true of someone who raises his spirit to God and takes pleasure in the same sex or alone (...) Carrying out these acts, which mistakenly are described as being unclean, is the true purity that has been ordained by God, and without which no human being can gain knowledge from him." This quote is an expression of how ancient matriarchal knowledge could remain intact throughout the centuries in spite of all alienation and persecution through the church and the Inquisition.

It is this elementary sexual knowledge, which is vehemently announcing itself.

As a woman, I will develop myself culturally and historically to where I am a powerful organ for the care of Mother Earth. I will see to it that a mental-spiritual field and consciousness for this issue arises in many women. The earth is as physical as we are. It is a matter of body knowledge, a cellular knowledge. We can access it through the right kind of wakefulness, perception, and presence for each other and by becoming sensually present for this earth. This consciousness will give rise to an entirely new concept of ecology.

Finding Elementary Trust Again

Here, we find the elementary trust that we lost a long time ago. It is the trust in the elementary forces of nature itself. Based on this trust, it is possible to connect with these forces in such a way that they give us their protection.

The connection with these forces provides us with a great opportunity for fulfillment. It requires that I place myself fully in the service of the earth with all its creatures. I must do this in spite of the great powers of destruction that are currently, at the end of the patriarchal era of the 20th century, accelerating more and more.

In this sense I can willingly subscribe to the biblical statement: "Follow me, for I am with you all days, until the end of the world." In this case I am not following a guru; instead I am giving myself with full trust to the loving aspects of the earth, the Goddess. Imagine the sensual trust that enters into our cells when we follow the statement in such a way that no fear can creep in, because we can perceive the protective powers of growth in nature and consciously and physically connect with them.

This view gives rise to a spirit of discovery, and I feel challenged as a woman to develop and establish life connections that re-create the basis for this elementary biological trust. Of course this is only possible by including and affirming the sexual reality. As long as a woman has to take a stand against her sexual reality out of fear, she will take a stand against material reality as a whole, and experience the elementary forces of life as a threat that she must protect herself from. If, however, we can follow this path fully, then we arrive at the basic cellular knowledge of our female cells. They carry the information that is necessary for our fulfillment. It is like the memory of an old archaic dream, of a pre-historic state, in which a culture of peace has already been dreamed.

Based on this new perspective, I am engaged in finding a new relationship to myself as a woman – a historical being. I am being guided, but this time not by leaders and not by the laws of patriarchy. Instead, I am guided by the universal powers of growth and the guiding powers that are inherent in the earth's and matter's original dream of paradise. In this sense my freedom and my necessity place me squarely in the service of Mother Earth.

Chapter 5

The Concept of Healing

The Whole and the Holy

Healing is a result of switching over
from the matrix of fear and violence
to the Sacred Matrix of life.

The Sacred is the Whole. Healing comes from being connected with the whole. A divine energy resonates through this connection, even in the most profane of activities. Healing is sanctifying, and sanctifying is healing. In this equation, we find the self-healing powers of life. The more we relate to the matrix of life instead of to any momentary defects, the more healing power can take effect within us. Healing means to enter into a higher and wider energy space. The greater your energy space, the freer your body and soul is. In the matrix of life every event, every owl that flies by, every pattern on the bark of a tree, becomes an event in the greater energy space. One is basically not alone any more. This closeness, this lifting of the separation, brings about healing. Wherever we encounter the Sacred, transformation occurs immediately, something touches our entire being, and its information enters into each of our cells. With every action we take within the Sacred Matrix, we set healing forces into motion. That is the method used by all true shamans and all knowing healers, and it is the principle involved in all so-called faith healings. Every action with which we take in and honor the Sacred in ourselves results in our own healing and in the healing of others, no matter what illness might be present. We should not forget that by taking such action we change our inner matrix. We thereby use an entirely different "program" or "software" to take in and process the universal energies and information that come together in us. Always and at every moment, our inner matrix determines what energies and what information is taken in and how it is processed. Through the matrix of fear and violence, a process of selection is initiated that corresponds to the state of separation. Through the Sacred Matrix a different process of selection is initiated, corresponding to the state of connection. To the extent that we become conscious of these inner processes, we control the switch that takes us from one state to another. Up to now, we usually left this up to the moods and events that occurred in the environment. We left it up to fate and thus to powers that were foreign to us, and they then determined if our lives became good or bad. In order to achieve permanent healing we must learn to take the switch back into our own hands. Here, the word "autonomy" has a very deep meaning. It is a key word in healing. Only we can determine which matrix we want

174

to follow. God, Goddess, and the powers of Creation can only intervene once we have made the corresponding decision. The decision to lead a sacred life is our own to make; everything else we get from the universe.

The Principle of Entelechy in Healing

Once healing has been correctly triggered, it is life itself that carries it out. All healing methods that we have developed are designed to impact an organism so that it can open itself optimally to the self-healing forces of life. This applies to the organism of a human being, an animal, a plant, a landscape, a community, a society, humanity itself, and the entire earth. An organism that consists of many individuals, such as a biotope, a landscape, or human society as a whole, can thus also be impacted so that the healing forces of life can flow into the whole organism. Whether dealing with therapy, ecology, or politics, we always face the same task: to treat the overall organism in such a way that the "Mana" forces in life, the healing powers of the Sacred Matrix, can enter the organism in an optimal way. We thereby always work according to the principle of **healing through entelechy**. It is the goal of global peace work to treat the entire organism Earth, including the human being, in such a way that healing through entelechy can occur.

Entelechy is the inner Gestalt or goal image of a living being. It is a kind of blueprint of the organism and is present as an inner program in all its cells and organs. It controls growth and development, corrects deviations and defects, reacts to disturbances with suitable countermeasures, and re-establishes the inner balance in all situations. An organism's power of entelechy operates as an inherent power of self-healing.

All beings – plants, animals, and human beings – have this power of self-healing through entelechy. The healer's task is to awaken and fully unleash the diseased organism's powers of self-healing by introducing an energy vibration, a mental-spiritual input, or information. That is the healing principle behind all so-called "miracle healings", and it is the healing principle used by Jesus, by the Huna healers of Hawaii, in the faith healings in Lourdes, and in the healings that we ourselves have experienced in our healing work. It is actually the normal healing principle in life, for the healing forces are present everywhere. Had we not so successfully destroyed or suppressed them through a misguided cultural development, we would not need any of the medical methods and instruments so separated from nature.

The powers of self-healing take effect in a space of trust that is free of fear. If the healer succeeds in creating a situation in which trust is greater than fear, then he finds himself, together with the patient, in the spiritual space of healing. At this moment, one experiences a clear inner relief, a holistic power of vision and awareness, direct communication, and a state of closeness and joy, and it is immediately shared with the patient. Sometimes tears of relief flow, sometimes tears of insight. The organism is in a state of basic trust. Now its entelechy, its blueprint, can take effect fully. All inner processes, including cellular processes, together organize themselves in this direction. Spontaneous healings, such as those that we know from the Bible, become possible. Almost all illnesses can be healed in this way. It is only a question of how much healing power one can create in this situation and how freely the healing information can enter the patient's organism.

Since we are dealing with a sacred process, we have thus entered into the most elementary experiential space of the religion of the future. It is probably the oldest religion on earth, mankind's original religion: the experience of inner closeness to the healing, sacred universe and to the Mana powers of Creation. This experience gives rise to trust and love, which are the universal healing forces of all life. These forces organize the world and by re-discovering them, we can build the world anew. This is how we are to work, pray, love, and live together. This is how the new communities are to emerge and grow together.

The necessary healing work on earth requires that we create social and mental-spiritual spaces in which the healing powers of entelechy present in us and in the world can be optimally triggered and grow. These spaces should be accessible to everyone who comes to our project with an authentic inner desire for his/her healing and for the healing of the earth. In the beginning, it is important that the future facilitators of the healing process themselves experience and understand the principle of healing through entelechy. They will form the growing inner ring of power in the future centers.

Life's Healing Powers

The seeds are sprouting as they always did, the trees are growing, and the flowers blossom. The sun shines as it did a thousand years ago. How can it be that after five thousand years of patriarchy the birds still sing, the children still play, and lovers still feel as if they were in seventh heaven? Something in life seems to have remained intact through all the agony and blind alleys of history. It is something healthy and sacred, perhaps something eternal, that comes from the Universe and not from human beings, and yet it has been entrusted to us in the deepest roots of our soul and body. Probably every single human being on earth knows it subconsciously. We live in the presence of a global massacre of humans, animals, and nature, **but we clearly also live in the presence of an entirely different intact and sacred world.** Healing consists of reconnecting with this other world, which is our most original and our very own world, and bringing it fully into life on earth.

Healing in Guatemala

Norbert Muigg is an Austrian who was initiated into the healing path of the Maya by Indian shamans in Guatemala. He is the author of the book "Sprache des Herzens – Begegnungen mit Weisen der Maya" ["Language of the Heart – Encounters with the Wise Ones of the Maya"]. In it, he describes his experiences with Indian healers in a sober and convincing way. They follow a path of power, which gives them special healing abilities. All true healers and all true shamans from all peoples on earth have in one way or another walked this path and we, too, will learn to walk it when we are fully prepared to make this inner journey. We will accompany it with other rituals, we will use other methods and other thoughts, we will establish other social spaces and work with other technologies, but in principle, we will do the same as they. We will let ourselves be guided through the secrets of life by the inner voices of the world, and we will find the doorways through which we can enter into the mystery that we call "Creation". In this way, we will learn to participate directly in Creation. Healing is often a re-discovery of the path that reconnects us with God, Creation, our Higher Self, and that of others. One can see healing as a religious issue, not in the old sense of pious submission, but in the original sense of a deeper and higher connection to the sources of life. Such a connection results in the new concepts that we need for our peace work.

The healing successes that Muigg writes about come close to miracles; it is a similar world of miracles to the one we know from reports about Philippine, Hawaiian, or Brazilian healers. We of course also know of this world through Jesus and through all those who have worked and healed through spiritual means. It teaches us much. We, for example, learn that there is practically no pain if one is in a fully trusting state. While the patient watches and converses with the healer, operations are carried out without anaesthesia. The cuts, even deep ones, do not result in a blood bath, and the wound is healed after a very short period of time. One of Muigg's sons was operated on by a healer without anaesthesia while he was lying on his back observing the events with open eyes. Muigg describes the process as follows:

According to the healer's diagnosis, his bladder had to be raised. For many years he had had problems wetting his bed. Don Chepe opened his abdominal wall and asked Florian to look away so that he would not be nauseous. But the boy, who was maybe 10 years old at the time, was very curious and later told us about the precise course of events during the operation. Don Chepe had spoken with him and had thereby had his eyes closed. Florian had seen his own open abdominal wall and had felt a slight pain deep inside when Don Chepe had cut into his body. Directly after the operation he went with me to a restaurant; I had had to promise him that beforehand. The years of bed-wetting were over forever.

For Don Chepe healing is a calling. He was not called through an academic education, but through initiated Mayas and their associates in the beyond. He says that he only listens to the instructions from within. The presence of healing spirits and powers create a situation in which the human body follows entirely different laws than normally. I would hardly have believed these reports if we had not experienced similar things in our own work. Whenever we give the healing forces of the world the opportunity to enter into our lives, they carry out their work promptly, quickly, and in an extremely undogmatic way. They are not tied to any textbooks, any specific rituals, any disinfection, or any scientific or occult beliefs. Shamans and healers all over the world simply have the task of allowing these healing forces to enter. In this sense, many of us – once we have gone through a deeper training in life for some time – could become shamans and healers.

What is Life?

Human society can perish, but life cannot. We should be clear about the fact that life represents a cosmic dimension that is not bound by any conditions set by humans. Life is not the result of something; rather it is the original process in the universe - it is the foundation of the universe. The entire universe is alive. Life did not come about through a complicated composition of matter. On the contrary, just like the stars, the galaxies, and all material objects, these complicated protein molecules have emerged from life. It is not matter that has given birth to life through a long evolutionary process. Rather it is life that has brought forth matter in a (less known) process of evolution. This absolute priority of life before other things is one of the currently emerging insights, which are shaking the view of modern science in its foundations. Life is not a material process, but a universal, cosmic, and spiritual process; yet one of its peculiarities is that it also repeatedly appears cloaked in matter. This seems to constitute a special thought of Creation. The earth, our home planet, seems to have been chosen to realize this thought.

We have a sense of what dimension is involved when we speak of "life". It is the dimension in which healing lies. Life forces are healing forces. In life itself, we find the universal process, which, just like the sun, keeps on operating, beyond all destruction. Life is polar and full of opposites, but in life itself we find the higher levels of the Sacred Matrix, in which the opposites have a creative and not a destructive effect. Life itself, with its trillions of beings, contains the entelechy of a perfect world in which all the parts are aligned with each other in a healing way. This entelechy exists as basic universal information in every seed, every egg, and every being. It is the Sacred Matrix. It functions on its own, once it has been correctly triggered. In life, we find all the information that a cell, an organ, an organism, or a community needs. Despite all my previous experiences, this thought was so overwhelming to me that I needed a long time before I began to follow it.

It is life itself. I am aware that this enigmatic statement, which cannot be proven, has a metaphysical and almost sphinx-like quality. But, is it not so that as we approach the center, things can less and less be proven externally and at the same time they become more and more obvious internally? (I know how this type of argumentation can be and has been misused by religion to dull the minds of people. Yet I hope that the many other arguments in this book provide enough substance that one can see deeper into what is meant.) It is the sacred path of life itself which brings healing to those who know how to follow it.

Experiences with Self-Healing

We have repeatedly studied healing processes in ourselves. The healing forces are always present. Whenever we stop disturbing autonomous life processes, the process of self-healing begins. We can achieve this by tuning into a certain peaceful frequency, for example through prayer or a healing trance. Already this can achieve surprising spontaneous healing that one would characterize as "miracle healings" if one did not know what is happening.

We lived for three years with a group of forty people in the Black Forest, and during this time, we successfully worked with the method of self-healing through entelechy. We thereby noticed that there are hardly any objective limits for this type of healing. All limits that we encountered were subjective and caused by restlessness, fearfulness, or resistance in the healer or the patient. My partner had an accident in which she almost lost her thumb, which got caught in the door of a Mercedes as it closed. The thumb hung limply like a piece of flesh from her hand. She knew of this kind of healing mechanism and immediately switched over to the "healing frequency". The result was that the thumb came back to life, and within half an hour it was fully healed. I know how difficult it is to believe such things, if one has not experienced them oneself. Some of us have had accidents that we probably would not have survived if our inner voice had not immediately taken control. The healing power of entelechy often makes itself heard through one's inner voice.

Also in the healing area, there is an "Archimedean fulcrum". If it were possible to create a situation during which, even just for a moment, a high dose of the healing frequency were to penetrate the entire body, then the body would immediately be healthy. There are reports of such events from Lourdes, the Catholic place of pilgrimage, as well as from certain so-called "spiritual healers". The hologram of a healthy and sacred world can be accessed everywhere. The limitations are only set by the limits of our knowledge and consciousness. It should be possible to correct this mistake, for the mind can be healed. Humankind has spent several millennia to imprison the mind, suppress the autonomous processes in life, and thus switch off the natural healing powers. We carry this legacy of history in us, and will therefore need some time to dissolve the limitations that we have placed on ourselves. But we are in the process of developing efficient methods. This task must be accomplished, for there can be no peace without healing.

Healing is Possible in Every Situation

Life is a continuum. Let us remember that life is never over. No situation, no illness, no accident, not even death can put an end to our lives, for we are on an endless cosmic journey. Everything always continues. Even temporary dead end streets, stagnation, illnesses, and relapses are simply moments within a continual process of life and development. If you have fallen far, then you can enter the process at the level to which you have fallen. Nothing is incurable, and the deepest part of us, the divine "I", is "always intact" (Immanuel Kant).

Thanks to its feedback loops and control circuits, life has an answer to every situation. For every injury, there is healing, for every false direction, there is a correction, and for every question, there is a constructive answer. This is true at every age and we can rely on this welcome fact, for it is a part of the system of life. We are in a state of permanent feedback with the whole. Everything that happens in the whole elicits new information and new healing forces from the reservoir of universal wisdom. Only an organism that has definitively given up can no longer be reached by the self-healing forces of life. We all carry the information matrix of our own healing, our "blueprint", or "entelechy" within us, and it immediately initiates self-healing, provided we are not standing in our own way. It does not matter what our initial condition is, for there is a correct next step for every situation. Every situation, every accident, every illness, and every crisis in love can be the starting point for a healing process of renewal. We only need to learn to listen within and step out of the old habits we have acquired.

We can imagine being a hamster in the wheel of life. Suddenly one makes a mistake and falls. One lands a few steps lower, and the wheel keeps on turning. As soon as one has recuperated from the shock, one immediately finds oneself in the wheel of life again. Every step has its own direction, upward or downward, at an angle or horizontal, slow or fast – depending on the place where one happens to be. This is true for the different situations in life in which we find ourselves as recuperating beings. Life determines the direction and speed that is necessary at a given point in time in order to initiate the healing process. There is no punishment and no eternal damnation. There is only insight and alignment with the inner process of development of our health and perfection. If we have committed a great sin, then there is a place where this mistake can be corrected in a meaningful way. To do this we may need the courage to do things that others would not do. What is good for one person may be bad for another – here, there is no dogma. While one person may need to accelerate their speed, another may need to slow down, etc. There is no set of identical rules for everyone, neither in our spiritual life practice, nor in sexuality, nor in our nutrition. Some swear by fried food, for it supports the forces of Yang, whereas others swear by raw fruit and vegetables. What usually helps here is not the diet itself but the belief in it, and that is sacrosanct. Beyond all prescriptions, there are some very unconventional inner instructions that we can access when we have learned to listen to what is often called our "inner voice". It is our program of entelechy, also called our "higher self", which speaks to us and protects us from exaggerated demands. Nothing is expected of us that we cannot fulfil.

In some cases, it is necessary to step out for a while from our habitual life circumstances and activities, maybe even from our circle of friends, in order to go fully into seclusion and find the spiritual exercises that reconnect us with our own authentic life process. We then do things that we could hardly do in the presence of others; we take the time to listen to the kind of inner perception that is overheard in the frequencies of everyday life, and we register fine nuances that lead us in new directions. We must especially learn to stop the inner dialogue and step out of the eternal ping-pong of our thoughts and feelings. The powers of self-healing work best in a frequency of deep calm. Peace workers, who are active in the world, need such a retreat, where they can recharge their inner batteries at the cosmic generator.

For those who are on a spiritual path or want to be on such a path it is helpful to know that we are never alone on our path of healing. During our stay on earth, we are connected to spiritual beings and helping forces with which we can communicate and cooperate, once the two sides have found the right frequency. Sometimes they are simply there, even if we have not called them. Then we are like researchers, delving into the unknown area of healing, looking for signs and signals. We can always feed back information about where we are at the moment and what we need. We here often deal with precise information (see Chapter 9: "The Effectiveness of Prayer"). If a researcher does not know how to continue, s/he can always ask for help and instructions. This is how people in the past conducted their dialogue with the spiritual world, with "the ancestors", or with the Goddess, and this is how we, too, can dialogue with our cosmic interlocutors. We call this dialogue "prayer". Learning how to engage in this kind of spiritual cooperation constitutes one of the changes in the direction of our lives that we need in order to handle the difficulties and negativities of our times. We are almost forcibly led to the insight that healing does not result from our own efforts but from the kind of change and opening in our lives that lets us enter into resonance with the healing forces of the world. Healing, then, is not something that we earn. Instead, it truly occurs as a gift. This reflects the fact that we have received life, not because we have earned it, but as a gift of Creation.

Love is the Archimedean Fulcrum

Love is the ultimate goal of the universe
and the Amen of history.

Novalis

If I speak in human and angelic tongues
but do not have love,
I am a resounding gong or a clashing cymbal.
And if I have the gift of prophecy
and comprehend all mysteries and all knowledge;
if I have all faith so as to move mountains
but do not have love,
I am nothing.
If I give away everything I own,
and if I hand my body over so that I may boast but do not have love,
I gain nothing.
(…) So faith, hope, love remain, these three;
but the greatest of these is love.

Apostle Paul in Book 1 Corinthians, Chapter 13

The more intelligent you are,
the earlier you will realize
that no relationship can fulfill you.
Why?
Because every relationship is but an arrow
flying toward the last and highest love relationship.
Every love relationship is a signpost
toward a greater love
that lies before you.

Osho

Love begins
wherever we can truly do something for each other.

Gabriele Brüggemann

There are two states of being: one with a closed heart and one with an open heart. Love is the opening of the heart. The worst truth about the patriarchal era is that it prevented love. The misery of western society lies in the fact that no permanent love is possible, because from very early on open hearts are bombarded with unimaginable disappointments and meanness. At first children have open hearts, but little by little, they close them off because adults today usually have no idea how to deal with open hearts. Events in childhood are often like a drop of acetone that falls on an amoeba. It closes off its openings and pulls back its tentacles. This pre-programs the organism to close itself off in the future too. In their first love, youths have an open heart, but often they soon experience that it is better to close it off again, because the experience hurt too much. Adults are usually only prepared to open their hearts fully under certain precisely calculated conditions. Since these conditions are incompatible with true love, their heart closes itself off by itself and then remains more or less closed forever.

A humane world can only come about through open hearts. In this sense, we can say that the determining point for the realization of the Sacred Matrix on earth is love.

However, this also marks the beginning of the drama, for none of us has closed off his/her heart without a reason. We are taking a risk by opening it up again. We are afraid to do so, because for generation after generation we have had bad experiences when we have done so. The greater the longing, the greater the fear. Ultimately, billions of people have learned to conquer their longings. In its place we put vicarious fulfillment that is compatible with the system: entertainment, the media, consumption, tourism, football – and sometimes war.

Many bad things result from unfulfilled love. Revenge arises from a love that has been betrayed. Clinging, blackmail, jealousy, the fear of abandonment, distrust, and mutual spying on each other: these are elements of a modern syndrome affecting our love relationships, and they are the result of bad experiences during a time when our hearts were still open. Wherever there is a spark and the heart wants to open up in a fraction of a second, there the inner opponent is often faster. Instead of love, the result is anger or fear, because the pain, which once was connected to love, is stored in the subconscious. For millennia, the fate of love has been tied to disappointment and separation, betrayal and lies, suspicion and meanness, murder and manslaughter. This resulted in a collective psychological structure, which reacted to love with the fear of separation, to the fear of separation with false promises of faithfulness, and to false promises of faithfulness with anger and revenge. This fateful connection lies at the foundation of today's society and of its concepts of love and rules of marriage, its morals, and its strategies of war.

There can be no peace on earth as long as there is war in love.
Betrayed and unfulfilled love constitutes a core element of the old matrix. Should a heart opening occur in spite of these conditions, then we often soon see the corresponding by-products that are a part of the old matrix: unbridled passion, claims of ownership, fear of abandonment, comparisons with others, competition, violence, and revenge. Operas, tragedies, movies, and magazines are full of them. So are therapeutic advice centers, hospitals, psychiatric wards, and cemeteries. Here we find a horror without end; a horror that nobody can bear to look at for very long. It is too terrible. For most people who are caught in the structure of the times there is no escape, no perspective, no chance for love. Even fifteen-year olds sometimes take their own lives because they have realized this.

Many groups have tried to practice free love or free sexuality. Yet they always failed when it came to love. If one practices free sexuality based on mutual agreements, this is an impulse in the right direction, but it cannot replace love. Free sexuality can occur without an opening of the heart, but love requires the heart to be open. It requires this risk. The groups that practiced free sexuality were thus for a long time faced with the conflict of representing something that was different from what they truly wanted deep inside. In addition to free sexuality, something entirely different waited, moaned, groaned, and cried out in their souls. It was the longing for intimacy, for a feeling of home, for love. But that had to be kept more or less secret, for it was still associated with the old image of absolute faithfulness between two people. One had already suspected that this image no longer corresponded to reality.

It was not the most stupid ones who had found each other under the banner of free sexuality. They knew that love could not function based on the old ideas. But they did not know of any real alternative that they could believe in. They knew of alternatives when it came to sexuality, but they did not know of any alternatives in love. As I see it, this was a main reason for the failure of such groups (such as for example the Austrian Friedrichshof). It also underlies the difficulties that almost all co-workers of a healing biotope have to work through, understand, and solve – and they can be solved if one goes about it intelligently. However, the effort that is required to solve the love issue goes far beyond one's initial expectations. We are dealing with a project for saving love. That is not a private task, it is the project of the century.

The most beautiful friendships between men have broken up over a woman. The most beautiful friendships between women have broken up over a man. As long as love was stuck in the restraints of the old matrix, it was a destructive force. In reality, however, its healing power is greatly superior to all other healing powers. It is the true elixir of healing. One could easily think that we are here facing a hopeless situation. On the one hand healing can only occur through love, and on the other hand, love leads us into all the conflicts that we wanted to escape from. But this calculation is wrong, for it operates with a false image of love. Healing is a part of the new matrix, not the old one. We must therefore seek the image of love that leads to healing in the new, not the old matrix.

One of the experiences of the new matrix is the discovery of the higher task for which one has incarnated this time as well as a corresponding professional category in the newly emerging human community. As long as I only exist as a private person, I will never be able to solve the secret of love. Love, even when it appears between two human beings, is always a universal, divine power, and can therefore only be realized in a universal state of being (see Chapter 7). Love does not require the fixation of two pairs of eyes on each other. Instead, it requires parallel eyes directed toward the joint higher goal. Love is more than a feeling; it is a state of being. It comes from the field of connection and not from that of calculation. Almost all people alive today find themselves – either consciously or unconsciously – in a field of calculation when it comes to love. The inner dialogue then goes something like this: "If I allow myself to totally love this person ... and if then somebody else comes along and also loves her/him ... and if s/he loves the other person more than s/he loves me ... if s/he is Number One for me, but I'm not her/his Number One ... nonoIcannotandIdon'twanttoandbrrbooo." That is the thought, which keeps the heart closed. Free love has always failed because of this inner structure.

Inner and outer peace work requires that we integrate the issue of love in a new way. The groups of the past did not know how to deal with the power of this issue. Their mistake consisted of seeking a solution for the issue of love where it could not be found. Free love, which does not calculate, compare, or ask for something in return, is a part of the Sacred Matrix. It can therefore not be achieved with ideas and methods that come from the old matrix. We cannot earn it through arduous inner transformation exercises. Instead, it manifests to the extent that we step into the new matrix of life. We find the matrix of life, fulfillment, cosmic teachings, guidance, and love also outside of couple relationships. The same is true of the creatures of Creation, and by engaging with them, we can learn about the secrets of love. This makes it easier to understand and accept love in the concrete situation with a person that one loves.

The Healing Biotope project began 25 years ago with the idea of establishing a project for love, in which lovers, who have separated from each other, can meet each other anew, again and again. We sometimes simply called it a "project for saving love". It was clear to me that we had to take a completely new path for this to occur, and that we could not just remain focused on the topic of love. Ultimately, it was a question of creating an entirely new life space, making it possible to switch over from the old to the new matrix. At the time, I did not know that it would take so long for the new image of love to be imprinted into our cells. In no other area do people so obstinately try to hold on to the old matrix; nowhere are they as conservative as they are in love. They build railway stations in space and use the same images for their ideas about love as their great grandparents did: high tech in war, Neanderthal in love.

We have become acquainted with the new matrix in many areas of our project and we have seen to what extent it differs from all old concepts. We have also seen how easily it comes to us once we are ready for it. We have gotten to know it when dealing with animals, when communicating with rats and snakes, when attempting to influence the weather, and when healing injuries and illnesses. We have experienced how a community in need sticks together, how dangers are overcome jointly, how financial bottlenecks can suddenly be overcome, and how spiritual helping forces keep intervening when our own power is not strong enough.

In spite of this, it took a long time for the first ones to dare to fully come down on the side of love. Yet, from the point of view of the matrix of life, it is so simple. If you notice that you love a person, then follow this love without any conditions. Whatever is done out of love, is done rightly. That was one of Vincent van Gogh's key phrases. You must begin by trusting. As for the rest, "let God do"; the Sacred Matrix will do the rest for you. It is not difficult to do this; it is easy. Difficulties can be overcome through ease. Follow love and take the risk of running into turbulence of the soul, which you will then probably go through. You should know that the person whom you truly and honestly love is probably truly and honestly loved by some others, too. It would be strange if this were not the case. Endure this tension, and remain faithful to love. You will have entirely new thoughts, and you will find a joy and a relief that you did not think was possible. You will make discoveries that you hardly can communicate to anyone. You may seem to be deep in thoughts or even gloomy, but a completely new kind of joy is making its way through you and your life. Ask your friends not to be surprised if you act a bit strange or seem slightly deranged for a while. Tell them that you enter a plea of insanity, and explain to them why. Learn to remain connected, even in the midst of this turbulence.

The right thing happens automatically when you know the Sacred Matrix and if you are increasingly willing to follow it. Entirely new knowledge becomes available to you. Jealousy, too, is a matter of knowledge. From a certain level of knowledge on, you can no longer be jealous. You now know that jealousy is not a part of love, and you know this not only theoretically, but also in a cellular way, with every cell in your body. The chains of information in your genetic code now rearrange themselves so that there is no longer any place for the information of jealousy. Your whole body knows this. You also know that love has to do with surrender, with giving, serving, and helping, and not with demanding and forcing. The old patterns of mutual blackmail no longer exist, and the old ideas of separation, competition, and jealousy have fallen away from you. The old matrix has disappeared all on its own.

I have repeatedly experienced how easily these things occur. It does not require any therapy; one only needs unshakable patience and growing knowledge. One could say that one needs to be absolutely faithful to the issue of love. The Sacred Matrix knows that fear of abandonment and precautionary measures are not a part of love. At some point we know it, too. Thus begins a new and deeper healing path with entirely new perspectives. From this point on, we begin to establish the healing biotope. We now know what it is about and why we are doing it. We begin to understand and love great people who have loved so uninhibitedly: Vincent van Gogh, Leo Tolstoy, Selma Lagerlöf, Frère Roger, Ernesto Cardenal, Nelson Mandela, Ruth Pfau ...

Finally, I would like to quote some gifted words about love, written by Elisabeth Kübler-Ross:
The essence of learning to live in the right way is to learn to love.
True love does not make any claims of ownership, nor does it set any conditions.
The only thing I know that really heals people is unconditional love.
It is love that gives life meaning.
Death is nothing that one has to fear. In reality, it can become the most

incredible experience of your life. It only depends on how you live your life here and now.
The only thing that is important here and now is love.

And, simply because it fits so well, some final words by Meister Eckehart:
The most important hour is the present one.
The most important person is always the person in front of you.
The most important action is always love.

Tears of Healing

When a person's inner structures dissolve, tears are often the result. When a process of insight, sympathy, and love reaches one's innermost core, our entire organism reacts with a new opening. A stream of new life flows through the cells and produces tears.

I would like to say a few words about healing that do not come from any theory, but directly from life itself. They are a continuation of the previous section about love. In love, there is an opening, a recognition, a fundamental experience of encounter, which immediately touches our cells so deeply that tears come to our eyes. Here there is no romanticism or sentimentality; instead, we find the original recognition between two or more people – the original sanctification and revelation. Those who have experienced it know what love is. It is the full opening of two souls for each other, and in this opening, the opening toward life occurs. So does the opening toward universal love and toward the one great state of being, which connects us all. Could a boy, who has loved a girl in this way, kill a rabbit? Could a mature man, who has discovered love in this way, ever become cynical?

In her book, "Women Who Run With the Wolves", Clarissa Estés tells a wonderful Inuit fairy tale about the fate of love. It is called "The Skeleton Woman" and describes the situation that arises when a man sees a woman after his heart has been frozen for a thousand years. The man is an Eskimo fisher and the woman is nature itself, which is so emaciated that only a skeleton remains. I would like to quote a few passages:

As he slept a tear ran down his cheek. The Skeleton Woman crawls clumsily over to him and thirstily drinks the tear from his cheek. What, we ask, could the fisherman be dreaming for him to cry a tear?

Tears contain powers of creation. In myths, worlds are created through the shedding of tears and what was separated is reunited at an emotional level. When tears are shed in fairytales, the rivers overflow their banks and flood the dry land. When they drop onto wounds, they heal them and if they drop onto blind eyes, they regain their power of vision.

When a lover has arrived at this point, he has revealed and opened himself so far that his deepest empathy, his deepest silent understanding for himself and for the others can no longer be held back and overflows. It is only this silent overflowing that can quench the thirst of nature itself, which has become as emaciated as a skeleton. It is only in his innocent and unprotected form that a human fisherman of love is able to quench his partner's thirst.

The fisherman is busy with the emotions of his wounds; he touches them where they hurt, even if the wounds are old, stemming from his childhood, from yesterday, or from the day before yesterday. This is how he can shed the tear of limitless sympathy, for in his own pain he recognizes the echo of the pain of all other creatures.

It was this point that Friedrich Nietzsche experienced one morning in the year 1889 in Turin when he broke down and embraced a horse in front of a carriage because it was being brutally beaten by the carriage driver. After that, he never spoke another word again until he died in the year 1900. Empathy with an animal broke the heart of the creator of the great Zarathustra. Or maybe it opened it. From then on, he was a different human being.

I continue with Carlissa Estés' words:
He sees what barricades he has erected within himself against the immediate feeling of pain. He sees how many opportunities to get love he has missed because of these barricades. And he realizes that the same is true for everybody else.

This is what women long for in men; this admission through which all projections on the partner are dissolved and a man faces his injured relationship toward his own basic nature. This admission causes the liberating, healing tear to flow from his eye, for now he recognizes that in the future he can heal himself, and he no longer longs for the woman to stop his tears. He no longer thirsts for his deeper self, for he has found it. (...) Now something new can arise in him, something that he can give to his life partner as a gift: a great, oceanically feeling heart.

Here lies a source of all healing. Let us use all the sensitivity, intelligence, and power we have to see to it that a new society is established in which a heart that has just opened does not have to shrink back and close off again. At that moment, when the tears of insight flow, the barricades against love are lifted and the energy of the new matrix flows through all the cells. Healing is occurring here and now. It seems to me that every other form of healing is less powerful.

Regaining Lost Power

The shattering causes a fright for a hundred miles.
And he drops neither sacrificial spoon nor chalice.

I Ching, Comment to Sign 51

You can look at the world with the eyes of a victim
or as an adventurer on his way to the treasure

Paolo Coelho

Healing means regaining lost power. When I speak of "power" I do not mean power over others, but the presence of one's own power, the presence of perception also in critical situations, the presence of an image of a higher self without vanity, and the presence of a higher connection. It is not the power over others, but the power over ourselves. It is the ability to make the decision to stop an emotional movement that pulls us down, to think or not to think a thought, to carry out a reaction or not to do so. It is the ability to step out of the old reactions of fear, anger, or revenge, and to be so deeply connected with what we wish to achieve that it cannot be taken away from us.

So what do we want to achieve? For example in love? In the encounter with someone we desire? At a political conference? In a tense situation with our friends or opponents? In our personal and professional lives? Before attempting to answer these questions, we must first find some of our lost power, for we need this power to both understand and answer the questions.

The peace movement is dependent on the personal power of their protagonists. It is dependent on their presence of mind, their boldness, their positive way of dealing with their own and others' mistakes, their ability to love, and not least their sexual powers. In all areas, it is a matter of not "falling out of one's Hara", i.e. not giving away one's own power to others, not becoming a victim of the perception of others, and of retaining "the blue sphere of power" in any situation. Their opponents, both human and political opponents, have their power only as long as others are afraid of them and project on them. The whole world of fear is a virtual world in which images of the past are projected onto present or future situations, thereby giving power away to others. Good mental training is required to see through these connections. No fear is based on an objective reality.

195

Instead, every fear is based on a projection that only becomes real if it is seen as real and if one reacts to it with fear.

These are central insights that come from years of studying our connections in life. Every good Samurai warrior knew of them. These things need to be learned and practiced so that they can be applied at the right moment. Up until now, many opportunities in our lives have been lost because we give precedence to our powerlessness instead of our power. We slip away and are simply not there for long periods of time in everyday life. We are then so absent that we go into a supermarket and believe that what we find on the shelves is serious reality. In this case, we have given our power away to things. Or else we believe that we simply have to have a special dish. Such seemingly normal needs and desires are well suited to quickly disconnect us from the higher frequency and imperceptibly dump us at a lower frequency where we may like our food, but where we are not equipped to deal with an unforeseen situation of fear. Maybe it is enough for a beautiful woman to appear for us to fall into neediness and lose the "blue sphere" on the spot. We will then be so scared that even the best morsel of food will get stuck in our throat. That is normal for us mortals, but it doesn't have to stay that way.

There are clear indications for how to regain power and for how a peace worker can gain inner victory. First, we should be fully clear about the fact that we always have access to the desired power if we do not chase it away, for we are the children, the partner, and the organs of God and the Universe. Then we should be clear about how we humans have lost our power and what we can do to regain it.

A part of our power was taken away from us already in early childhood. Our parents thought that we were very irrational, sweet little children with snub noses. In reality, we are cosmic beings, who have come from the other world, and first of all have to learn to cope with life on earth. For this, we were well equipped through our mind, our perception, and our ability to learn. At the time, we were more awake and alert than we have ever been since. If you look into the eyes of a baby, you see an incredible wakefulness. In many ways, we knew much more than our parents did, for the memory of our existence in the cosmic space was still fresh. It was not until we had gone through years of a strange kind of "upbringing" that we learned to be as "reasonable" and as narrow-minded as they were. When we were trivialized and treated as small and therefore insignificant beings, we often reacted with desperation or attacks of rage. We could not do more, for the adults were much larger and stronger. To the adults, our unruliness was yet another reason for making us conform to their norms. They thereby became a higher authority for us, and we began to believe that we had to be like them. Even if we rebelled, we still became like them. They, themselves, had already given away most of their power, but how were we to know that?

The continued dispossession of power occurred through three things: by restricting our drive toward insight (curiosity), by restricting our urge to be active, and by restricting our sexuality. Curiosity, the urge to be active, and sexuality are all parts of the fundamental power with which every human being comes to earth. How much true power a person can develop during his/her life depends on to what degree s/he is able to follow these three basic aspects of power and integrate them into his/her life. Let us remember with what eagerness we once wanted to know what was hidden behind a castle wall, where the entrance to a cave led to, or what was inside a chestnut. As children, we have an almost metaphysical curiosity that seeks and finds something quite interesting behind the exterior signs in life, almost in the same way that Parcival sought the Holy Grail. S/he who is curious, lives in perception. Strong curiosity can overcome almost any fear. It is a true power in life - a power of healing and of liberation. Providing people with ready-made answers to the most elementary questions and prohibiting them from carrying out their own investigations was a diabolical measure in human cultural history. Those who sought answers that were different from those provided by the state and the church risked their lives. Truth was punishable by death (see Giordano Bruno and the entire history of the heretical movement). Maybe this – in addition to the sexual restriction – was the strongest method used to take power away from people.

Healing means regaining one's lost power in all areas. This may sound like a heroic definition, but deep down it touches a core issue, and why should we not be a bit heroic? It means that we must find a "path of power", which immunizes us positively against our old susceptibilities. Don Juan (Carlos Castaneda's teacher) calls it the "path of heart". Here, power and love, strength and heart do not contradict each other; instead, they come together. The path of power consists of following the energies of life and not external laws or emotional moods. Every situation contains a certain amount of Mana energy, which we can use either for or against ourselves, depending on our behavior. Those who take the path of power learn, step by step, to connect with these energies. This does not mean that they will always have external success, but they will gain power. Jacques Lusseyran, the blind resistance fighter during the French Résistance, wrote that for some time he went "victoriously from defeat to defeat". This is a very unusual learning process, for we keep running into situations where our old habits have resulted in paralysis instead of empowerment. We are faced with entirely new learning tasks, especially in the areas where we so far have reacted with fear, anger, and defiance. We are beginning a basic training course of life. Eventually this training will make it possible for us to gather so much power that we no longer need to react to dangers with fear, for we are in good hands and safe through a higher form of connection. We no longer need to avoid the old zones of fear in our lives, for they contain what we need to learn to gain final insight and peace. The whole world is now the stage on which our amazement about existence is played out.

In our exercises, we have often practiced following and retaining power. I can recommend this exercise to everyone, without exception. One evening, during a trip through the Algarve in southern Portugal, I went to play billiards with a female friend of mine. I was looking forward to playing in such a way that my power stayed with me, and I secretly enjoyed the idea of showing her how good I was. It began well, but after a while, nothing seemed to work any more. Somehow, I could not hit the balls correctly. Several times, I found myself saying "Shit!" in a totally serious and identified way. Not even the woman's erotic flair could keep me from doing that. I was in deep disagreement with something, I felt that life was treating me unfairly, and I became irrationally angry at the game and at the world in general. "That always happens when one feels good!" I soon noticed that I had completely lost my focus. A few bad shots had been enough to throw me off my path of power.

In his wonderful book "Thought Forces", Prentice Mulford describes this process when he unsuccessfully tries to push a wheelbarrow along a garden path without any inner agitation. Every day of our lives, we waste our power by automatically surrendering to our inner habits and dialogues. After the game of billiards, I met the gaze of a spectator and lost my power through my eyes, because I was ashamed of my bad game. It happens that easily. It took a while before I could regain the frequency of power and return to being connected. It was a teaching. This is what life can be like if one is engaged in this kind of training to regain lost power. One can easily imagine in what inner confusion one can suddenly find oneself when engaged in this training in the area of sex and love. There are, in reality, two world processes that we go back and forth between: one is the process of the ego world and the other is a process of the universal world. Freedom definitely emerges – also when playing billiards – on the side of the universal world.

Regaining lost power. This power is not one's own power in terms of the strength that one has, it is the power that one has naturally through the connection with the powers of God and the universe. There are no limits to this power; it has gone through many people, and has resulted in many "miracles". Why did Jesus have the power to heal the sick, and why did Rüdiger Nehberg have the power to cross the Atlantic in a pedal boat and survive his incredible adventures? Why did Reinhold Messner have the power to conquer all 14 mountains in the Himalaya that are higher than 8000 meters? Why did Johannes Hus have the power to sing as he was burned at the stake. Why did women such as Hildegard von Bingen, Elsa Brandström, Maria Theresa, Ruth Pfau, and others have the power to carry out their great healing work? Because they were all connected to their higher power. They, and many more, provide living testimony to what human beings can do if they have reconnected with a higher power. Ghandi was a single individual. He succeeded in liberating the large subcontinent of India from British colonial rule. Would it not be possible for us today to liberate ourselves from the old civilization and its false matrix?

The Unused Energy Potential

We do not suffer from a lack of energy,
but from an excess of energy.
Illness is the unused, blocked energy
that is stuck in our bodies and cannot find a way out.

Healing always relates to an organism's energy supply and energy transformation. How does the organism exchange energy with its surroundings? Is it blocked or is it open for the energies of the world? Energy is present in any amount, for the cosmic energy reservoir is inexhaustible. Usually, we do not suffer from a lack, but from an excess of energy. We are here dealing with life energies that the organism cannot integrate and use, because they do not fit the moral and social norms. They are the great energies of sexuality, the often great energies of rage, the energies of the highest vitality and speed, and the energies of curiosity and of overcoming limitations, all the way to having transcendental experiences. These energies cannot flow freely, they cannot unfold and move in their own way, and they often block each other, leading to paralysis and congestion. An inner "yes" and a simultaneous inner "no" – for example relating to a sexual impulse – can split the energy flow into two opposite directions, thus paralyzing them or damming them up. The inner blocks, dams, confusions, and aberrations of our life energies then result in the typical symptoms of our times: irritability, sleeplessness, tiredness, headaches, asthma, a tendency toward hysteria and occultism, a lack of energy, stiff limbs, flabby tissue, vegetative dystonia, bouts of insanity, and feelings of acute meaninglessness.

When dammed up energy blocks off body tissue for a longer period, the result is inflammations and uncontrolled cell growth (cancer), which Wilhelm Reich characterized as "biopathies" and "congestion illnesses" (see his book "The Function of the Orgasm" and "The Cancer Biopathy"). The excess energy, which has nowhere to go in the body and which clogs up its channels, results in extreme forms of bodily changes. Many bent spinal columns, many forms of limping or unusual swinging of the arms when walking, many undeveloped thorax or too large rear ends, as well as other deformities are due to energetic constipation. The body does not know what to do with the energy signals, for it is receiving conflicting information based on desires and morals. Especially the well-known forms of extreme obesity or underweight and the unconquerable pads on the thighs or the abdomen (that sometimes are not so unattractive) are the result of excess, un-integrated life energy. Diets then usually do not help, for the problem lies in a basic disturbance of the energetic dynamic equilibrium.

A blockage of energy output is also the reason for unexplained illnesses. There is then too much "dead" energy in the body. A healthy organism is in dynamic energy equilibrium. The energy from the world can then flow in and out freely, so that there is a balance between the inflow and outflow of energy. If this balance is disturbed, "dead" energy collects in the body and can no longer be transformed into motion, power, and action. The entire population of Western civilization is suffering from un-integrated energy in one form or another. In the corsage of today's civilization, the rhythms of output and breathing out, the functions of energy release and ventilation are disturbed. Usually, we do not notice our blocks much. We notice them if we, for a brief period of time, come into a highly energetic state that mobilizes all our life forces. It is incredible how great the reservoirs of power are that we then suddenly have access to. They seem to be practically limitless. All pioneers of great bodily experiences, from the polar researcher Fridtjof Nansen to the extreme mountaineer Reinhold Messner, describe such experiences.

We should be aware that our infirmities, our bodily weaknesses and de-formities, and our tiredness and depressions are not a part of our nature. Instead, they are cultural illnesses that separate us from life's vision. We are wrong if we believe that the body has to become weak and withered with increasing age. We are wrong if we think that inflammations can be treated successfully only with antibiotics and that obesity can be healed only through diets. These thoughts stem from the state of being of an organism that has already separated from the matrix of life; they come from the matrix of fear and violence. If our sexual circulatory system is blocked, we need different diets and different medication than if it is unblocked. The prescriptions that we find in regular health books are based on the assumption that they are dealing with the normal state of being of people today, i.e. with a blocked sexual and energetic circulation system. They usually do not really heal, but they do make the situation more bearable. Those who suffer from obesity will regain their natural figure if they can give off more constructive energy and create a larger energy space around them, which is in resonance with the cosmic space and with their own entelechy. Their bodies will regain their natural form when they regain their full ability to act and to discharge energy, and when they are no longer hindered by secret thoughts, vanity, contrariness, or miserliness. It is usually a question of releasing energy in the right way.

Those who have a goiter [enlargement of the thyroid gland] can get rid of it by speaking correctly. This is not easy in the world as we know it, for we have had good reasons for learning to keep many things secret. A humane space must first be created, where it becomes possible to speak the truth about deeper and more sensitive issues. Usually we cannot find any words when it comes to topics that have to do with rage and sex. Permanent healing requires fundamentally new life spaces, in which the human organism can freely reconnect with the cosmic energy because it is no longer blocked by the organism of society. **The biosphere and the sociosphere, life energies and social energies, must match for the human body to be forever liberated from its inner contradictions.** It then automatically fills up with the power that has been lying paralyzed and unused within the body.

An essential part of the energy circulation of a freely flowing life energy is the great sexual circulation, which connects the heart with the genitals (more precisely, the heart chakra and the sexual chakra). In the matrix of violence, this connection has been almost totally severed. This results in many of the common sexual illnesses, all the way to the chronic inflammations of the uterus and the abdomen. Many sexual diseases of our times – including the resulting secondary illnesses – come from a sexual energy circulation that is too small. If the sexual chakra and the heart chakra are energetically and spiritually separated from each other, the space for the incoming energy is much too constricted, and this inevitably leads to congestions and inflammations that are then said to be due to some kind of "contagion". As we know since the research conducted by Lachovsky and Reich, the dammed up tissue itself often produces the pathogens. Many sexual diseases disappear when sex and heart come together again. Making this possible is an important task especially for communities with free sexuality.

We need power to fulfill the tasks at hand. The question of how much power I can access is not primarily dependent on how strong I am, but on how much power can come together in me and how much I can discharge. The more power is liberated from the blockages, the more power can be focused toward a conscious goal. Cats have their incredible leaping powers and precision from a completely open state of relaxation. The cosmic energies are free to flow in an open organism that is connected with the Sacred Matrix. It is then not a question of excess energies, but of work energy that is readily available and that constantly connects us with the cosmic energy reservoir. It heals all body parts, for the matrix of healing is present as entelechy in every cell. I insist on this statement: cosmic energy heals every cell of the body if we open the path for it. There is no reason for suffering, there is no reason for depression, there is no reason to brood about the meaning of life, and there is no reason for illness and disease - if we find this opening. The icons of suffering are based on blocked energy.

Working on Oneself

*We have to apply the correctives
that are necessary for the earth
to ourselves.*

Dieter Duhm

*It is only if one does not change,
that one is working against nature.*

Vincent van Gogh

*We, ourselves, have to be the change
that we want to see in the world.*

Mahatma Gandhi

Illness is not a private problem. But it must be dealt with by those who are afflicted, if they want to be healed. To work on an illness always means to work on one's own character, and we can only spread as much healing power as we carry within us. Healing workers work with the healing powers that they can mobilize within themselves. Peace workers work with the powers of peace that they have created within themselves. And servants of the community work with the "communitarian" powers that they carry within themselves. As inside, so outside. In the life of an individual, there are certain powers of attraction that promote peace and health. Such powers are for example love, trust, the power of good, the desire to give, a high physical energy, and a positive self-image. There are, however, also other habitual powers of attraction that have the opposite effect. I call them the "attractors of illness", because they have to do with an inner disposition that attracts illnesses. Such negative attractors are, for example, a bad conscience, fear, a lack of perspective, a lack of challenge, not being needed, negative body energy, and a negative self-image. These attractors are usually connected with each other and give rise to an image of a symptom (a syndrome) which today characterizes the lives of countless people. Especially in the alternative movement, it was difficult for most groups and projects to develop goals, convictions, tasks, and professions that elicit a feeling of joy, a sense of purpose, and power. The contents in life that are chosen remain more or less within the framework of personal whims and never attain the dimension which would give the participants higher energy. The ideology of spontaneity and of voluntariness, with which most actions are connected, is quite unsuitable when it comes to erasing the participants' fear and providing them with a higher image of the value of their work. The strengthening of the individual is oriented toward the issue with which they are confronted. A small issue does not result in much strengthening. Great issues cause a strengthening that can overcome all boundaries. In his book "And There Was Light", Jacques Lusseyran, the French Résistance fighter, writes of the life-threatening, almost super-human work that he and his group carried out in order to establish a secret organization against Nazi terror in Paris.

In the beginning of our project we wrote the following on a wall: "Why are we afraid? Because we do not have an issue." This has to do with a rule of thumb for success-oriented groups: give your co-workers tasks that challenge them. See to it that work projects are formulated precisely enough, so that everyone knows where s/he belongs. See to it that there is enough resistance within the work to mobilize the powers of the participants and to raise their motivation. In the long run, work that is too easy leads to a low energy. Work that is too difficult leads to discouragement. We need a continuous positive energy in order to be able to solve the life issues of the Sacred Matrix. Even human issues such as free love, the willingness to trust, or drug use require a certain minimum amount of inner energy for them to be able to be solved. How much energy a group can bring together and how energetically they can design their work projects is of essential importance for the emotional climate in a group, the health of the participants, and the solution of the conflicts at hand.

Work on oneself is successful if it is carried out under suitable energetic conditions. The first guideline is thus to act so that you assemble a maximum amount of energy, "mana", or life force. This includes learning to live in such a way that one does not have a bad conscience, not even subconsciously. In many cases, a latent bad conscience, which is usually hidden from others, acts as a severe energy damper. A bad conscience arises from doing things that one knows one should not do and therefore hides them from others. If we look at our lives through a microscope, we can find any number of such small things. Together, they form our dark continent that nobody is allowed to see. This life practice, which automatically results from the structures of our culture and which is present in varying degrees in practically everybody, has a very special consequence: we do not believe in love. We do not believe that others would love us if they knew everything about us. Our subconscious computer makes its calculations whereby we always fail. If we have to hide ourselves in order to be loved, we can never trust love – that is only logical. Because we then do not believe that we are loved, we will become suspicious, clinging and blackmailing. We will behave in such a way that we truly do not seem to be very lovable. The belief that one is not loved is therefore usually fulfilled due to one's own behavior. If we in this sense put the pieces of our own lives under the magnifying glass, we usually do not arrive at a very praiseworthy result. It would, therefore, be wise to step out of this double-entry bookkeeping and finally come clean with oneself and with the world. For this to occur, we need a decision that we can only make if we know exactly what for. We need a vision of a different life, and we need a concrete task in order to realize it. The success of an enterprise always also depends on if the participating co-workers have been assigned the right tasks. For, as the saying goes, you grow with your responsibility.

We know of the new possibilities to regenerate and develop power that result from reconnecting with the Sacred Matrix. We know of the miracle of the mysterious processes that occur all by themselves under the guidance of the forces of the universe. We are then faced with the question: what do we need to do, in order to connect with this matrix? The sibyllic answer is that we must make the decision for it to occur, we must open the way, and we must give up the old resistances. As Dhyani Ywahoo says: "It is through the conscious decision to live in a sacred way that we attract the teachings, the information, and the understanding that help us to unfold all our gifts for the good of all." It obviously starts with a "conscious decision". The entire spiritual process of development referred to here begins with making a conscious decision and consists of repeatedly making new decisions. It means adopting a spiritual life practice, a communitarian life practice instead of a private one, and a new image of love. It means renouncing old life habits and consumer habits, old comforts, and distractions. It means stepping out of complicity and taking on new ways of living, a new language, and a higher, more energetic, and intelligent kind of pleasure and joy of life, etc.

Once the conscious decision has been made and you remain faithful to it through all the decisions that follow, the new path opens up all by itself, for now the laws of the Universe begin to operate as they are meant to in "God's circuit" (see Chapter 9).

In reality, the decision that we need to make is easy and clear. It only becomes difficult through the power we have given to the habits and distractions that surround us. We are still standing with one leg in the old world of dualism and separation. There are so many reasons to forget the sacred decision. However, there are also many reasons to no longer allow this forgetfulness. A peace worker is a professional, who does not let her/himself be thrown off course by the moods of fate. The power of our decision-making ability goes very far. Indian fakirs have learned to stop their pulse with their will power. Circus artists ride on a bicycle across a tightrope and make a handstand on the handlebars. Now that we are connected, many questions in life become a part of our area of decision-making. We can decide to no longer think any judgmental thoughts, no longer allow any fear to enter us, and no longer lie. We can decide to no longer fall into the habit of being lovesick, but to place our lives in the true service of the earth and of all creatures. At a higher level, I can even decide to not fall ill any more. Free human beings regulate their lives through their own decisions. They do this through the strengthening that they experience within a powerful community and that they find anew within the power of Creation in the Universe. The will of the world operates within every decision that already contains its own realization. Here we have both: the desire and the achievement.

Will power is a strange thing. There are different kinds of will: one kind that has an effect, and the other, that has no effect. If we want to achieve something, then we really have to want it. This statement seems to be trivial, but it means a lot. One should check to see if one really wants what one says that one wants. If one lives in a marriage, one should check to see if one really wants this. If one lives in a community and maybe even facilitates community courses, one should check to see if one really wants to live in community or if one would not rather live in a private house with open doors. Here there is often a lot of static in one's inner thoughts, stopping us from taking effective action.

We can continue with any number of examples. Do I really want a non-violent relationship to animals? Do I still want it if I have a juicy steak in front of me? Do I really want free sexuality – and do I still want it when I have fallen head over heels in love? Do I really want to get rid of the habit of judging – and do I still want it when I have been insulted and offended? A will that quickly reaches its limits is not a will that counts in the Universe. The divine, universal power can only enter into us if we truly want something fully. Then the will opens the door for the authority of our actions and our impact. A full will does not come from us; it comes from God within us. Many religious leaders have learned to suppress their will because it is created by humans. They have simply placed will on the side of the ego and thus created a rift between human beings and God. In reality, both the will and the achievement come from God. We must get to know this process in order to believe in success. If my will is deep enough, then the world will achieve what it wants within me.

In a dream, one of our female co-workers once saw the four heads of evil over Guatemala. She saw that the whole world, from all four directions, has followed these heads of evil since millennia, have subjected themselves to them, and have worshipped them. As long as they ruled, the earth would remain dark. She then received the following question: Is it your will to deprive these icons of evil of their power? Is it your will to gain so much power, that you are able to do so? If it is not your will, can you then say that you truly want healing to occur? If it is your will, then can you still waste your energy and your time with private love dramas? In the dream a laser cannon was then directed at the icons of evil with the words: This is the ray of consciousness that you need in order to deprive them of their power and to establish new icons. Are you determined to establish such a laser power in your consciousness? Use, practice, and train this ray of consciousness. Make it irresistible and give it power, will, permanence, truth, and rage. Also, give it as much love, humor, magic, and art as you possibly can. Make it a topic in your schools.

We have drawn up "ten commandments for peace workers" in the political ashram in Tamera that are to serve as personal orientation:

1. Resist hatred and serve love.
2. Do not let any thoughts of fear enter you..
3. Help your friends and you will help yourself.
4. Do not react or judge before you have understood the situation.
5. You live in community with all beings. Care for them and protect them.
6. See the higher image in your fellow human beings; respect them and support them.
7. Do not commit any cruelty, neither against humans nor against animals.
8. If you see how a being is suffering, help it.
9. Step out of complicity. Do not use any food or products whose production involved cruelty against other living beings.
10. See to it that you are in a good physical and emotional state so that you can believe in the success of your work.

Dealing with the Inner Enemy

A morning prayer by Sabine Lichtenfels

It is time to take a strong step forward. Do not give your faults and weaknesses nourishment any more. When you begin to see them and when you look into the hidden parts of yourself that you have never looked into before, then they have the tendency to first inflate themselves greatly.

If fear, jealousy, or hatred begins to besiege you, then do not allow this. Choose what you surrender to.

It makes no sense to blindly give yourself into the hands of your inner enemies and yet believe that your surroundings are to blame.

Direct the willingness to fight, which you in the past applied to the outside, to your inside. And especially, do not believe that you are a victim. You are not the victim, but the perpetrator of your life.

Your fight needs new inner strategies. It is no longer enough to fight against something. If you have just silenced an enemy, another one will appear elsewhere. This is true both outside and inside. The old strategy of extermination no longer works, just as spilling blood never can be a true solution.

Recognize to what extent cruelty comes from despair. Transform your own wild energy, which would like to break out in a blind rage, into power and composure. Step into perception. Assemble your energy.

Dare to look your enemy in the face. Recognize his/her true face behind his/her many masks. Recognize that your enemy is a part of yourself: a piece of abandoned, neglected, unfulfilled life within yourself.

Now you will recognize the true meaning of the power of reconciliation. At this deepest level, healing truly occurs through reconciliation. This reconciliation can only occur when you prepare the way for your enemy, so that s/he can change and regain his/her original power.

Go into vision. Go to where your enemy says goodbye all by him/herself, or where s/he gets a right to live within you in a way that serves the whole.

In many enemies you will find the distorted and disfigured face of those who originally were your friends.

If you discover what needs to be done inside, then your power and impact on the outside will increase dramatically. You have healing knowledge within you that is urgently needed. Access it.

End Psychological Suffering

We owe it to the people
in the basements of Grosny,
to stop our private suffering.

All our psychological problems would cease instantly
if we were to see
what is happening at this moment on earth.

I am in the cosmic classroom
and I see everything as a part of my training.
    Peace School Mirja

There are enough bad things happening on earth; we do not have to increase them through our own suffering. The following text is about the vision of a life without suffering, and it describes the reason why our habits of suffering are based on a mistake. If I suffer or not, not only depends on if I'm feeling fine; it is also a question of consciousness, knowledge, and willpower. One of the first tasks of a powerful peace movement could be to practice the avoidance of suffering. We must learn to deal with our inner conflicts more effectively than through suffering. There is no natural law that forces us to turn conflicts into a source of suffering. Conflicts are there to inspire our intelligence, our wakefulness, and our learning ability as well as to make decisions that are more aligned with the needs of the earth.

Psychological suffering stops where true suffering begins. If you are present after a traffic accident and you see how a child is trapped in the wreckage, you go there and help. At that moment there is not a trace of psychological suffering in you. If you have physical pain, such as for example severe tooth pain, you also do not have time for psychological pain. No matter how simple and trivial it may sound, I think that it is worthwhile to think about it. Could it be that our psychological suffering is a Fata Morgana, i.e. something that disintegrates as soon as we are confronted with something more real? Is it possible that psychological suffering is something that fills the lives of people when there is nothing else with which to fill it? Is it almost a kind of substitute action or even vicarious satisfaction? Is it a social game that provides us with mutual recognition, understanding, and participation? We live in the era of psychotherapy. For a part of today's western society, psychological suffering has become a kind of popular sport and a source of money for millions of therapists. During the first pioneer phase of our project we had written a saying on the wall "Why are we afraid? Because we do not have an issue." If we were to make peace work our issue, could we not see the possibilities of intervention and act on them as directly as we would in the case of the child in the wreckage? Why should we become accomplices in bringing misfortune to ourselves and others? We have understood the deep meaning of the noteworthy statement: "It is your spiritual duty to be happy." Is there any reason to hold onto our collective emotionality, which neither leads to clear feelings, nor to clear thinking? Who has seduced millions of young people to focus on their own navels in misery instead of forcefully driving off the old monsters?

Note that I am speaking of the psychological suffering of those who are not subjected to any real suffering. I am not speaking of the emotional suffering of those who have been torn apart by war, have lost their friends, and have had to watch as their own children died. I am not speaking of those who have had to watch helplessly as international corporations and their henchmen destroyed their homes. I am speaking of us, of those who have been spared, of those who still have time to think about the world and, for example, read this book. I maintain that those who have set high goals for themselves and who have taken on real tasks are no longer preoccupied with their own psychological suffering. Peace workers will put their psychological suffering to rest to the extent that they fully take on their task together with the corresponding responsibility. For a peace worker, there are only two types of real psychological suffering. One comes from the compassion or empathy with the suffering of others. This is true compassion. The other is the suffering that results from the loss of a beloved person (or animal). Compassion and grief are the two forms of suffering that healthy persons with an open heart experience when they no longer avoid the pain of the world. This suffering will accompany them professionally and it is one of the tasks of their spiritual discipline not to give in to it too much, for with the world the way it is, it could devour them.

What are the troubling issues that the alternative groups in the 20th century have been grappling with ever since Monte Verità and that have caused most of them to fail? What were the issues that the co-workers of our own project brought in front of the group for decades? They were conflicts with authority, a lack of self-worth, fear of sexual rivals, jealousy, bouts of meaninglessness, a lack of perspective, fear of being passed over, fear of losing out in love, anger at others, anger at oneself, anger and a feeling of resignation in all directions. They were also fear of manipulation, fear of conforming, fear of freedom, fear of a lack of freedom, fear of negative energies, fear of positive energies, fear that others know more than oneself, etc. Thirty years ago, we realized that revolutionary work did not make sense without transforming one's own person. What became of this? The result was a general moaning and groaning about phony personal questions that only arise because one is looking in the wrong direction. We demanded that work be done on one's own person and we developed new methods for dealing with conflicts. For a few years, it was a productive adventure for the entire group. Then we noticed that the topic of personal conflict had taken on a life of itself. Those who had previously never spoken of their personal issues now did not want to do anything else. They did not stop wallowing in their own personal difficulties. A wave of habitual wailing and moaning about oneself had engulfed us as well as thousands of other groups, and for many years, it characterized the mental-emotional life of the groups. Some people were like dry sponges, whose only function was to absorb anything that could be problematic. They never missed a chance to suffer, for every new reason to suffer was new material for discussion and contact. Under these circumstances, the artistic, spiritual, and political goals of our project could no longer be understood. It was a difficult time for those who were still serious about the political or even global peace ideas. We had committed ourselves to deal with our own personalities because it was absolutely necessary in order to be able to carry out efficient peace work externally. We had included working with our personal difficulties as a part of our concept in order to solve them, not in order to perpetuate them. Yet we underestimated the entertainment value of this measure and the communicative importance of the suffering game. Being ill, frail, or confused and mutually supporting each other's personal weaknesses had become a collective ritual. One can gain a lot of attention through this game, and it is played so intensely and so constantly that one starts believing in it oneself. And so, ever since the therapy movement was initiated in Esalen in California, many million believers united around their unbearable situation. Because of this unity itself, they could not change the situation, for their sense of belonging was based on their common suffering. Their common creed was:

I am not loved – I cannot – I am afraid of being controlled – my brain has understood it, but my guts haven't – I do not need any new ideas, I need contact – I can only begin to do anything meaningful once my personal needs for love and warmth are fulfilled – I carry a karmic wound in me – I am afraid of authority.

We, who have not yet been afflicted by war and destruction, live in a world without real danger and we speak of fear. We live in a world of abundance, and speak of neediness. We live in a time of incredible perspectives, and we speak of boredom. We are facing elementary tasks in all directions, and we do not know what to do? Maybe this is the main mistake that we must correct in order to establish powerful peace work. We need to correct our belief in emotional suffering, the belief that this suffering is authentic, that it has a substance of its own, and that suffering is a part of us and our existence. We must also let go of the belief (which I shared for a long time) that this suffering only can be overcome through long and hard work. Martin Heidegger moaned incorrectly that suffering constitutes the basic pattern of human existence. This mythology of suffering has blocked the path of insight and liberation for far too long.

The suffering that I am speaking of has no substance of its own. It is a structure that is projected from my fantasy, a Fata Morgana, a confusion that I create in the moment. It disappears immediately if I let go of the confusion. I create suffering myself, usually subconsciously, and its scope and power depends on how much scope and power I give it. At every moment, I have the possibility to increase its power or to take power away from it. A large part of suffering is self-produced. Behind every suffering there is fear, a bad conscience, a lack of self-worth, hatred, or resistance – i.e. an emotional process with which my ego rebels against the world. Do I have to behave so that I have fear? Do I have to behave so that I become jealous or so that old fears of separation are mobilized? Does a trauma that we have experienced in the past automatically have to be re-awakened in the present? Do I have to follow my contrariness, my hatred, my desire for revenge? Who has nailed me to this path of ego, who, except for myself and my strange ideas about life? Maybe there was an original traumatic experience, but who says that I have to follow the direction that was defined by that development? Do we really know what we are doing when we say, as if it were the most natural thing in the world: I am jealous, and that is just the way things are? Let us take the famous example of impotence: Are we aware of the fact that sexual potency comes about all by itself if we stop thinking about this individual show that we feel is necessary in order to look good? Do we know how much we really are perpetrators in situations where we feel like victims? Are we aware of how we in every moment are creating what we are suffering from? Are we aware of how we do this through false thoughts, by holding on to false ideas and expectations, through the habitual trivialization of our own person, and by constantly turning down offers of friendship, spiritual cooperation, and divine support? By self-created distractions? By complicity in a social game that has become meaningless? If we no longer know all this, then we should do everything in our power to see through it. Otherwise, we are participators in this strange insanity of our times, where we only react to the circumstances instead of changing them.

Even in situations where our emotional suffering seems to be natural, for example in cases where we are grossly ignored, insulted, or humiliated, we have other options. The saints of the earth, the freedom fighters, the true revolutionaries, the great discoverers, and the true believers have all shown us how to retain an unbroken, almost joyful heart, free of suffering, even under the most difficult circumstances. Of course, we do not lose our cooperation with the higher powers if we are humiliated or persecuted. We only lose it if we give it up ourselves. True peace workers – no matter in what area they are working – quickly find themselves in clear opposition to the customs of our society and they are correspondingly denunciated. Hans de Boer, the radical fighter for human rights (see his book "Gesegnete Unruhe" ["Blessed Restlessness"]), who has intimately experienced the practices of our current society, once said: "If you are a Christian, and if the Office for State Security still has no file on you, then you have lived falsely." No matter how we look at it, no matter how much meanness and blame we find in the world, it is ultimately our consciousness and our inner decision that determines if we react with psychological suffering or with strengthened willpower. It is only if we react with suffering that we are vulnerable.

I just had an interesting conversation with Petra, our medical doctor. She said something like: "But if you love someone and if this person doesn't pay any attention to you, then it's totally normal that you suffer, isn't it?" Is it? Is it not more a habit and a quite common emotional structure to react to unrequited love with suffering and worry? Lovesick – is that really a meaningful word? If I truly love, then I am not sick. And if love is not returned as desired, why should one suffer? Why not react with increased interest, increased perception, new motivation, and new learning? Maybe I overlooked some things, maybe I have to take care of a few things first, or maybe I was simply too fast, too intense or too much for this person at this moment? Maybe s/he senses a love awakening in her/him and does not know how to cope with it yet. There are many possibilities, and instead of suffering, it would be more productive and supportive of love to accept the situation and look for solutions. If we did not have this program of suffering in our cells, then a thousand possibilities would open up for us to reach fulfillment. Even if our most beloved person were to leave us, we would then not truly be abandoned, for divine presence is with us as long as we do not refuse it. We are only abandoned if we define ourselves that way, thus solidifying a momentary situation, which otherwise would be just as changeable as all living things in the universe.

Is this asking for too much heroism? No, it is not heroic. Once we accept the greater version of life, it is very sober and normal. I do not have to courageously suppress my tears, keep a strong upper lip, close my heart, and swallow my disappointments in order not to show my wounds – for I have no wounds at all. I do not have to use all my power to turn things in the desired direction any more, for I am living in cooperation with divine forces. I am given what I need, I find myself on a new continent, and I am learning to navigate anew, especially in love. I live in a cosmic classroom and take all things as a learning opportunity. I am an organ of the universe and receive everything that I need for my further development. Here, an inner paradigm shift has occurred which could hardly be deeper. It entails changing from a suffering-oriented to an insight-oriented state of being, and it is a change from a life of deficiency to a life of abundance.

We live in a decisive situation; the earth is at stake. There is no point in regarding oneself as a scarce commodity, giving away one's responsibility by referring to one's own inadequacy. I remind you of Marianne Williamson's great words. It no longer makes sense to pretend to be small or great toward each other; all these subjective perspectives come from the category of rulers and subjects, not from peace workers. Now we need the other version of life. It is already fully present as a possibility. It is only we who can decide to no longer follow our conditioning and our habits. If necessary, we will make this decision a hundred times a day. Instead of reacting with stress, fear, or envy, we will speak an inner "thank you" to the little tyrants, who remind us to stay on course.

I can begin to create
what I am seeking.

Leaving the Hologram of Fear

It is only seldom that I can overcome
my separation from the world,
and feel at one with the universe:
when I'm mountain climbing.
And even then,
only when through the greatest effort and concentration,
and in the greatest of difficulties,
I reach a state where my "I" is dissolved.
These are the moments that I am addicted to.
In order to experience "not-being-separated-from-the world"
I have to go to the limits of my physical ability.
My greatest enemy on this quest is fear.
I am a fearful person and,
like all fearful people,
I long to overcome my fear.
Three times I set out for Nanga Parbat,
three times I turned around out of fear,
before I had the power to overcome it
and reach the summit.

    Reinhold Messner

Healing is to leave the world of fear. The world of fear is tied to a hologram of life images, which we have internalized during the last thousands of years. It is the hologram of fear. Since the methods with which humans have tried to impose their will against each other and against nature were associated with the experience of violence and terror, the image of life that was stored is a hologram of fear. It is the hologram of the current overall civilization on earth. We are all – from our ideas about love to the medical and technical methods that we use – stuck in a hologram of fear. Because of karmic atrocities, we are all conditioned to react according to the hologram of fear. We interpret the information that we receive about life based on an automatic fear reflex, and we react to the world and to the elements of nature with an almost inborn need for protection.

The hologram of fear surrounds us daily because we illuminate it daily, thereby making it into reality. We then believe that it is the only reality. In truth, however, like all things in the holographic world, it is a virtual reality, which can immediately be transformed into another reality by changing the settings of our cosmic movie projector. It is only so visible because we have focused our thoughts and actions on it so strongly that hardly any other realities can penetrate into our everyday consciousness. In this late phase of patriarchy it is the only reality that is constantly illuminated, which is why it seems so powerful. It does not have this power of itself, but through our illumination. This is similar to the chains of information that we find in the genetic code. They contain many life possibilities – as virtual realities. Which of them are realized depends on which parts are actualized (illuminated). Based on the genetic overall information, we could, in theory, switch instantaneously from one life program to another and would have immediate access to all the necessary information.

If we want to leave the hologram of fear, we must change the program. This is possible because we carry in us not only one, but many virtual holograms as so-called "parallel realities" or "parallel universes". The hologram of fear mirrors reality in the state of great separation. Yet there is also the opposite hologram, which mirrors reality in the state of great connectedness. This hologram contains entirely different axioms of life. It is based on entirely different experiences, which we all – as participants in the universe – have gone through and are still going through at parallel levels of reality. The hologram of connection is a hologram of trust and of cooperation with nature and with Creation. In short, it is the hologram of peace.

In the beginning, we may operate in a kind of gray zone in which the old information is mixed up with the new. The result is that the changeover from the hologram of fear to the hologram of peace occurs tentatively and with inner contradictions. We need some time of practice and inner perception, before we can find the right "gates" through which we can step over from one hologram to another. Then special discoveries may be made – for example about the topics of love or community, vegetarian food, the soul of animals, or God – that all of a sudden illuminate the overall image of the hologram of peace. From then on, piece by piece, the entire hologram crystallizes and becomes material reality. Now it becomes an empirical (manifest) reality, just as the hologram of fear was before. The previous hologram of fear has now dropped off into the world of virtual holograms that are no longer illuminated and therefore are no longer actualized.

The existence of different virtual holograms makes it possible to change our entire way of living, not only to undertake a partial correction. Once we have found the gate through which we can switch matrix, we no longer need to stagger from one difficult decision to the next, from one conflict to the next, from one headache to another, for the new life principle that we are seeking, the Sacred Matrix, is already there. The divine world, the connection, the grace of love, the beauty of a body free of fear, cooperation with nature, and the world of trust are already present, fully and completely, in the "implicit order" of our existence. From a certain point on, we simply "slide" into this ready-made hologram. The transformation that we are seeking is then a process that happens all by itself. It follows a blueprint, which is already present in us. It is present not only in humans, but also in all our fellow creatures and in all that exists. The holographic leap from one reality to another is fully prepared.

For us personally, to step out of the hologram of fear means to step out of the image of smallness and normality and to step into the higher gestalt of our own entelechy or goal image. It already exists, here and now. Perceiving it is a question of frequency and opening. Entering into the hologram of healing, of reconnection, and of peace means to regain the power that we have given away to the world.

The hologram of fear and the hologram of peace correspond to two different configurations of the world, two different states of being, two contrary images of life. Both are virtual, both are real, and both can be retrieved and actualized. Today we live at a turning point in time where the transformation of one state into another is a prerequisite for our continued existence on earth. The new world, whose matrix is waiting to be realized, emerges entirely on its own when we leave the era of fear behind. We will then notice what ghosts we used to believe in and to what extent our reality to date, with its very real complications and agony, was the way it was because we could not see the other possibilities that the universe holds for us.

Illness is Not a Private Issue

An illness can be an important factor in our development. It depends on what we make of it. There are illnesses that become important because we cannot get rid of them. Some common examples: migraines, depression, impotence, sexual perversions, chronic abdominal problems, fear of speaking, asthma, skin rashes, heart pains, uncontrolled fits of rage, alcoholism, poor eyesight, etc. Such illnesses relate to specific aspects of the afflicted person. Yet each person is connected to the whole. To illustrate what this means, I remind you of the turbulence that we find on the surface of a pond. This turbulence is present at every point of the pond, and yet it creates a different pattern everywhere. In the continuum of the world, every individual phenomenon is connected to all the others, and thus every illness is connected to the totality of all vibrations and interferences on earth. Long-term illnesses are always also an individual expression of the overall situation of life on earth, for each of us is a part of the whole. Every body is a part of the entire body of life of the biosphere, every emotional excitement is a part of the overall excitement, every fear is a part of the overall fear, and every rage is a part of the overall rage. Prolonged illnesses arise through an interference pattern of inner agitation and conflicts that can no longer be expressed by one's own body in a meaningful way. In the same way, worldwide agitation and conflicts cannot be expressed in the living body of the earth in a meaningful way. Just as the individual symptoms of illness arise in us, the global symptoms of natural catastrophes, social catastrophes, and collective violent eruptions arise on earth. This holographic view leads to new consequences.

Our illnesses and chronic life problems are not private issues. They are signs of our connection to the totality of human civilization. By healing them, we not only heal ourselves, but contribute to the healing of a certain aspect of the world. We work as representatives of everyone who is suffering from this or a similar problem, and every piece of healing work that occurs consciously brings a part of the healing field onto earth. In the framework of the global peace and healing work, which we will carry out in the healing biotopes of the future, it is therefore not meaningful to conceal the problems and to try to get rid of the illnesses with medication as soon as possible and at any cost. On the contrary, it is necessary to treat them with much deeper and less hesitant healing work. The unsolved life problem or the illness that someone has is not his/her private fault; it is a public and political task. Through their own specific problems, all participants of a community represent a special aspect of the global healing task. The problems and illnesses complement each other, and there are hardly any spiritual, emotional, or physical areas that do not affect someone. If all participants of a healing biotope take on this task, then a holistic healing field is created, which communicates with the global life body through its holistic structures (as described in Chapter 11 about the "Political Theory").

This is a new way of perceiving an illness and provides a new possibility to accept it with dignity and almost with joy. We need new insights into the inner processes of our souls and bodies in order to be able to follow this path. In the emerging healing biotopes, we thus need professional medical knowledge and a new kind of healing knowledge. This especially includes knowledge about the healing powers of an organism that is connected to the Sacred Matrix and about the right way to activate the connection. Without this connection no broken bone can heal, no broken branch can grow back, no cut dandelion leaf will ever grow back, no caterpillar will turn into a butterfly, no sprout of grass will ever burst through a layer of concrete, no spider will build its web, and no human being will use his/her intestines. The design of Creation is based on the interplay of the individual with the whole. The power and the knowledge of healing come from the connection with the whole. The knowledge that we need has always been present in the holon of life, it exists as information in every cell of the body, and it lies in the entelechy of our entire lives. The crucial question that we are faced with is: are we willing to change our lives so that the healing powers can enter? This often requires a transformation of deep-lying character structures (see the section: "Working on Oneself" in this Chapter). When I speak of healing in the healing biotopes, I do not mean healing in the classical sense, whereby a patient for example takes the medication that a medical doctor has prescribed.

(In Chapter 9, which deals with "God's circuit", I describe how and why prayers have an impact when they come from a connected state of being. In this sense, we need a spiritual life practice in order to be able to pursue a path of healing for ourselves and others. As Sabine Lichtenfels writes, spiritual development requires a life practice that is free of lies. We must step out of deeply engrained habits that come from the old matrix, in order to see what healing means and in order to understand our own issue, under which we have suffered for so long. That is the purpose of our courses at Tamera.)

Every unsolved life problem and every chronic illness challenges us to change our lives and to establish the state of connection from which healing arises. We carry the connection in us as an instinct or an intuition, as an inner voice and prayer, as the power of thought and the power to make decisions. We re-establish the connection by following these inner instructions rather than the habits of an outer desire. We find the corresponding spiritual life practice by summoning up the will and the joy that comes from abstaining from playing our habitual roles and instead presenting ourselves to Creation and to our fellow human beings in our true image. For this, we originally developed the method of "Self-Expression"; it is the beginning of a public form of healing work, which definitively breaks the private framework surrounding illness.

Illnesses that have an unclear cause are usually connected to unsolved problems in love and with disruptions in the circulation of sexual energy. They have to do with a deep disappointment, a deep rage, and a deep fear that have arisen in these areas. They are thus directly connected to several thousand years of male fight against all things female, against sexuality, against love, and against original nature. We all come from this era, and we all carry its scars and wounds. For this reason alone, it is not our private but our political task to rid ourselves of these illnesses and create conditions in which they can no longer arise. If we want to heal illnesses, we need a new perspective for life, which enables us to love without fear and to live a lively sexual life without suppression or humiliation. Those who are on a different path of healing, and who have stopped trying to solve their problems and illnesses by going to psychotherapists and doctors, will also help to establish new life spaces, in which illness is no longer necessary.

Sexuality and healing – this will be a central issue for all future communities. Here, new experiential paths, new social institutions, and new professions will be developed. Here we cannot hesitate, for too much suffering, too much illness, and too much cruelty and war is linked to the sexual issue. There is no healthy community without sexual healing. There are no healthy human beings without the healing of the releationship between the sexes, and there is no ecological healing as long as there is fear and strife in these core areas of the human soul. We are here facing a truly fundamental decision, which is historically new in terms of its clarity: do we want to continue with our moral pretenses and with the inner ambiguity of our lives? Do we want to continue to deny and suppress the greatest part of our sexual desires, and do we want to continue to use religion to compensate for the lack of fulfillment of our sensual longings? Do we want to continue to regard the resulting illnesses as our own private issues? Or do we want to begin to create a real, fulfilled life in free sexuality, free love, and true partnership? I would like to emphasize that we are here dealing with a medical issue in the deepest sense of the word. Medical doctors should be aware of this issue and should work for true healing, rather than simply applying medication. In addition, every person, who wants to participate responsibly in the establishment of healing biotopes, must find a decision here. This entails taking a firm stand against one's own thought habits and against the lies and swindles that one has grown accustomed to. I do not believe that any of us can avoid this issue.

The same thing applies to the area of sexuality and love as to every healing: not through one's own power. Among the fundamental cosmic powers of life, sexuality and love show us most clearly that a power is at work that we have not created and that we therefore cannot control as we please. Sexuality and love grab hold of us like the forces of nature, for it is the power of Creation that is grabbing hold of our souls and our bodies. The Swiss deep psychologists C.G. Jung and Erich Neumann both spoke of the "numinous", which reaches every fiber in our bodies if we just come close to it. There is an entelechial form of sexuality and sexual love, of partnership and free love, as well as of every living being, and we must find this form in order to achieve healing. It is the form of the Sacred Matrix. It already exists as a basic archetypal pattern and as virtual reality. There is already a blueprint for a liberated sexuality, for free love, for a life without the fear of being abandoned, for an existence without illness, for the connection with the divine powers. We only need to make the switch and stop thinking privately. Here, too, we are faced with the topic of a new spiritual life practice. This time the issue may be more urgent and more profound than ever before, for we are dealing with sex and love, the very same forces against which the spirituality of the patriarchal era was directed.

Healing often consists of providing release for organs that are energetically blocked and creating good paths for the inner energies of motion to flow out into life and into the world. This is true for asthma as well as for chronic abdominal inflammations. It is always a piece of unlived life that is plaguing us in our illness. But it is not only my own unlived life; it is also that of millions of other people. Up to now, it was often our own laziness and our addiction to the comforts of middle-class life, which kept us from thinking about this lost piece of our lives. Even if we could have found it, we also did not have much hope that we could realize this missing part of life. One of the main reasons why the psychotherapy movement failed was that it could not offer the patients any possibility of realizing their unlived lives in the future. The post-therapy space was missing, and in this case, this space would have had to consist of an entirely new life space. We are now establishing the healing biotopes in order to be able to live this unlived life. If all members of a single healing biotope succeed in seeing and healing their illnesses as topics of humanity, then a morphogenetic field of unforeseen strength will arise. We give thanks for this possibility.

Jacques Lusseyran

I could no longer afford
to be jealous or unfriendly.

Jacques Lusseyran

Lusseyran! A great name in the history of knowing love. A name that can move us to rethink the goals in our lives.

Lusseyran was blinded as a result of an accident at the age of 8. From then on he became seeing, he writes. During the Second World War, he joined the French resistance movement and worked against the terror of the German occupying forces. He was 17 and led a group of young people of his own age. They risked their lives passing on information and at the same time continued their normal lives as high school students. This overexertion led to a strange liberation:

Since we began taking part in the Résistance, our mental-emotional abilities had increased. All types of dark problems had lightened up. Our memories had all improved tremendously. We read between the words and in pauses. Operations that two months earlier had seemed impossible to carry out and that blocked our path like walls or ghosts suddenly turned into easy little actions. Georges was right when he described this state as "a state of grace". On my part, I felt that my consciousness had connected with the consciousness of hundreds of others and that it grew with their suffering and their hopes.

The group was betrayed, and its members were arrested. Some disappeared forever, and Lusseyran was taken to the Buchenwald concentration camp. Of the two thousand Frenchmen who were sent to Buchenwald with him, only about 30 survived, including Lusseyran himself. "I do not know how. It is not I, who guides my life. God guides it. I did not always understand how he did it." The reason for his unusual ability to survive in the middle of torture and terror was that he was constantly present and perceptive in a way that was not clouded by fear or hatred. "I could no longer afford to be resentful or irritated." From this state of immediate perception, he could react differently from what was expected. He thus constantly created new situations to which his tormentors, with their old patterns, could not react. Fate had forced him to live continuously in the present. This gave him the unusual calm of insight, non-judgment, and survival.

How did this unusual development occur? After becoming blind, he discovered an illuminated screen in front of his eyes, which always grew dark when fear, anger, or bad thoughts appeared. He could thus always monitor his feelings and thoughts. As time went by, he learned to keep his calm, even in difficult situation, thus keeping his screen illuminated. His book is called "And There was Light".

Through his blindness, he discovered the light, and the discovery of light led him to be birthed into a new life.

I was aware of a radiance emanating from a place I knew nothing about, a place, which might as well have been outside of me as within. But radiance was there, or, to put it more precisely, light. It was a fact, for light was there.

I felt indescribable relief and happiness so great it almost made me laugh. Confidence and gratitude came as if a prayer had been answered. I found light and joy at the same moment, and I can say without hesitation that from that time on, light and joy have never separated in my experience. I have had them or lost them together.

Here, he describes an aspect of the Sacred Matrix: the basic experience of light. Let us continue to read:

Sighted people always talk about the night of blindness, and that seems to them quite natural. But there is no such night, for at every waking hour and even in my dreams I lived in a stream of light. Without my eyes, light was much more stable than it had been with them. As I remember it, there were no longer the same differences between things lighted brightly, less brightly, or not at all. I saw the whole world in light, existing through it and because of it.

Then he discovers how the light is driven away, and how the human being loses his/her inner ability to see:

Still there were times when the light faded, almost to the point of disappearing. It happened every time I was afraid. (…) What the loss of my eyes had not accomplished was brought about by fear. It made me blind. Anger and impatience had the same effect, throwing everything into confusion. The minute before I knew just where everything in the room was, but if I got angry, things got angrier than I. They went and hid in the most unlikely corners, mixed themselves up, turned turtle, muttered like crazy men and looked wild. As for me, I no longer knew where to put hand or foot. Everything hurt me. This mechanism worked so well that I became cautious.

When I was playing with my small companions, if I suddenly grew anxious to win, to be the first at all costs, then all at once I could see nothing. Literally, I went into fog or smoke.

I could no longer afford to be jealous or unfriendly, because, as soon as I was, a bandage came down over my eyes, and I was bound hand and foot *and cast aside. All at once a black hole opened and I was helpless inside it. But when I was happy and serene, approached people with confidence and thought well of them, I was rewarded with light. **So is it surprising that I loved friendship and harmony when I was very young? Armed with such a tool, why should I need a moral code? For me this tool took the place of red and green lights. I always knew where the road was open and where it was closed. I had only to look at the bright signal, which taught me how to live.** (My emphasis.)*

I was not afraid. Others would say that I had faith. How could I not have had faith – faced with this miracle that was constantly renewed?

Art

Art is the true metaphysical act of human beings.
    Friedrich Nietzsche

To create –
that is the great redemption from suffering,
making life lighter.
    Friedrich Nietzsche

Art and worship are the original forms of venerating and cooperating with the Gods. Art and sexuality are the true forms of Eros.

Very little can be said verbally about art, because it lies outside of the categories of thought from which generally understandable words come. From the beginning of our project, we have held art courses with the single instruction to not speak about so-called personal problems for the duration of the course. Throughout the years, all participants have gladly followed these instructions, which have had a great liberating effect. Art is an area that lies outside of personal problems. It is a fundamental dimension of human life, which we re-integrate into our existence in order to reach fulfillment. Art is a dimension that is as specific and elementary as sexuality or religion. The one is not the result of the other, but they belong together.

Art is a response that human beings give to the world when the world goes through them and emerges transformed. Nature needs this kind of answer, it needs art as a mirror, a stimulus, and an accelerator of its development. Art belongs on every ecological property, on the walls of ruins, on the walls of metal workshops. Systems where art is missing definitely bypass the principle of Creation. I do not mean this as dogmatically as it may sound, for art comes from an exuberance of a joyful, clear spirit. In a special kind of way, it objectifies life and one's own person and releases us from our identification with everyday things and with ourselves. Therein lies its immense healing power.

Those who are immersed in art have a different relationship to life: life is their material, their profession, their constant challenge in terms of new creation. Life is everywhere, Creation is everywhere, and we awaken it by participating in it. An artist is the opposite of a victim. As an artist, I do not follow the rules of society; instead, I follow the continuum of life, which has no name and does not follow any preconceived notions. In the creative continuum, all things lose their everyday quality. I discover the metaphysics of a seed. I am touched by the great presence that lies in these small things. I must respond. I can do nothing else. As an artist, I transcend moral and religious slogans. I constantly break my own habits and those of my fellow humans. The grim faces that I then encounter are then not an interpersonal problem. Instead, they form an arabesque of a flowing, living, artistic world. **I solve problems by no longer participating in them.** So many things solve themselves if we become creative! I experienced this during three weeks on the island of Corfu, and I wrote about these experiences and painted pictures that appeared in the book "Buch Sidari" ["The Sidari Book"]. We also experienced this during an art course on the island of Lanzarote, where we chose a scrap metal dump as our base camp. We documented this joint adventure in an art book entitled "Die Wäscheleine" ["The Clothesline"].

Mostly we use the medium of painting in our art courses. Here, as in authentic music, dance, and theater, we experience a special kind of interplay between our own power and the powers of Creation. In her book "Kunst und Gestaltungstherapie in der pädagogischen Praxis" ["Art and Creational Therapy in Educational Practice"] the art educator Gertraut Schottenloher has found beautiful words to describe this interplay:

If I pick up a brush and paints, I do this with joy, provided I am free from the thought that I must fulfill a task or achieve something. The deeper I go into the painting process, the less I think about why I am doing it, how I am doing it, and how I am feeling. If I truly immerse myself, the merry-go-round of thoughts, which usually circulates in my head, stops, often without my noticing. There is silence. I am totally in the now, totally perceptive in the process of creation, in the transformation of form and color. In this silence, in this state of perception and contemplation – beyond all thoughts – a deep knowing arises in us and takes form in a process of creation. It is beyond reason, for the language of art is of a different dimension.

Henri Matisse has summarized the search for original truth in art with the following words:

In art, truth and reality begin when one no longer understands what one is doing or what one knows, and when there remains an energy that is all the stronger for being constrained, controlled and compressed. One must therefore offer oneself up in all purity and innocence, almost devoid of memory, like a communicant going to communion. It seems that we must learn to leave our experiences behind and at the same time retain the freshness of instincts.

These are elements of an original process of discovery and healing which have to do with art. But art goes far beyond that. In art, we discover the joy of celebration. Art is a sigh of relief in the gift of life. We have all internalized the icons of suffering through the artistic images of crucifixion, purgatory, hell, martyrdom, and damnation. In order to get used to the state of suffering, human beings had to create incredible images of the soul in their hearts, depicting trials and tribulations. Now we want to create the opposite: icons of the joy of life, sensuality, love, and community. The larger topic of art, which I want to dedicate myself to during the next decades, consists of replacing the terrible icons of the past and of the old churches with new icons of life.

In the beginning of 1999, during one of our art courses, Sabine Lichtenfels spoke the following words during a morning prayer:

Art is not a question of ability. Art comes from the encounter with true, non-judgmental perception. In this sense, the artist is a true Zen master. The fact that you understand your craft does not yet make you an artist. Your craft is your tool of power that you need to be able walk the path of art.

Art comes from the deep connection with the world as Creation. It comes from an inner willingness to constantly release the old and open up to the new. True art is always a rebirth. You participate in the aspect of the "I" of the world that always creates anew.

Art is not a question of ability. It comes from the inner willingness on the part of the students to keep their inner eyes so open that they see and perceive the newness of reality on a daily basis. That is the great and true ability of an artist, and it lies beyond trends and tastes. Art is always a rebirth. Be prepared. The rest occurs all on its own.

Do not worry about your ability, for it comes all on its own as soon as you let go and learn to go along with and be with what you perceive.

Do whatever you do, fully. Do it consciously and clearly, for then you will rise above the fog of naturalism and notice that the world is never what you believe it to be. Use humor to destroy your many old ideas and images of what the world should be, until a childish awe and a joy of doing take you back to yourself.

Art is Creation's celebration. Art is prayer and reverence. Art is the deepest connection to the state of pure beingness, and it has no further agenda or goal. When you truly become an artist, you will rise up to a level of insight that allows you to see and understand more deeply the connections involved in true peace. In this sense, art is always work on oneself. At the end we have the true life artist.

The outcome is a person who has joyfully and calmly integrated the many aspects of existence as a creator. The result is a deep reconciliation with oneself and with the world, and this reconciliation can lead to true change. An artist is no longer a victim, neither of her/himself nor of the world. From this connection, you will integrate the real joy of life into the simplest aspects of your everyday life. This joy of life is deeper and quieter than the first phase of jubilation that you experienced in the beginning.

Whereto after Therapy?

Whereto should one release the patients,
once they are healed?

When engaged in healing work, one must see to it that the healing can continue once the therapeutic process has ended. This is true for the healing of human beings, as well as for the healing of nature. We always need a therapeutic space in which the healthy organism can remain connected with the healing forces. If this condition is not met, the result can easily be relapses that can no longer be healed.

I would like to describe two examples that illustrate the importance of such a therapeutic space. First, the movie "Awakening" by the director Penny Marshall. It is based on a novel by Oliver Sacks, which in turn is based on true events. Coma patients, who had fallen into a coma through a strange collective illness, could be awakened from their coma after several decades. They experienced a new joy of life, of music, dance, and sex – and they noticed that their surroundings reacted to this with resistance and a lack of understanding. They then fell back into a coma and died.

Secondly, we have the reports by Wilhelm Reich. After having been healed, his cancer patients experienced a new sexual energy. They had bad experiences with this, fell back into the illness, and died. These reports are undoubtedly true. Every person, who has ever worked seriously with therapy, is aware of this issue. Conditions in society are usually so pathological that they can make even the healthiest person sick again. Even a stable organism, with a healthy information matrix, cannot forever resist the pathological frequencies, which are produced daily through the existing forms of work, consumption, love, and communication. We need spaces, wherein the basic rules of healing can be upheld. It would be wonderful if such spaces could be established not outside, but within existing society. I encourage all those who feel that they could create such spaces, to do so. In this way, natural cooperation could occur between the centers of the new peace movement within and outside of society. The healing forces are everywhere, even in the large cities, but one needs good friends to be able to walk the path of healing. The energies of trust, of a life free of fear, of human truth and solidarity, and of spiritual guidance are the elementary energies of healing. They bring the power of healing into every cell. Under current conditions they are not simply there; they have to be created.

That is one of the main reasons for establishing healing biotopes. We want to create a healing environment, in which the reasons for illness disappear for good. The emerging opening of the heart, the emerging sexual opening, and the emerging spiritual opening are to be encouraged and promoted. What used to be the task of spiritual welfare and psychotherapy is now a task for the overall social and cultural design of our co-existence with our fellow humans, with nature, and with the universe. It is no longer a question of developing new forms of therapy, but new forms of life. That was the concept that we developed at the end of the non-parliamentary opposition thirty years ago, and at the time, none of us were up to the task. In the meantime, thirty years of learning have passed. In our project, decades of uninterrupted research involving trial and error and trial again have made the new life forms that we are seeking concretely visible (see Chapters 7, 8, & 10). The methods and possibilities of stepping over from the old to the new matrix of life are slowly but surely emerging from the fog (see Chapters 5 & 11). Today, we are no longer facing the question: How can it be done? Instead, we are faced with an inner decision that has far-reaching consequences, both for those who live in cities and for those who decide to take the new path into the healing biotopes.

10 Tenets of Healing

1. You can have as much healing impact toward the outside as you have within you.

2. In the circulatory system of life, every disturbance brings forth a measure (or a series of measures) to correct it, and every illness brings forth a measure (or a series of measures) for its healing.

3. You can enter into the healing process at every step in life, in every situation, and at every age, for the healing (sacred) matrix is ever-present.

4. All healing is self-healing. As peace workers and healers, it is our task to correctly "nudge" an organism towards healing – be it a human being, an animal, a group, or a biotope – and to create the optimal conditions for the principle of self-healing to take effect.

5. The most effective basic condition is trust. Trust is the fundamental healing power for all beings. Healing biotopes are "greenhouses of trust". One basic task of our times consists of establishing spaces in which mutual trust is established between human beings, between human being and animal, and between human being and the world.

6. One of the strongest self-healing forces is sexuality. The full healing of sexuality therefore lies at the heart of the healing work. Healing biotopes are human habitats for the healing of sensual love.

7. Healing is the reconnection with the whole. In this reconnection, we experience the Sacred Matrix. The whole and the sacred belong together. Healing is always a spiritual process, which connects us with the sacred

8. Healing work always entails working on oneself. We must apply the corrections that the world needs to ourselves. I cannot have a meaningful image of a whole and healthy world if I do not have one of myself.

9. By dealing correctly with your personal issue, you are at the same time dealing with a topic of humanity, for you are a part of the continuum.

Every solution to a personal issue constitutes a part of the healing work for all of humanity.

10. Inflict no violence against our fellow creatures. Every act of violence comes back to us as fear or illness. The healing of life consists of the fearless and non-violent cooperation among all living beings.

Chapter 6

A Project for Global Peace Work

Origins of the Project

The two halves of the human being have sought each other;
they wanted to find and love each other.
For this fundamental reason, the reason of reasons,
we stood up for the healing of love
and for a historic project,
that is in the service of this healing.

It began in the year 1974. The revolutionary Left had disintegrated once and for all. The new alternative movement did not have a vision, the ecology movement did not have a political concept, and the new esoteric movement was seeking salvation in spiritual introspection without any political connection. One did not care about social conditions or about the situation on earth, but about the inner light (which could not be found in this way). Many former comrades had gone to live in isolated rural communes and were seeking to heal their souls by drinking herbal tea and milking cows. The situation was desperate. It looked as if the established system had won the fight once and for all. The beginning globalization, the worldwide elimination of any opposition, the increasing tendency toward global brutalization, and the destruction of indigenous peoples in the name of international corporations all pointed toward a global holocaust. This development could not be stopped using conventional methods. It was no longer possible to speak with old friends about politics. The Marxist Left, which I had belonged to for six years, did not have an answer to the new situation. We needed a new inner foundation, in order to find new outer concepts. The three books that I published during this time, especially "Angst im Kapitalismus" ["Fear in Capitalism"] were widely read, but could not contribute to turning the situation around.

In spite of three different offers for positions as university professor, I left the university. I could no longer hold my marriage together, and I abandoned my political work. I visited new projects, among them the Austrian AAO commune, founded by the actionist artist Otto Mühl, the anthroposophical Third World Project (Achberg) at Lindau on Lake Constance, the project network for harmonic research in Germany and Austria, as well as some centers for Zen Buddhism and meditation. After two years of learning and traveling, I needed to gather my impressions together. I decided to spend some time in seclusion in order to think about everything. I thus moved to a hermitage in Egglham in Lower

Bavaria. Here, I reached the decision to undertake the project that we are working with today.

During my travels I had met fascinating people, who were involved in discoveries in the areas of energy, water, light, sound, horticulture, architecture, and healing. I wanted to establish a place, where these developments could come together. But first a community spirit and a functioning group had to be created. Who was to lead the group? Who was to mediate in the fights and competition that arose? How would sexual territorial disputes be solved? We would soon be dealing with the same human issues that almost all groups had failed to solve.

I rented a farmhouse in Southern Germany (Leuterstal), and we began the long process of creating a group. After four years we had a core group of 10 persons, with which we could take the project to a new dimension. We moved to a large house in the Black Forest (Schwand) and there we began our great social experiment with 35 people. We wanted to stay together for 3 years and address all the basic issues of our time: sexuality, family, children, ecology, food, healing, art, energy technology, a new world view, a spiritual life practice, and politics. By having experiences of our own, we particularly wanted to learn how to build stable communities that could deal with the challenges of our times. By now, the project was well underway. Hardly anybody left, and some more people joined. The idea arose of creating a larger network for peace work: the Meiga Project.

In order to carry out the project, we had to use unusual methods. We were not cowards, and we were prepared to do almost anything. During this adventurous community process, our thoughts around healing kept changing. In the beginning, we focused on using music, theater, and self-expression in front of the group as a method to break through the body armoring and to liberate and shape the emotions that were buried underneath. The establishment of the group began with the method of "self-expression" ["Selbstdarstellung" or "SD" in German]. The group came together every evening for an SD forum in a converted attic. These evenings were the glue that kept the community together.

Yet after a few years we were forced to realize that the emotional and bio-energetic methods that we used were not enough to change people and to heal them. A high mental-spiritual power is required in order to channel and integrate the liberated emotions; otherwise the result is chaos and anger that smolders under the surface. The true path of healing always consists of an increase in one's **mental-spiritual** power, resulting in increased insight, self-insight, participation, responsibility, overview, humor, and art. It also leads to an increased ability to communicate and think in a communitarian way. These **mental-spiritual** processes determine if trust arises in a group or not. **Mental-spiritual** processes and forces also determine if true love, true Eros, and true surrender or self-abandonment become possible in a community. The mental-spiritual development that the group participants have gone through determines if free sexuality can function or not. If they have not gone through any mental-spiritual development, they will always end up stuck in their emotional body and will finally give up or get married.

We are cosmic beings, and we are all on a cosmic journey with a stopover on planet earth. We recognize our joint cosmic classroom, and no longer want to stand in judgment. In this classroom we begin to get to know each another in a different way. Simply getting to know each other – that of itself is almost a new discovery. The more we get to know each other, the more our common humaneness enters into our interactions.

The greatest obstacle was holding on to the old habits and thus carrying the old structures over into the present. To avoid this, we invented month-long spiritual exercises, during which we gave ourselves new names and gave each other crazy tasks to carry out. The highlight was the so-called "master/slave game", which went on for several months, because those who were in the role of the "slaves" did not want to stop. Our lives had become a constant process of crossing boundaries and overcoming old limitations. For example, one had to serenade an unknown woman at a café in the city of Basel. One had to ask a policeman for some change for the parking meter. One had to sing a love song to the mother of someone in the community who came for a visit. One of us had to get down on all fours and go crawling and barking into a baker's shop, and ask for some bread for his mistress. Surprisingly enough, it always worked; there didn't seem to be any limits. One had to do the things immediately, without thinking about them. A group of 10 people decided to take a trip to the south of Spain without any money. It was a never-ending voyage of discovery. The greatest discovery was that without fear one could do almost anything.

We invented a new form of theater, where we presented historic themes such as the Roman Empire, Nietzsche's "Genealogy of Morals", Hitler's megalomania, the church's suppression of sexuality, etc., in a way that illustrated our own involvement. For a while, the theater was an indispensable instrument for the creative dissolution of old life problems. We were full of enthusiasm. We established a choir of our own, built art studios, invented energy machines of our own (that tended not to work), and converted our basement into a music room where we played music of our own. We had destroyed all recorded music and the corresponding equipment during an actionist celebration.

In the meantime a sexual permissiveness had taken hold, whereby we made up for what we had been denied for centuries. We could mutually allow one another to live out fantasies that so far had been hidden away in secret closets. Especially the women used this opportunity with abandon. We had common property, community rooms, community automobiles, and finally also communal sexuality. We gave ourselves fairly strict rules for everyday life, in order to remain focused and clear while pursuing all these new things. We lived an unusual life, which we called "cultivated schizophrenia", and we had very specific visions of a new way for people to live together. We had new experiences in contact with animals, and we began to develop a very caring relationship to all our fellow creatures. Finally, we gained insights and knowledge of healing with which we could heal our illnesses on our own. I have mentioned examples of this throughout this book. We clearly stood under protection and guidance.

New Basic Research Using Unusual Methods

The project had turned into a research project. Together, we were doing community research, healing research, and art research. Taken as one, we called it life research. To us, Creation seemed to be a piece of art, in which new facets could constantly be discovered. If we did not look at it with our old glasses, we could see new images, and to do that we did not need any hallucinogenic drugs. We experienced a deep resonance between thinking and reality. We were able to access other realities by changing our thoughts, and we used these insights to elicit unusual healing processes. In order to bring about a healing process in a person, it can suffice to change his/her "world view". So-called "reality" will then present itself differently for him/her. Illnesses that are consciously or subconsciously connected to the belief system of the old world view will then disappear. Old issues around anger can suddenly disappear, when the liberating thought or the corresponding information is allowed to enter the organism. We called this interrelation between belief and healing "objective magic".

We discovered the principle of "sudden kaleidoscopic change" from the matrix of fear to the matrix of life. As is the case with kaleidoscopes, a slight twist was enough to turn an existing pattern into an entirely different pattern. Everything seemed already to exist as a latent pattern, a "blueprint". We used music, singing, and art to practice this. We established art studios and built a music room in the basement. We practiced systematically extending our limits. In winter, when the ponds were partially frozen, we lay down in them and meditated in ice water, staying there for up to thirty minutes.

We had discovered that what happened to us largely depended on us, our thoughts, our fears, and our concepts of limitations. In reality there were no limits. We especially discovered the so-called "field effect", which became a key piece of our political theory. It follows that if one lives in a functioning group, one does not have to be able to do everything oneself. If a single member of the group goes beyond a certain limit, then all the others can do so, too. A single action is enough to access the information about this possibility.

Our curiosity and enthusiasm skyrocketed. For many, it was the first time in their lives that they experienced true research and conscious participation in the secrets of life. They practiced fire-walks, jumping into the ocean from cliffs, and other tests of courage. They became interested in biology and physics, philosophy and history. We discovered new methods of rejuvenating the soil in the energy web of the earth. We discovered radiesthesia, the secret of dowsing and using pendulums, and the reality of things that we had so far categorized as occult. We succeeded in finding old water pipes that were buried 3 feet below the surface. We saw the connections between ecology and geomancy and developed far-reaching concepts of earth healing, at first as mental experiments, for we did not have the possibility to implement them. We realized that water is a fundamental carrier of life information, and we began to become interested in the places on earth where in the past humans built their sacred temples. We began to study old sources and we developed new thoughts about ancient human knowledge. We built unorthodox gardens and developed highly imaginative composting methods. When the vegetables were ripe it could happen that we forgot to harvest them out of sheer exuberance. They began to blossom and go to seed. Instead of a vegetable garden we now had a wonderful flower garden. Blossoming – fertilization – seeding – sprouting: what a wonderful new world!

We bought powerful microscopes, in order to look deeper into the secrets of Creation. We noticed, saw, and smelled that it was all interconnected to form one great unity. We began to understand that a human community can only function, if it integrates these connections into its life. In the survival-adaptive communities of the future, the social order must be connected with the cosmic order. Also, interpersonal conflicts can ultimately only be solved under the protection of a community that is connected to cosmic forces. Through these connections, fear disappears, and in its place we get a growing consciousness of a universal community. "Higher consciousness is a more encompassing consciousness", said Teilhard de Chardin. There were times when we felt the truth of this statement every day. We sensed the universal connections between all living beings, and began to have deep thoughts about our eating habits, especially about the issue of eating meat. Once we had discarded our ideologies and preconceived values, we now slowly found new paths that led us back to very old, maybe eternal values. "Thou shalt not kill." This ethical knowledge already existed on earth, and now it awakened again in us in its original depth. We began to follow it even in our behavior toward small creatures while working in the garden. Deep in the innermost part of all things there was something sacred that one had to care for and protect. Deep in us, there was a sacred being, which was in resonance with the sacred core of all other beings. We weren't very pious people, but nonetheless we did begin holding religious ceremonies that we earlier would have felt were only embarrassing. We developed new forms of interacting with each other and with all creatures. Love was no longer just a phrase. It had become a true power that played an important part in our healing work.

Sometimes one could not sleep at night because of all the exciting new experiences. One night around 3 am, without having made any arrangements, all 38 members of the group congregated in our library, which doubled as our living room. All of us had somehow gotten up to see what the others were up to. Something was always happening – even at night. One did not want to miss anything. The world was alive and on the move. The members of the project began to get up earlier and earlier, without anybody telling them to. An old "friend" had shown up, whom we had known in childhood: the joy of anticipation of tomorrow. We noticed that whatever we did, we were basically dealing with the same thing, i.e. with the rediscovery of life in all things, the connection to the whole, and how all things belong together. We were tracking down the sacred matrix – and in some happy moments we were fully immersed in it. That was when the so-called "miracle healings" occurred, and we understood how the whole and the sacred are connected. We approached the entirely realistic vision of a non-violent life, in the form of a new human community. We felt a growing sense of thankfulness and an anticipation of things to come, such as we had never felt it before. Now we knew that it is possible to create a whole and sacred world, and that it was not an illusion. Of course we also felt a strong impulse to preach this knowledge, for "out of the abundance of the heart the mouth speaketh." A vision of a great network of such communities was born, as was the dream of a new earth and a new heaven. Deep inside we knew that we were not the first ones and not the only ones who knew this dream. This is how the larger outline of Project Meiga came about.

The Cult Debacle

Then came the cult debacle. We were denounced, and the worst rumors were spread about us. I will briefly describe the events in order shed light on an aspect of today's reality that we had underestimated: the cult craze. The actions that were taken against us were not unusual; they were the norm, when it comes to dealing with new projects that break down old barriers. I want to emphasize that there is hardly any positive news coming from many new developments - from both the cultural and technological areas - because their proponents have been isolated and eliminated using similar methods. I ask all friends of a humane culture of the spirit and the mind to help spread the word about these conditions.

One morning in the beginning of July 1985, a local newspaper from a neighboring town published a full page article about the "Sex Cult" from Schwand (the name of the place where we lived in the Black Forest). It contained reports of sex orgies, child kidnapping, and a command hierarchy. It contained everything that an average newspaper reader conjures up when it comes to a cult. The result was a chain reaction. More than forty newspapers published the story. They copied from each other without checking the story, and they invented new delicacies. Illicit sexual relations with dependants, child abuse, and incitement to sex with children - there were no limits anymore. A newspaper in Berlin published a story saying that cult members spent their days on drugs, lying in the sun, engaging in all kinds of excesses. We could not stop the chain reaction. We failed due to the legal paragraphs about the freedom of the press and due to a lack of money. In addition, we were baffled and upset, and could not react very well. We experienced close up and personally what it feels like to be denunciated. It takes a while until one can take slander with humor and see and understand it from the necessary distance.

The avalanche continued for ten years. We were attacked with such relish that we began to wonder what was happening. Who was behind it? Why did the editors so completely refuse to let us publish our view? Who protected them so that they could risk publishing such false stories? We had few possibilities to correct anything. Appearances at public events, lectures at conferences, presentations at church conferences, and lectures at universities - all these were called off without notice. We were publicly banned. What happened followed precisely the script for every persecution of a cult. Our non-profit status was withdrawn, the authorities demanded exaggerated back taxes for the last 3 years, and our ability to make money diminished greatly. Teachers who were friends of the project were transferred elsewhere and our children were mobbed by their fellow students. At various events, tables with our books and publications were demolished, signs about our seminars were destroyed, posters were torn down, and invectives were spray-painted over them. At night we had to put up guards. There was violence in the air.

Did we go too far in our provocations? Should we have expressed our thoughts, especially those in the sexual area, more carefully, in a softer way, or more humbly? Probably, yes. It was not only the latent fascism in society that caused it, it was also mistakes that we had made that now came back to roost. Obviously, we found ourselves in a new kind of teaching. When we were supposed to appear on TV in Freiburg, we could not enter the building, because it was blocked by a chain of young people. Two of them were distributing flyers that stated that we had called for sexual violence against women. Those who distributed the flyers were just like us a few years earlier, when we blocked the streets and the universities to protest against the Vietnam war or against the emergency laws. Why had they so easily let themselves be hounded against us? Who had sent them into the streets? They probably believed in what they did, because all they knew about us was the falsehoods that had been written.

Slowly the word spread that the news was false. More and more journalists began to doubt the truth of the slander, but they could not help us. They had been instructed in advance to write a harshly critical report. If, in spite of this, they had the courage to write positively, their stories were discarded and other articles were published instead. Interviews with journalists from respectable newspapers were not allowed to be published if they provided a positive image of our project. Instead, they published interviews with a well-known priest who was charged with denouncing cults. He delivered the Christian promise: "I'll get them." – We documented all these events in the book "Sommercamp im Wilden Westen." ["Summer Camp in the Wild West"].

In addition to the slander, there was a second tendency: one started to demonize us. We had successfully carried out a three year group experiment, we had established projects and studios, and we had ordered a sailing ship built in order to research the communication with whales and dolphins. Those denouncing us all agreed that there must be something fishy going on behind all this. They thought that only a cult, a secret organization equipped with dubious power and money, could undertake such projects. The guru of the cult – with that they meant me

– had supposedly bought a yacht in order to be able to flee to the Canary Islands in time. (I found this role to be almost flattering.)

When the Berlin wall came down in 1989 and when the former Soviet Union under Michail Gorbachev took further steps toward Perestroika, a group from our project started a larger project to deliver relief aid to Russian hospitals and orphanages. These actions could be carried out thanks to the generosity of trucking companies. We had to stop these deliveries because the German media warned the public against them. Supposedly, the project was a cover for a suspect psycho-cult. – What a strange world! And all we had wanted to do was to help. By now we had practically run out of possibilities, and we were even denied permission to carry out work on our own property. Building a biological water treatment plant using swamp plants was seen as a cover for something else and stopped by the authorities. It was not possible to publish corrections in the media, because most newspapers refused to print them. We knew that we still had many friends, but they laid low and hoped that we would make it through the difficult times.

Today, I no longer believe that there were any paid agents behind the campaign. I simply believe that we touched the sore points in our society, true points of pain, too hard. What those points of pain were has been described in the previous chapters of this book. We had disrupted the defense systems that injured people had established in order to protect themselves from a return of the inner pain – especially in the areas of love, sex, and partnership. Our society, i.e. we all, still suffers from the fatal basic structure of reacting to unsolved conflicts with rejection and violence. This structure has been well described by Wilhelm Reich in his book "The Mass Psychology of Fascism" and by Theodor Adorno in "The Authoritarian Personality". This attitude, which we used to call "fascistoid" during revolutionary times is not a question of political party affiliation. Instead, it is a historically rooted human structure, and it can be found across the entire political spectrum.

One of the arguments that were repeatedly used against us was that we were a cover organization or a successor organization to the notorious AAO commune, founded by the Austrian painter and action artist Otto Mühl (see also chapter 3). I had, in fact, visited this unusual commune a few times during the Seventies. I was both repulsed and fascinated, for up until then I had never seen a project that dealt with the topic of sexuality in such an open and radical way. I got to know Otto Mühl as a very radical human being and artist. I liked his love of the truth, his uncompromising attitude, and his grandiose, indisputable artistic genius. But I took exception to his quick judgments and his despotism. Too many issues relating to a more sensitive, spiritual, ecological, and human culture were excluded, for any cooperation to have become possible. The last time I visited the commune was in November 1979; after that we took very different paths.

The cult campaign was the beginning of the most difficult (and maybe most important) part of our work. Now that there were hardly any positive outer connections left, we had to find a new direction internally. The matrix of violence was everywhere. It was in me, too, which I noticed through my inner reactions. If we wanted to avoid it, we had to find a new way to react and a more careful way of conveying our new contents. We are all aspects of the one existence and we are all parts of the same continuum. There is always an aspect of us in our opponents and there is always a part of them in us.

This was the foundation for a new way of thinking. We were engaged in a new kind of existential basic research, which was to encompass everything that was important in life. The cult debacle now became the object of our research. From now on we had to integrate the reality of these human structures into our work. Our peace work had received a new dimension, for it had to be in a position to overcome latent fascism from the core. We also had to deal with what remained of the matrix of violence in ourselves. We still had impulses of fear, anger and delineation in us, which were in resonance with the collective structure of our society. It is dangerous, almost suicidal, to touch the hot points in a society, as long as one still has fears and projections that one has not dealt with. External peace work can only be effective to the extent that one has created true peace within oneself. One finds true peace by fully overcoming fear and hatred. This truth cannot be taken too seriously, for it determines if any peace work meets with success or failure.

If the public campaign of slander had not produced this inner reso-nance of negative feelings and thoughts in us, it would probably never have continued for so long. If we had been able to engage with the slander with composure and humor, then it would have been much easier for us to use it to achieve our goals. We saw ourselves as peace workers, and yet we suddenly found ourselves filled with un-peaceful thoughts. We wanted to act to promote healing, but we had violated some of the principles of healing, especially the principle that one may only heal if healing is desired. We had also gone against one of the principles of the future revolution: that it comes softly and does not parade around with its goals on its banners. Finally, we had misjudged the inner balance of power. We did not really know to what extent one has to be connected with the higher powers of the sacred matrix in order to successfully engage the matrix of violence. This learning process is still going on. In terms of the creation of a new global force for peace, political work requires that the participants undergo an inner change, which can only be measured and understood by carrying out the work itself. Today I know why the revolutions to date have failed: because their protagonists did not undergo the corresponding changes in their own lives.

In one of our morning prayers (by Sabine Lichtenfels: "Quellen der Liebe und des Friedens" ["Sources of Love and Peace"]) we can read about how to deal with those who seem to be our enemies:

You can be sure that former friends are among those who are fighting you today.

You can be sure that former enemies are among those who love you today.

You can be sure that you have once fought against that which is fighting against you today.

It is also possible that you yourself at one point were someone whom you today would regard as your enemy.

You can be sure that your enemies also serve your development, as long as you remain connected with the soul of the world.

Ultimately, there is only the path of reconciliation, for there is only one existence.

Recognize the enemy within you. Recognize the enemy in your best friends and learn to conquer him/her – then you will recognize your potential friend in your enemies.

Do not nourish their hating eyes through your fear. Know that behind their hatred, too, there is an unfulfilled longing for love that is calling out for life. Fear gives rise to constriction; constriction gives rise to violence.

It is important that you first of all become quiet. Without having become quiet inside, your every reaction only feeds what you are reacting against.

Do not give the fire of hatred, which comes from destructive passion, any nourishment through your all too hasty anger.

You know quite well the hopelessness of an anger that keeps you chained to your emotions like a puppet. By then you have given away your power a long time ago.

Sacred rage does not hate. It is not stuck in the chain of reactions. It comes to you when you have become quiet enough. (...)

Recognize how in your thoughts and words you yourself have challenged the opposite. (…)
Take back your power fully. (…)
The best path to this fulfillment is your humor and your unwavering joy of life.

Further Developments and the Founding of Tamera in Portugal

The consequences of the cult campaign were incalculable. Our rental agreement was put on notice, our sources of money dried up, public appearances were no longer possible, and there were rifts in the group itself. It had become obvious that under these conditions it was no longer possible to continue the project in Germany in a meaningful way. But "emigrating" was a strange thought for many members of the project. The time of our "diaspora" began, during which there was no unified project anymore. But the community experiences had been so strong that one could not simply suppress them. Various project groups were formed, which continued the original thoughts in the Black Forest, at Lake Constance, and in Switzerland. A process of reflection and individuation began for many members of the group, and some found their own profession, which temporarily led them away from the project. But most of them soon wanted to get together again. The political plan of global peace work had come too far to be given up again.

Although we were dispersed, the concept continued to be developed. One group moved to the outskirts of Berlin and founded ZEGG (Zentrum für experimentelle Gesellschaftsgestaltung [Center for Experimental Societal Design]). Sabine Lichtenfels began to organize desert camps twice a year, during which prayer research and new community experiences created a basis for the continuation of the project with different methods. Together with some friends, I moved to Lanzarote for a few years in order to have the peace and quiet I needed to prepare the next steps. I needed a long time to overcome the pain and to lay aside my bitter thoughts. I noticed that I had reached a karmic point in my life, which had repeated itself many times in similar ways during past lives. I now had to find a different path for myself and for others, in order to forever step out of the chain of hatred and violence. I knew that we had to find totally new ways for this to happen and I was thankful for the opportunity to do this in an incarnation where I did not have to fall victim to violence. I began to understand how much one must give up internally, how much vanity, vulnerability, ego, and impatience one has to give up in order to be able to work effectively for peace today. I thank Sabine Lichtenfels, my faithful partner, for the mental-spiritual support that I received from her through her unshakeable rejection of every form of hatred or resignation. I would not have given up in resignation, but I experienced what it feels like if one becomes hard. It is not a bad feeling, for it gives you power, but this is not the power of peace. Many of those, with whom I have conducted regression trances, became hard in this or similar ways. Many lived and suffered as early Christians, as members of religious minorities, as Cathars, or as Russian revolutionaries. In spite of the best of intentions, they all experienced the treadmill of violence. In their present incarnation they came to our project in order to solve this karmic issue. We have all reached the innermost point where we definitively can no longer allow ourselves to react with fear or hatred. To learn and understand this and to replace the old power of anger with a higher power has become one of the deepest tasks of our emerging peace project.

During the spring of 1995 we moved from Lanzarote to Portugal, where we bought a barren piece of land of 140 hectares (350 acres) under unusually reasonable conditions and began to establish Tamera. On the property there were mostly rock roses, thistles, and cork trees, as well as some ruins and enough ground water. This was where we were to create a center for our planned peace work, our first healing biotope. The property lies at an important geomantic point, where the power lines (ley lines) of the earth and energy lines from old cultural centers meet. As matriarchal seers have stated, it is a place of the Goddess, where age-old peace knowledge from prehistoric times wants to be accessed. In Marco Pogacnik's and Sabine Lichtenfels' medial research, the female source and the spiritual matrix of this place turned out to be part of an encompassing network that was connected to many large centers from ancient times (before the great separation). It thus suggested itself to conduct trances and regressions, to collect archeological knowledge, and study old sources in order to access the Sacred Matrix that latently existed at this place. It also suggested itself to create a global peace network to maybe function according to similar principles as back then. The creation of a global network constituted a part of the peace thought, even if one has one's main focus on a single place. The idea of the healing biotopes became clearer. Once again, research work was initiated that was to go on for many years and which confronted us with the elementary forces of life and of human history. We discovered a plan of Creation for human society, the "elementary historic utopia", which exists as a basic matrix today as it did ten thousand years ago. This plan of Creation is shown in the stone circle at Évora.

Then – during the night from January 31 to February 1, 1999 – our enormous warehouse building burned to the ground. This building contained practically everything we had. It was 260 feet long and contained the community kitchen, the laboratory, the library, the art archives, the lecture hall, and many other things. The entire group slowly assembled around the inferno, but we could save nothing. Strangely enough we all felt an unusual calm. It was unimaginable how much material and mental-spiritual value had disappeared in an instant. But none of us felt that it was a catastrophe, for we were in the middle of a development that had made us strong and resilient. Something had just gotten even more serious and even stronger.

After a year of intense rebuilding, we established the IGF (Institut für globale Friedensarbeit [Institute for Global Peace Work]) and the Mirja School for Peace. Now, the mental-spiritual and political concept for the creation of a global power for peace was developed. We were faced and are faced with the concrete questions around a new model of human cultural creation. On what infrastructure, what economy, and what principles of co-existence is a functioning community based? To what extent is the principle of self-sufficiency applicable? How can we achieve clear communication and cooperation with other living beings? How can waste water be cleaned, how can ground water be cleaned? How can we access the energy that we need? How can we build generators for the use of free cosmic energy? What does non-violent technology look like? What would nourishment that is free of violence look like? How can we develop a model of consumption that is free of complicity? How do we raise our children, and how do we train and teach our youth? These are all basic questions for the new survival communities. All ideas that are developed around these issues must be tested in practice. And so we are in the middle of a futurological research project, whose success could determine much.

Now, a great number of people are following the project with growing interest. They have not joined in yet, but they are hoping that it will succeed. We have been preparing the project for 25 years, and now, in the year 2000, we are beginning a phase of expansion. We view the developments on earth with deep concern. At the same time, we see the great opportunities connected to the further development of the healing biotope project with anticipation and optimism. We see a developing global network in our connection to a growing number of other centers and groups on earth. We believe in the holistic concept of healing, which is described in our Political Theory (see Chapter 11). It is the globalization of a new peace idea.

Chapter 7
The Universal State of Being

The blind beggar in front of the church – that could be me. The same energy flows through all of us, including through me and the dog, through me and the plant, the rock, and the stream. Everything is one continuum. Based on this insight, neither judgment nor violence makes any sense. They stop existing.

The Holographic Human Being

I am not fat.
   Obelix

My circumference and the circumference of the universe are identical.
   Dieter Duhm

To find an identity,
which truly can encompass everything that is manifest.
   Ken Wilber

I really love being a part of the whole.
   Monika

Take any point in time in your life history,
from incarnation to incarnation.
From there you can look in all directions,
backwards or forwards,
into the past and into the future.
Into the cosmic space or onto earth.
Why should it be any different today?t
   Dieter Duhm

The human being's future state of being on planet earth, in this chapter defined as the "universal state of being", is a question of experience, memory, vision, and insight. Before I describe it, I would like to say a few things about the new image of the human being and the kind of life that corresponds to this experience.

   We live in a time when thought based on experience and thought based on scientific thinking join together at a deeper level than they did thirty years ago. Before dealing with the experiential issue around the universal state of being, I would like to show that, and why we are different from what we thought we were. I described some of these thoughts in a book that I wrote 25 years ago, entitled "Der Mensch ist anders" ["The Human Being is Different"]. We are truly completely different. The mistake that separates us from reality is that we believe we truly are the way we pretend to be, and we truly lead an existence that is as separate as we have been taught to lead. Yet we live in a holographic and cosmic world.

We are holographic and cosmic beings and therefore in a sense limitless. We do not stop existing at the surface of our skin. If we understand both our holographic existence and our cosmic existence, then we understand the universal state of being of all beings. This foundation itself produces solidarity with all our fellow creatures.

The human being is a holographic condensation of the universe. We are something like a cosmic railway station, a receiving station of all vibrations, energies, and information contained in the universe. All information in the universe is imprinted in our body. In the Gospel according to John it says: "The Word became flesh and dwelt among us." The "word" is the translation of the Greek word "logos". The logos of the world has become flesh and lived – in the form of Jesus – among us. But it did not only live in Jesus, it lives in us all, to the extent that we have not closed ourselves off from it too much. The logos of the world is the Spirit of the universe, the Sacred Matrix. It lives in all beings. Every thing, every egg cell, every marigold, and every mole is a holographic condensation of the universe. All these condensations are connected with each other in an eternal holographic movement. It is through this movement that the whole, Spirit, Brahman, or God, keeps flowing.

In its original image, human community is also a holographic image of the universe. The Almendres stone circle at Évora in Portugal unites the cosmic order with the social order of the prehistoric community. The universal frequency, with which the world was perceived and understood at the time, was still clearly free of interfering frequencies. The architecture of the great Egyptian pyramids (as well as the architecture of termite structures, which are very similar), the plan of ancient cities, and the choice of places for the sacred centers and oracle temples were based on a cosmic pattern (see Robert Temple's book "The Sirius Mystery"). The original foundation of the sacred center on Malta was undertaken about 30,000 years ago, long before the temple was built. It belonged to a network of similar centers that encompassed the earth. Here, too, highly developed spiritual beings followed a sacred hologram and spread it over the earth in the form of a sacred pattern. Later, maybe 7,000 – 5,000 B.C. these higher beings (who in reality are more encompassing aspects of ourselves) left the island and handed over the continued work to the priestesses. The famous Maltese temples were established, as was the blossoming advanced culture, which Sabine Lichtenfels discovered there and described in her book "Temple of Love".

The holographic view of the world leads to a fundamental change in our concepts of space and time. In a world of holographic projections and condensations, there is no objective time or space, for everything is contained in everything. Everything exists at one point. These points are everywhere. The panorama of the world unfolds from every point into all directions of space and time. Past and future are held in the present at every point. The holography of the moment makes all projective movements possible in all directions of space and time. There is, therefore, also no objective past or future in the old sense. As is the case for all objects that we perceive holographically, what was in the past depends on from what angle we direct the "reference beam", in what direction of consciousness, and with what frequency we perceive it. It is this that determines the images that then become visible. It also determines the supposed time periods that lie between us and the past. For example, according to traditional historic views, the erection of the stones of the megalith cultures occurred 6000 – 3500 years ago. But what about the stone circles that were found off the French Atlantic coast 16 meters [50 feet] under the surface of the ocean? During this time, there was ocean there, and the inhabitants would hardly have built their stone circles under water. To date, hundreds of such bewildering findings have been made, and they lead us to develop a new image of reality, which is connected to a different view of history and of historical time. (Again I would like to refer, somewhat cautiously, to the unusual book "Darwin's Mistake" by Hans-Joachim Zillmer and to the many mysterious phenomena and findings of Erich von Däniken and others.) How old things appear to be depends on the viewing point and the angle from which we direct our focus (reference beam) onto the holographic film of the universe.

The holographic structure of the universe has consequences that we will only fully understand during the coming decades. The overall information in the universe, for example, can be found at all space-time points. In his book "The Pulse of the Universe", George Leonard writes:

As every particle in the universe constantly produces wave fields, and as every organized combination of particles emits its own unique fields, the number of intersecting waves is practically infinite. Theoretically, one could create a kind of super hologram at every point in the universe, which receives information about the entire universe from this point of view.

At the right frequency of our consciousness, we would thus be able to access the entire information of the universe at every point in the universe. This is exactly what every cell in our organism does, what the spider does when it weaves its web, and what the colony of termites does when it builds its incredible cities. We live in a world of endless networks of light and information. If we could introduce our conscious mind into this process, we would be all-knowing. Maybe we will be so one day, for the structure of our brains, with its almost infinite number of neuron connections and synapses, also seems to be a holographic image of the universe.

The concept of an individual "I" was developed during the time of the great separation. The human being had the thought that s/he is alone on earth, alone and dissociated, without the holographic tissue that connects him/her with everything. Over time, this is how the narrow and distorted image of human beings was developed, an image with which we cannot solve the problems that are facing us today. We are the heirs of a mental-spiritual history gone wrong. We believe that the human being is what we find in ourselves: our individual body, our individual soul, our individual life, beginning with birth and ending with death. If we only see that, then we see only a tiny part of the whole, which began a long time before our birth and extends far beyond our death. And the whole is – as a holographic condensation of infinite times and spaces – the human being. This whole is **we, ourselves.**

In order to know how we can create this new earth, we must re-create the real world in our consciousness. This means that we must again find the connection with the systems that we belong to and from which we emerge holographically at every moment. It is the entire human being, this condensation of the entire universe, of which the world said that it is the image of God: **"Adam Kadmon".** This human being is as large and as wide as Creation, with which he is holographically connected. His being appears in the most varied levels and forms of holographic condensation – one could say in the most varied states of matter. 50,000 years ago, the inhabitants of Atlantis lived in a different material state than we do today. According to Rudolf Steiner, the earth to date has existed in seven "tellurian states", i.e. in seven different states of matter. All these states of matter today exist as holographic parallel universes. Everything that has ever existed, the entire series of time lines, exists at another level as simultaneous events. We find the longitudinal section of history in the cross section of the present.

It is this **entire** human being who has brought forth the unexplainable miracles that von Däniken and others speak of. There is truly a message in these miracles, unexplainable pictograms, and edifices, a message that stems from the experience of the whole. The message says: do not forget, you earth beings, that you are a part of the whole and that it is the whole, in the form of human beings, which has carried out these feats that you today see as miracles before you.

The world of things and events is a result of holographic condensation. The images that we see are holographic projections of things that appear different depending on the setting of the reference beam. We thereby play both the role of projector and that of receiver. A UFO, for example, is a holographic condensation of "something". UFO's have the reality of projective images; they are therefore in this sense without a doubt real, and they can at times be seen, photographed, and touched by real people. At the same time it may occur that others are present and yet see nothing. Neither side is lying; they only find themselves at different points of projection and reception. The same is true of the famous apparitions of Mary. Some experience them as concrete reality – they can even take photographs of them – whereas others do not see anything. This is not because one group has drunk more liquor than the other, but because the different participants are at different levels of consciousness and have programmed their sensory system with different frequencies.

The children in our project have seen real "little people" around our sweat lodge. They refused to deny this and saw to it that a little house was built for them. In a similar way, many people have seen the so-called "devas", i.e. the elves and nature spirits, at the famous garden of Findhorn. There is no doubt that they saw something "real". What they saw was a certain condensation of the holographic movement of the world, which at this moment appeared to them as elf beings. They did not make this up; they truly saw an aspect of the holographic reality. The question whether such beings exist or not can be answered clearly: yes they exist, but you only see them if you are on their frequency. The only thing that does not seem to exist in the holographic world is the form of objectivity and lack of ambiguity, which we like to require, in order to have proof. We only have that if we are all at the same point in space-time and at the same frequency, and if we look at the same object from the same direction. In addition to that, there are only realities which we either access or do not access. If we access them, we still do not have any proof of their absolute existence, and if we do not access them, this is in no way proof of their lack of existence. True reality is always an interplay between our mind and the holographic movement of the universe, in which a practically infinite number of images (i.e. of possible realities) can be retrieved.

Jürgen H., one of our co-workers in Tamera, is a technician with special abilities. He seems to have a special connection to psi fields and thereby access to unusual powers. He could not do all the unusual thing he does, if he were not connected to a special system of the holographic world, from where these powers stem. Since he is connected to such systems – I suspect, for example, to the "Sirian" system and to that of Atlantis – he has access to knowledge and abilities that he needs for his work. In principle, this process occurs in all of us. It is the type of connection that we have with overall systems, whose holographic condensation we are, that determines what will-power, abilities, and knowledge are available to us here and now. The better the connection is, the greater are the feats that we are able to carry out. (This explains why people can carry out great feats in areas in which they have not had any training.)

The world is in a state of development. That, which manifests everything – the Hindus call it Brahman – runs through all of existence and creates its holographic condensations at the various space-time points: here a proton, there a blue algae, a desert fox, a human being, or a galaxy. Everything is connected to everything else through the holographic movement of the world, and everything has something of all the other things, with which it is connected. In that sense, I am truly also a little bit in the spinach that we are harvesting today or in the rats with which we spoke yesterday morning. In reality the rat is a holographic image of me, just as I am a holographic image of the rat, for we are both holographic images of the same whole. We are both images of the same goddess, of the same divinity, and of the same world consciousness. The projector, which brings forth both images, lies in the holographic movement of the whole, which both beings belong to. Let us enter into nature in such a way that we do not bring any fear, destruction or poison into these connecting channels of life.

Our Cosmic Existence

One must accept that one is divine.

Sabine Lichtenfels

As people, we are not only citizens of a state or a society, nor only citizens of the earth. First, we are members of the universe. We exist on earth only during the relatively short periods of time that we are incarnated in a physical body. We are here in a kind of school, in order to learn certain skills, gain certain knowledge, and carry out certain tasks. If we go through life on earth with this perspective, some things look different. If there were only this life on earth, then many things would not make sense, and they would look like coincidences. But the essential things that we experience here on earth are no coincidence; they are a part of a meaningful context that we can understand only if we have a sense of what happened before and afterwards. In our group, we have carried out over thirty regression trances in various groups, and thereby we have gotten to know the karmic patterns through which certain issues and tasks repeat themselves until we solve them. The friends we meet, the partners we go through life with, the people we fell in love with already as children, the preferences we have for certain places to travel to, certain eras and certain cultures, the choice of our profession, the choice of our gender, the role we play as a victim or a perpetrator, as rich or poor, and even the shape and size of our bodies, are to a certain degree predetermined in a life plan that we have designed together with other souls before we came to earth. We sometimes meet someone who immediately seems to be well-known and familiar to us, although we both agree that we have never seen each other before. Such "déjà-vu" experiences are often the beginning of longer love relationships. When they are authentic, they are based on the simple fact that one knows each other very well from earlier incarnations or from the cosmic group that one has been a part of for a long time.

The outline of a concept for our current life on earth already existed before our cosmic soul entered the embryo from which we emerged physically. It is, however, possible that we have forgotten the concept, due to all the difficulties and conflicts that we are exposed to in life on earth, and that we therefore have chosen wrong paths that we have to correct in later incarnations. Such deviations often show up as accidents, illnesses, inner crises, a bad conscience, and the vague feeling of never reaching one's goal. We notice that something is not quite right in our lives. If we were on our death-bed, we would often know quite precisely at what points in our lives we diverged from the right path and abandoned our task or suppressed any knowledge of it. It is often due to a negative emotional reaction such as fear, hatred, or simple contrariness. Usually surprisingly trivial things lead us to life-long deviations. During one regression trance, a patient found herself in a church in Marseille, to which those who had the plague were taken. She herself was a victim of the plague (end of the 18th century); she was surprisingly calm and a bit cold, and seemed to always want to tear out her hair, because she had given up her will to live due to jealousy. Then she had to laugh at such incredible stupidity and added that she had committed this stupidity in earlier incarnations, too. She said: "I know exactly that I will keep coming back and suffering, until I let go of this idiocy."

Because of our forgetfulness, which was caused by misfortunes and by our deviations, we no longer know anything about the original plan and the original mission with which we came to earth. We may seek help from doctors, therapists, or priests, but usually this does not lead to any real solution. The result is that we keep returning to earth with the same issue, until we are in a position where we no longer forget it, but recognize and solve it. This is a karmic process, and it is almost a spiritual law that makes us keep running into certain unsolved issues, especially issues of love, power and vanity, of victim and perpetrator, of chronic fear, or unquenchable sexual longing, etc. It tends to follow an almost identical process, until we step out of forgetfulness, recognize the plan, and solve the issue. It is possible that lovers, who have hurt each other deeply in an earlier life, now try to get together again with new roles, such as for example by switching gender roles or encountering each other as family relatives. Some examples: a woman incarnates as the daughter of a father whom she earlier had loved passionately, but then betrayed. A man incarnates as the son of a mother who used to be his lover. A woman and a man experience a strong sexual attraction to each other, combined with the desire for a joint child. The karmic analysis shows that during the Spanish Reconquista she was on the side of the Christians and he was on the side of the Muslims and that he killed her in spite of their love for each other. There are many parent-child conflicts, in which both sides no longer know that they are connected through a long karmic love story.

I would like to repeat that these constantly recurring topics in our karmic life story are not private issues. They are closely connected to human history, which we all have experienced in our incarnations on earth. They are often associated with such intense emotions that we simply erase or forget our cosmic existence, because we are fully identified with the current events. We then no longer ask about a higher existence; we are only focused on love or revenge and on stopping the pain. We definitely need a way of life that makes it possible for us to avoid these emotions and – like the French resistance fighter Jacques Lusseyran – to keep a high level of consciousness even in the most difficult situations. Acquiring this ability is one of the first goals for many more highly developed souls during their current existence on earth. We need to take one step after the other, reach one level after the other, and conquer one area after the other, when it comes to building universal life here on earth. Some have therefore begun to change their food intake, to step out of their smoking and drinking habits, as well as their drug habits. They have begun to clean their bodies and train their mediumistic skills of perception. Among other things, we need cleansed, purified, and transparent bodies, in order to awaken the cosmic memories and let the messages of the Sacred Matrix rise up in us.

Human evolution is moving in a direction from which we can hardly deviate, no matter how skeptical we are and how great our distress about the conditions on earth may be at times. We are here to make earth into a paradise – a mental-spiritual and sensual paradise. The old religions were intent on fleeing from this earth. Salvation was not to be found on earth but in heaven. The new religion, however, is the religion of life. It no longer leads you into the beyond, but right into the here and now of our senses. The earth and the human being belong together cosmically. A great adventure has been going on for eons, and today we are slowly becoming aware of it. It is the adventure of turning our planet into paradise. Once we humans have begun to discover this earth and settle on it as conscious, cosmic beings, we no longer need Nirvana, renunciations, and comfort in the beyond. The beyond is already here, between the glittering dew drops in the morning. Once we have succeeded in breaking the curse of forgetting and in bringing the spirit of eternal life onto earth, we will create a different type of love and a different culture.

At the age of four, my daughter Vera fainted when a group of people around her were singing a German love song and came to the lines: "this is what your beauty has done, it has made me love with a great longing." She was touched by such a deep memory and longing that her mind could no longer hold her body. It is the same memory that the German romanticists clothed in the image of a blue flower, it is the memory of Werther and Lotte, of Hölderlin and Diotima, of Novalis and Sophie. We all know this memory, and we have all done much to repress it. Yet we can never suppress it entirely, because it contains a real promise that is waiting for redemption. Even Augustine, that terrible church father, in his text entitled "Meditations", describes this constantly recurring longing, which could not exist if its goal did not exist in reality. Every true religious experience and every deep erotic experience is a fulfillment of this promise. It is so new and so overwhelming, that the joy can hardly find an adequate expression, and yet deep down we feel that we already know it. Stunned, one has the feeling of: "Oh, that's what it is, that's really it! It really exists!" That is what everybody is waiting for. It is Eichendorff's song, which sleeps and dreams in all things. It is Mignon's land, where the lemon trees blossom. When the divine thus shines into the present, we know why our cosmic home is here on earth. We have arrived. Our planet is waiting for this kind of cosmic arrival on earth.

As long as we live in a physical body on earth, we are more or less identified with our bodies, our physical appearance, and our age. But who is actually older, a newborn baby or an old man? Right now, of course the old man. But what if the old man reincarnates onto earth in thirty years as the son of the present baby? Then the present baby will obviously be thirty years older. In the cosmic space, there is no age as we know it on earth. All cosmic beings are without age, and so are we. It is therefore a good idea, already here on earth, to learn not to identify too much with one's momentary age. This is only a passing phenomenon. Those who are young today will later be old, and those who are old now will some day be young again. We sense the freedom, which lies in this insight. The same is true for the physical body, for we only have our body on earth. But without it we exist in an equally real way, equally conscious, and equally individual. The experiences that we have in the non-incarnated space are just as concrete and precise as those we have on earth.

I know how skeptical one is, as long as one has not experienced these things oneself in some way. I therefore recommend Raymond Moody's book "Life after Death," in which true experiences are described by people who were clinically dead and returned to life. There is an especially touching book entitled "Return from Tomorrow" by George Ritchie and Elizabeth Sherill, in which the wanderings of a soul without a body is described so movingly and authentically, that even skeptical readers have the feeling that they already know this state of being. Seen from "the beyond", our experiences on earth seem like a distant, unreal dream, which is soon forgotten. The opposite is also true: seen from life on earth, the experiences in the cosmic, non-incarnated space appear as fantasy. Our entire existence suffers from this separation of our two spaces of existence – the earthly and the cosmic, the physical and the non-physical.

The souls on earth and those in the beyond are suffering from it. This separation is one reason for the many meaningless ideologies, which people on earth have to develop, as long as they cannot recognize the continuum between the two worlds. Today, it seems that one of the most important prerequisites for the emergence of a whole, healthy world is that channels of communication be established between the two worlds. We need a lively conversation and permanent cooperation between incarnated and non-incarnated souls, between the "living" and the "dead". We will therefore do all we can to make this possible, and we will prepare ourselves for it already in our present lifetime on earth. When friends of ours die, then we want to remain in contact with them. They can help us, for they see the other space. If we ourselves were to die, we would also want to remain in contact and do all we can from the cosmic space for the continuation of the peace work on earth. The groups that have been created for peace work here on earth will also meet "over there". One is never separated for ever.

The Universal State of Being

Universal consciousness is present everywhere.
One cannot see it, just as one cannot see radio waves.
Tune your consciousness to the universal frequency
and enjoy the floating attention.

    Dieter Duhm

Under natural life conditions
all wild creatures are in a state of bliss,
for they are true forms of expression of the great Unknown,
which, for lack of a better word,
we can call infinite consciousness.

    Prentice Mulford

The previous passages point to a new form of existence on earth. We are no longer private beings, but organs of a universe which is always with us and in us. We leave behind the great separation and enter into a state of connection with all things. The following is a summarizing description of this universal state of being.

They were not afraid of animals. To them, animals were sacred. They knew of the healing power of the snake, and they knew that it was the guardian of sexual knowledge. They understood the calls of frogs and other creatures, and they knew that their communications were messages from the Goddess herself. Since they learned how to connect with the innermost essence of the animals, no danger threatened them from the animal world. Animals would only become dangerous to human beings if fear were to come to earth and if, with the fear, a separation would occur in the unity of Creation.

    I am speaking of the human beings who erected the stone circle at Évora in Portugal some 7000 years ago. They lived in a universal state of being. To them, their highly differentiated social system, documented through the arrangement and size of the stones, represented an eternal order of human community and of its co-existence with the beings of Creation. In the universal state of being, they correctly saw a timeless form of human life on earth, which is not tied to any cultural era. It is the part of the overall cosmic information that we can regard as the "entelechy of human community and society". Life in a universal community is constructed out of such elements as are depicted symbolically here in the stone circle. The universal community of humans on earth consists of such communities. This was concrete utopia in a conscious and vital form, realized in an ancient advanced civilization, from which we today can learn almost everything. It could only be destroyed by a fundamental separation in the unity of Creation. This separation occurred during the time of the patriarchal revolutions, in which male power rose up against the female sources of the cultures to date (see Chapter 3). As male dominance began, it destroyed the unity of humans and their fellow creatures, of human being and human being, of human being and nature, and of human being and Goddess. The basis for a non-violent human community was thus destroyed.

The universal state of being is a state of connectedness with all things. The power that the people had, who erected the great stone circles, came from this connectedness. Their astronomical knowledge, their ability to feed themselves with wild plants without being poisoned, their lack of fear of animals, and their ability to heal came from their universal connectedness. The aborigines of Australia had this connectedness and so did the Tsalagi, the ancestors of the Cherokee Indians, who lived in the Andes 10,000 years ago. Universal connectedness was obviously a global characteristic of human life on earth before the time of separation. We cannot achieve healing without universal connectedness. Today we are faced with the task of achieving a fundamental reconnection.

In the book "Traumsteine" ["Dream Stones"] by Sabine Lichtenfels, the Goddess Nammu, who at the time was connected to all life, speaks to us today, in spite of the separation:

Your dilemma, during these times when you are alive, consists of the fact that you hardly know the universal process, and that you instead take things extremely personally. You have developed a totally false understanding of the individual "I". You thus keep contributing to new misfortunes. Love cannot be experienced only on the personal level. Every human being inevitably fails in this, for love is of itself a universal process. Therefore, only universally structured tribes have a chance to survive. Those forms of society that have separated from the universal structure of the human being will sooner or later perish, for they have separated from the universal source of survival and of love.

Here, something is said about the concept of the "individual I", which usually provides the basis for our understanding of a "free individual".

The individual freedom, which we have today, is mainly the freedom not to do all the things that we actually would like to do if we had the power, the beauty, and the courage to do them. It is a term of endearment for the habit of staying in one's old rut, rather than trying something new. It is a cover word for the cage of isolation in which we find ourselves ever since the separation. The individual I, as it is understood today, is the Ego. The Ego is a very isolated and therefore very fearful form of existence. The transition from the ego human being to the universal human being is the transition from the smaller to the greater version of life. This transition is a prerequisite for every healing. This includes the healing of our fears in the areas of love and sexuality. How could one solve the problem of potency through ego powers? Sexuality, like love, is a universal process and requires shifting one's inner assemblage point. "Not out of one's own power", but out of the power that comes to us, when we are connected. That is the power of (universal) love, and we then do not need to worry about any extra love. Even when two lovers experience the highest bliss with each other and in their over-enthusiasm promise each other eternal faithfulness, they are still a part of a universal process, which touched them and united them with each other at this moment. If they are wise, they know that, and they take care not to bind themselves too closely to one other. For one should not lock up a universal process in a private cage. The personal relationship, that two lovers develop, can only have permanence if they come together as two universal human beings. Only then does the high development of Eros begin, where even the most personal love between two people does not result in jealousy. A love that is connected to jealousy is based on a mistake (see the more detailed analysis in my book "Der Unerlöste Eros" ["Eros Unredeemed"]).

The universal state of being is the fulfillment of erotic life, and it extends the limitations of our bodies. Universal actions are almost always erotically important, for the world of universal existence is a love affair. We experience actions that come from the identity of universal connection as beautiful. We therefore like the movements of cats and dogs so much, and it is why we are so fascinated by watching pigs wallow in mud. When we dance, we can sense if we are doing an ego dance for the eyes of the others – or if we are dancing out of the universal connection with the music, the light, the colors, and the flows of the world. It is worthwhile to learn to dance freely and to forget all the rules of dance classes, for a free dance is an opportunity to briefly feel the universal state of being. Maybe dance should be incorporated into the learning program of future monasteries.

We live in a historic movement toward individuation, in which the individual emerges from the collective, and one of the tasks of future communities consists of seeing and supporting this process in children. But the true individual always has a universal structure, for s/he always remains connected to the universe, from which it came. True freedom consists of this universal connection, for it is only then that we have the power and fearlessness that we need in order to be free. The universal connection is freedom, and all beings that live in this connection are free beings. The blackbird, which sings out of this connection, is a free animal. There is no reason to believe that the process of individuation is in contradiction to this original connection. On the contrary, wherever true individuation occurs, the human being becomes aware of this connection and uses it to develop special powers and abilities and thereby to serve the whole. The individual plays a very special melody in the great score, and receives the ability to find the right tones from his/her connection with the whole. The individual's "I" is in resonance with the world's "I", just as it is in resonance with the communal "I" of the community.

The universal structure of human beings is expressed in the universal structure of the community, which develops its activities and organizational forms from this connection. The development of such universal communities has become a survival issue for humanity. The universal community is the basis for the coming healing biotopes and it is also the basis for the future inhabitants of the earth.

There Is Only One Existence

The highest feeling is the experience of union with everything-that-is.
This is the great return to truth
that the soul longs for.
It is the feeling of complete love.

Neale D. Walsch (in "Conversations with God")

In this chapter, too, I will summarize the foundation for the entire book: the teaching of **one** existence and **one** consciousness, in which all things in the world are connected with each other.

There is only one existence. This statement, stemming from mystical revelations, is one of the mental-spiritual experiences, which can liberate us from all fear and fully heal us within. It comes from the cosmic library and belongs in the base camp of humanity's healing knowledge. All things, all elements, and all beings are connected in one great existence. In meditation this connection appears to us as pure light. Here, we experience the "pure beingness" that Osho spoke of so eloquently. The healing power comes from the connection with all living things, whereas the destructive powers come from the separation. It was through the connection with an unconditional cosmic brotherhood that Francis of Assisi spoke with the birds, with all creatures, and even with those who had the plague. He could therefore embrace them without catching anything. The statement contains the basic experience of every true mystic, every true cosmology, and every true communication between the beings of Creation. There is only one existence and one consciousness, which flows through all beings and unites them from within to form one great body of life, which we call the "biosphere". This biosphere encompasses not only the plants, the animals, and the rivers of the earth, it encompasses our entire solar system, the galaxies, and the entire universe. For the entire universe is alive. The same existence and the same consciousness pulses through a molecule, a galaxy, a worm, and a human being. This is why we can make contact with all beings, why we can love them, and why we can heal them. Internally, they all react in the same way, and they are connected with the same dream of existence. Joseph von Eichendorff, the unwavering poet and dreamer of the Romantic period, expressed it in the following beautiful verse:

There sleeps a song in every thing dreaming on and on,
And the world will rise to sing, just find the word of magic.

271

Whenever human beings were touched by the **one** existence, the great figures of the true history of religion were born. For in this touch we touch God/dess, and this can forever change the direction of our lives. The knowledge of the one existence was a part of the foundation of life in the ancient advanced cultures, and today again it is the power base for the new era that is about to begin. 700 years ago, it was the basis for the great sermons by Meister Eckehart, and today it is becoming a core thesis of modern science in the areas of holography and chaos research. The Greek Pre-socratics, such as Pythagoras and Empedocles, knew of the one existence and made it the foundation of their systems of teaching. Pythagoras and Plutarch, the last oracle priest in Delphi, translated it into an absolute ban on killing animals, since we are all connected in a cosmic brotherhood. The same was true for the Cathars. Their vegetarian way of life came from a deep knowledge of our connection with all animals.

In the unity of all existence, everything is an image of everything else, the whole comes together in every being, and the human being becomes a holographic condensation of the entire universe. This, too, i.e. that the human being is an image of the divine world, was natural to the human mind, as long as s/he was connected with the one existence. The statement in the biblical story of Creation: "So God created man in his own image, in the image of God he created him" constitutes one of the original feelings of unity of mankind. In the structure of our brain, our nervous system, our energy circulatory system, and the incredible coordination of our cells and organs, we are truly a condensed universe. In a certain way we can therefore sense in ourselves how the universe functions. Hildegard von Bingen, the great German Benedictine nun, mystic, and healer, described it as follows:

God has created human beings according to the building plan of the structure of the world and of the entire universe, just as an artist has certain forms, according to which he creates his vessels. Just as God measured the giant instrument of the universe according to balanced measures, he correspondingly measured human beings in their small and short form.

(In this quote we see how, in the consciousness of the people of the Middle Ages, a separation was made between the Creator of the world and his/her Creation. As heralded by Meister Eckehart, this separation was dropped as the view of the one existence was developed further.)

All beings are aspects of **one** existence and **one** consciousness. Together they form an organic and healthy unit. All beings that I encounter are aspects of the whole that I myself am a part of. I can, therefore, also say that they are aspects of my own existence. This is true even if they come at me in a form that threatens me. Why do they appear threatening? Because we project something dark onto them. This darkness, however, comes from our own soul. We project the evil and the darkness that we carry inside of us (as a result of history) into the figures, demons, or animals of the exterior world, which thereby appear threatening. By fighting them, a truly threatening situation arises. Here, we have one of the central vicious circles in our falsely developed civilization. It is now absolutely imperative that we understand and dissolve this vicious circle. In the course of the development of human cultures, human beings have split off certain dark aspects of their souls and projected them into other beings that they now use as enemies to focus their fears and aggressions on. For thousands of years, they have projected their repressed drives, thoughts, and cruelties onto people of other races and religions, onto evil spirits and demons, and onto animals of all kinds: predators, snakes, rats, spiders, octopus, sharks, etc. They believed that they had to pursue and annihilate them. By doing this, evil was created on both sides, and they wanted to protect themselves from this evil. It was through projection that they themselves had created the danger, and then they crusaded against this danger with fire and sword. That is the cruel vicious circle, with which the band of the one existence and the one consciousness was broken. That is the self-created separation of human beings from the powers of nature, and today it lies at the heart of their fear and rage. The massacres, which make us and the earth ill, were caused by this spiral of repression and projection, fear and violence. We are all the organs of one body, and the violence that we inflict on our fellow creatures comes back to us as counter-violence, fear, and illness.

Understanding these connections constitutes a part of the basic training for global peace workers. Based on this understanding, human beings can only stop global violence by taking back their dark projections and by integrating and dissolving their dark spots. There is no other way. For there is only **one** existence. The darkness that I encounter would not be dark to me, if I did not also have it in the deeper layers of my own soul. It was through the drama of separation that the human being had to bury or hide a part of his soul deep inside. The unconsciously raging pain produced the demons, with which the separated human being began to disfigure the entire world. In spite of all education and science, still today we find superstition and the fear of demons deep in the basements of the souls of humanity. The separation was not overcome through science; instead it was entrenched, for now there was a definitive separation between a subjective world in me and an objective world outside of me. Due to this separation, the common band could no longer be seen, and healing was no longer possible. The human being was definitely moving in the wrong direction. If we today again begin to include religious or spiritual elements in our healing work, it is in order to reconnect the broken band. We will not be able to permanently stop resorting to violence until we have finally understood that all things that we fear or are disgusted with, and all things that we judge and hate, constitute aspects of ourselves that we have not yet dissolved and transformed.

The Two World Processes

I have this rose in my hand. Who made it? It hasn't made itself. Neither is there a builder, who created it from outside. So who or what created it? If there is no such subject, then from what did it emerge? We have the same questions regarding ourselves. Who or what has made us? We have clearly not made ourselves, for we do not even know exactly how we function. If I yawn, who is then using my yawning equipment? When I breathe, who or what is then using my lungs? Who or what has organized the billions of elementary particles of my body so that the whole can function? I know that neither I nor an external builder has created all these things. Neither is "God" an answer, for we want to find out what it is that we call "God". There does not seem to be an understandable answer to the question of the subject of things, at least not through traditional thinking. The true answers lie at a different level of logics. The closer we get to an answer, the more clearly an entirely different world emerges in front of our inner mental-spiritual eye. There must be a world process, which produces everything and yet can never be separated from the things that come into being, because it can also be found in these things. There must be a world process at work in me, in my pulse-beat, in the peristalsis of my intestines, and in my basic biological and mental-spiritual functions. This world process has created me and keeps me alive every day.

There is no Creator, who stands outside of Creation in the way that an engineer stands outside of his machine or an architect stands outside his building. This is a mental-spiritual discovery, with which we have to struggle, because it goes fundamentally against our habitual structures of thinking. Yet it was the first modern thinkers, as we see it, i.e. the Milesian (Greek) nature philosophers before Socrates, who first expressed this thought. It was formulated the strongest by Xenophanes (born in the middle of the 6th century B.C.), who said that there is no Creator God, but that God is what is inherent in all matter. In the limitless world of the universe, there is no separation of subject, object, and predicate, as our everyday thinking would stipulate. There is only an endless co-vibration and interweaving of mental-spiritual energy fields that condense here and there to bring forth the things and beings of the world. This whole is the subject which lives in all things. The whole is God, and God is the whole, and the whole is nobody, neither a thing nor a person, nor a definable size. This is why in the East it is called absolute emptiness or "Nirvana". The whole is the whole; therefore, it cannot be something individual, nor can it be outside of the whole. The whole is present and active everywhere, in every movement of my pupil and in every line in a mussel shell. The smallest whirlpool of water in my sink is colored by the whole. I myself may have caused it to exist by the movement of my hand, but first of all I, too, am a part of the whole, and secondly I only caused the movement, not the form of the whirlpool. The whirlpool form follows the matrix of the whole. The whirlpool in my sink or in the drain of my bathtub is a universal event, a world process. It is also a universal event or a world process that causes my blood to circulate. Even my thoughts, when they are authentic, are brought forth by a universal process. It is the universe which is thinking in me. Thinking is one of the basic activities of the universe. (By the way, the widespread fight against thinking, which runs through the media, our culture, religions, and the therapy and alternative movements, are a part of "Big Brother's" secret strategy of domination in Orwells novel "1984". Our culture is not suffering from too much thinking, but rather from too little thinking.)

The whole is the subject, and the whole is Creation occurring constantly. But this whole is not an automaton with built-in holographic mechanics, but a living, conscious whole. The whole is full of consciousness, just as I myself am full of consciousness. The whole is a mental-spiritual organism with a cosmic "I", which we also call the "soul of the world" or "God/dess". I am constantly connected to this soul of the world through my own "I".

By following these connections, we inevitably enter into a new mental-spiritual connection with the rest of the world. We enter into the mental-spiritual space where the individual "I" and the "I" of the world co-vibrate in a universal score. The divine and the human are connected to each other in a constantly present union. But the divine lives in all beings, and in this sense all beings become our natural interlocutors, for they are all related to us through their connection with God/dess. This is the space of the religion of the future (which we then will not call religion any more, because it is identical with life itself). The great version of life emerges from this connection with God/dess, i.e. from the connection of the individual things with each other and with the whole. Here, we have the world process, which gives all beings their beauty, their naturalness, and their effortlessness, their movement and their stillness, their structure and their power. Here we find the mysterious functions of Creation that we admire in its creatures: power without effort, beauty without vanity, concentration without tenseness. This is the overall creation of our world. Nobody is doing it, and yet it is done.

Here, powers operate all on their own; they do not need to be forced into action. Here, the soul of the beings remains empty, free, and filled with the whole. Here, we find the religion of birds and of fish, of dolphins and cats, of children and newly born adults.

The whole repeats itself like in a holographic film in all its parts and organs. No matter how individually the individual organs may behave, it is always universal information and universal actions of the whole that find their expression and are taken further in a unique way. Whenever the actions of the whole are expressed through the natural actions of an individual, a harmony arises, and the result is an inner power and coherence, which, at the deepest level, we can describe as health.

If an individual organism, which lives in this connection, is disturbed or injured the self-healing forces, which are controlled by the whole, take effect in order to heal the wound. This is true for the organism of the earth as well as for the organism of a single human being, an animal, or a plant. The individual beings – except for human beings – do not have the possibility to withdraw from this circulatory system of healing. They all act in accordance with their inner goal image (entelechy) that connects them with the whole and through which the whole operates in them. Due to its entelechy, the stinging nettle will always develop into a stinging nettle, and the spider will always build its web according to the same pattern. The mussel will always follow the same vibratory matrix and the snail will always build its spiral housing according to the same cosmic symphony (world harmonic). Yet they are not built by the spider or the snail, but by the functions of the universe, transformed into the specific actions of a spider or a snail. The building of the spider web is the universe's own activity, expressed through the medium of the spider. The peristalsis of an earthworm is the universe's own activity, expressed through the medium of the worm. Taken together, all these actions, which are both individual and universal, constitute an overall process, which we call original "evolution" or "creation". It is the universal process, into which human life was integrated during the time before the great separation.

In addition to this natural, universal world movement, there is a second world movement that does **not** come from the whole, that is not connected to the divine source, and that is not aligned with the inner movements and goals of Creation. It is the movement of human civilization since about 7000 years (invasion by the so-called Kurgan people, sexual divergence from the tribal order, emergence of the concept of property as a result of agriculture and animal husbandry, creation of the realm of male gods, political power blocs, etc.). This second world movement arose through a cultural dam, which the male human being has erected against the original universal flow of the world. This dam has fundamentally changed the entire circulatory energy system and the circulatory consciousness system of human society. The human being was no longer a part of the whole, but a split off part, which saw itself as the subject. Where there had been universal thinking, in which s/he had been connected with the cosmic whole, we now gradually had individualized ego thinking. The higher self, which connected her/him with the whole, was reduced to a small but violent capsule of a private "I". I quote from the morning prayers in the book "Quellen der Liebe und des Friedens" ["Sources of Love and Peace"] by Sabine Lichtenfels:

The human being, who wants to exclude the soul of the world from his/her life, is behaving like a plant that separates itself from its source. The result is an ego, a piece of separated life, which is separated from the source and now believes that he/she is the source itself. The ego begins to run amok. For a while it has the resources it needs to nourish itself. But at some point these resources are used up, and it no longer finds a source from which to feed itself. It resorts to artificial nourishment, which makes it puff up, for no artificial nourishment contains the Mana of eternal life. But the human being exists in the face of eternity. At some point it will have to return to the source, either in this life or the next, in order to be able to survive.

The connection to the original source was lost through the split into the many ego worlds. Millions of private egos brought chaos into the world and led it to the edge of global destruction. The result was the development of exploitation techniques, wars, systems of domination, protection, religion, morals, justice, and money, as well as intelligence services and military strategies, with which the state of separation was to be locked in forever. Ego collectives emerged that were prepared to kill any life that might stand in its way. This is where we stand today. There are no limits on this path. The so-called crisis of our times, which in reality is moving toward a global holocaust, consists of the split between human civilization and the rest of the world. The actions of individuals are no longer connected to the original world process. Together, they form a kind of counter-world, which possibly will only end through the foreseeable breakdown.

The healing task is clear enough. The two world processes, the universal one and the individual one, the cosmic one and the societal one, must come together again. Human culture and society must again become the place where this connection occurs. Both world processes, that of the universe and that of humans, must again be fed by the one flow of great evolutionary energy and the one great cosmic consciousness. All our instructions, our teachings and programs, our concepts of life, love, living, working and celebrating, of community, ecology, and politics, our individual actions, from our morning exercise until our evening prayers, from gardening to organizing public conferences, should actively contribute to re-connect us with the great divine flow of the world. **That is the ultimate imperative of our times.** When the two world processes, the human and the divine, the individual and the universal, come together again, then we can finally follow the great path that our species has already followed in the past and that – by entering the patriarchal era - we have left for several thousand years. It is the path of "ancient memory" and "ancient utopia", the path of ancient advanced cultures, of the stone circle at Évora, and the temple on Malta. We will not return to the old times, but we will reintegrate the principle of universal connectedness. We will bring the divine world process onto earth so that – in concrete cooperation with all earthly and cosmic forces – paradise emerges, a paradise for which our round planet with all its colors and scents is so wonderfully suited. We will do it by recognizing our function as organs in the whole and by receiving the support from the whole that every organ receives from the organism that it belongs to. We can only solve the human, technical, ecological, and mental-spiritual tasks that we are facing by learning how to lead a universal existence.

The Universal "I"

In truth, we are this one Spirit,
we are the self-consciousness of the universe.
At that moment when we feel this precisely,
nothing can separate us from our Godhead.

Jasmuheen

Every being has some kind of an "I". All beings are connected to each other through their "I", for the "I" is the true divine authority which runs through them all. This was one of the great discoveries made by Rudolf Steiner as well as Teilhard de Chardin. In order to understand ourselves and our real possibilities, it would be good to rediscover and understand this fact about Creation. The "I" is of a universal dimension. The whole has an "I", just like I do. I could not have an "I" if the whole did not have one and if this whole were not in me. We take part in the overall "I" of the world through our own "I". As Teilhard says, the "I" is God's inner station in all beings.

The "I" of individual beings and the "I" of the world represent both polarity and unity. All processes in the world occur between these two poles. It is through our individual "I's" that we all experience each other as different from each other. Once our individual "I" is no longer integrated into the greater whole, it appears as an ego without an easily recognizable divine origin. In reality, the existence of an "I" in all beings shows that we all come from the same source, that we all are organs of the same life, and that this one great life, with its transcendental core, shines through all of us. The cosmic "I" is the endless loop, "God's roller coaster", on which all individual "I's" are riding. The "I" is both individual and universal. The personal and the transpersonal aspects of the world are inseparably connected through the "I". The "I" is the mystery of the world. There is no explanation for the "I", for every explanation presumes the existence of an "I". If there were no "I" in the world, then there would be nobody who could explain anything. The "I" is immanently woven into all universal actions.

Could it be that our difficulties, our fears and worries, our unsolved knots in life, and our susceptibility to illnesses all stem from a mistake that all of us are making on a daily basis, and that we therefore no longer notice? Could it be that there is a kind of collective mental illness, which has to do with our historical heritage, and which we must dissolve in order to return to reality? The confusion consists of the fact that we say

"I" and we mean our person, whereas in reality the great whole operates within this "I". Who or what sees, when "I" see? Who is looking at the landscape when "I" look at it, who or what hears, loves, and thinks in me, when "I" hear, love, and think? Who or what wants in me, when "I" want and when it is a part of a true, great will? Let us see what the consequences are, if we assume that this mysterious subject is separate from my personal ego. We immediately get a sense of a certain excitement, a clear twist in the situation. The constriction that so far was connected with the little word "I," is no longer there. We still use the same concepts, but they feel different, they are filled with a different quality. Even suffering, should it still be there in this situation, does not break my personal heart. It is clear that our "Buddha nature", our "Chechina", or our universal "I" has been touched here. It is the divine human being, Adam Kadmon, the fulfilled one, who exists in this state, and it is obviously a part of our basic nature to be or become like the Sacred Matrix.

We leave the jungle of our ego world and enter into a clearing. The "I" is the center of the Sacred Matrix, the gate that connects us with the divine world, our channel to the universe. Here one stands still and creates an opening through which light can come in. A light falls through us onto everything. We see things anew; we see them with the eye of God. The difference between us and everything decreases. We see them as a part of the body that we ourselves belong to. The stronger we can keep this opening, the more we understand through this light. So this is how cosmic consciousness works! So this is what is meant by a connected transpersonal existence! It is full of power, reality, and presence. One could almost say that it feels quite personal. It is not without my person, but with it, and it is illuminated far beyond the boundaries that limited it up to now. It aligns me with the Sacred Matrix. This is the goal of the liberation. It is the goal of every liberation, every religion, every development, and every healing. It is the correction of a historical mistake. Once we have reached this state, there is no longer any separation between religion and science, theology and anthropology, or science and the arts. There is only this one limitless path of discovery. One would like to live for another hundred years in order to have enough time to walk this path without being in a hurry. But according to the same process of insight we have time, for after death we continue this path into other spaces. We have no age and no end.

A human being is beautiful when the light of the universe shines through him/her. The universal forms of the Sacred Matrix are beautiful. The blindness of the mind begins when we want to be something all on our own. We do not achieve things with our own powers; they are achieved by the powers of the world. It is not the "I" of our own person, who takes a stand for our deepest will; the "I" of the world operates in us and makes the decision. The world has created both the will and the achievement. Our plan becomes ugly and confusing when we no longer know this, but it becomes pure and powerful when this consciousness is present. We do things, not out of our own power, yet we are fully empowered. This statement now makes sense, for I and God/dess are now one.

Entering into life, entering into the healing matrix, and finding reality anew means to rediscover the source from which everything comes that we are and that we have. It means to rediscover the greater whole, from which every molecule of our bodies comes. This is a positive reversal of the fatal distortion whereby we no longer see what we truly are, and instead believe that what we are not is the only reality. It means that we reconnect with our lost sources and that we definitively change our assemblage point from the ego-"I" to the universal "I", which is fully connected to the other "I's" in the world.

Does this mean that we hereby enter into the area of religion? Perhaps. But I am not speaking from the point of view of a certain religion, but from a logical viewpoint. In his lectures under the Bodhi tree, Buddha taught us about the logic of the greater "I", which lies behind all our personal characteristics. The statement that we are a part of the holistic universe, and that we are nothing without this connection with the whole, is not an expression of religious dogma, but of pure insight. Every breath, every pulse, and every atom of our bodies comes from the great studio of the universe, and this connection has not been made up, for it is active in every moment. Even our most meaningless words are sounds that emerge from the eternal "becoming" of the world, although they are often constricted and distorted through the narrow pipeline of our own person. We are the living organ of a transpersonal subject, which inhabits every being. The statement that we ourselves are destroyed if we destroy our fellow beings is not some kind of moral moaning and groaning; it is a holistic law. The idea of stepping out of the existing cul-de-sac and creating a new world is not a pipe-dream, but a definitive decision.

Individuality

Individuality is a community endeavor.

(Statement from chaos research)

Every being has two sides, a universal and an individual side. Every being is universal, because it is a part of the whole. But every being is also – as Teilhard de Chardin so clearly formulated it – centered in itself and therefore individual. Life occurs within this polarity. Osho once said that the individual is like a piss in the ocean and that after its death it dissolves into this ocean. This is the Eastern point of view, not the Western one. I would like to demonstrate the story about the piss in the ocean with a physical experiment. We take two glass cylinders with different diameters and place one inside of the other. We then pour glycerin into the space between the cylinders and add a drop of ink to it. We now turn the outer (or inner) cylinder. The drop of ink lengthens, becomes thinner and thinner, and after a while it disappears. But has it really disappeared? We now turn the cylinder back and experience a minor miracle. The drop reappears, at first as a cloudy stream, which then condenses to form the original drop. The drop had not really disappeared; latently it was still there. David Bohm, the physicist and philosopher, would say that it switched from the explicit to the implicit order and then re-appeared by turning the cylinder back. The individual exists even if we cannot see it, for it is a part of the implicit order of the universe. Individuality is a part of the building plan of Creation. As the regression trances keep showing – we humans continue to live as individuals after death.

A nice example is provided by the formation of vortices in a stream. If there are stones or branches in the water, vortices are created behind them, and they drift down the stream without changing their form. The have a form of their own and seem to be very resistant against change by the rest of the world. They are clearly "individuals" with their own size, their own rotational speed, and their own ability to survive. And yet they are a part of the whole (the stream). They consist of the same stuff (water), they have emerged from the whole, and they flow with the whole.

Individuality is created through an inward rolling motion. Every motion contains its own counter-motion, said Heraclitus. In the structure of the world, we are thus always dealing with two movements: one that expands and one that centers; one that diverges and one that converges, one that explodes and one that implodes, and one that is universal and one that is individual. The individual one is of course also in a sense universal, for it is a part of the building principle of the universe.

In nature, individual actions are often controlled by a higher organizing power. This, too, can be illustrated using an example. A hundred ants are carrying a part of a sweet biscuit to their colony. They all make their individual movements, and one cannot discern any commonality, and yet the heavy piece moves toward the colony. There is clearly an overall coordinating principle, which guides the chaotic individual motions. This is true for people, too. Unless we have shut down completely, a higher coordinating principle controls our individual actions and connects us with the goals and the direction of the overall movement of the world. Let us look at the world as a holon and the motions of the six billion people and trillions of other individuals in the world as an expression of a connected super-hologram movement in terms of a co-evolution of all things. This corresponds to the modern view of the holistic quality of the world. The statements in the Political Theory (see Chapter 11) are based on this view.

Through the process of inward centering, a type of individuality can emerge, which says no to the processes of Creation. It can separate to a certain degree from the whole and create its own structures, as the human being has done since the time of the great separation. In terms of a meaningful development, we of course conclude that individuality should in no way be dissolved. On the contrary, the individuality of the human being should be promoted and increased so that those involved can use their own minds and experiences to recognize their connection with the whole, and are able to correct their lives correspondingly. **It is the task of a new type of functioning community to no longer suppress individual differences, but to accelerate the emergence of healthy, strong, and autonomous individuals.** Under the conditions in existing society, this cannot occur privately, because the collective pressure in the public world is too great to allow the development of autonomous individuals. The breeding-ground for a healthy human development has always been and is a healthy community. Individuality does not occur out of itself; it is a community endeavor.

A Principle of Creation: Congruence of Pleasure and Purpose

Nature clearly operates in a different way than human beings do. In nature we find a great wealth of colors and forms, of incomprehensible structures, and fantastically precise processes. From the microscopic radiolaria in the depths of the oceans, to the processes in a biotope in the Alps, everything functions with a breathtaking beauty and precision. Nature is quantum leaps ahead of humans when it comes to precision, effectiveness, and functionality. But there is no master builder, sweating as he builds all its structures. In some mysterious way, everything occurs "on its own". The highest feats of precision are the result of very imprecise methods, such as feeling, circling, and oscillating. Everything looks like a great, unsystematic, chaotic game, where nobody seems to seriously exert him/herself or to follow a plan. How is this possible? What is happening here? One central principle of the universal state of being is the unity of functionality and the joy of existence. Cosmic intelligence has organized things so that the various beings can best interact with all the others if they follow their own pleasure and joy. (This is true for those beings, who have retained their universal quality, but not for the human being, who has separated from Creation.)

Nature operates in a different way than humans do. But is not the human being also a part of nature? If nature works differently, could then not the human being also work differently?

If humans want to achieve something, they make an effort. For this, they need various things: an intent, a will, discipline, and follow-through. They especially need rational, result-oriented thoughts and actions. Because they believe that they always have to achieve something, they always practice their rational, result-oriented behavior. They call this "realism". I do not dispute the importance of these values, but in the name of the new culture, I would like to note that Creation has designed entirely different methods to achieve goals. If left alone, plants and animals always reach their goal, and they do not need to exert great effort, will, or discipline. The song of a lark comes from its joy of existence, and at the same time balances its energy household. A dog jumps around back and forth in great leaps; it does this out of joy, and at the same time this promotes its bodily health. If a dog has lost its master, then it enjoys its freedom, it sniffs around in circles on the ground, peeing here and there, and does not worry about which way to go, and yet it finds its way home before its master. It also finds its way back in foreign territory, without arduously having to look for the way and without having memorized the way beforehand. Animals obviously have a high congruence between what they need and what brings them pleasure. They do not reach their goals in life by setting goals and following them, but through their elementary way of being, of living, and of joining in the dance of the great circle of creatures. They do not need any extra plans for their lives, for they carry the plan within them – as entelechy, as their drive, their curiosity or greed, as joy or high spirits, and as patterns of motions of their bodies and souls. They do not calculate, they do not take preventive measures, and they do not worry. "They do not sow or reap or store away in barns, and yet your heavenly Father feeds them." The same is true – at a different level – for plants. There is no apple tree that refuses to start growing roots because 50 cm under the surface its roots will hit a rock. It is the inner entelechy that guides and drives the growth processes and solves the difficulties that arise. Its connection to the whole, to the overall matrix of Creation, operates through this entelechy. There is no sprout of grass that loses heart because there is a layer of concrete above it, for it doesn't think about the difficulties that this may bring. Its entelechy, its built-in growth plan, and its ethereal energies lead it here and now through all resistances, until it either fails or breaks through the layer of asphalt. There is no caterpillar that stops spinning its threads to form a cocoon because it thinks that it will never turn into a real, flying, multi-colored butterfly. It is working in the richness of unlimited presence and goes through transformations, which it could not have reached based on its own power and its own goal. An animal automatically does "the right thing", for what is effective is also pleasurable, and what is pleasurable is also effective. This is true, not only for eating, drinking and having sex, but also for all other movements and activities. Animals follow the general principle of **congruence of pleasure and purpose.** This is one of the deepest original thoughts of Creation. In reality, it also holds true for humans.

Children speak their mother tongue almost perfectly already at the age of three, without ever having to study vocabulary. They are not often seen with books on grammar, either. They learn playfully, and thereby find themselves in the basic creative process of Creation, just as animals do. They repeat what they hear, and sometimes they repeat it wrongly, simply due to their high spirits. They laugh at how funny it sounds and yet they learn it correctly. They carry out the seemingly most meaningless things with an incredible seriousness, and yet they do not take anything as seriously as we adults do. They are not yet in a process of judgment but still fully in the process of universal existence and abandonment. There is not yet a difference between them and their actions. If we do not force them to go into the wrong direction, our children and animals, i.e. our natural gurus, lead us to the path of the new existence.

We adults are not supposed to copy animals and children, but to understand their state of existence. Once we have fully understood this universal state of being, and once we again know what it means to learn playfully, to act without intent, and to reach one's goals without effort, then we have reached the goal. The principle of congruence between pleasure and purpose is a basic principle of Creation, which can lead to an entirely different concept of human culture. It contains ancient elements of Zen Buddhism, combined with unspoiled elements of sensuality, contact, and the joy of existence. In art, when singing or dancing, during martial arts or gymnastics, when having sex and making love, we start being good when we stop thinking about the meaning, purpose, and goal. The Zen student's arrow hits the bull's eye when the student no longer thinks about the goal.

And yet qualities such as will, intent, setting goals, effort, etc. are necessary qualities in our human lives, and we would hardly be able to survive without them. If we did not have them, we could no longer get out of our current cul-de-sac. We cannot simply lie down in a meadow and lead a fulfilled existence. The basic cultural and societal patterns are missing for this pleasure to be afforded. Our most elementary drives, wishes, and longings would remain unfulfilled. The hippie era has passed, at least for now. If we today again want to connect with the secrets of the universal state of existence, we need a way of thinking that takes us to the edge and that does not close its eyes to any possibilities, no matter how fantastic they may seem. It is only through this extreme intelligence and awareness that we can make the decision to leave the old pattern of existence and enter into the new one.

This decision must be made. The new things that are needed for a future concept of human life on earth require a new kind of health, a new power of insight, and a new willingness to act, and these cannot be attained through effort and sweat, by fulfilling one's duty, or through outer discipline. It is our "duty" to be happy, writes Dhyani Ywahoo. But this duty is very different from the one we know from school, from professional life, and from the military. The happiness is different, too. It is the happiness of a higher connection and of a higher sense of security. Every plant, every animal, and every child exists in this happiness

– and so does every adult, if s/he has chosen the inner path toward it and has found it. Humanity, or at least a part of humanity, has lived in this happiness for a long time. Up until the Minoan era on Crete (second millennium B.C.), the cultural foundation there was the celebration of the joy of Creation.

We can obviously not immediately change over from one state of existence to another. We still live in duality, and we still need to consciously set our goals, which in reality exist inside of us as entelechy. We still need to use our willpower with focus and intent, in order to get the life engine going, which has been disturbed and damaged for so long. There are still many situations where pleasure and purpose are incompatible, and where we have to make decisions that go against our pleasure, at least in the short term. There is still a small difference between the things that we like to eat and those that we should eat for health reasons. But we should not worry too much about this, for the other level, where what both tastes good and is healthy, what is necessary and pleasurable, can already be felt and seen. The deeper we go into the spiritual area without losing our sensuality, the more we discover the level where necessity and joy, and duty and freedom, come together. Historically speaking, we are in a state of transition, in which the past and the future sometimes still remain irreconcilable. We are transitional human beings. In this historical phase of transition we must now learn certain things that we need, in order to be able to fully carry out the transition. Experienced transformational workers have therefore developed humor and tolerance toward their occasional relapses and contradictions, which sometimes cannot be avoided. Sometimes we go victoriously from failure to failure, as Lusseyran said. With each time, our body becomes somewhat more sensitive, our will a bit tougher, our knowledge sharper, and our vision more realistic. Subtly, we notice that something new in us has slowly but surely taken over: the one existence and the one consciousness. We feel it through the arrival of a deeper joy.

Matriarchal Powers of the New Culture

A new women's power is not directed against men,
nor against our love for men.
But it definitively bids farewell
to the structures that have contributed
to the worldwide destruction of life and love.
It is now up to us women
to take on the political and sexual responsibility
that has been missing for so long.
We invite all committed men
to join us in our peace work.

Sabine Lichtenfels

The life form of the coming era is given by the laws of universal existence. It is tied to the Sacred Matrix and to the life functions of Mother Earth. I have described the original image of such a way of living through the example of a highly developed ancient culture (Chapter 3, last section). It has distinct matriarchal characteristics. No matriarchy will arise today, and we do not want to revert back to past cultural forms. But there are matriarchal sources of human culture that each culture must rediscover, if it is to find a meaningful way forward. When we today speak of free sexuality, we touch a matriarchal principle of life. There was a clear historical connection between free sexuality and a matrilinear order of living together. For both genders, polygamy was a part of the sensual stream of life, and it was therefore natural. If a child was born, it was usually not known who the father was, but the mother was always known. It therefore suggested itself that the children stay with their mothers. This is how the matrilinear tribes, villages, and cities of humanity arose, all the way into the Neolithic Age. The foundation of the social structure was the genealogy of its inhabitants. The natural size limit was determined by the clarity that was needed regarding the relationship between relatives. Once the size limit had been reached, a group moved further downstream or founded a new tribe, a new village, or a new "daughter city". This is how the organic growth of matrilinear society functioned. There was no foreign domination, no state, and no church that towered over the people.

There was a natural ethic of being there for each other, based on this order of relationships. One shared what one had, helped each other in times of need, and served the good of the people, not the good of a system. True ethics only arise from true human relationships, not from tablets with commandments and systems of justice.

One central human value was motherliness, a caring relationship toward all creatures. Motherliness was not tied to the female sex. In societies with a matriarchal orientation (such as for example the Iroquois native Americans), a man could only become chief if he had enough motherliness. Here we should stop for a moment and stay with this image. (One can briefly compare it to the image of a division head or the CEO of a company.)

I am describing these simple things because I believe that they belong to the Sacred Matrix, and that therefore they will determine life in the communities of the future. Today, when we establish the new healing biotopes, we will no longer build simple matrilinear structures. But neither will we live in an unstructured way in the long term. Groups will emerge that are based on relationships. Most people come from a cosmic or karmic clan, to which they still belong. As a community reconnects with its cosmic roots, the mental-spiritual or cosmic relationship connections take hold, creating larger circles of friends and "family circles".

A part of the original matriarchal ethic is the joy of giving. Mother Earth is full of gifts for hunger and thirst, for love and beauty, for the needs of the body and of the soul. According to the plan of Creation of the Sacred Matrix, humans and the earth live in a symbiotic relationship. The earth gives people what we need, and people give the earth what she needs. These are two mental-spiritual organisms that are meant for each other. Every healthy economy requires two movements: one of giving and one of receiving. These are foundations of the Sacred Matrix, and we will understand and happily follow them when we have re-established our natural connection to our fellow humans and to nature. If we today are asked about the economic concepts for tomorrow, we can hardly provide any answers at all, because the economy of connection will be a fundamentally different one from that of separation.

The matriarchal view of the world is different from the male view. If, in the morning, clouds of steam rise from a warm lake into the cold morning air, then this is not just a physical event relating to the differences in temperature and the thermal forces. It is a living spiritual process between water and air. It is living spiritual energy, in the form of orgone steam figures, that is doing its morning dance. We find living spiritual energy everywhere in nature; there is no other energy. This connection with everything that exists is the basis of (matriarchal) universal love. This love is a biological fact, a state of existence. It is both a sensual and a mental-spiritual love. It is the unsentimental love, with which the new human beings will encounter each other when they visit another tribe, another center, or another healing biotope. Here, one can sense the freedom and the openness. There is no need for masks, for there is no need for caution or pretense. Here we meet again, from source to source.

It is not by chance that we were guided to Portugal as the place for building the first healing biotope. In the rural areas, the matriarchal powers of the past are still so visible, that one tends to enter into resonance with them immediately, in order to support it. The cult around Nossa Senhora is not so much a cult from the Catholic Church, as a cult of the pre-Christian joy of life. Old sources, caves, and places of pilgrimage testify to a reverence toward the female that is probably unique in Europe. This is where the voyage of discovery of advanced early matriarchal cultures began, as described by Sabine Lichtenfels. On our property in Tamera there are toads, snakes and owls - all signs of an especially intense presence of the Goddess who once breathed life into this whole land.

In the larger communities of our times, we usually find more women than men. The communal life form was the source of the matriarchal era. The historical cycle, in which we are living today, is again moving in this direction. The powers of cooperation and resonance that we are rediscovering today are the basic forces of the matriarchal culture. They are not gender specific, for the entire Sacred Matrix lives equally in both genders. The only thing that was gender specific was the war that was waged against it by the male mind. A new, softer way of thinking will also increasingly dominate classical male domains, such as mechanics, technology, political work, or conducting seminars. Especially the new forms of political networking are characterized by the methods of gentle power. If a level of humor and gentleness can be attained, then human or ideological contradictions and conflicts do not have to be solved immediately. Some women have the ability to not take anything completely seriously, since for them political opponents are first of all human beings, no matter how much they act like despots or puppets. They must therefore not be judged. It is impressive to see how some women deal with their opponents. If needed, they suddenly access a matriarchal power, against which a man can no longer use his old war axes.

It is not least this female power that we are betting on, when we today are counting on an historical victory for the peace movement. A deep reallocation of the old roles will occur in the power system of the new centers and movements. Women will also become more active in the choice of their love partners. A prerequisite for this is a new, more deeply rooted solidarity between women, which does not stop when two women love the same man. Men will align themselves with female power, without losing their male powers. They will thereby discover themselves anew. They will develop their mental-spiritual, physical, and sexual qualities as men in the service of life and in the service of woman. This is true courtship of a different kind. Men, who no longer romanticize women, but who concretely and physically love them, will support and serve them with all their powers.

Due to the larger number of women, there is naturally a certain deficit in terms of men. This is not easy for women who are in the process of opening up to their sexual powers, which had to be kept locked away for so long. The leading women of the new centers will no longer respond to this deficit through renewed neediness and through submission to the men, but by working actively with the men, seeing to it that a new type of maleness can develop. For this, we have occasionally created what we call "love schools", where men are instructed by women in the art of love. Male uncertainty or dominance often transforms into an almost childish longing for a matriarchal, superior, protecting woman. Obviously, men have some catching up to do when it comes to what the male child never had: the absolute love for "Mother". This means that certain parts of the gender roles are almost fully reversed. The women will learn to respect this situation for a while and will use their female abilities to make partners out of their immature men. To do this, they themselves must take an important step: they must leave their old neediness toward men. They will no longer be fixated on a single man and cling to him when they have him. They will no longer fight each other over a man. Future communities can only function if a powerful "woman's field" of solidarity has been established. That is an irrefutable postulate of the new culture. Even when they are in love, the new women will be partners to the men and tell them the truth. Every true man needs women, who tell him the truth (and vice versa). When the women in the new communities have learned to behave in this way, and when they no longer give their independence away to a man as soon as they fall in love, then the great turnaround will occur and many men will come. Once the patterns are clear, there will no longer be any lack of men. Here, a deep kaleidoscope is being turned, and all those involved will rejoice when they see the new pattern. A new world will arise between woman and man.

Sabine Lichtenfels has written 24 theses for a new women's movement. She has also written the book "Weiche Macht – Perspektiven für eine neue Frauenbewegung und eine neue Liebe zu den Männern." ["Gentle Power – Perspectives for a New Women's Movement and a New Love of Men"]. Right now, as I am writing this chapter, some events are occurring that could contribute to the realization of this thought. The Women's Conference at ZEGG (Center for Experimental Societal Design) in Belzig, not far from Berlin, the publication of the first issue of the magazine for women entitled "Die Weibliche Stimme" ["The Female Voice"] by Leila Dregger and Christine Meissner, and the Summer University at Tamera, which is facilitated by Sabine Lichtenfels. During the daily morning prayer, spoken by women, Monika Alleweldt today spoke the following words, accompanied by a slow drumbeat:

Everything is one existence.
I am a part of this one existence.
I am connected to the rocks and the stones,
to the water, the plants, the animals, and all human beings.
I am connected to the weather
and to the most distant galaxy.
Everything is one existence.
As a human being, I am a part of the self-consciousness of the universe.
It can understand itself through me,
and it can change through me.
I do not belong to myself.
I place my life in the service of all those
who now need my help and my empathy.
I am in the service of oppressed peoples.
I am in the service of starving children.
I am in the service of tortured animals.
Through my thoughts and actions,
I must and want to contribute to peace on earth.
It is not war, but peace, that requires the full commitment of my life.
I give thanks for the abundance that we live in.
I give thanks for the clear water.
I give thanks for the community and for all those
who are helping to establish a ring of peace around our earth.

Chapter 8
Cooperation with Nature

What Does It Mean?

Once again, to regain our focus: all of life together constitutes a whole, a continuum. What we do to other beings comes back to us in some form or other. We cannot destroy an organ of the body of life, without injuring the entire organism. The violence that we do to other beings comes back to us as violence, fear, illness, or a weakening. There is a fundamental contradiction in today's civilization. It is fighting a war against so-called pests, in order to produce healthy vegetables. It tortures laboratory animals, in order to protect the health of humans. The daily work in a single animal laboratory creates more illness in the living body of the biosphere than can be healed by the insights that are gained in this laboratory. The cruelties committed in the animal laboratories damage the entire "biobody". For both scientific (holistic) and ethical reasons, we are forced to find new directions when it comes to healing the human being and the earth. The Sacred Matrix is based on cooperation.

According to estimates by modern day ant research, the total mass of all ants on earth is greater than the overall mass of human beings. Can we cooperate with ants? Could we work with them as allied partners for global peace work?

Water veins course through the earth. Can we cooperate with the water? Could we work with it as an allied partner for global peace work?

The world's oceans cover more than 70 percent of the earth's surface. They hold an inexhaustible animal world. Can we cooperate with the inhabitants of the oceans? Could we work with them as allied partners for peace work?

The material world, including our atmosphere, with its weather processes, is filled with flowing, living energies. Could we cooperate with them? Could we work with them as allied partners for peace work?

The plants and trees of the world are spiritual beings. Could we cooperate with them? Could we work with them as allied partners for peace work?

That is what I mean, when I speak of "cooperation with nature". It is a question of winning over all of nature as an allied partner for the global healing work. It may sound like a science fiction novel, but it is not science fiction. It is the building plan of Creation. All beings on earth are organs of one body, and they are the minds of one mind. The biosphere is a holon, a unified, spiritual organism, in which life is designed for cooperation and symbiosis, just as the organs and cells of our body are.

All cells and organs of a body cooperate with each other. If we no longer input the information of violence but instead the information of peace and cooperation into this body, then its beings, which are all an aspect of the Goddess, will align with it naturally. Just like us, all these beings, from the large mammals down to the microbes and bacteria, are a condensation of spiritual, planetary, and cosmic energy. Information from the Sacred Matrix can be accessed from all of them. If we turn toward nature, nature turns toward us. If we turn a bit more, we will witness a living, almost personal divine presence, which surrounds us permanently through the beings in nature. While experiencing this presence, cooperation is not only possible, but totally natural. All beings in nature are waiting for this to occur.

Together with his wife, the Austrian Sepp Holzer has established the Krameterhof in Lungau in Austria. Here, at 1200 – 1500 meters [4000 – 5000 ft.], we find the largest functioning permaculture garden in Europe. This is the best illustration of how nature accommodates human beings when they do the right thing. Here, surrounded by a monoculture of spruce trees, nature is exuberantly celebrating the feast of its diversity. Plant and animal beings unite with ponds, rocks, and rotting branches to create a paradise garden with unique abundance. Now, lemon trees grow where spruce used to be. Nature shows us how its beings mutually support and sustain each other, if the human being cooperates with it. Neither pesticides nor fertilizers are used at the Krameterhof. The result is a very large harvest. The productivity of this 45 hectares [about 110 acres] mountainous property is greater than what has so far been deemed possible.

(Incidentally, Holzer has repeatedly been reported for offences against the forest laws and against forestry office regulations. His project has been operating for the last 35 years. At the time, nobody spoke of "permaculture", and it was hardly ever mentioned in ecological magazines or at seminars on permaculture – this seems to be the fate of all great innovations.)

Cooperation with Water

Thales of Milet (600 B.C.) and Viktor Schauberger both agree that water is the basic substance of all life and that all other forms of life come from water. Anyone who is connected to water is connected to the secrets of life. Understanding water is one of the foundations for the creation of a new culture.

From where does a salmon get help orienting itself when it returns to its source from the wide ocean to spawn? What enables it to swim against the strongest of currents and to leap up waterfalls that are 10 meters [33 feet] high?

In the worldview of the coming era, water will have a new meaning. It carries the information of life into the material world. In addition to light, it is life's most important carrier of information. Moving, natural water gives rise to countless segments, whose surface areas act as sense organs for cosmic information (see Theodor Schwenk's book "Das sensible Chaos" ["The Sensitive Chaos"]). All information in the ether of life, be it of cosmic or terrestrial origin, is received and transmitted further by water. The Japanese Masuru Emoto influenced water with musical pieces, texts and individual words, whereupon he froze the water and photographed the ice crystals under a microscope. What he found was highly differentiated crystal patterns that varied greatly from one crystal to another. This means that the water took on the information (from words such as "love" or "hate") and, through its immanent formative forces, translated it into a coded image (see the magazine "raum & zeit" No. 107, Sept/Oct 2000). Water is a living spiritual being, which absorbs the information that we input, for example through singing, praying or writing, and passes it on to the biosphere. Roland Plocher's process for cleaning pond water is based on this type of information technology. If we want to strengthen the information of peace, it would be reasonable to input it into water. It will then spread this information in its own way.

Water is not a chemical formula, but a central organ in the biosphere that contains practically all the secrets of the universe. All living structures have come from the forms of motion of water. Water contains the patterns of all life possibilities that have been actualized, and maybe also of those that have not yet been actualized. Water constitutes a special state of universal life, within which the world of light and that of matter touch each other and connect. Water therefore has qualities that go against all physical rules, especially when it forms vortices, when it flows upward within subterranean channels, or when it produces unknown forces of levitation in the middle of waterfalls. A hundred years ago Viktor Schauberger began his breathtaking studies of water. He discovered a whole new world (explained in detail in the book "Living Energies" by Callum Coats and in the book "Living Water" by Olof Alexandersson). The mysteries surrounding water have not been solved yet, and they are only now being recognized. But already now we know that in a future world culture, the human being's whole way of living will be connected to the laws of water in a new way. Drinking clear water will be a part of the future bodily culture. Cleaning and energizing water will be of great importance in the overall work of the healing biotopes, the spiral and hyperbolic vortex forms will create new structures of sound and space, and the spiritual information technology will make natural contact with water as a carrier of information. In all areas, cooperation with nature is at the same time cooperation with water.

Cooperation with Matter

"First and foremost among the inherent qualities of matter is motion, not only as mechanical and mathematical motion, but even more as a drive, as the spirit of life, as tension, or to use Jakob Böhme's expression, as the agony of matter."

This sentence was not written by a mystical dreamer, but by Karl Marx (in his book "The Holy Family"). Matter is a universal energetic substance in condensed form. This universal substance is of a mental-spiritual nature. If matter is mentally-spiritually anchored, then it can also be influenced mentally-spiritually. This phenomenon is well-known in parapsychological research and is called "psychotronics". Psychotronics is the influencing and changing of material objects through the mind. In future technologies, it will be as natural as it is to make a phone call today. The experiences in psychotronically influencing matter that have been reported by Uri Geller go far beyond bending spoons. He is seriously thinking of using psychotronic powers for global peace work – for example to disarm all atomic warheads. Let us not smile too soon, but instead read his book "My Story".

In American and Russian military laboratories, psychotronic experiments have been carried out for several decades. It seems that it was natural to deal with matter psychotronically during the era of the early advanced megalithic cultures. The sacred stones and dolmen were probably erected using mental-spiritual powers to a high degree. According to our knowledge to date, one can no longer dismiss the idea that the positioning of the enormous blocks of stone of the Egyptian pyramids and the incredible precision of its joints could only have been achieved with the help of mental-spiritual powers. Matter consists of energy. Even protons, the heaviest and densest particles of matter in the so-called nucleus of the atom, consist of fields of highly vibrating energy. If one succeeds in impacting this energy with the right frequency, then matter changes. The psi abilities of artists such as Houdini seem to be limitless. From this point of view the question naturally arises if there are any material limits to human actions. Are we here dealing with limitations that ultimately are limitations of our consciousness and that we will some day overcome? Albert Einstein once said that everything that can be thought, can also be done. This statement contains a truth that is almost frightening. It concerns the deep connection between thinking and reality, which is a result of the mental-spiritual nature of reality. How thoughts can transform into material objects was impressively demonstrated during the 1980's by the Montauk experiments, which were kept secret for a long time. Here, I must add that as far as I am aware, it has not yet been independently confirmed that these experiments truly took place.

Material objects have their own tensions and forces of motion. The artist and Bauhaus student Hans Hoffmann-Lederer made metal sculptures that consisted only of the inherent motion in thin metal plates. They rolled and twisted like cardboard, when they were cut into strips. The future human being will enter into contact with these powers, which are inherent in matter, in order to shape his material surroundings through vibrations and resonance. We will no longer break the resistance of material beings, but enter into resonance with their own inherent forces. Resonance technology and psychotronics are the foundations for future non-violent cooperation between the human being and matter. (We do not need to implement everything at once. Often, developments begin with a well-founded and realistic vision. This, then, attracts the knowledge needed for its realization.)

Making Peace with the Animal Kingdom

The fear of you and the dread of you
shall be upon every beast of the earth,
and upon every bird of the heavens;
With all wherewith the ground teemeth,
and all the fishes of the sea,
 into your hand are they delivered.
Every moving thing that liveth shall be food for you;

    The Bible, 1st Book of Moses, 9,2

As long as there are slaughterhouses,
there will also be battlefields.

Leon Tolstoi

As long as humans torment, torture, and kill animals,
we will have war.

Bernard Shaw

Just like human beings,
animals experience joy and pain, happiness and unhappiness;
they are moved by the same emotions as we are.

    Charles Darwin

The issue of animals (...)
is inextricably intertwined with the issue of human beings,
so that every improvement in our relationship to the animal world
infallibly constitutes progress on the path
toward human happiness.

    Émile Zola

The day will come,
when humans will judge the killing of an animal
exactly the same way
that they today judge the killing of a human being.

    Leonardo da Vinci (and similarly by Albert Einstein)

I can imagine a world – because it has always existed –
in which human beings and animals enter into a covenant
and live together in peace and harmony,
a world that day by day is transformed by the magic of love,
a world that is free from death.
This is not a dream.

    Henry Miller in "Sexus"

The dog that we expected has arrived.
Where she was before, she must have been beaten;
she is terrified of everything.
The kisses that she gets from Marie-Sonaly do not help.
She does not succeed in settling in
Her name: Pity.
One could almost translate this with compassion.

    Frère Roger (in Taizé)

Sunday morning. I used to have to go to church at this time. Today, I go to my bathtub. (Are we dealing with the same person?) In any case, I am in the bathtub and I notice some tiny animals on the tiles on the wall. They are very thin and maybe 3 millimeters (1/8 of an inch) long and they have many legs. I decide to regard them as ants. Where do they come from? What do they eat? What are they doing on this wall? I become curious, for they are my fellow creatures in evolution, they are real living beings, and they are a part of the one existence, so they must be cosmically related to me in some way. I watch them on their Sunday walk on the vertical wall and I see how they disappear into a little hole. That is their apartment. They have actually built themselves an apartment in the plaster between the tiles. What occurred in them, as they did this? Where did they get the enthusiasm and the power to be able to do something like that? Normally one sees them as a pest and cleans them off.

Here, two worlds collide with each other, and one of them, the older one, has to give way. This may be fully in line with Darwin, but is it also right in a higher sense? Do we humans really have the right to destroy an element of life as if this were natural, just because it doesn't fit into our own system of life? Is the ants' system of life wrong – or is ours? Maybe our own system of life is not quite correctly adapted to the higher order of Creation? Is there a possibility for non-violent co-existence? Just a few decades ago such thinking would have been characterized as absurd, but with every further consideration, and with every new experience, it today becomes increasingly relevant. Maybe there is a possibility for a kind of co-existence that encompasses all living beings? We will see. Chaos research has taught me one thing: things that collide on the existing level of order can harmonize at a higher level of order. If enmities arise within a certain system, they can transform into friendship at the level of a system of a higher order. The solution of many issues consists of finding a higher level order.

On days when I am lazy, I lie down on a meadow, push aside the grass, and observe life on the ground underneath. I have sometimes used a magnifying glass because I have been so surprised and awed at what I saw. The earth is alive everywhere. I do not know how many hundred or thousand little beings inhabit a single square yard. If we take this entire layer – containing bugs, ants, worms, snails, spiders, lice, all the way to the microorganisms – and add it all up, then we have a population that we can no longer ignore in our future plans for peace on earth. We must assume that they play an important role in the organism of the biosphere. From this point of view, it is no longer natural to cover the earth with concrete or to build a house somewhere, without first contacting the inhabitants there.

There have been times and cultures when this kind of thinking was still clear. According to ancient philosophers such as Thales, Pythagoras, or Empedocles, the unity of life was a natural fact that they perceived mentally-spiritually. This fact made it clear that there is a kinship between human beings and animals, just as we find with St. Francis of Assisi and the Cathars, and it resulted in a correspondingly ethical approach to the animal world. In the following I will describe to what extent we today can confirm this approach and use it for our work.

Peace Work in the Garden

All over the world, the agrarian production of food is connected to chemical warfare that human beings are waging against "pests". These are innumerable small living beings, who inhabit every field and every garden, and naturally want to partake in the harvest. There are, for example, worms, caterpillars, snails, bugs, aphids, mice, moles, etc. Chemical warfare is not aligned with the Sacred Matrix, for here the human being is destroying other organs that belong to the whole just as s/he does. There is an alternative, which has proven itself effective in small model projects.

There are non-violent gardens on earth. They are described in the book "In Harmonie mit den Naturwesen" ["In Harmony with the Nature Beings"] by Eike Braunroth. The principle is based on communication with the so-called pests, not on their destruction. The peace gardeners use neither pesticides nor any other methods of deterrent against the small creatures. Peace is established through an agreement between human beings and their fellow creatures. Jürgen Paulick, for example, a student of Eike Braunroth, thus made the following agreement: "I have planted a bed of lettuce, it belongs to all of us; I will harvest 12 heads of lettuce and you can have three." Sometimes he put down such agreements in writing on a piece of paper that he then placed in the garden. I can imagine a nice heading in a tabloid newspaper: "Alternative Gardener Writes Letter to Pests". At first we may react similarly and shake our heads. The only thing is that it works. We in Tamera have had contact with animals in a way that one would not have believed was possible if one had not experienced it. It is based on the fact that we all – animals and human beings – are parts of the one existence and of the one consciousness. The information must be unambiguous and consistent. It must come from an authentic spirit of peace, not from reluctant concessions. In the surroundings, too, there must be no signs of violence or destruction, also not in the form of so-called complicity products, for whose production animals had to be killed.

Do snails know the number three? Probably not, but neither do they have to know it. A computer also does not have to understand what one inputs, and yet it does the right thing, because it was programmed to do so by a higher authority. We have a similar situation with the snails and the other animals. If we formulate our request clearly enough, and if it makes sense, it will be taken up by the information pattern which controls the snails and will be transmitted to the snail as a behavioral impulse. The same is true for a spider that is building its web. Does the spider know how to construct a web? The meta-intelligence, which operates in the body of the spider through the spider's information grid, knows how, and in the circuitry of Creation, that is enough.

In the case of the peace garden, horticulture is a spiritual process of information and cooperation, from beginning to end. Everything is one existence and one continuum: the garden soil, the plants, the animals, the human being, and the world of the microbes are all parts of one life body. All subjects that participate in this life body are connected with each other through the right frequency in one information circulation. There are probably further subjects that are involved in this system, such as the so-called devas, or plant and animal spirits, which are something like a group spirit of a species. We know of these devas from Findhorn, the well-known spiritual community in Scotland (see Dorothy McLean's book: "To Hear the Angels Sing"). Today, the devas are almost an integral part of spiritual descriptions of nature. The landscape healer Marco Pogacnik and his daughter Anna Pogacnik work with them and see them as their natural partners. The devas seem to be able to consciously absorb the information that has been input and pass it on to its beings. They are also able to come up with suggestions for improvements that can then be understood by individuals who have natural mediumistic abilities.

The place where a garden is to be created is already inhabited by a multitude of small living creatures. There, in the skin of the earth, just under the surface, in the shade of grasses and herbs, they have their natural home. There, they live out their symbiotic relationship with the organism of the earth. All beings, including the smallest ones, react to communication, for all of them are a part of the whole. Therefore, in terms of Creation as a whole, it makes sense to inform the beings of the plan of the garden in advance and to ask them for their cooperation.

One of the basic thoughts of non-violent gardening concerns the abundance of the earth. There is enough for everyone. The agreement that we enter into with the small living beings is based on leaving them a generous part of the harvest. Eike Braunroth writes:

When I myself carried out research in this area about 20 years ago, I gave the nature beings some 10 percent. This is a good measure. (...) Based on the experience that nature reacts to generosity, I raised the voluntary gift to 30 percent. It is nature's way to think and act in ever-greater dimensions. From the third year on, I thus invited all the Colorado beetles, snails, aphids, field mice, voles, rabbits, etc. to live with me and to also tell their relatives that they could live with me and partake of the food. That was the moment when I let go fully. From then on our harvests kept on growing and the fruit became increasingly healthy, tasty, and beautiful, and it did not spoil.

For making physical contact with the nature beings, he recommends an attitude, which one can also practice among humans:
Send out love in advance, and only then, touch!
Send out blessing in advance, and only then, touch!
Send out joy in advance, and only then, touch!
Send out a welcome in advance, and only then, touch!
Send out goodwill in advance, and only then, touch!
Send out the desire to get to know them in advance, and only then, touch!
Send out the desire to share in advance, and only then, touch!
Send out the desire to do good in advance, and only then, touch!

Cooperation with Rats

As happens almost everywhere, when a settlement is established, the rats appeared in Tamera. The methods they used to make our lives more difficult, especially at night, became more and more conspicuous. It was not possible to sleep in the spaces that the rats had conquered. One rat seemed to have specialized in loosening little stones from the mud wall and letting them fall down on us. Since they could not be chased away, but came closer and became louder every night, our attention was awakened. They truly seemed to want to tell us something.

Then, during a trance event, their message came through. They, or their deva, suggested that we not simply drive them away, but that we enter into cooperation with them. It was very clear and precise. We received the message that the rats could build up immunizing energies, and therefore could help us to neutralize harmful substances. We also learned that rats are important carriers of information, that they can go almost anywhere, and that they are willing to serve as carriers of information for the peace work. In return, they asked that we make available living quarters for them as well as enough food. From then on, a communication was established, which we would never have believed possible. Once again a reality opened up for us, which was so different from what we had experienced before, that one could only believe it if one had experienced it oneself. We built them a place to live in an old ruin, and they actually soon began to use it. The nightly commotion disappeared, for the rats had moved out. During this time we learned that there are rat temples in India, which were specifically built to serve as living quarters for rats. I suspect that this tradition goes back to the Indian emperor Ashoka, who united the empire around 200 B.C. and who established many animal asylums during his Buddhist renewal of the empire.

Another story: one day in our storage cellar we discovered a rat's nest with five naked baby rats. Imagine a rat's nest in the storage cellar, surrounded by fruit, bananas, vegetables, and bread! The woman in charge of the kitchen placed a sumptuous plate with fruit and rolled oats on the floor and put a letter next to it, in which she asked the rat to eat only that food, also explaining why. After a few misunderstandings, the rat began to focus exclusively on the plate. We could without hesitation let it stay in the storage cellar. In her book "To Hear the Angels Sing", Dorothy McLean describes her communication with the rat devas. She could, however, not get through with her suggestions for cooperation in the community of Findhorn, because the prejudice against rats was too entrenched. For millennia, rats have been seen as enemies of the human being. Humans fought them instead of realizing that their constant closeness has something to do with a desire for contact and for a symbiotic relationship between human beings and rats. The situation regarding snakes is very similar. We will not be able to make up for the cruelties that have been committed in the past, but we can do everything to make it stop, and we can replace them with cooperation and friendship, which was obviously the intent right from the start. Rats could become allies and partners for global peace work.

The Spiritual Natural Law

Not only does the human being seek cooperation with nature,
but nature also seeks cooperation with the human being.
Not only does the human being seek healing herbs,
but the healing herbs also seek the human being.
Not only does the one who is thirsty seek water,
but water also seeks the one who is thirsty.

Is it not a miracle that the human being finds on earth everything that s/he needs to eat and drink for the sustenance of his/her body? In nature there is a correspondence for every need of our bodies. The body of nature and the body of the human being are finely attuned to each other, for they come from the same divinity (divine whole). All things correspond to each other in the holographic continuum of life: what appears as hunger in one place appears as repletion elsewhere; what appears as a longing in one place appears as fulfillment elsewhere; what is desired here is done elsewhere. There could be no thirst, if there were no water. In the following chapter about the "Effectiveness of Prayer", we will return to this topic. The Sacred Matrix has designed a symbiotic relationship between the human being and nature. The human being who desires encounters nature that fulfills – and nature that desires encounters the human being who fulfills. The activities of both sides are guided by subjective drives, desires, longings, and needs. Both sides enter into contact and communication with each other through their "inner side" (Teilhard de Chardin). The dead natural laws of physics do not exist.

In the physical laws of nature, physical bodies react to each other. In the spiritual laws of nature psychic (or spiritual) beings of things react to each other. Old science asks about the characteristics of a thing, a plant, an animal, a stone, a metal, or a river. The new science asks the question: what is this being **doing?** All things are engaged in an activity, even if this activity is sometimes so slow in our way of perceiving that we cannot see the activity. Every form of a plant is a gesture. Every thing is a phase of motion in a universal development. Together, they are all engaged in a great common activity, which we call "Creation". Creation is a continuous process, and it is occurring at every moment. The so-called natural laws are not really laws about things, but about their habits of behavior. These habits of behavior do not change, as long as conditions in their environment remain the same. But they can change suddenly if something new occurs. They can, for example, change from stillness to movement, from fear to joy, or from repulsion to attraction. Objects that normally follow gravity can suddenly follow levitation and float around – such cases are often reported in psi research. Animals or plants that have so far avoided human beings can suddenly approach them, if a friendship arises where there was previously enmity. (In the case of enmity, however, they can also bother them until they change and become friendlier; then they leave them alone, back off, and keep a friendly distance.)

There is no dead matter. Everything is alive, everything is consciousness, and all things reacts to each other. Nature reacts to the human being, just as the human being reacts to nature. Every being in nature is happy when we are good to it. Nature is not something that the human being faces, as an autonomous, independent world. Instead, it is involved in a joint evolution together with humans. Herbal healers say that the plants that human beings need for their health establish themselves around new human settlements. Stinging nettles seem almost to follow humans around. Maurice Messègue, the famous French herbal healer, goes one step further. He states that, in the case of a longer illness, those plants that are suitable for the healing will appear close by.

Not only do human beings enter into cooperation with nature, but nature also enters into cooperation with human beings. Once, after we had cleared a piece of land, the naked earth covered itself with new herbs that nobody had sown there. When studying them closely, we found that they were all valuable edible wild vegetables. The plant devas had called their plants to us. They reacted to the friendliness, with which we had previously treated nature. Everything is prepared for communication and cooperation. Let us enter into this world.

Chapter 9
The Effectiveness of Prayer

God's Circuitry

Watch the distraction;
maybe it is an attraction.

We live in a world full of magic and miracles. If we want to build a new culture, we need the power that lies beyond our ego. We know that this power exists and that it is available to the human being. In order to establish healing biotopes and future communities that can survive, we need knowledge that enables us to use this power to heal the human being, nature, and the earth. A correctly spoken prayer is an efficient method of realization. How does it work?

Once again, I will briefly summarize the basic thoughts. The universe is a living organism. As long as it is not too greatly disrupted, it operates according to the principles of the Sacred Matrix. Provided they have not separated themselves from the plan of Creation, all beings in the universe are connected to each other within **one** existence and **one** consciousness, like the cells and organs of a body. The organism is filled with **one** "I", **one** control center, and **one** world soul. It exists in the whole and in all individual beings. The individual beings are the feelers, the antennae, the eyes, and the thinking organs of the whole. What they perceive, what they do, and what they need and desire is always reported back to central control through a great control circuit. Central control then sends out the impulses and information the individual beings need in order to function properly. All these information processes are ultimately mental-spiritual processes, and they are based on a cosmic control circuit, in which mental-spiritual impulses and consciousness energies run back and forth between the parts and the whole. The world would break down in an instant if this control circuit were no longer to function properly.

In this connection we can recognize the function of prayer. A true prayer is a function of the control circuit (which I call the "divine control circuit"), which has been translated into conscious communication. It connects us with the central control of the whole. The prayer occurs on both sides. When we truly pray, then central control also prays in us and through us. Sometimes we receive the answer already while we are praying. This is central control praying back to us. Both poles need each other. I need central control, and central control needs me. If I stop working, then the specific information it could gain through me is missing. It needs this information to be as clear and unadulterated as possible. It is therefore important that I operate correctly, that I do not make any false reports, and that my body and mind are able to transmit undistorted information to central control. It needs this information in order to be able to support me. The information must be provided with the greatest possible clarity and awareness, so that conscious cooperation can be established between the organ and central control.

God/dess, central control, or the soul of the world, needs my perception, my thoughts, my desire, and my feedback at a fully conscious level. At the biological level, the feedback occurs constantly anyway. At the conscious level it has been more or less cut off ever since the great separation, and today it must be re-established at a new level. This is a historical necessity. We must learn to pray. This means that we must learn to inform central control and the whole of our perceptions, thoughts, and desires in a clear way and at the right frequency. This is the only way that the cosmic control circuit, "God's circuitry", can again begin to operate at a conscious level. Only then can the "mountains be moved" that stand in the way of liberation, including the mountains inside of us.

If I want something very deeply, then it is the will of the whole. Otherwise I could not want it very deeply. Since it is the will of the whole, the whole (God) will take the measures that are necessary for its fulfillment. I will take note of these measures and report back correspondingly. Thus begins a joint process of navigation between me and central control. If we together remain at the right frequency, we are on the path of realization. This is a logical result of the holistic structure of the world. Whether we take this spiritual path or not is not a question of hope or belief, but one of insight. It is the result of our insight into the operating procedures and connections of Creation. A spiritual life practice has nothing to do with sentimentality; it is an efficient method of realization. All those who participate in creating a new earth will sooner or later connect with an everyday spiritual life practice and will set their priorities and make their decisions based on this practice. Consciously putting the divine control circuit into operation again is a prerequisite for success when it comes to global peace work. It is also a prerequisite for waking up from the fog of the material era and finding one's way toward reality.

I would like to illustrate the idea of the divine control circuit with an example. Let us assume that we are deeply in love with a certain person and that we desire nothing more than to be in contact with him/her. We now pray for the fulfillment of this desire. In order to believe in this fulfillment, we need to know three things:

First: If you have this desire deeply, then it is not only your private desire. Rather it is the world in you, God or Goddess, who has this desire through you. It is a desire of the universe – a universal desire – that you unite with this man or this woman. The whole world (of which you are a holographic condensation) wants this desire and this prayer from you, and therefore the whole world also wants it to be fulfilled. This follows from the unity of God and human being, from the unity of the "I" of the world and the "I" of the human being, and from the fact that our own person is an organ in the body of the universe. It is true for all authentic desires and all true prayers.

We come from a long religious tradition of so-called "selflessness", and we may have scruples about praying for "selfish" things. We must change our thinking. That, which serves the organ, serves the whole. For its work of creation, the cosmic "I" needs our being, our longing, our will, our prayer, and our feedback. It cannot function without our "I want", "I need", "I seek", etc. We are on a cosmic journey and we are dependent on a functioning navigation system. For it to work, we must say what we need. It is quite possible that one needs a certain love partner for this. Our experience will show what things we can and may pray for. We will find the connection to our higher self, and this connection provides us with the correct frequency. We sense this through the expansion, the calm, and the confidence that fills us at this moment.

Second: The information in the prayer is recorded and passed on by central control. The universe orients itself towards it – just as the human body orients itself toward the desire of one of its organs – and it reacts with a strategy for its fulfillment. Things then happen that we often do not immediately understand and that at first may not look as if they serve to fulfill our wish. We have often experienced these things in our prayer research. Only when we have learned to avoid quick judgments and disappointments do we begin to understand the ways and methods that the universe uses when arranging the fulfillment of our prayers. We are then initiated into the principle of perceiving mindfulness, for everything that occurs from the time of our prayer could serve its fulfillment. We enter into a state of "floating attention" (Simone Weil), which for example was practiced and described by Hildegard von Bingen, the great, almost revolutionary, mystic. We experience a chain of small and large events, and, as soon as we begin to see in them the early signs of the desired fulfillment, they get a meaning and a special kind of tension. It can be anything: children playing, maybe a red ball, a scene from a dream last night, a bird singing, the scent of a flower, the smell of an apartment, a neighbor's words, an unexpected phone call, a quote in a calendar, the name of a street or the license plate of a car. It can also be negative things: a little accident, a car breaking down, a forgotten watch, a missed plane. It is a chain of permanently changing situations – a "creative continuum", which leads to the desired goal, provided we are awake enough to see the individual situations and its possibilities, and do not falsify them through our habitual judgments. This chain will lead to the goal, because it follows a guidance and direction that corresponds to the prayer. Sometimes the consciousness of the world knows a bit more about the path to fulfillment than we do. It therefore chooses methods that we would never have thought of. Even atheists must admit that the universe has an advantage in terms of knowledge. The individual links of this chain of events often have no perceivable purpose. Instead they serve to retain the energy that is necessary for the fulfillment on both sides. Just like in a crime novel, we recognize in retrospect the logic of the events that were caused by our prayer. As one enters more fully into these connections, one can sense what kind of life we are approaching. We are here so clearly faced with a concrete utopia that we can almost breathe it, and we begin to understand the concept of "spiritual perception". When praying for the fulfillment of a great wish, every human being in his/her right mind will begin to perceive the most everyday things spiritually.

I do not want to hide the fact that the ability to perceive spiritually has to do with the constitution of our bodies. We need a light, cleansed body to be able to fully align with the fine web of sensual and spiritual perception. This is not least an issue of nutrition. All those who enter into the process of prayer and who are moving toward transformation, will of necessity be faced with the issue of nutrition (which I will not deal with in this book, in part since there are no ready-made prescriptions that are applicable to everyone). Plutarchos, the Greek historian and last oracle priest in Delphi (around 100 A.D.) recommends a light body in order to be receptive to the light of the world. He writes: *If we see the sun through humid air filled with a thick mist, it appears to us not in its clear shining, but in a pale, foggy, dying light. In the same way, the joy and light of the soul that goes through a fat, over-stuffed body must become cloudy, mixed and muddled, because it loses the light and the strength to sense the fine and invisible quality of things.*

Third: Do not get fixated on the desired object and on the fulfillment of your wish. Let go! This surprising statement is very important, and it follows from what has already been said. Fixation is a process that makes us blind to everything that in our opinion does not correspond to the desired goal. We then overlook and ignore the many finer, smaller things, which – if they had been perceived – would lead to the fulfillment of the prayer. The spiritual logic is often as simple as that. It is important to understand this thought.

By walking this path of prayer and by opening your senses to perceive the present moment, the cosmic spirit, which ultimately was the source of your prayer, could walk with you on this path of fulfillment. The concept of God's circuitry is almost a tautology, for in the holographic structure of the world serious prayers can hardly do anything but be fulfilled, provided that the path of mindfulness, as described above, is taken. There would otherwise be a crack in the world. Together, God, the world, and the human being form a holon. The subject, which brings forth and guides everything, exists in all three. If the subject wishes something, this wish is like a thermostat setting in the cosmic control circuit. The events, which then occur in the control circuit, are directed toward the realization of the specified value.

The universal intelligence, which we have received from our higher self, is often heard through a special medium, which we call our "inner voice". It becomes all the more audible the more we align with its frequency and the more we are prepared to follow it. At times we have heard our inner voices so clearly that we contemplated using them to create a new form of theater. That would be a meaningful, almost brilliant continuation of what was so far the self-expression in front of the group. I assume that this will occur. As an example, here are some statements that the inner voice spoke to one of our co-workers: *If you receive me fully, then I will give you directions and situations in which you need me totally, and where there is no room for forgetting me or doubting me. I am the voice of love, who wishes to speak in you and through you. Love is nothing sentimental. It is the other principle of living and acting (...) If you let me act through you, I am the voice of basic trust in the course of things. I have an answer to your every question (...) Therefore, do not worry about tomorrow, but remain with me, no matter what your past was like and what worries you may have about the future. I know your fears precisely, and I will not provide you with anything that you cannot deal with. Live so that you can believe in yourself; then the fear will slowly disappear.*

Not all prayers are fulfilled. They must come from our authentic core, and they must be compatible with both our own entelechy and with the building plan of Creation. We must all learn to pray in plain language about our true wishes, our true intent, our true joy, and our true goals. If there are falsehoods, bad habits, or superficiality in the prayer, there is a hiss in the channel and therefore no fulfillment. We need trust, truth, and precision in order to be able to believe in the fulfillment of our prayers. Finally, I would like to quote a morning prayer by Sabine Lichtenfels:

You know that there is fulfillment for your longing, provided that you connect with it fully and recognize it fully. You should know that your longing is unique and that it can only be fully recognized by you. As long as you see the longing of others as your own, you cannot find fulfillment and you will remain separated.

But you have stepped out of comparisons and you let your own longing speak for you. You know that your becoming speaks through your true longing and that this is the becoming of the world. You know that fulfillment is inherent in your longing as the water is inherent in the one who thirsts. The true knowledge of your entire self lies in your longing.

Since you know this, you have become calm, strong, and clear. You keep the seed of your power clear and unclouded. The gnawing longing and the impatience have left you, and you can calmly, day by day, listen to the answers that the world gives you and that take you closer to your goal, day by day.

Your true and unveiled longing is the voice of your cosmic being, which guides you safely and gives births to the self that you are.

An addendum to this section:
For those who think stringently, the following question may arise: if an individual wish results in reality moving toward its fulfillment, what happens when we have two different individual wishes, or ten, or six billion? Does not our whole reality get confused? Can there be a principle in the structure of reality which sees to it that the individual wishes and the prayers of any number of people are fulfilled, without creating total chaos? The question is legitimate from the point of view of the old dualistic logic, but it does not conform to the dialectic or holographic structure of reality. The individual actions that occur within a unified organism, for example the many different prayers, can be totally different and yet together they form the overall stream of life. It may be that a man's authentic individual wish does not immediately conform to a woman's authentic individual wish. If they both remain in the universal frequency, a chain of events will occur between them, which dissolves the contradiction. The individual wishes will complement each other instead

of colliding. This is true for all beings, if they are a connected part of the whole. They are like individual organs in a super-organism, and, if the overall control circuit is functioning, they cannot create any mutual disturbances. The same is true for the billions of cells in our bodies: they can fulfill opposite functions, but not contradictory functions.

We live in the eternally spinning fabric of a multidimensional holo-gram, in which every event has its own meaning for each subject, depending on its place within the whole. There is no contradiction bet-ween these meanings; instead, the result is a chain of events, a creative continuum. "Contradiction" is a static category of formal logical thinking, but in reality there are only processes. Georg Friedrich Wilhelm Hegel was the great discoverer of this different "dialectic" world. Today's discoveries in the field of holographic research confirm this view. Speaking a prayer is in itself the beginning of its fulfillment. If there were no fulfillment for a prayer, it could not be spoken with conviction. I will deal with this topic further later in this chapter, under the heading "The Haifa Manifesto". The things that we formulate as a wish or a prayer already exist as a possibility or a blueprint for the further development of reality, for we are a part of this reality.

The Circuitry of the Body

If we want to know how the universe operates, it is sometimes advisable to look at our bodies to find out how it really functions. All the wonders of the world are also in our bodies. What is special is that we ourselves are in this body and, if we learn to direct our attention toward the processes in our bodies, we can observe its way of functioning from inside. It is easy to understand the simile of the body. If we were to keep on enlarging the body we would finally have a system, which like the universe almost only consists of "nothing". The seemingly solid pieces of matter, such as bones, muscles, etc. would dissolve into a galactic fog with more or less dense energy fields. In between there would be nothing. It seems, then, that matter consists of "nothingness" in motion, i.e. of energy motions. Our body is like the body of an energetic vibratory system, in which all individual vibrations are in resonance with the whole.

There is something very mysterious about our bodies. If, for example, my little toe itches, then how do I know the place that is itching, and where does my ability to scratch the right place, even with my eyes closed, come from? Here, finally, we can no longer get around holographic thinking. It is no longer physiological or mechanical models, but holographic ones that provide the necessary answers. It is no longer the familiar world of linear cause and effect connections, but the new world of endless intertwined loops, circles and holographic projections that we need to enter in order to understand the living world. Here the real "course in miracles" occurs, in which every step we take as we discover our bodies can lead us to a new universal insight.

Let us go back to the itching toe. Somewhere in the body of the universe something is itching and my holographic positioning system recognizes where: it is the small toe of the left foot. The little toe cries out into the universe: please scratch! That is its prayer. Now something incredible happens, something that one needs to contemplate for a long time in order to understand and to believe that it is possible. The entire universe reacts to the prayer; the entire body bends over in order to scratch the toe. Is it not incredible what power such a small part has over the whole and how this whole puts its entire power and skills in the service of this tiny part? The universe bends over and – thanks to permanent feedback in the circuit between central control, the finger, and the toe - the finger finds the right place. All particles, all energy vortices and galaxies of the body, participate in fulfilling the prayer that the little toe cried out. Everything is put into motion to fulfill the prayer, and yet it all remains as well coordinated as it was before. We must let our mind dwell on this for a long time in order to get a sense of what is happening here. It is the most perfect demonstration of the art that is inherent in a holographically constructed world. At the same time it is the perfect demonstration of a prayer being heard.

In principle, it makes no difference if the prayer is sent as a neuro-physiological impulse from my little toe to my brain or if I consciously send a prayer to central control, for I, too, like the little toe, am an organ of the whole. Just as the universe of my body hears and fulfills the prayer of my body, my prayer is also heard and fulfilled by the universe of overall Creation. I regard this simile as being correct and precise. It shows the immediacy with which permanent communication and feedback occurs between a part and the whole. It especially shows us that a correctly spoken prayer **cannot** remain unfulfilled in an intact overall organism, provided the overall organism does not decide to injure itself. The little toe's prayer of "please scratch" cannot but be fulfilled unless there happens to be an important reason to postpone scratching, because other things have to be done first. We must allow the soul of the world this time, for it may say: wait a little while, for certain other things must first occur. If someone, for example, prays that the love with a desired partner may blossom again, then it is possible that the soul of the world, in the form of his/her inner voice clearly states that there is something that must be dealt with first. There may, for example, be a certain swindle or lack of integrity that must first be eliminated in order for trust to be able to grow. For this we do not need to make our way through any putrid swamps of the soul or fall into profound broodings, for the helping voice is often very clear and simple. One cannot doubt the existence of the inner voice. The broodings usually do not stem from any deep problem of existence having to do with the theory of insights, but from the fog of our old habits and ego games.

The fulfillment of prayers is not a question of our beliefs, it is a spiritual natural law. We are at the beginning of the development of a spiritual science, and the further we go, the more the basic knowledge of humanity comes up to meet us. During the developmental phase that lies ahead we cannot avoid discovering and using the laws of the spiritual world, just like the laws of a mechanical world have been discovered and used. For this, however, we need an inner ability that is clearly different from those that we have used before. We need the ability and the inner willingness to connect in everyday life with the vibrations of life and love. We need the ability to contact and communicate with the world. If we are in the state of separation, we cannot use the spiritual laws in a meaningful way.

Prayers only function in a state of connection. The divine world needs this connection in order to provide us with its wisdom and its power, just as the body needs the little toe.

The Meaning of Truth in the Divine Circuitry

Open the body, yours and that of the other,
through the "Mana" of your words.

The little toe that was just mentioned cannot provide false information to central control. It cannot lie, and it also does not have a psychological problem which makes it calculate and consider the reactions of its surroundings. It says what needs to be said. Central control receives a clear message, and it can therefore react just as clearly. With us it is different. We have a harder time with the truth, even among our best friends. We are afraid of the consequences of the truth, and when we are asked how we are doing, we usually choose the answer that is most socially accepted. Instead of admitting that we are suffering because we have a sexual longing for the partner of another, we say: "I have a back problem", "I just read this horrible article in the newspaper" or "I think I need another concept in the area of love". Instead of saying that one is engaged in an inner fight with a secret rival, one speaks of reacting to changes in the weather or of one's hormones being out of balance. The explanations that we all come up with are fit for a comic series. We all know these sayings, with which we "open up" to each other. Sigmund Freud called it "rationalizations" of a problem that could not or may not be named. We have to admit that we usually do not feel quite comfortable when making such false statements. We may be a bit bored, certainly a bit frustrated, about the fact that nothing much changes, but in the end we are usually pleased that nothing is stirred up. There are many people today, both men and women, who know of no greater fear than that of having to speak the truth in front of a group. In order to be able to speak the truth with joy, one needs a different social background and one needs to be embedded in a new human environment. One of the tasks of the new peace movement is to bring forth people who are able to speak the truth and to create spaces, in which it becomes possible to speak clearly and without ambiguity. I am referring especially to truth in the areas in which truth has seldom reigned: sex, money, and power.

When praying, we have a similar problem. Do we really dare to speak the truth to our highest religious partner, to God or Goddess or whoever it may be? Do we not have age-old fears of punishment and feelings of guilt that make us suppress the most intense things and "smooth over" information in order to be able to include it in our prayers, even when we are alone?

The issue of the truth is not a moral issue; it is an existential one, and – if we think of the terminology of the cosmic circuitry – it is a technical one. A prayer can only operate in the desired way if the information that it contains is true, if the wish that is expressed is true, and if what we are praying for is really what we mean. In all other cases there is interference in the circuit, and it therefore delivers false and undesirable results. People then say that their prayers did not have any effect. Before we say something like that, we must check to see if we were in a state of truth when we were praying. This is a kind of preliminary exercise for a spiritual life practice, which underlies the coming healing process. We cannot avoid the issue of truth. It is truly a decisive question.

The issue of truth is a problem. It often comes across as being moralistic and it becomes embarrassing and sounds like a confession. We can still remember the smell of such pious situations, and we're not interested in a repeat performance. I would like to emphasize that the project Meiga developed artistic group methods specifically to spare us such false piety. On the other hand we are truly dealing with something sacred. We are dealing with the truth and with the deep inner, religious power, which is connected to it. The truth can move mountains. We have often experienced how a whole group is transformed and the entire energy suddenly changes, when a person begins to speak from a state of truth. This is a mental-spiritual and bio-energetic state, which is immediately communicated to all those who are present, because we are all meant to be in this state. With every true statement that we make about the more sensitive things in life, healing occurs. Every such statement dissolves some of our historic armoring, which has blocked our energies. In the future, healing will occur through truth, not through more therapy. I do not mean the dogmatic truth of the founders of organized religions, but the elementary truth that children know – applied to the issues that we have as adults.

What has made our work with our unsolved problems and fears so difficult has been the fixed idea that we are dealing with private difficulties that are somehow due to a private defect, and that one therefore should hide from others as much as possible. I touched on similar issues in the section "Illness is not a Private Issue" in Chapter 5. In a holistic world there are no private problems. Every time we deal with a problem inside of ourselves, we heal a part of the world. That is the approach which we take toward ourselves, others, the world, and God. Here, too, there is a message. If you speak the truth, deeply and without holding back anything, then a power of entelechy overcomes you, which creates a chain reaction. None of the things that you feared would happen, and that were the reason why you hid the truth, actually happen. They only occur if, in addition to the truth, you allow for secrecy and swindles that would ruin you if they were discovered. Those who enter into authentic prayer are also determined to reveal these secret places and to clear them out. From then on, whenever one speaks the full truth regarding a decisive point in one's inner life, one is no longer the person one was before. The truth is contagious, and the human environment in which healing biotopes emerge will no longer react to truth with condemnation but with gratitude and liberation. We need truth and transparent information for our joint navigation on the new continent. **Truth creates trust, trust opens our channel, and an open channel creates understanding.** This is true both for communication between people and for communication with the divine world.

The Haifa Manifesto

Everything that we are truly seeking,
has been seeking us since eternity.
   (Old proverb)

During a trip to Israel, we stayed overnight in a monastery in Haifa, which had been converted into a hotel. There was a sign in the garden of the monastery, with the following text:

There would be no thirst, if there were no water.
There would be no hunger, if there were no food.
There would be no question, if there were no answer.
There would be no longing, if there were no fulfillment.
There would be no faith, if there were not the Divine.

What is formulated here is one of the deepest truths about the holographic world. The statement: "There would be no thirst, if there were no water" does not make sense with conventional logic, for what does the phenomenon of thirst have to do with the objective phenomenon of water? What do the subjective stirrings of my soul have to do with the facts of the objective world? In the holographic world, on the other hand, the subjective and the objective world belong together like an image and its mirror image. This leads to strange, but true statements, for example to the statement that the fact that there is a religious belief is the proof that there is a divine world. Or: the fact that humanity has this longing for love, home, and salvation proves that there is fulfillment. The fulfillment may not exist in objective reality, but as a possibility that is present in the building plan of Creation. It may lie in a different direction than expected, but it exists, for if it were not to exist, then the mirror image longing for fulfillment could also not exist.

Our inner longings, thoughts, and images are a reflection of the outer world and – I hardly dare say it – the opposite is also true. The outer world is a mirror of our inner thoughts and images. There is no objective world that exists on its own, there is only what we perceive when we set our movie projector in a certain way. The inner and the outer are two aspects of one reality. It is a "holo-movement", an evolutionary movement, which brings forth the "subjective" images of our soul on its inside and the "objective" images of the physical environment on the outside. Every longing is in resonance with what is needed in order to fulfill it. Every thirst is in resonance with the liquid that can quench it. We therefore say:

327

"Not only does the one who thirsts seek the water, but the water also seeks the one who thirsts." Thirst and water have emerged from the same basic mental-spiritual movement of the universe. They are connected in the same way that bees and sage are connected – a symbiosis that has been described perfectly in an article by Jürgen Dahl. Such symbioses result from a development which brings forth both the sage and the bee.

Once we have begun to pay attention to it, we find this unity and complementarity, for which we lack an explanation in a mechanistic world, everywhere in life. In the holographically intertwined world structure, two seemingly totally separate things form a unity, in which one cannot exist without the other. The story about the one who thirsts and the water is one of many. Certain healing plants, for example, start growing where people build their settlements. Furthermore, it has been observed that the healing herbs that are needed to treat certain chronic illnesses started to grow around the patients' houses. Here, too, we find the eternal principle of resonance in the spiritual world. Nothing exists on its own. The outer world and the inner world of humans are closely related and have the same origins. We all come from these origins, we have all recorded the knowledge of these origins in our cellular system, and we all have a corresponding longing for the source in us.

The clearer we can look our true longings and our real visions and goals in the eye, the clearer we see the image of a reality, which is waiting to be attracted and created by us. What we see may still be utopia, but by seeing it, we are already on the path toward realizing it. If I say to a patient: "Visualize your health" and if s/he is actually able to do this, then I know that s/he is on the path of healing. The transition from a vision to reality is flowing. What has once been seen is in a state of manifestation. One could not have seen it, if it did not (latently) already exist in reality. The Haifa Manifesto is the reflection of a great inner certainty. It is not just comfort for the tired and the poor; it is an insight into the structure of the world.

Chapter 10

Communities of the Future

Community as a Universal Way of Living

Only tribes will survive.

Vine Deloria Jr. (Native American spiritual teacher)

The original community of humans is not the family, but the tribe. The original community is the human vessel, into which all human life, including the family, is embedded. The community is a part of the Sacred Matrix. In it, the cosmic order connects with the social order. It is not bound to certain times or cultures, rather it is an integral part of our human social existence that lies beyond history. It could only be destroyed through violence, and it is only when we have found a full equivalent to it that is aligned with our times, that we again can enter into full and wholesome relationships with each other.

Community is the universal organ that has experienced the greatest damage. It is a necessary part of the whole, which was destroyed worldwide. Everywhere, where people were abducted, enslaved or sold, communities were annihilated, thus destroying the life nerves of entire peoples. This process began with the Kurgan people's invasion of Neolithic river settlements 7000 years ago. It continued as the Native American peoples of North America were annihilated by the European invaders during the 17th century, and we find it right up to the present day, when the last indigenous peoples on all continents are being driven out and destroyed in the name of commercial interests. The disappearance of human community left behind a bad wound in human civilization. It was through the destruction of community that humans lost their authentic morality and sense of responsibility. People were torn away from organic communities. Piece by piece, this also separated them from their own higher selves, from their higher knowledge, and from the higher orders of life. Community was and is the natural breeding ground for trust and solidarity. If this humus is missing, the uprooted human being becomes violent, evil, and ill.

The real power of the individual comes from community. A true process of individuation, which does not resort to the use of asocial methods, can only occur in community. Individuality and community are not opposites; instead they are mutually dependent and one cannot function without the other. Community without individuality leads to terrible collectivism (see fascism), and individuality without community leads to individual despotism or to the loneliness of a beautiful soul. Without community, the foundation for a full and healthy development of the individual is missing. Without community, the development of the individual always has a quality of forlornness, loneliness, the fear of separation, and general fear. One expression of the lonely soul was, for example, French existentialism. Our basic fear will most certainly only be fully overcome once we have succeeded in building new, functioning communities.

Community is an intermediate stage in the scale of life, and it cannot be skipped. It connects the individual with a higher order and sharpens her/his sense of the whole. A healthy community reflects a universal order, with which we can then connect easier. It is through this connection that a functioning community gets its high field-creating power. We find an original image of this order in the stone circle at Évora. The 92 (originally 96) erected stones reflect a tribal order and at the same time a cosmological order, which is possibly valid for all times (see Sabine Lichtenfels: "Traumsteine" ["Dream Stones"]).

The universal community is a unified organism, and the individual people are its organs. The liver acts differently than the kidney and the brain differently than the heart, and yet they all belong to the same organism. The people, who live in such an organism, do not live according to the principle of comparison and competition, but according to the principle of supplementing each other mutually. The system could not function otherwise. As the new organism emerges, a new mental-spiritual subject develops: the communitarian "I". This "I" is at a higher level order in the spiritual hierarchy of life than the individual "I". The communitarian "I" contains the knowledge and the power of all individual "I's". It also contains the structure of the order of the Sacred Matrix and it therefore guarantees the survivability of the community. All co-workers that are solidly a part of the community are connected to the communitarian "I" and its mental-spiritual powers, and they can therefore access survival abilities that they could not have developed alone.

When the first humans again enter into the state of community and when it again becomes possible to think and act based on this connection, then this will have a high field-creating and healing power. In a living universal community, the entire universal peace knowledge is developed, which once existed on earth and which is needed again today, in order to change the world and the souls. We learn the laws of universal peace by learning the universal rules of the community.

Individual and Collective

Today, communities have a bad reputation. It is believed that they are not compatible with a developed individuality. It is one of the core beliefs of the whole Western world, that individuality and collective are two irreconcilable opposites. In reality the situation is much more complex. Nature does create collectivist communities, in which the individual hardly plays any role at all (herds of animals, etc.) But it also creates communities, in which the development of a highly specific individual is a prerequisite for the functioning of the community (biotope, etc.). I call them "communitarian" communities. If people today resist communities, then they are thinking of collectivistic, not communitarian, forms of community. In reality, in human history to date, only collectivistic communities have existed. In the past, the development of the individual and the historical process of individuation had not progressed far enough to make communitarian communities possible.

The universal community is a communitarian community. It can be likened to an organism in which the individual people are its organs. The organs of a healthy organism have different tasks and functions; the liver acts differently from the kidney. The organism is a unified system, and the organs are characterized by their individuality and their differences. The unity of the organism is achieved by the individuality and difference of the organs. In other words, it is only when the full individuality of the members is developed that a healthy community can emerge. Community and individual are not opposites; they are prerequisites for each other. The prerequisite for a universal community is an autonomous individual, and the prerequisite for an autonomous individual is a community. That is the natural order in the building plan of Creation.

The structure of future survival-adaptive communities is always connected to the self-development of the individuals involved. The more they develop their individuality and the less they let themselves be ruled by preconceived dogmas and false authorities, the easier it is for them to recognize their chances of development in the community. At some point a deep process of individuation leads all human beings to not see themselves as private persons, but as organic elements of a human community. For it is through individuation that human beings experience not only what separates them from others, but also what connects them at a much deeper level. They dare to rediscover and accept this. It is as individuals that they find their universal dimension, and it is as individual human beings that they experience their connection to the universe.

Without individuation a healthy organism cannot develop. Instead we get conforming collectivism in which individual differences are not promoted but instead suppressed. Collectivistic systems do not tolerate individual autonomy. Instead, both toward the inside and the outside, they fight everything that does not fit into their ideology. The process of individuation must be suppressed, because it would disturb the prescribed uniformity. The inner cohesion is achieved by dissociating from others and through the fight against so-called "enemies". This is how the cruel collectivistic systems in history up to today have operated, be it the Christian church, Islamic fundamentalism, orthodox communism, national socialism, or every form of racism, but even such things as "party lines", "common sense" and bourgeois sexual morals. Today, the collective human being has been trained to react to other symbols – the symbols of fashion, lifestyle, consumerism, and commerce – but the principle remains the same.

Today, we are facing a historical turning point when it comes to the creation of communities. The old structures no longer function and the new ones need to be found. To what extent such structures can be developed determines if the human being can regain the basic values of living together: truth, trust, solidarity, and mutual support. Functioning communities of autonomous individuals are the basis for a humane world. In them, love, both emotional-spiritual love and sensual love, will be able to develop in a new way, for personal love begins to blossom wherever we begin to recognize each other in our specificity and individuality. A mature community will always protect this love.

Trust as a Life Quality

Healing biotopes are "greenhouses of trust". That is their deepest meaning. Communities function if there is trust between the members; it does not function, or only seemingly functions, if there is no trust between the members. They break down if the trust was bought through conformism or hypocrisy. The survival abilities that a future community develops will be effective to the extent that there is trust within the community. The methods that a community develops to further its inner cohesiveness are ultimately judged by if they are able to increase the substance of trust. That is the yardstick. Trust is the core power of a community. Without trust it can maybe take forceful action in the short term, but in the long run it will perish. Through hundreds of exercises and practices, through feasts and rituals, and through sweat lodges and nights of inspirational drinking, we have ourselves noticed to what extent this is determinant for everything that is important in the community. If true healing occurs in a community or not, and if the community can make human, mental-spiritual, and political progress or not, depends on the trust between its members. I am speaking of trust between the sexes, between love partners, between adults and children, trust in the authorities or leaders, trust between the center and the periphery, and between different project groups and age groups. If free sexuality is good or bad depends on if it produces trust in the community. If introducing joint finances is good or bad also depends on this.

Today, one often attempts to arrange things through slogans and through organization. If an organization is good or bad depends on the trust of its members. We have had a lot of time to discover connections in which true trust can arise between people. This consisted of joint preparations for theater productions, traveling together, going swimming together in winter, long volleyball parties, joint public appearances, painting pictures together at garbage dumps, fasting together, being ill together, being excited together. Especially the art courses and the spiritual courses created a special feeling of belonging, all the way to love. Right from the start, the most outstanding method to create transparency and trust in the group was the so-called SD (German: Selbstdarstellung [self-expression]). We do not have any easy answers. As can be seen in Chapter 6, we have tried out new paths to create a life without fear. We cannot connect a certain result with a certain method. Overall, a collective layer of trust emerged in the community, a trust that has slowly grown on its own.

Trust is deeply related to human truth, transparency, and the ability and willingness to allow oneself to be seen. If one is truly seen, this usually means that one is accepted. One strong requirement that is necessary in order to create trust is that all essential processes in the group be made transparent. There cannot be any secret fights and complicities regarding money, power, or sex.

Creating trust is not easy. The oohs and aahs with which people today fall in each others' arms as often as possible, celebrating the flow of warmth where there is none, are not a suitable method. Many groups fall apart because of too much sweetness, with which they cover their wounds without healing them. If one has the courage to stand up against the old habits of hypocrisy and bootlicking, one will have to be very persevering. Groups need a highly developed mental-spiritual and human concept in order to be able to create true trust. If they do not have a concept and instead put their trust in the spontaneous development of their positive emotions, the old powers will ultimately win. Almost all groups in the 20th century fell apart because of their inability to deal with conflicts in the areas of sex, love, power, money, and recognition. Due to this historic fact, the issue of trust has become a basic topic for our continued existence. We therefore had to develop the unusual that I described in chapter 6.

Trust is the primary healing power of the soul. If one is fully trusting, one does not need psychotherapy or any other special methods. The soul heals itself if it can breathe and exist in trust. There is no power that can set the self-healing forces into motion more powerfully than the power of trust.

For the creation of communities in the new culture, there is no higher goal than to create trust. It is an unprecedented adventure, for the qualities that we bring from existing society are not at all suited for this. We had to disguise ourselves in order to survive. We need functioning communities in order to learn to trust again so that our powers of peace become more forceful, allowing us to survive. In the structure of the future communities, we step by step access the sacred knowledge which enables us to connect with the universal powers and the higher orders of life. We thereby enter into the highest level of trust: the true, daily, trusting cooperation with the divine powers. Before that, we should clear out the paths between us. May the following two chapters show even more clearly what possibilities we have at our disposal to achieve this.

Community as a Way of Enlightenment

True community with people
must come about through cosmic participation.
It is not the special actions of the "I", but it is the goals of humanity
that bring forth lasting community among people.

(I Ching)

One of the strongest powers of survival is the spirit of the community. When an "I" can be replaced with a true "we", a different state of being begins. One's private biography is replaced by a communitarian one. We are here dealing with one of the most fundamental transitions from the old to the new form of life. The only place where we find similar transitions is in the areas of Eros and religion. Many people, including the most committed ones, needed decades in order to understand and undergo this transition. This is not surprising, for the conventional structures of living together in society forced the individuals to protect themselves from others instead of opening up to them. These defensive structures became second nature to them, so that a different type of existence was hard to even imagine. One can imagine twelve people going on a sailing trip, having joint experiences in the desert for 10 days, or staying at a base camp in the mountains, maybe even taking part in an experiential workshop for several weeks. This is all imaginable, but living in community for one's whole life, always with the same people? Maybe we can help in overcoming these worries by taking a closer look at what community will mean in the future.

Community is a "Tao", a path to enlightenment. Like all enlightenment, this enlightenment is slightly different from what one imagined after having taken one's first LSD trip. It does not immediately bring the eternal light, but it brings a new human quality that one can trust. One becomes a human being that one can trust. The others notice this. The Goddess notices it too, for she loves such people. People, who have lived in community for a long time, stop saying unnecessary things.

The communities that I am referring to are never static; they never stop developing, but are constantly growing. They grow to encompass a certain size, and then they split in order to be able to continue to grow freely. We do not need to speculate about a critical size, for we will notice this soon enough through experience. In my experience the number is not around 50, but rather around 500, maybe more. It depends on how strong the idea is, which has brought the people together and how strong the people

336

are that constitute the core group. The upper limit is reached when the people begin not to know each other. This is probably the case at a size of around 3000. We thus arrive at a maximum size of future settlements that approximately corresponds to the largest settlements in the Neolithic era, provided that they have grown organically and are not based on male dominance. In the beginning, the first healing biotopes will consist of a few hundred people. But that is enough to fall in love again and again and to find interesting partners.

We can take our time when it comes to finding our so-called partner for life, for we will be together in any case. The fact that we stay together has an unusual and deep effect on the soul. We no longer need to make an impression. We can take our time and be thorough. Nobody has to make a bond for life after having experienced the first fantastic night together. The most decisive questions can be approached calmly and in sobriety. The continuity of living together means that people get new faces. We can no longer think of wanting to own someone, neither sexually nor in any other way. We can sense the issues with which individual persons have come to earth and the place in the community that gives them the best chances to develop. We can sense which people belong to the same cosmic group and therefore are connected to each other in an especially deep way. We can see possible groups of friends, and we stop throwing sand in the gears. We see the possibilities that open up in a community, as soon as it has clearly passed the limit of about 20 members and has entered into a stage of having a conscious joint will. Human solidarity and mutual support arise naturally, if we have been together long enough and if we have had enough time to peek behind all the masks. The ethic of the love of our neighbor no longer comes from moralistic laws such as the Ten Commandments, but from people living together organically. Many moral goals that we had to fight hard to achieve as Christians become very easy to fulfill. Participating in the communitarian "I" is participation in a higher order, in which we find the values that were destroyed through a false cultural development.

The highest values are trust and cooperation. More than anything else, they guarantee the survival of the community. They form the foundation for a necessary spiritual life practice. We need spiritual powers to survive the coming apocalyptic times. Also, a healthy spirituality requires healthy and truthful relationships between people. One of the main aspects of this is truth in sex and love. Again: human beings will learn to be truthful in areas where they so far had to swindle – in the areas of sex and love. They will learn this to the extent that they become a part of a true community.

By this I do not mean truthful in terms of confessions and moralistic truths, for life is full of play and high spirits. I mean the inner, true, existential truth, which shines through in human relationships when one no longer needs to pretend. There is maybe no greater relief than this.

Peace Work in the Community

If we want peace on earth, we need functioning communities. If we want functioning communities, we need – simply said – a revolution of our image of the human being and of our concepts of life. This follows from what has been written earlier in this book.

Peace and healing mean almost the same thing. When I speak of peace I do not mean paying lip service to peace, nor do I mean being morally upset about existing injustices. I mean true peace, which fills us with joy and power. This is a power, which no longer is afraid of the forces of violence because it can stand up to them and is superior to them. Building a power for peace is connected with an encompassing new process of insight. We can only produce as much peace as we have peace inside, and we can only mobilize those powers of healing that we can create and realize within ourselves and within our communities.

Peace work in the community is mutual healing work and support of those involved. A community develops a growing power for peace if its members engage with each other in a healing way. Healing here means to be creative, full of humor, alive, and truthful. We needed many years in our community project to find out what an active power for peace truly is, in addition to simply being the absence of strife. The real path of healing consists of an increase in a **mental-spiritual** power, through which true trust, true unity, and truly free love can become possible (see Chapter 6).

A community becomes all the more healthy and powerful to the extent that it has solved the issues of trust and love. For the issue of love we need to make an excursion into the land of the soul. Fred Frerk, a plumber and electrician in Tamera, a real muscle man, who loves to go kayaking and play handball, once said: "For an edge-walker, the ultimate edge is love." Like many others who have gotten involved in our adventure, he has noticed that he is truly able to love. His yearlong partner, the belly dancer Birgit Schenscher from Stuttgart, was enthusiastic about his strength, confused because of his helplessness, angry about his clinging ways, and deeply touched by his honest staying power. Together, they will celebrate a "chymical" wedding. Tamera is a project for all lovers to come together, no matter how deeply they have misunderstood and mistreated each other. Sometimes short separations are good. We sometimes need this pause, this time of contemplation, in order to understand what love means. Once we have understood this, we can understand the purpose of the coming culture. But the lovers, who have separated temporarily, should have the possibility of finding each other again at a new level. That is one goal of our planned communities.

Love is more than an emotion. Most emotions tend to block our path toward love. By suppressing real feelings, human life became flooded with false emotions. Therefore, an emotional body stuck to our souls and our bodies, and it reacts immediately, before anything has really been observed and understood. Today, this emotional body is praised due to its spontaneous and supposedly honest qualities. What emerges from the emotional body is today called "culture", "literature", "music", or "love". In reality it contains all the hatred, disappointment, and mistrust that has accumulated in us during a very taxing historical era. The emotional body is praised in the media, and it is protected against intellectual analysis by referring to thinking as "mindfucking". Most media of our times have united in the fight against authentic thinking and promote the emotional body in one way or another. The thicker the emotional body is, the thinner the power of thinking is. It is the task of our future schools **to find a way for us and our students to dissolve the false emotional body, without losing the power of our hearts.** At the point where we are today in our historic development, this is a precondition for **true** learning, opening, understanding, and love.

The love that we aim for in our healing work arises through a long process of experience, mutual perception, and insight. It is often preceded by much despair followed by new hope, or by anger at a certain person, followed by gratitude toward him/her. Love is a mental-spiritual process, which lets us dismantle our emotions, our stubbornness, our anger, our vanity, our resentment, our fervent joy at the failures of others (which we all share), our arrogance, and our tendency toward hasty judgments. This is the beginning of an evolution, which is based on the slow unveiling of the secret, which we call "love".

In functioning communities, an invisible mental-spiritual subject arises, which slowly but surely takes over from our private thoughts and decisions, and changes them. I call this subject the "communitarian I". Those, who have begun to take on responsibility and to fully serve the community, take part in this higher level of consciousness that is referred to as the **"communitarian I".** Now an inner process of insight and healing begins, which is deeper and truer than anything external therapeutic measures can bring. One still orients oneself toward one's own, so-called "personal" interests, but one increasingly senses, seeks and finds the connection to "the others". One begins to look past one's own plate and to honestly take an interest in the lives of others. This is an experience all of its own, and it is usually a new one.

"The others", that we now begin to see, are the participants of our community, the guests that arrive, and one's friends. But also our brothers and sisters in the Ukraine, in Chechnya, in the Czech Republic, in Bosnia, in Kosovo, etc. Sometimes we thereby rediscover people who we had forgotten long ago, people from our own life history, earlier friends, relatives, or lovers.

This kind of participation in the lives of others is first of all a very new experience for many of those who want to join a community. They come from a world of homelessness, loneliness, and distrust, where they could remain above water only by using their ego power. At first they try to continue their habit of playing ego games. If it is a good community, they notice that this does not work. The egoism that they had worked so hard to achieve due to all their disappointments in life, no longer makes sense; it is no longer an "evolutionary advantage". Now comes the inner point of decision where they choose either the old or the new possibility in life. Many settle for their old lives, but they keep an eye on the new one that we are offering, so that they can maybe make a transition later, but still just in time.

The communities of the future need the necessary knowledge and a concept to take them out of today's antiquated way of thinking. In today's global and historical situation on earth, an antiquated way of thinking means to be stuck in old ideas of a private fulfillment of love, of a whole and healthy family life, and of sweet children. What a beautiful world could have arisen in the American Southwest if the builders of the "home sweet dome" had not had such a sentimental concept, but a realistic and revolutionary one! If the members of a community – once they have built their houses and created their gardens – retain their ancient way of thinking, their ideas of love and of home, their old ego games, their contrariness, and their competition, then no force for peace and no survival concept can be realized, no matter how beautiful their houses and their gardens are. There is no doubt about it: we all still love the romantic linden trees at the gate, the little flowing fountain, and the summer houses of love. There are feelings there that we do not want to lose, but we know that this is not enough to save us and our world. This will not happen until the necessary prerequisites have been fulfilled.

One of these is the first change of the inner assemblage point: the transition from the ego "I" to the communitarian "I". This transition has not been brought to a close in any community. It is, of course, not only an individual process, which everyone must carry out for him/herself, but rather a historical process, which is now being initiated. If we want to survive, we cannot bypass this historic step. We must walk the path of the communitarian "I", for the old collectivistic concepts of community are not workable. The newer concepts of the individual "I" and of the autonomous individual, as they were developed especially during the 19th and 20th centuries, were anthropologically false to begin with. They were connected to a false image of the human being – an individualistic image instead of a communitarian one. But there is no private existence in the universe, for all existence is communitarian. It is only on this basis that the individual forces, which every communitarian system needs for its self-preservation, can develop freely. Individual autonomy and community are not contradictions; instead they are mutually dependent and complement each other (see Chapter 7, "Individuality"). The strived-for freedom of the individual, which is connected to the concept of autonomy, can only be realized in community. Functioning individuality is not a private enterprise, it is a community endeavor. A functioning individual is not an isolated system; instead it grows from a web of multifaceted relationships and contacts. It is only in a functioning community that one can risk putting away one's mask and showing oneself the way one really is. This liberation from having to play one's old role is the first prerequisite for the development of a truly autonomous human being, who determines his/her own life. I wish all participants that they make this discovery and experience this relief.

The future community begins with community among people. But wherever it is experienced and understood, it has no limits. When we enter into connection with each other, we are connected with all of life, for we are universal beings, and our universe is ultimately the community with all living beings. It is in the union with the whole that the individual finds his/her highest fulfillment and his/her highest power.

That is a power statement for the future: It is in the connection with the whole that the individual finds his/her highest power and perfection. Teilhard de Chardin once said: "A higher existence is a more encompassing union." A new source opens up through the connection of the individual with the community.

The emergence of the communitarian "I" marks the beginning of the participants' crossing over of boundaries. It may be new in the healing paradigm of our time to see the desired overcoming of boundaries not as a result of private exercises, esoteric introspection, or therapy, but as a result of entering into community. This transition from a private to a communitarian biography initiates the decisive healing process. The communitarian "I" emerges, and I feel a new perspective for my own life. I "grow beyond myself". I get real visions of the one existence and of community with all living beings. Step by step we notice that we share a truly common life with the animals, the plants, and with every living thing, and also with all beings that we cannot see physically in our incarnation on earth. Step by step, the communitarian "I" develops and grows, and thereby incorporates more and more of the world. We begin to look at life in a new way, and we discover new connections. This process cannot end before we arrive at the source from which we all came, and this source is the entire living universe, it is eternal life, eternal divinity.

Those who have embarked on this process and who have understood it from within are engaged in a special kind of development, and they attain true humanity. They develop the ability to help others through very simple words or actions. By helping others they are on a secure path toward their own healing. In one of our early communities we said: "Tao is the path that one cannot abandon; the path that one can abandon is not Tao."

The possibilities of the communitarian "I" are greater than those of the individual "I". The communitarian "I" can develop abilities which the individual "I" either cannot develop or can only develop through extensive practice. Some examples of this are the ability to make it through times of need, to overcome crises, to love without jealousy, to not hate one's enemies, and to let go of feelings of revenge. The more the individual is connected to the communitarian "I", the more the law of the creation of fields comes into play. We experienced this principle very strongly during our project phase in Schwand during the Eighties. According to this principle, once we have succeeded in mobilizing the communitarian powers of the community, the basic forces of life, and the creative powers of the Universe, we no longer have to do and achieve everything through our own power. This constitutes a core thought of our political theory of global healing work, and it is the reason why functioning communities have high chances of surviving difficult times. There is no reason to die if one is well embedded. The original form of connection and protection is the human community.

Community Self-Sufficiency

How independent and self-sufficient does a community have to be in order to be able to survive during the coming decades? To what extent may it be dependent on the existing supply systems? In what areas should one as quickly as possible try to achieve full self-sufficiency?

Full self-sufficiency in all areas is only necessary once the existing supply and money systems have broken down completely. We do not know when that will be, neither do we at the moment need to know this. Self-sufficiency is important in the areas of water, energy and healing (and increasingly nutrition). This should be achieved as soon as possible in the communities and centers of the future.

Water: In order to guarantee the necessary amount and quality of drinking water, it is necessary to have a water supply of one's own, either from a source or well of one's own or from water tanks. According to Schauberger's insights and methods, the amount of ground water and spring water can be regulated (see the book "Living Energies" by Callum Coats). If one has free access to the water and to the landscape, it is probably possible to guarantee access to the minimum amount necessary by planting suitable plants and arranging for shade, as well as by influencing the tellurian flows (energy flows in and above the earth). Schauberger also made interesting statements relating to the origins of water. As our insights into this area increases, it is probable that we one day will have the knowledge necessary to make water ourselves. If we connect Schauberger's methods with those of anthroposophy (Rudolf Steiner, Theodor Schwenk) and the technical and spiritual methods of modern healers of water (Plocher and others) the necessary water quality can also be guaranteed. Even relatively polluted water can be transformed into good drinking water through suitable whirling processes, through the input of information, by creating certain vibratory and spiritual cleansing fields, and by artificially creating wild water courses that are similar to those in nature. We need to realize that water is also a life body. It follows that every stream and every pond has its water devas that one can ask for cooperation.

Energy: Future communities will develop their own energy systems, which are technically and mental-spiritually different from the traditional systems of energy supply. Already a hundred years ago, new possibilities for producing energy were developed through the work of Nikola Tesla.

344

Since then, all the research carried out under the name of "free energy", "cosmic energy", "tachyon energy", etc. has had the goal of accessing useful energy from the cosmic energy, which is present everywhere. The Methernita Group in Switzerland, the Damanhur group in Northern Italy, and other groups are working with these ideas, and some have developed functioning systems. In America and Japan the first free energy motors exist, supposedly delivering a few hundred horse-powers. It is only a question of time before we have a general field of self-sufficiency in terms of alternative technologies. The traditional forms of energy production, from hydroelectric and nuclear energy to using fossil fuels, cannot be used. They endanger the environment, and the conditions under which crude oil is extracted and transported in pipelines is barbaric. At ZEGG (acronym for Center for Experimental Societal Design), a community that we cooperate with in Germany, the cars have been rebuilt to run on normal plant oil. Their performance remains practically the same.

Here we are facing one aspect of the self-sufficiency issue: to what extent, and for how long, can we justify living from things that are produced under such inhumane conditions? According to our Political Theory (see Chapter 11), the coming healing biotopes can only function if their information of peace is free of contradictions. But it is not free of contradictions as long as we use products on which there is so much blood that we become accomplices. **Self-sufficiency is necessary for ethical reasons.** We would not like the taste of any bottle of milk if we could see the conditions under which it was produced. Unfortunately, this is also true for many technical devices that have become a natural part of our everyday lives. In terms of their organized exploitation and destruction of nature, the corporations that produce them are almost all criminal associations. The key question is increasingly clear and urgent: with whom do we want to cooperate, with nature or with corporations?

Healing: From what has been described earlier in this book, the need for self-sufficiency in the area of healing is obvious. The need to gain access to complicity-free products means that we need to increasingly separate ourselves from the products of the pharmaceutical industry. The healing knowledge of the new communities makes it possible to use very different healing methods than the ones used by established medicine. The understanding of life that is connected to the new matrix requires an entirely different way of dealing with illness and health than what is normal in society. I even suspect that, in healing biotopes that are well run, we will no longer have illnesses of the old kind. Healthy bodies and healthy souls will arise through a deeper contact between people, through a rediscovered trust in life, through the liberation of the organs through free sexuality, through cooperation with nature, through healthy nutrition, and by using locally growing healing plants.

An important area of self-sufficiency is the entire field of schooling, education, training, research and teaching. It is clear that the children in future communities cannot in the long term go to regular schools with their traditional curriculum. For their creativity and their sense of purpose they need an entirely different teaching program regarding nature, research, and art. It is also clear that the youth can no longer attend the training courses of middle-class society, for there they will not get the training they need as peace workers of the future. All future communities will establish their own primary and secondary schools, training centers, research laboratories, and universities, in which they themselves will develop the new research approaches of the new culture.

We are in the middle of a process in which we have to say goodbye to the life habits and consumer habits of the old world. The need for self-sufficiency requires a more spartan way of life. This is also desirable for spiritual purposes. It is surprising to see how easily and quickly a community can shift according to the new requirements, as soon as they have "gotten it". Taking full responsibility for developing a non-violent model of consumption without complicity requires that those involved make a basic decision whereby they can more solidly grow into the programs of the Sacred Matrix. Enjoying the wealth of the earth, promoting one's ability to enjoy pleasure, and at the same time developing a non-violent consumer model – now that's an interesting future.

Children in Community

We know that they come from another state of existence.
We will watch them
and we will learn from them.
We will give them guidance,
but we will not make up their minds for them.
We will see to it
that they carefully switch over to a new state of existence,
and that they thereby forget as little as possible.

Sabine Lichtenfels

I begin with a very conservative statement: children need someone to call MAMA from the fullness of their hearts, and they need someone to call PAPA from the fullness of their hearts. This is an immanent archetypal structure in life, which needs to be fulfilled in order for a child to be able to grow up healthy, without fear, and with a sense of security. In other words, the child needs stable structures, stable people to relate to, and a stable feeling of home. The more stable this home is, the more self-assured the child will be, when it one day makes its excursions to discover the world. Like a reeling young kitten, it always needs to be able to come back to the nest after such adventures. This kind of thinking is contrary to the way that children come into this world. Most of them are without a home right from the beginning. The solid structures that a child needs are as a rule provided neither by conservative nor liberal parents. Parents, whose love lives have died, can maybe give their children a stable home, but not a warm nest.

In functioning future communities, the children's nest is not limited to the family, for around it is an interesting community. Children, who feel at home, have a very generous concept of family. Sometimes, out of sheer fun, they seek out other mothers and fathers to live with for a while until they maybe choose others. That is normal, for if there is trust between the adults, then the children trust the adults. Like adventurers, if they are allowed to trust, children enlarge their terrain and their family. The basis for raising children in a healthy way is that the adults live together in a healthy way. Under the social conditions of the old matrix, this has not been the case for a long time. In order to be able to grow up healthy inside, children need the human environment of a good, solid community.

Children are cosmic beings, just like we are. They do not come to earth like sweet babies with a clean slate, but as mature spiritual beings, with a longer or shorter karmic history behind them. In this sense, we do not know if they are older or younger than we are. A newborn child, who is lying in front of me, could have been my great grandfather. Is it therefore older or younger than I am? This question of age according to the calendar has no meaning, and we would be well advised to see our children as cosmic beings and not artificially make them smaller than they are. We can learn a lot from them, if we regard them as cosmic beings. We can see how their way of perceiving the world is still connected to cosmic memories. We recognize the incredible alertness, with which they sometimes look at falling leaves or at clouds that go by. They are often on a real trip, and it would do us good to join them on this trip. We could thereby more easily find the inner space that connects us with the "beyond", from where we all come. Many of the things that children babble about come from experiences from "over there". They have forgotten much, but they still know the aura, the energy of the spheres, and light. They are awed at what they find every day on earth. If we could see things as openly and as freshly as they do, then we, too, would marvel at existence every day.

Children live in immediate contact with everything that is alive or that they see as being alive. They learn through observation and participation. But they do this in their own way. Otherwise, they could not learn their mother tongue in two years, without taking a single lesson. We must learn to understand what they are doing, for here we are being shown a way of life that could become ours one day, once we have rid our lives of stress.

Children must be protected from the too many desires for contact that the adults have. They must especially be protected from too early entering into the private relationships that the adults like to engage them in. A mother, who enters into a possessive personal relationship with her child, robs the child of its freedom and binds it to her rather than to the world. The child will react to the desire for relationship, and it will become demanding, impatient, whiny, and blackmailing. It will scream, not out of pain, but out of anger. The whole world today is full of the angry screams of children. They all have parents, who much too early entered into an almost symmetrical relationship to their children. In this way, the children lose their early role models and the possibility to orient themselves on earth. They only need to scream and the adults will come. This type of overprotection is poison for the free development of a child. If the child itself could see through these connections it would cry out and beg: "Please do not follow me around just because I'm screaming. I don't need any puppets. Be the solid anchor, to which I can always return. I need you, and I must be able to trust you. I am a child and I need adults that I can believe in." It is very difficult for many modern parents to understand this point. First, they had to set their authority aside, and now they are supposed to take on true authority again. I cannot help it; they need to learn it. A child needs positive authority and guidance from the adults to orient itself; it sometimes needs a clear rejection of its insistent wishes; and sometimes it needs a definite no! During a lecture I once told an outraged person in the audience: If you really call that "brutal", then children sometimes need this kind of "brutality", which consists of not being its servant all the time. Maybe I should have chosen my words more carefully, for soon thereafter the Bulletin of the Protestant Office for Philosophical and Ideological Issues published an article with the title: "Dieter Duhm preaches violence against children".

There are many mothers, who do not want their two year old child to call them "Mama" but to use their first name. They thereby unknowingly rob their child of its Mama.

If a child is drawn into the adults' wishes for relationship at too young an age, it quickly loses its cosmic existence and memory. If a mother wants to have her child for herself, the same thing happens as between love partners: the child develops an incomprehensible anger toward its mother and at some point it goes off into the world as a warrior and fights the Goddess. The child must be protected from the emotional advances of the adults. Usually, this insight is most difficult for the parents themselves. There is another thing that is difficult for them: that the child does not belong to anyone, not even to its parents. The child has sought out a certain parental home, in order to realize a life plan and not in order to belong to these parents.

One cannot capture a child for oneself, neither through overprotection, nor through excessive offers of gifts and other goods. At some point a child will react to this with hatred. The uncontrolled consumerism, with which the children of our consumer society are fed – even by fairly intelligent parents – brutally separates them from their source and turns them into little monsters that want to have everything. One day they will exact revenge for this deceit. Someone, who as a child has repeatedly received chocolate instead of love, cannot but become evil and cynical inside. These children then turn into adults who lie to and blackmail their love partners because they can no longer believe in love. The parents of these children, who themselves mostly grew up during the anti-authoritarian movement, have lost a great dream of life, for the movement did not achieve its goals. They now pass their resignation on to their children. The children notice that the parents have no dream or goal any more. What should they believe in, if their parents no longer believe in anything?

That is the situation of a child in today's society. Maybe I have described it too gently, for it constitutes one of the major tragedies of our time. Many parents despair and do not know what to do. The Sacred Matrix has an entirely different situation in mind for the children. We find this described in detail in Sabine Lichtenfels' book "Traumsteine" ["Dream Stones"]. The children live in community. The entire community carries the responsibility for the children. There are no property rights whatsoever between parents and children. The community creates a kind of circle, of which the children have a large part for themselves. There we find – to use today's words – a "Children's Republic". This relatively independent children's facility was an essential element within many highly developed cultures. In modern literature we have rediscovered it in reports about the Indian Muria tribe, which is now disbanded. There the children and the youths lived in their own village, the "Ghotul", and they determined their own rules for life and their own sexual order. During the time of the stone circle at Évora there was no static family membership, but the children were firmly embedded into the tribe and into a certain age group. In their age group they learned to connect with nature beings in their own way and to enter into a process of discovery. Under the guidance of adults, they learned the basic things about the plant world and the animal world, about healing plants and moon rhythms, and about geography, geomancy, and astronomy. Relatively early they knew what the ant roads mean, how they arise, and how they are connected to the weather. Early on, they could speak with animals and ask plants if they were healing plants. Our children today also develop surprising abilities in this area if we do not stop them. The knowledge that these early humans developed, can be found in us all.

Our children are the carriers of the new culture. I have experienced what joy they feel in the moment when they discover their parents anew, when they love us again, when they believe the adults again, and when they can trust their authorities again. They love the world in which parents are parents again, where adults are adults again, and where role models are real role models. They love being able to ask the adults questions and get meaningful answers or help. They are willing to do anything to help the earth, nature, the plants, and the animals, if we put our knowledge at their disposal without making their decisions for them. They are cosmic beings and they have the ability to learn incredibly fast. Maybe some of us will come back to earth as newborn babies when they, our children of today, have become old and wise. Perhaps we then will be their grandchildren and will listen reverently to their words. Some of them are such incredibly beautiful beings.

Grassroots Democracy and Individual Autonomy

Public opinion could always
stop the best from happening,
but never the worst.

    (Karlheinz Deschner)

The community of the future is an original, communitarian, grassroots democracy, free of domination. This follows from the basic principles of the universal community. But we must know what grassroots democracy means and what conditions must be met by the group members for them to be truly able to exercise grassroots democracy. The word "grassroots democracy" has become a catchword for all those who want to protect themselves from authority and domination. The concept has thereby lost its meaning. For many directionless people, grassroots democracy means that they settle down somewhere in a community, that nobody can tell them what to do, that they get to discuss everything even if they haven't got a clue, that nobody is allowed to be better than they, and that any differences that might exist are leveled as much as possible. The differences are always leveled down, never up. The success of this approach can usually be seen quite quickly: a sleepy group of bored characters who aren't really interested in anything and who therefore need stronger and stronger stimuli in order to do anything: alcohol, nicotine, stronger drugs, new enemies, going on rampages. If then the new thoughts of free sexuality and self-healing enter into their minds under such conditions, there is total chaos. Many young people, who in the beginning were truly committed, have today become depoliticized and resigned because of their participation in such groups.

We need a concept of community that makes it possible to dismantle the structures of domination and develop decision-making processes in which all community members participate. That is a very ambitious concept, for everybody must be able to take on responsibility and think productively about the issues that affect the whole. They can only do this if they have left their private status behind and entered into a communitarian status. As we have seen, this is a fundamental change of one's attitude towards life. Without this inner change, there can be no grassroots democracy. In order to become capable of democracy, people must change their inner structures. We come from a long history of domination and subjugation. One is the mirror reflection of the other. As soon as those who were subjugated came to power, they immediately began to subjugate others.

This structure is a part of the collective character of humanity and it exists up to today. This is one of the reasons why the leftist revolution never could have worked. It had not developed any truly new inner human structures.

People have learned to either exercise power or be subjugated. The German people's longing for a strong man (Hitler), the Russian people's longing for a strong man (Putin), the Catholic population's longing for a head of the family (Pope), the spiritual seeker's longing for a great master (guru), and people's longing for the highest leader and guide (God) constitute a piece of history that is imprinted in all of us, without exception. This longing for a (positive) authority has never truly been fulfilled, leaving behind incredible anger and disappointment. For many people, their original longing for authority has developed into an angry rejection of all authority, but that simply constitutes the reverse of the same coin. Anti-authoritarianism is nothing else than a fixation on authority with a negative prefix. In both cases we are dealing with an internalized "authoritarian personality", as Adorno called it. In both cases, the idea of true autonomy is not even present. It is rebellion, but not autonomy. Rebellion always needs an outer enemy. Groups, which are held together through rebellion, quickly disintegrate once they no longer have an enemy. If they are too weak to fight the real enemy, i.e. the societal conditions and those who uphold them, they create substitute enemies: people with a different skin color, from other countries, or with a different concept of religion or sexuality. Today we can see this principle in action across the political scene, from the right to the left.

Autonomy is independent of such categories, for it occurs within, and it is a part of the developmental process that every person goes through as a part of the phase of self-reflection. Autonomy is a process of insight and self-insight. It is the innermost process in a person's soul, resulting in a person taking responsibility for his/her life, no longer making others responsible for his/her actions. It is the decision of every true revolutionary. Once the decision has been made, one cannot simply rebel the way one used to, for one would first have to rebel against oneself. There is no point in fighting outer structures that one has not dissolved in oneself. If one is fighting an outer power, but would like to be powerful oneself, one is playing a false game. The same is true if one is fighting the abilities of others, because one does not have them oneself, or if one attacks the leader of a group, because one wants to take his/her place. It is not honest to get angry at being dominated, as long as one is not able to walk a true path of one's own. It requires courage and much thought to truly walk a path of one's own. Autonomy is a high goal. It requires a process of inner individuation, which liberates us (not verbally, but in reality) from every kind of domination.

People, who walk this path in a consistent way, are automatically attractive to others. People congregate around them, and they are natural forerunners and natural leaders – even when they do not want to be. By taking on the new role, they suddenly find themselves in a situation that they never wanted, for they share the anti-authoritarian point of view. They do not want to have power and dominion over others, nor do they want privileges and being waited on. They inevitably find themselves in a difficult situation, for now they, who have walked the path of autonomy, are attacked by those who used to be their friends and now accuse them of authoritarian behavior. The supposed friends from before inevitably make this accusation, for they have not themselves walked the path of autonomy, and they therefore react with anger and envy. This process is repeated a thousand times in all groups that do not have a concept. It is one of the main reasons for the failure of so many groups. In the name of autonomy, a merciless fight is fought against those who have the courage to walk the path of autonomy and to realize the declared goals in their own lives.

We must be clear about the fact that grassroots democracy has never existed in our culture of the old matrix, and that when people start to create the structures of a true grassroots democracy, something new begins to occur in the history of communities. From then on there can be no more followers, for grassroots democracy depends on the self-responsibility of its members. Here, I would like to quote a passage in the book "The Circle Way" by the Native American teacher Manitonquat.

In a small circle it becomes very clear that everyone has to see himself as responsible. Everyone must be a leader. It will otherwise be exhaustingly difficult for the one or the ones who carry the responsibility. They will be left in the lurch; they will feel overextended or isolated. They will soon be the target of anger and reproach. They are doing something good for everybody, and nobody is making it easier for them. They are hardly honored at all. What they need is the support of the circle; people who recognize and support them in their general tasks. They need everybody to take responsibility and think like a leader.

In a circle everybody is a leader. This means that everybody takes personal responsibility for the entire circle. To take responsibility means to think about what is needed and to share this with the whole circle.

I would now like you to consider the possibility of taking on leadership yourself and to design things the way you want them. If this seems to be overwhelming or impossible, then stay with me a bit longer.

Here we see the issue of grassroots democracy in a new light. It means to take on leadership for the issues regarding the community, to take on responsibility for the entire circle, to no longer engage in endless discussions, but to be a role model instead of waiting for others to do so. Here, personal qualities are demanded that in the beginning most group members are not prepared for. They must be learned. A strong and resilient community consists of those who have acquired these qualities. They are the natural authorities and the natural representatives of the community, and they are also seen as such by the representatives of other communities. Among themselves they choose the various group and work leaders. The leadership structures in a grassroots democracy are based on competency, contact, and trust, not on dominance. People who are stuck in the old power structures should not be given any leadership functions, for otherwise the result will be fear, competition, moral cowardice, and a lack of transparency in the group. In badly functioning groups, the problem is often that one or more people from the old power structure are at the top and nobody has the courage to do anything about it. These people are like a heavy lid on a barrel that is slowly but surely breaking up beneath them.

Grassroots democracy is a new force in a new world. It is not connected to antiauthoritarian behavior and private moods, but to the responsible participation in building the community and to the decision to create a self-responsible, autonomous, and communitarian life. The communitarian "I", which carries the community through difficult times, arises from all individual "I's" who have made this decision. It is through these individual "I's" that the new evolution is being prepared at this moment in many places on earth.

What Holds a Community Together?

After a hundred years of failed community experiments since Monte Verità in Ascona, Italy (which also failed), one is justified in asking: What holds a community together, what stops it from failing, and how is its power increased?

First of all it needs a strong idea, a concept, or a goal, which is more than a personal desire for contact and a feeling of home. Some examples would be building a peace garden, establishing a children's republic, a school of transformation, an encompassing energy project, an art center, a media and communication center, etc. The more its concept corresponds to an objective necessity, the more it will be supported by the universe.

Secondly, it needs good methods to deal with human conflict. It needs a mental-spiritual concept, which remains effective even when human relationships threaten to break down.

Third, it needs a few responsible people, who have the strength to stand up for the community idea even when many things go wrong. It needs an unusually strong staying power.

Fourth, it does not need any top dogs or territorial thinking; instead, it needs cooperation among those who have taken on the main responsibility. A prerequisite for the creation of any community that has taken on a larger task is a permanent circle of responsible people, without secret competition for power and position.

Fifth, it needs a clear infrastructure. Every member should know their place and their task. Like every organ in the body, every person has a special function within the whole. Once a certain size has been reached, it is important to have a precise division of labor and a clear assignment of leadership functions.

Sixth, it needs a leadership structure that is free of domination, consisting of persons who are natural authorities, because they have the corresponding human and professional abilities, and because they have the group's trust. The character of these persons must be so mature that they do not misuse their position for self-interest and power. People with the old power structure are not suitable to function as leaders, even when they themselves immediately want to take on leadership roles. Future communities should neither have an authoritarian nor an anti-authoritarian basis.

Seventh, it needs the professionalism of their members. For the whole to develop, it needs a direction and a will that is not influenced by the momentary feelings and moods of the members. Freaks and hippies were often quite nice people, but they could not create functioning communities.

Eighth, in order for trust to grow, all important processes and decisions must be transparent. Especially in the areas of sex, love, authority and power, money, and economy, it is necessary to create transparency using suitable methods (such as self-expression or forum) and clear communication. Otherwise, the community will soon fall victim to hidden conflicts.

Ninth, it needs sexual vitality and liveliness. It will otherwise become rigid, ideological, or boring. In the past, communities either fell apart because of the Eros or else they suppressed it. Community and Eros were two opposing concepts. In reality, a free and honest Eros can only develop on a communitarian basis. For this to occur, the normal hindrances must be overcome in an appropriate way (see Chapter 5).

Tenth, it needs the re-commitment to the human basic values of neighborly love, hospitality, trust, and mutual support. It needs the connection with the issues of humanity of our times and with the universal source of life. The more general human validity and meaning it has, the more power it will receive. The task then grows, the will strengthens, and new possibilities become visible. Behind every project – be it a peace garden, an art or a technological center - there is a life concept, which becomes more encompassing the longer we work.

Eleventh, it needs authentic songs, feasts, and rituals. For every community that develops and grows in a healthy way there comes a time when it celebrates its own feasts and finds its own rituals. This is when thankfulness and celebration naturally transform to a festive form of life. Suddenly the community finds songs of its own, its own icons, mantras, and signs that focus its power and joy of life. At some point, every community of the future will begin each day with a kind of joint celebration.

Chapter 11
Political Theory

Evolution through Field Formation

Life is a universe of unlimited possibilities. Which of them will be realized depends on what information dominates on earth and is at the disposal of living beings at a given time in evolution. Every new piece of information changes old facts and makes new ones possible. Boundaries that up until then had been seen as immovable are shifted. There are innumerable examples of this in the areas of science, technology, and sports. The phenomenon of field creation probably applies throughout the scale of life, from the greatest global changes down to the smallest things in everyday life. The development of the art of printing books, the invention of the steam engine, the discovery of electrical current or nuclear energy, and the development of lasers and computers all resulted in changes in the entire field of human civilization. The field of intellectual or physical abilities can also suddenly make a jump. When Armin Harry ran 100 meters in 10.0 seconds 44 years ago, a new "field" was created for sprinters. Sixty years earlier the field was at 12.0 seconds. The runners' personal efforts were probably about the same, for it is not primarily one's personal ability, but new information or a new field which brings forth the improved performance. A new "program" has taken control. In our group adventures, we used the advantage of field creation when trying out new things, such as jumping from towers, fire-walking, deep sea diving, or spending a long time in icy water.

Whenever a boundary is moved, all participants in the group are able to connect to the process. The performance to date can then be greatly surpassed without the participants needing to undergo any special training or effort. Throughout history there have been reports of almost limitless field effects relating to human resistance against cold, hunger, pain, and fire. Entire tribes have been saved from the most extreme conditions through field creation. An especially clear example of historic field creation comes from the time when the Gothic cathedrals were built. In the middle of the 12th century, the first Gothic cathedrals were built in France under the direction of abbot Suger, resulting in a chain reaction, which went far beyond the borders of France. Everywhere, Gothic cathedrals were built in a completely new style, based on new static principles, new proportions, and a new scale. The rules governing how to build were broken in almost all regards. How did this explosion of knowledge, skill, and art occur? A field had been created, prepared by the School of Chartres, the Templars, and the building lodges. Its power knew no limits, for it had touched a deep image of entelechy of the people of the Middle Ages. After a long period of inner maturation, the result was suddenly there. What is true for short periods of time is also true for the great epochs. It was always global fields that characterized the great stages in evolution and in human history.

The development of life on earth occurred in waves and steps. When amino acids had joined to form the first cell some 3 – 4 billion years ago, the field of single-celled organisms arose on earth, and the oceans soon teemed with them. At the next level, the cell nucleus developed, as did cell colonies and multi-celled organisms. Every new developmental stage is connected to a new set of information, which is quickly spread across all life on earth. Every new piece of information overcomes a boundary that was there before, opens up a new possible development, and creates a higher and more complex structure. The result was the emergence of fish and other larger inhabitants of the oceans. At some point they left the water and transformed into amphibians. They were able to perform the miracle of being able to live both in water and on land and also to breathe. A new field arose for the development of lungs instead of gills – of itself an incredible "technical" feat! At some point in this great laboratory of Creation, the field for mammals emerged, and then – according to the traditional calendar some 10 million years ago – highly developed mammals began to walk on two legs. The field for the development of human beings had been created.

The evolution of human beings also occurred in steps and through fields. The most important steps – such as the taming of fire, the creation of tools, burying rituals, building the first houses, and erecting sacred stone sites – probably occurred everywhere on earth at the same time. When the wandering nomad tribes began to settle down, domesticate animals, and grow crops (about 10,000 B.C.), a new global field was created: the field of the Neolithic revolution. Thus began a new phase of human cultural development that was characterized by storage, property, constancy, and tradition.

A particularly intense transition in the development of human life on earth occurred during the patriarchal revolutions. They created a new field of domination and violence. A field arose for creating metal weapons, conquering, killing, destroying nature, building great empires and monolithic power blocs, introducing the great world religions, subjugating women, suppressing sexuality, forcing monogamy onto the population, making life technical, industrializing, capitalizing, and today digitizing. The matrix of violence kept on developing from one stage to another until its last stage of "globalization" had been reached at the end of the 20th century. By reaching this stage the matrix of violence has triumphed. But this triumph cannot be permanent, for it destroys the foundations of life and thereby itself. The overall life on Gaia/Earth is in peril, and the outer cosmic order has been destroyed (but lives on in a "veiled" state).

We are now facing a new field creation of global dimensions. As was the case with the previous ones, this field creation will change global learning, as soon as the necessary information is available. The new developmental level that we are facing today consists of the re-connection of human life with the basic rules of the earth, life, and all creatures, and with the laws of Creation. The information that is necessary for this to occur is already present in the form of entelechy. We have it deep inside our "memory", and we can access and realize it. It is the overall information for the coming "universal state of being". Non-violent technology, cooperation with nature and its beings, holistic thinking, partnership of the sexes, free love, and a new spiritual consciousness are today no longer hypothetical concepts. They are real developmental stages of a global transformation, which is already underway. The healing biotopes have the historical task of acting as catalysts, amplifiers, and accelerators in this world process.

Overview of the Political Theory

The biotopes project described in this book follows a theory of distribution and realization, which we call the "political theory". In the following I will provide a brief description of its basic thoughts and its logical structure.

Worldwide peace work needs a global concept in order to be able to stand up to the existing economic and military concepts of globalization. Only a global concept can have the strength to disempower the global matrix of violence. The peace concept presented here assumes that the Gaia-Earth with all its inhabitants is a living unit, an organism. A unified organism can be influenced and changed through the introduction of suitable information. This input can be made from one or a few places on earth. If it follows the basic laws of life, it will have a field effect throughout the entire organism. The transition from the old to the new matrix will not follow the old principle of tests of strength and power struggles. It will follow the principle of changing information. Healing information, introduced at a place which has been blocked by the information of fear and violence, can call forth a change in the overall organism. Today, due to the emerging holistic world view, we have new healing possibilities that could have an effect on the entire planet. We live in a time when it is possible to realize the greatest ambition that the human being can have – restoring peace, freedom, and harmony on earth – in alignment with scientific thinking. We are thereby in a race with the opposing powers; it is objectively urgent. The Political Theory offers a concept with which the race can be won. It contains six parts:

1. the holistic structure of reality;
2. the unified structure of information of life;
3. the field principle;
4. the new information;
5. the reality of concrete utopia; and
6. the healing biotopes project.

1. The Holistic Structure of Reality

The holographic or holistic world view assumes the unity of all existence. The world is a unified whole. The structure of the whole, its information, and its laws can be found in all its parts and can also be influenced by all its parts. In his book "The Pulse of the Universe", George Leonard writes the following:

Since every particle of the universe constantly produces wave fields and every organized combination of particles also emits its own distinctive field, the number of intersecting waves is practically infinite. Theoretically, one could create a kind of super-hologram, which contains information from the entire universe from this point of view.

In other words, the overall information of the universe can (in theory) be accessed at every point in the universe. If we were able to see into the innermost depths of a single place in the universe, we would see and understand the entire universe there. In addition, what occurs at a single point in the universe is determined by the overall events in the universe. Also, the entire universe can be influenced from every point in the universe. These are logical conclusions from the quote above.

The whole exists in all of its particles and the super-hologram of the world can be seen in its every detail: in the structure of an atom, in the spiral structure of a snail-shell, in the neuron connections in the brain, and in the molecular composition of the genetic code. The stamp of the world is everywhere as a kind of high density cosmogram. Everything is an aspect of the same one existence and the same one consciousness, which exists in the whole. In a religious sense we could also say: the world soul, which operates in the whole, also operates in all its parts.

2. The Unified Structure of Information of Life

In the biosphere there is a place where the overall information of life is imprinted in a special way: in the genetic code of the nucleus of the cell. In all living beings the basic mathematical structure of the genetic code is the same. It only differs in its level of differentiation. This means that the same basic information of life in a mussel also exists in a cherry tree and in a human being. This is truly awesome! What modern natural science research has brought to light corresponds to a true "course in miracles". The Political Theory takes note of such miracles. Here we have a sure indication of the unity of the bio-body that all beings belong to. There is only one existence and one consciousness. We can therefore – provided we use the right frequency – communicate with a snake, a toad, a rat, and even with flowers and trees. The inter-species communication which we are seeking, the cooperation with animals in terms of global peace work, has been provided for by the plan of Creation. This possibility results from the fact that there is a universal structure of consciousness operating in all beings.

Here, I would like to point out an interesting discovery that was made thirty years ago: the striking parallel in the mathematical structure of the genetic code and that of the Chinese I Ching oracle. In two such different areas we find an almost identical world formula. The unity of existence could not be illustrated better.

3. The Field Principle

New information that is introduced into a unified organism operates in all its parts. New information that is introduced into a part of a unified organism operates in the entire organism. New information that is introduced into a population operates in all its individuals. New information that is introduced into an individual operates (latently) in all individuals of the population in question. All members of this population take part in this learning process. For all of them a trail is blazed, making it easier for them to learn the new behavior. An example of this is to climb Mount Everest without oxygen – an important piece of information for the population of mountaineers. Once Reinhold Messner had achieved this, many others could do it, too. Certain paths in the neuron patterns of the brain and certain connections in the chain of molecules of the genetic code are activated, resulting in an increased readiness to behave in the new direction. The principle of "morphogenetic field creation" is applicable to cultural, political, and global developments. If the population consists of all of humanity, then new modes of behavior, which are important for all of humanity, will create a readiness to behave in a new way on a global level.

The biosphere is a unified organism. If I introduce suitable information into it, then this information operates in all its elements, i.e. in all humans, animals, plants, waters, etc. If the information stems from the Sacred Matrix, it will reach all beings, either openly or in a hidden way, for all beings, including humans, are at least latently in resonance with the Sacred Matrix.

(The biosphere consists not only of its materially visible forms, but also of invisible spiritual beings (devas) and the energetic and spiritual lines of connection between the beings. One can thus easier imagine their spiritual unity, which Teilhard de Chardin called the "noosphere".)

If we introduce a new, well tested, and proven set of information of trust and cooperation, then this information operates in the sense of new field creation. In all elements of the whole, a certain behavioral readiness is now actualized and the probability that this new behavior will emerge is increased.

In summary: the Gaia-Earth is a unified body of life. Its organs belong together like the organs of my body. In a sick body, a single pill may suffice to animate all the cells and organs of the body in the direction of health. The pill introduces healing information into the body, and all elements of the body follow it as in a field. What is true for the body is also true for the entirety of all bodies in the life body of Gaia-Earth. The field effect is based on the holistic building plan of Creation. This is a great opportunity, which we have today; it may be our only chance. If we follow it, we are entering into a completely new direction of political thinking. What is, then, the "pill" that we need to introduce into Gaia-Earth in order for peace and healing to occur?

4. The New Information

The new overall information, which is to be introduced into the bio-body, concerns the central areas of human co-existence and co-existence between humans and nature. Key concepts for this information are: community without domination – solidarity and the coming together of the sexes – trust instead of fear – cooperation with nature, animals, and all creatures – nutrition without complicity – non-violent technology – a spiritual life practice, and a universal state of existence. The new overall information comes from these areas of experience. It emerges when the individual sets of information from these areas become congruent and begin to vibrate in the same direction, i.e. when they become coherent. Then, a unified, coherent frequency of thinking and acting emerges, which enters the noosphere as overall information. It is the information of trust, unity, and cooperation. The result is a fundamentally "universal" state of being, in which all life is connected, communicates, and cooperates with each other. The peace workers, who work in these areas, find themselves in a common vibrating, coherent frequency of consciousness. There may be no contradictions in the new overall information, which we introduce into the noosphere, or else there will be "static on the line". Here, high ethical standards are placed on peace workers. One of our slogans is: "If, as a peace worker, you do something that disturbs your own inner peace, then at this moment you are in a contradiction."

It is necessary to re-think all areas of life. If, for example, we truly want friendly cooperation with animals, then we must stop seeing them as consumer products. We will use (vegan) products that are free of complicity; we will use less and less cosmetics and medicines that have been tested in animal laboratories, etc. We do this, not due to an outer set of morals, but because of the logic of facts. Every peace worker, who understands this logic, will be glad to follow it. One should know of these things, but not immediately turn them into dogma or laws. If one does, the result will be inquisitorial structures. First, we need to understand, then act on a trial basis, then understand deeper, then act more thoroughly, then understand fully, and then act radically. If we act consistently, there are further consequences: We cannot live in a vegan fashion and at the same time watch how animals are killed in the world without doing something about it. We will thus continue to build the information of peace by taking certain actions in the world, maybe already in our neighborhood. Living in a rural area such as Alentejo in Portugal, some of us in the healing biotope have begun to visit those farmers, who let their donkeys and horses run around on their fields with their front legs tied together, speaking to the farmers about it in a friendly manner. If we do not do things like this, then in a sense we are in a contradiction and there is static on the line again. Following the Political Theory requires that we consistently engage in new behavior in the small details of our lives. If the actions that we take are not aligned with the great overall information, they have little effect. But if they occur within the framework of the overall information, they resonate with the great system, Creation, the bio-body of the earth, and with its structure of information, its basic functions, and its spiritual laws. These actions are in resonance with the dream of the world (see next point). Such actions, taken day after day by a strong community, together form a power that enters the life body of the world and sets a new course for all beings. It creates a new readiness to act, opens a new direction for development, and makes new decisions possible. It is the goal of the healing biotopes to make this happen.

5. The Reality of a Concrete Utopia

We do not have to invent the desired future, for it is – latently – already contained in the present. It must be accessed, seen, and made conscious. This is a true process of envisioning. The young Marx wrote the following to Ruge:

It will become plain that the world has long since dreamed of something of which it needs only to become conscious for it to possess it in reality.

This means that we only need to become conscious of the world dream in order to "possess" the content of the dream, i.e. realize the dream. We find a similar train of thought in the beautiful poem by Joseph von Eichendorff:

367

There's a song slumbering in all the things, that now dream on and on, and the world commences to sing, if only you find the magic word.

In all things there is thus the same song of the world, the same dream. It is a question of recognizing and realizing this dream of the world. Ernst Bloch called it the "nondum", the "not yet", the "utopian latency" or "concrete utopia". This nondum has a latent (veiled) but real existence. It is a subtle matter image of reality, which is inherent in all forms as a real blueprint and a real possibility. It is as with holography, where the original image – in a latent or "veiled" form – remains untouched behind the distorted images of a holographic film. If I direct the reference beam toward the film at the right angle, the undistorted image emerges through the distortions. The same is true of people: if I look at a person with the right attitude the true image of his entelechy appears.

The existence of concrete utopia makes our work easier. Our efforts to develop new life structures are met from within by a power, which guides us and makes it possible to do things that we otherwise could not have done. There are many examples of this. We are sometimes overcome by a complete calm and sense of security during an automobile accident. What is that? In the middle of a tumultuous situation with someone who so far has been my enemy, I suddenly experience feelings of understanding, sympathy, and true compassion. What is that? In a violent revolutionary situation, I suddenly deeply experience that this is the wrong path. What is that? – It is the real presence of our "higher gestalt", our "light gestalt". It is a real part of "concrete utopia" or of the Sacred Matrix, which is always present. This is important in terms of dialectic and holographic thinking: concrete utopia is not only a subjective or arbitrary human vision; it is a real blueprint of reality. In the holistic concept of reality, the objective and the subjective aspects of the world belong close together. We saw this in the Haifa Manifesto: "There would be no thirst if there were not also water to quench it."

A dream, vision, inner image, and concrete utopia constitute the inner light of a coming reality that is already present in real latency and that has incredible effects. It lies behind all metamorphosis in nature. According to the aborigines, the plant is the "dream" of the seed. The cockchafer is the "dream" of the larva. The butterfly is the "dream" of the caterpillar. We can see what a powerful dimension is at work here.

A real piece of future reality comes to light in a vision that has truly been seen and found. It is through the vision itself that the realization comes closer. The Russian mystic and scientist Solowjew stated that all actions and thoughts that are aligned with the harmony and unity of the world promote their manifestation.

6. The Project of the Healing Biotopes

Healing biotopes are places on earth where a living system is developed according to the basic qualities of trust, a sense of belonging, and solidarity with all living beings. They are birthplaces and transmitting stations of the new information, places to learn and experience the Sacred Matrix, and social and ecological vessels for collecting (and disseminating) healing energy. In order for the right information for a non-violent way of existing to be transmitted to the noosphere, the healing biotopes must have enough complexity, duration, experience, and members. (As mentioned earlier, the smallest number of co-workers necessary to bring forth the overall information probably lies at around 300 - 500.) Many years of practical experience are needed for those responsible and the co-workers to know clearly what it is all about and what changes are needed in their own way of life. When they begin with such a project, a process of revelation begins, challenging them to constantly take new steps and look in new directions.

Healing biotopes emerge when the time is ripe. This seems to be the case today. The idea of the healing biotopes is not a private invention; it lies as a "mental-spiritual blueprint" in the spirit of the times. It has a high "utopian latency" and a high drive toward manifestation. What runs through us as an idea and a will corresponds to a tendency in the universe.

Once the information of the healing biotopes has been developed far enough, we will probably see a global chain reaction: as soon as the new information that is developed in the first healing biotope reaches a critical size in terms of energy, density, and precision, the probability increases dramatically that similar centers emerge in other places on earth. This occurs of itself based on the field principle (see point 3). As soon as the new matrix has materialized at one place on earth, there is a high probability that it materializes at other places too, due to the field principle. It is still difficult to express this process in numbers. Maybe 10 further centers in 15 or 20 years? It is not so much an issue of the number of new centers; what is important is their power and the cohesion of their information. The more encompassing the new information is, and the more precisely it comes through, the more probable is the possibility that the existing system "topples". The noosphere is then, so to speak, pregnant with the new information, and the old information of violence no longer receives any projections and dies. The outcome of the power struggle between the old and the new matrix is determined by processes of information. The new global civilization will emerge from places such as the network of new centers. To the extent that they conform to a blueprint of the universe, the healing biotopes are the real germ cells of a new era. Wherever new beginnings are possible - after all the dead end streets, wars, and destruction – the healing biotopes can be the enzymes of a new era.

The Non-Violent Overall Information

The overall information that is introduced into the continuum by a healing biotope consists mainly of the insights that have been made in the areas of sex and love, community, cooperation with nature, spirituality, and art. Here, the key experiences take place that lead to new life forms. From a certain level of maturity and experiential explicitness, the overall information is taken in and transmitted further by the continuum, provided that it fulfills the necessary prerequisites. What characteristics must non-violent overall information have, in order to be able to be taken in by the biosphere and by humans? What characteristics must it have in order to lead to a global change in consciousness?

1. It must be **complex.** It must be high up in the mental-spiritual hierarchy and thus have a guiding power. What does this mean? A certain set of information is higher in the mental-spiritual hierarchy the more knowledge, the more aspects of reality, and the more life force and meaning it encompasses. In short, the more complex it is. Complex does not mean complicated, it means encompassing. Complex things can be very simple, such as, for example, a cell. Wherever in evolution two contradictory sets of information meet, the more complex one will prevail, as long as the following conditions are fulfilled.

2. The new information must itself be **without contradictions.** Some simple examples: if a vegetarian does not eat meat for ethical reasons but still walks around in a fur coat, s/he is sending out contradictory information. If someone takes part in a demonstration for peace but inside is full of hatred and thoughts of revenge, then we get static on the line. If medical healing work is connected to mass murder of laboratory animals, no positive healing information can result. If a society creates a law saying: "Thou shalt not kill", and if the same society produces weapons, then this can only result in the creation of an information field of lies. The mental-spiritual ecology of the entire planet is today suffering from such false information. This is not material, but mental-spiritual environmental pollution.

3. It must be **compatible.** Its structure and developmental direction must be compatible with a higher system. It must also correspond to the "software of Creation", i.e. with the possibilities inherent in the whole, especially the possibilities for change. It must also conform to the inner

371

forces of germination and processes of Creation at a given time, as well as its direction of development and perspectives. This depends on the historical state in the evolution of consciousness. Today, for example, it must correspond to a planetary tendency toward overcoming all boundaries of race, religion, and nationality, toward holistic and spiritual thinking, and toward an ecological consciousness that sees the earth as a unified being.

4. It must be **necessary.** It must correspond to a deep need of the human being and of all other living beings. It must comprise an encompassing answer to the cry for help by the human being and the earth. The concept of necessity should not be understood superficially as the short-term alleviation of distress, for this often increases the long-term distress. If we today ask evolutionary theorists what characteristics have proven themselves in the overall fight for life, they will, among other things, mention such qualities as cunning, mistrust, deception, and violence. These qualities were necessary under the life conditions of the matrix of violence. But seen as a whole they were not advantageous for evolution; they were an immense obstacle. The global necessity for the new information of peace unites the life interests of all participants at a common, more conscious level.

5. **It must work.** It must prove itself in practice that the information of peace works and that it is superior to the old information. This requirement is obvious. It is true for the new concepts of love and sexuality, as well as for those of ecology, technology, healing, etc. The new overall information can therefore not be developed at the computer, for it must result from a life practice that is as multifaceted as possible. Its superiority can be seen in the growing powers of love, insight, and survival ability of its responsible members. Ye shall know them by their fruits...

If a set of information fulfills these five conditions, it has a good chance of asserting itself worldwide. We are dealing with "genetic" information, true information of Creation, which determines the further course of evolution. From now on, we ourselves are responsible for the further direction of evolution of life on earth, for we live in the era of globalization. We have the real possibility of globalizing the forces of peace. If they are carried out correctly, local actions have a global effect. Up to now, we have believed that God knew what needs to be done. Today, we know that this fully automatic God does not exist without humans. It is we who are a seeing and reflecting organ in the universe, and it is our perception, decision, and ability to introduce new information into the body of the world that determine what will follow. Once we have understood the idea of the Sacred Matrix and follow it, God or Goddess, life and the universe will meet us with all their powers. They are following the higher functional logic, which has been described as "God's Circuitry" (see Chapter 9). We then no longer work against the world, but fully with it. Those who understand these thoughts understand something about the project of the healing biotopes.

Not through One's Personal Power, but through Field Power

The caterpillar does not become a butterfly
by its own power.

This is wonderfully related to fields. It relieves us from the necessity of knowing how to do everything ourselves. Without being able or wanting to do a lot of explaining, we here discover a secret of our entire evolution, a universal method of becoming. The field is the instrument with which the universe has reached its goals. The field is a power which helps life do things that nobody could have done on their own. It operates everywhere and at every moment. If we ask a spider how it builds its web, we will hardly get a meaningful answer. This is not just a language problem but also a problem of competence. When the spider is building its web it is not following its own intelligence; it is following a global spider field. We can go up and down the ladder of evolution and everywhere we find organs, living beings, behavior, and survival strategies that do not come from the intelligence of the beings, but from the field of information, that guides their actions. This is also true for humans. If somebody believes in God or in Marx, or in exclusive love between couples or in free love, is a question of the field that s/he belongs to. If s/he thinks materialistically or spiritually, if s/he practices violence or non-violence, if s/he seeks the highest life energy in war or in love, is a question of the collective field. Today, for example, there is a collective field for the belief in the Big Bang. After Einstein there can be no intelligent scientist who has truly thought about this and seriously believes in the Big Bang, for s/he will immediately know that a linear concept of space and time has here been projected onto the origins of the world in an improper and un-relativistic way. Yet they follow this nonsense, for there is a field for it on earth. This is an example of a negative field at work.

On the positive side we have the indisputable fact that we do not have to learn everything with great effort through our own power, as soon as field forces are at play. This is true for sports, technology, and culture. It is also true for spiritual and emotional issues. If someone finds her/himself in a community in which jealousy is not a part of love, s/he will at first resist it through especially intense attacks of jealousy. If the field is stronger than her/him then s/he will accept the message with great relief and after a short period of time be amazed at how easy it can be to love without jealousy. It usually takes a while to believe it. Mental, emotional, and spiritual processes, too, follow the field principle to a great extent. We have thereby made a surprising discovery, which we only can present as theatrical satire: that most of our problems and our issues of love, especially those that seem to be completely honest and dramatic, in reality come from an old collective field that keeps operating until there is a convincing new one. As soon as the new field is developed enough, the venerable old problems fall away like leaves in autumn, if we allow them to. There is something like a spiritual gravitational force that is directed backwards. It makes us repeat the same problems and face the same difficulties again and again, although in reality a new situation has arisen that could liberate us completely from this old film. Sometimes one must simply wake up from a long sleep consisting of repeated habits, in order to notice that a new life pattern lies ready.

For the communities of the future, it is of central importance what fields they create. Once a certain level of inner development has been reached, it will, for example, be necessary to leave the old ideas of love and sexuality, nutrition and consumption, all forms of complicity, the supposed natural laws of jealousy and competition, the habits of smoking and drinking alcohol, and emotional suffering. We know how much inner conflict is connected to such a transition, if it is done individually. In a functioning community, the transition can occur immediately without any difficult cases of relapse and withdrawal. It is the field that does the work for the individual. During our art courses, we regularly experience how people, who have never painted, paint incredibly good pictures. In the Mirja School for Peace we experience how people, who have always had a problem speaking in public, suddenly hold grandiose speeches. These are all field effects. They occur in all areas, for example when it comes to learning foreign languages or songs, new eating habits, getting up earlier, changing one's working times or work load, punctuality and precision, humor and tolerance. The community must know what it wants to prioritize and then deliberately begin to create fields. This makes unnecessary discussions superfluous and creates a climate of good and high energy. We can clearly see the effect of fields in the healing work. If a community has created a healing field, people become healthy without having to do very much. Good group facilitators have the noble task of building a good field for their group.

All this is also true for the high and complex goals of global peace work. It is not through our own power, but through the power of the field that we can spread the new thoughts and life forms. It is not through our own power, but through the power of fields that the old matrix will transition to the new one. It is not through our own power, but through the power of fields that inner spaces that so far were occupied by our ego open up to divine powers. What has been said above about the overall information is also true for creating a field force. The same five conditions apply when it comes to a field asserting itself globally. A further condition must be fulfilled: it must be supported by the undivided, unambiguous will of the participants. True will is the gate through which the cosmic forces can enter into our work. Our old mentor Prentice Mulford has the following to say about will: "For those who desire, the whole universe is the placenta for their work."

15 Essential Points for Peace Work and the Political Theory

If one works for God one doesn't count the hours of overtime.
  Gothic master builder

Here I would like to summarize some of the basic thoughts about peace work that have been expressed in this book. Maybe one or the other statement can contribute to making the journey easier. The statements that count are always those that our minds and our hearts have understood.

1. You can only bring about as much outer peace as you have realized peace inside yourself.

2. Your personal problems are not your illness, but your task. You serve the whole earth by taking them on and solving them.

3. Inner peace comes about through the sense of security and connection with something greater: connection with life, community, the universe, and divinity.

4. Reconnecting our lives with the Sacred Matrix is therefore one of the prerequisites for successful peace work for a non-violent world culture.

5. It is through this reconnection of the earthly world with the divine world that we receive the power and the authority that we need to overcome the difficulties that otherwise would be insurmountable. The stronger the connection, the greater the power is that is on our side. It has no limits. We should be tolerant of our own doubts and relapses.

6. It is through this connection that we receive the power to change our thought habits, let go of our secret thoughts of violence, and no longer react even to the greatest meanness with thoughts of revenge.

7. We overcome fear through connection. If we remain centered even in the middle of dangerous situations, we are protected against all dangers. "The wild buffalo's horns find nothing to gore, the tiger's claws find nothing to tear, and weapons' points find nothing to pierce" (Lao Tse in Taoteking). Full connectedness leads to a high level of psychological and

physical invulnerability. Even if we feel that this is taking things too far, it is still a direction which is given by the structure of reality.

8. If we succeed in breaking the chain of fear and violence at a single point, then the entire chain loses its stability. There is then a high probability that it breaks at other places, too. The unexpected then occurs, and love enters where there used to be enmity.

9. If you succeed in replacing the old reactions of fear or hatred with an act of peace at a single point in your life, then you have carried out an exemplary change that has a field impact on other people.

10. In this sense, working on one's own person always has an added political dimension. Even the smallest twists can have a field-creating or even global effect, if it is in resonance with the matrix of life and with a possibility for all humans.

11. Every thought and every action sends information into the ether. It is transmitted like radio waves. If it is in resonance with the Sacred Matrix, it operates in all things. That is the basis for the political field theory and for the idea "Act locally, have a global effect."

12. It is a matter of creating encompassing information of peace that corresponds to the basic laws of sacred life. Once it has developed to the point of being unambiguous and without contradictions, it has an effect at all points on earth.

13. In order to create such complex, unambiguous, un-contradictory, and realistic information of peace, we need social and ecological spaces of our own, in which this information can be developed. We call such spaces "healing biotopes".

14. According to the laws of field creation, as soon as the first healing biotope exists and is functioning, there is a high probability that similar centers will arise at other places on earth.

15. This is how the new network of humans on earth arises; it is the federation of healing biotopes and of all groups who operate in this sense. They form the core of a new human civilization in real cooperation with all creatures.

Tamera – Establishing the First Healing Biotope

The Healing Biotopes Project has been described in its various facets in the earlier chapters of this book, so I do not need to describe it in detail. In summary:

Our existing civilization has spread the code of violence over the earth. Healing biotopes spread the opposite code: the code of trust, cooperation and solidarity with all living beings. For this code to have a global effect, a field must be created that is in resonance with the plan of the earth (and with the matrix of Creation). For this field to appear, the code must be understood, transmitted, and realized by a sufficient number of people. This is the next step in the new direction of human evolution. We must also create places on earth, where the basic information for a non-violent earth can be developed in a meaningful and efficient form and be input into the ether or noosphere.

In order to find and implement this new unit of information into concrete life practice, we need communities that realize the life principle of healing biotopes at different places on earth and on different continents. These communities will be connected with each other through a living network of contact, information, and cooperation. Together, they will form a new global "field", as described earlier (Chapter 11). It is through this global field that the next level of human development is initiated. It already exists in the information plan of our cells, as the Sacred Matrix in the building plan of Creation, as a real future in the cosmic data bank, and as an ancient utopia. Healing biotopes are places on earth, in which the changeover to the new matrix is implemented through the highest possible commitment of all the inhabitants, so that it can occur worldwide. They are crystallization points of the new society on earth.

The basis for the work is the creation of functioning responsible communities with a human and technical infrastructure that can handle the coming tasks. Herein lie the greatest challenges and difficulties, for it is here that the old concepts of living together and of harmony must be most fundamentally replaced, as described earlier in this book. Maybe one could say that this is the true pioneer work of our time. Concepts that so far have been used as catchwords for a desired ideal society must now be tested and implemented in reality. These are concepts such as "grassroots democracy", "trust", "non-violence", "individuation", "free love", "self-sufficiency", "reverence toward life", "cooperation with nature", "spiritual life practice", etc. The "concrete utopia" must now be realized. Its foundation is the paradigm of the Sacred Matrix. Replacing old beliefs and behavior patterns, which have etched themselves into the human being during seven thousand years of violent history, with new values, new basic ideas about life, and new behavior, is an unusual enterprise – especially if it is to be done in a few decades. Those responsible for such a project need great staying powers in order not to lose their focus in spite of all the inner and outer friction, resistance, misunderstandings, and dangers. Those taking on this task are trained in a university that was created specifically for this and which is described later in this chapter under the name "Mirja School for Peace".

Once we had spent twelve years working in our project, which started in 1978, the task for the next phase became clear: establishing the first healing biotope. It could be formulated as follows: "Find a suitable place in the South, establish a community, and see to it that the ideas of the healing biotope are realized. Do everything you can to see to it that the beings living with you – humans, animals, and plants – come together in full trust. Do it as well as you can and as quickly as you can. The earth needs healing biotopes before it is too late. Do not worry, you are being guided." It took a few more years for a suitable place to be found in Portugal. On the outside, the place did not immediately live up to the ideas of a healing place: 140 hectares (350 acres) in a diseased landscape with cork oak trees, rockroses, blackberry bushes, and thistles, a few ruins of a planned meat processing plant (!), overly acidic earth, and general erosion, but with a sufficient amount of ground water and some artificial ponds.

Yet the place was beautiful and powerful. Over time we scouted out the geomantic location and the early history of the place where we had settled. Up until then we had followed a form of guidance that we had not quite understood. Slowly, the reason for the choice of this place was unveiled. We found ourselves in the middle of an ancient network of sacred sites, in which the original cultures had been connected to each other several thousand years ago. The connecting lines and the "ley lines" that came together here continued far beyond the borders of Portugal. In her two books "Traumsteine" ["Dream Stones"] and "Tempel der Liebe" ["Temple of Love"], Sabine Lichtenfels has described the meaning of this discovery. We found ourselves at an energy center, which is one of the five great energy centers in Portugal. Ancient matriarchal and spiritual knowledge was stored here and was accessible. We were in Alentejo, one of the poorest most rural areas in Portugal, and at the same time we were at one of its historical sources. Through medial input, which today is fashionably called "channeling", an entirely new image of human evolution and cultural development came to view.

It took another few years until we had constructed the necessary lodgings, meeting rooms, workshops, facilities, installations for water, electricity, etc. and, as one can imagine, the process is not complete by far, for more and more people keep coming here. We cannot yet let everybody stay, for the infrastructure and the mental-spiritual field creation must first be expanded and stabilized for us to be able to take on the number of people that are necessary for a healing biotope. We estimate that we will be a few hundred people in 15 years. By then several other healing biotopes will be in the process of being created. Due to the fields that it creates, a project such as that of the healing biotopes will initiate a global chain reaction.

Since two years, five new facilities are being created in Tamera: the Institute for Global Peace Work (German acronym: IGF) as a center for global networking – the Mirja School for Peace to train peace workers – the political ashram to train the students mentally and physically – the Youth School for Global Learning (German acronym: JGL), and the Art Center (on Mount Tesla). Four further projects that constitute central parts of the healing biotope are being planned: the children's republic, the peace garden, the permaculture garden (forest garden), and the new technology lab. Tamera is currently being built up by about 50 permanent co-workers. In order to fulfill the tasks fully, we need qualified co-workers in the following areas: horticulture, permaculture, and landscaping – computer and Internet – information technology – energy technology (especially subtle energy systems) – flow/vibration research – chaos research and holography – water technology. We need talented qualified people who think for themselves and who can or want to integrate themselves into the community. We also need committed sponsors who wish to invest their money in the development of peace instead of war.

A basic thought that led me to found the project 25 years ago was to create a place for all true pioneers of our time, where they can pursue their thoughts and developments in a common direction of peace. The universities had become intellectually desolate and empty. During my travels I had met several people – such as, for example, the Austrian Sepp Holzer (see Chapter 8) – who were working on great developments, unnoticed by the public. The list of great mental and spiritual adventurers and discoverers of the 20th century, including such names as Rudolf Steiner, Albert Einstein, Nicola Tesla, Sigmund Freud, Wilhelm Reich,

Viktor Schauberger, Alfred Wakeman, etc. lives on. I was fascinated by what was happening behind the scenes of public science and with what unwaveringness the preparations for a new civilization were being made. I was, however, also surprised at the extent to which these pioneer achievements were either ignored or attacked by other groups or by the establishment. It was clear that we had to create the possibility to bring together all these future developments in science, ecology, technology, medicine, spirituality, and art. I would therefore like to appeal to all the great minds of our time: introduce your genius, your intelligence, and God's gift to you into a meaningful context! Give up your position as a lone fighter! Let us work together for a comprehensive model for future thinking, living and building!

An international meeting place will be created within the framework of the IGF (Institute for Global Peace Work), where people from all countries come together to work at developing a global concept for peace. We are thinking of people who have committed themselves to working on the question of how, during current conditions, it is possible to save and heal planetary life on earth. This will result in the creation of a simple kind of conference center for global peace work with a focus on the main topics mentioned in this book. I will again enumerate them: sexuality and Eros – a new women's movement – community – cooperation with nature and Creation – a spiritual life practice – creating global networks and fields – changing oneself and individual transformation. Every year in August we organize a Summer University, to which all are invited who in some way want to participate in the healing and peace work. I urgently encourage all committed people, including the young and the untrained, who could imagine participating in the development of such a planetary healing center, to do so. One should not be dissuaded by the size of the task, for it corresponds to the appalling dimensions of our time. For those who would like to get to know the project in order to possibly participate in this kind of global peace work, we have created a regular series of courses: community courses, art courses, spiritual courses, theoretical courses, the Summer University, and work camps for participation in the individual working groups. Youths, who are seeking a meaningful perspective for their future and who want to participate in the global peace work, can find a spiritual and human home in the "Youth School for Global Learning (JGL).

We ask all new centers and community projects, who understand the idea of global peace work and would like to take on a task in the healing biotopes project, to enter into synergetic cooperation with us. We have all noticed that the time of disassociation is long gone. For years we have focused on the different aspects of the great task; now is the time to complement each other mutually. We have climbed our common mountain from different directions, and now that some of us are approaching the summit, we see that we all have the same goal. I give thanks for future cooperation.

In the name of warmth, for all beings that have skin and fur.

The Mirja School for Peace

The Mirja School is a school for peace within the framework of the Tamera project. It is located in the Alentejo region of Portugal. Here, a new concept for global peace work has been developed over the last several years: the Healing Biotopes Project. Healing biotopes are cultural centers with a few hundred inhabitants, in which new forms of cooperation between the human being, nature, and Creation are developed. Their power of survival is rooted in a principle of life, which can be described as the universal state of being. The Mirja School teaches the knowledge and skills that are necessary to establish functioning healing biotopes and a worldwide network between them. The school is associated with a political ashram, in which the thoughts underlying the basic training are deepened through mental and physical training.

1. Our current human civilization is at the end of its tether. Financial and political globalization is a globalization of violence. Democratically elected governments participate in genocide. The global plutocracy feeds itself by annihilating its victims. The inferno gets closer every day. Tormented tribes, individuals, and animals have no protection, and they have no forum where they can make themselves heard. The basic values of human co-existence - truth, trust, empathy, solidarity, and help for those in need - are ruined.

We no longer need reforms; we need peace. Peace is not reform; it is the most complete revolution of our circumstances in life. The human species needs a new settlement concept and a new cultural concept for its existence on planet Earth. We need to be embedded in the whole of Creation in a new way. We need a new order of human community, a new concept for sexuality and love, and a new kind of political networking. We also need to enter into a fundamental understanding with all other creatures on Earth.

2. The Mirja School is a training and education center for the creation of a global force for peace. Here, peace workers are trained for the cultural and political tasks that will be facing us during the next years and decades. It also serves as a vehicle for finding one's profession within the framework of a new planetary culture of peace. The thoughts and goals of this peace work are described in the **"Tamera Manifesto"** (see next section).

All co-workers of the Mirja School - both students and teachers - are in a state of higher apprenticeship. Learning occurs in a creative continuum, where all signs and impulses - be they dreams or daily events, political news, or an unexpected phone call - are integrated into the training. As Martin Buber would say: We pray, and God answers us through the events that we are confronted with. Prayer research – the exploration of the connection between prayer and fulfillment – is a part of the basic training at the Mirja School.

All students at the Mirja School have previously attended various events at Tamera. Once they have gotten to know the basic thinking of the project, they can decide to take part in the intensive training. The minimum course of study at the Mirja School takes one year. It consists of three months of basic training, followed by nine months practical training. The practical part occurs in the various work areas that are necessary for building healing biotopes and for the creation of a global network: water supply – energy supply – workshop with carpentry shop, metal workshop, etc. – horticulture – healing work – art – group facilitation – working with children – technology and research – networking – computer and Internet. During this time, the students, who are mostly between 20 and 40 years old, receive an overview of the Healing Biotopes Project, other international projects, the various tasks they might decide to take on, and the professions that will be needed in an emerging culture of peace. The basic training serves to prepare them to work within the global network for peace, such as participating in the work of Tamera, cooperating with other communities and centers, making contact with old peace tribes, or participating in humanitarian interventions in areas of crisis. The students especially study the theory and practice of implementing possible future non-violent cooperation and co-existence with all creatures on Earth. The foundation of the peace work that is developed here consists of the "universal state of being", i.e. the re-connection with the higher order and the sacred powers of Creation.

In one way or another, all students are working for the establishment of functioning human communities, for it is only in alive and vibrant communities that the knowledge of peace that we need today can arise. Only those who are able to live in community are in a position to see the solutions for the current social, sexual, spiritual, and ecological problems of our time. An autonomous individual, who is able to create a life for her/ himself that is free of fear, is not a private, but a communitarian being. All existence is of a communitarian nature, all developments occur in community, and all evolution is co-evolution. The prerequisites for healthy co-evolution are perception and trust. In this way the development of theory and life practice come full circle.

The main topics in the training program of the Mirja School are therefore:
- creating trust among human beings;
- cooperation with plants, animals and spiritual beings;
- the creation of sustainable future-oriented communities;
- the re-integration of human life into the universal order of Creation;
- the healing of sexuality and its liberation from all fears and degradation;
- inducing profound spiritual and bodily healing processes;
- breaking the worldwide chain of fear and violence through the development of concrete information of peace;
- group facilitation;
- global networking; and
- the political theory of healing biotopes.

3. The re-integration of human life into the cosmic whole requires overcoming deep-seated fears that have accumulated throughout history. If we wish to overcome the worldwide chain of violence and fear, we must first overcome it in ourselves. During dramatic regression trances the group participants experience - sometimes as perpetrators, sometimes as victims - the extent to which we are all entangled in this historical chain of fear and violence, and the consequences this has for our current lives. The deepest entanglements lie in the sexual area. It is here that the patriarchal era of the last 5,000 years have used the most brutal methods to establish fear and violence as tools of power - first against women, then against all those who are seen as being "inferior", "unruly", or "sinners".

It was only a few hundred years ago that the men of the church began to seriously exterminate the female sex through witch-hunts and the Inquisition. Add to that the brutal anti-male slogans with which modern feminism struck back, and we sense the difficulty of the heritage that we all - men and women - are faced with in the sexual area. In all male religions and states the suppression or trivialization of sexuality has become the number one tool of domination. This is also the prerequisite for the unbridled consumerism, which is consuming our children, nature, and the planet. This is why the healing of the human being and of the Earth is possible only if we succeed in healing sexuality and in restoring the sexual energies to their sacred order. A new culture is rooted in a new relationship between the sexes.

The reform concepts that are being offered today no longer have the power of true renewal. They do not respect the fact that healing has to do with a reintegration into the sacredness of existence, and that mental-spiritual healing can succeed only if it is connected to a healing of the senses and vice versa. These are not empty words; they are serious requirements that we place on our own work. The communities of the future will either have solved the sexual issues - or else they will not exist. Religion and Eros were the sources of our existence. We need a new concept for both, so that they can be restored to being that again.

In this sense, the Mirja School is an "exoteric" mystery school, wherein ancient knowledge is combined with the requirements of a new cultural era. At its core, we find the transformation of violence, the re-connection with the sacred powers of Creation, and the re-discovery of our Gaia-Earth as a unified, spiritual, conscious, living body. The individual learning steps are often accompanied by unusual contacts with animals. Animals are aspects of Gaia's Spirit, and they are seeking to cooperate with us. Once we truly see this, we automatically enter into an aware, caring, and vegetarian way of life.

4. A central area of study at the Mirja School is the establishment of functioning communities. Here, we need entirely new concepts. None of the old concepts of leaders and followers, affiliation and exclusion, collectivism and uniformity, inner cohesion through outer enemies, etc. can fulfill the needs of a non-violent human co-existence that is free of fear. The concepts of "authoritarianism" vs. "anti-authoritarianism", "centralization" vs. "decentralization", and "hierarchy" vs. "grass-roots democracy" yield little when attempting to establish positive, sustainable foundations for a new type of trust among human beings. It is obvious that the new communities are grassroots democracies, but what inner qualities of truth, responsibility, and communitarian ethics must a community develop, in order to be able to truly behave like a grassroots democracy? The communities of the last 30 years did not fail because of outer enemies; they failed because of inner conflicts and rivalries.

If we want to survive the ecological and social crises that we have brought forth, then we are forced to enter into a totally new and dramatic community experiment. First of all we need to establish community among humans; secondly, community with all living beings; and third, although it may sound strange, community with the spiritual forces of the Universe. Teilhard de Chardin, who studied the higher and more stable order of life, said that a higher state of existence means to be in a state of more encompassing union.

The basis for a functioning human community is trust. Trust is a result of truth, mutual support, and transparency of events, especially transparency about existing power structures, decision-making structures, and sexual structures. We can find some good models for human community in the fields of holography and chaos research. Community life in nature has arranged itself as a non-linear, open, and very complex system. By studying such systems, we find the necessary parameters for the functionality, survivability, and growth potential of human communities. They are all the result of the connection and compatibility with the next higher structures in Creation.

This higher compatibility with the universal order enables a process to occur, which is determinant for the further evolution of humankind: the blocked energies, that were constantly discharged "downward" in the old systems, resulting in destruction and wars, can now move "upwards" and can have an effect on a higher level of order. The ordering principle of chaotic life forces is no longer below, but above the ordering structures of societies to date. The desired stability no longer excludes our elementary driving forces, but expressly includes them. This eliminates the disastrous moral ambiguity that human society had to live with for thousands of years. These are connections that will be thought through and developed in a variety of ways at the Mirja School.

One can see why a certain amount of elementary theoretical studies needs to be part of any training program for the new centers. What is being developed here is not just more academic knowledge, but new knowledge in terms of a new overall orientation: a new type of general course of studies. The (approximately 30) participants of a 3-month course come together to create a small community, within which the new principles can be understood and tested. The research work in the Mirja School is therefore always connected to concrete personal experiences.

"Only tribes will survive". This statement by a Native American leader (Vine Deloria Jr.) may be somewhat exaggerated, but it does put its finger on the heart of the matter, provided we do not associate "tribes" with cave dwellers, but with highly conscious crystallization points within post-capitalist humanity.

5. An essential part of the training consists of "working on yourself". We can only achieve as much outer peace as we have achieved inner peace. The conflicts that we experience in the outer world are reflections of the potential for conflict that we - being a part of history and a part of humanity - carry in ourselves. This is true also for the prevailing perpetrator-victim structures, which are deeply rooted in us and in our karmic history. Today, we often encounter our enemies from the past as friends and vice versa. Things repeat themselves until they are solved,

and we must solve them, in order to avoid further chain reactions. The solution begins with us. We must take farewell of the many games that the ego in its isolation has learned to play, and of the dearly held habits of blackmail, being offended, and contrariness. As soon as we are filled with something greater, we take farewell of these things naturally. We learn to get rid of our deep-seated fears, our swindling, our bragging, etc., in order to enter the functional circle of a stable community. We say goodbye to our thoughts of hatred, revenge, condemnation, and defamation, and we connect with a higher functional circle of trust and human solidarity. For the professional co-workers, the issues usually concern releasing deeply stored fear and anger that has stood in the way of their empowerment and their love lives. Love relationships are popular arenas for private bottlenecks and conflicts. Two lovers can never on their own correct what many generations before them have created. The historically based compulsion to pretend and to suppress oneself has inflicted too many wounds and has resulted in too many fears of separation, for two people to be able to cope with them alone. Yet there can be no peace on earth, as long as there is war in love. The students learn what it means to see these conflicts not as private conflicts, but as a part of an historical issue that affects more or less all of us. Whoever solves his/her conflict is doing this work on behalf of everyone else and is therefore serving peace. This is a wholly different view of one's so-called "private problems". It makes it possible for peace workers to stop hiding from others.

The work on changing oneself is supported by the group. The Mirja School has developed various methods for this. They range from various methods of "self-expression" in front of the group to healing trances and regressions. Special places and lodgings are provided by the political ashram for all peace workers who temporarily need an inner sanctuary to deal with themselves and with their world.

The coming transformation requires a frequency of transparency, openness, and cleansing of the soul and the body. A continuous training camp (including a sports gym) is being planned, in which the mental, emotional, and bodily energies can be supported and increased as part of the basic training. We know that we get help from the universe if we are prepared to receive it. "Not out of one's own power" is therefore a motto for the emerging spiritual life practice.

6. The mental-spiritual framework of our work is the **Political Theory** (see Chapter 11). It is the theory of healing biotopes and how they can multiply on earth. It describes, in theoretical categories, the creation of

a new planetary culture. The concepts of "morphogenetic fields" and "morphic resonance", which were developed by Rupert Sheldrake, are valid not only for the creation of new patterns of behavior in nature, but also for new developments in the human area. New systems of ecology, social systems, and mental-spiritual systems are established through the creation of fields, if they are aligned with a latent developmental direction for the whole.

The world is a unified whole. Every point in the universe is of a spiritual nature and reflects the whole. Here, we are not following Newton's physical worldview, but rather that of Giordano Bruno. The forces and the order of the whole impact each of its parts. Even in distorted and broken images, the whole can still be perceived, just as it can in holographic film. It can be viewed through the correct perceptional attitude (in holography referred to as the "reference beam"). What we see when we focus our minds on the undisturbed whole is what we in the Mirja School call "prehistoric utopia", or the "dream" or "entelechy" of things. The students practice this perceptional attitude in their daily experiences with their fellow human beings, animals, plants, myths, religions, and communities, and in the study of history. History, too, follows "the whole" and carries the seed of the whole as "prehistoric utopia". It consists of the concrete possibility that Ernst Block called "utopian latency" or "Nondum". Since we are the eyes of the whole, we have the possibility of seeing and recognizing this prehistoric utopia. This makes it possible for us to realize it tentatively at certain chosen locations. We call such locations "healing biotopes". If the information for peace, which is developed there, is aligned with the whole, then an immediate field effect occurs and it has an impact everywhere. It affects the organism of the biosphere, just as medicine does in the organism of the human being. It affects the energy system of the world, just as a correctly placed acupuncture needle does in the energy system of the body. This "law of fields" applies to the evolution of life on earth and to the evolution of the human being and human community, and it is the basic thought behind the Political Theory.

In order to heal the overall organism of the biosphere, we do not need to treat all its parts. It suffices to introduce a "medicine" or an input with the right content at the right place, in order to introduce a healing force into the whole. The task then becomes one of establishing healing biotopes in which a comprehensive set of information about non-violence, co-evolution, and trust is developed in real life. Once this information has reached a certain level of maturity, and if it corresponds to the immanent building plans of Creation, it has an impact in terms of morpho¬genetic field creation. Similar healing biotopes will then appear at other places on earth.

The healing biotopes that are being established globally constitute the seeds of crystallization of the new era. A network of planetary healing biotopes organizes itself into a pattern for a new planetary community of all living beings.

The Mirja School is firmly connected to various parts of Tamera: to the "Institute for Global Peace Work" (German acronym: IGF), the political ashram, and the Art Center (Café Tesla), in which new approaches to perception and Creation are practiced. Art plays a large role in our work, since it liberates creative forces that are intimately connected to the healing process. In addition to the professional training in the Mirja School, there is the "Youth School for Global Learning" (German acronym: JGL). This school coordinates the youth work of different groups, organizes extensive journeys, and contacts peace-loving tribes, international peace projects, individuals committed to the protection of animals, and environmental groups. The young participants gain knowledge about the global situation of life on our planet and about the possibilities for meaningful work.

The Tamera Manifesto

for a global culture of peace

This text is being sent to representatives of various human rights organizations, environmental and animal protection organizations, peace projects, and future-oriented communities, as well as to dedicated individuals, who have committed themselves to working for global peace. With this text we ask for support and cooperation for the development of a global concept for ending the worldwide massacre of human beings and animals. The fight against the global mutilation of life, the fight for the liberation of peoples and minorities, the work for the healing of human beings, and the work for healing nature must be coordinated in a meaningful way. This text contains some thoughts for the creation of a global force for peace and a corresponding perspective for a humane future. We ask you to pass this text on to committed friends.

Tamera is a property of 140 hectares (350 acres) in Southern Portugal (Alentejo), where for the last several years work using unusual methods work has been carried out for the healing of the human being and the earth. The most important facilities are the "healing biotope", the "Youth School for Global Learning" and the newly created "Institute for Global Peace Work" (German acronym: IGF). The work follows the ideas and goals expressed in the Manifesto. Some 100 volunteers are constructing the buildings and installing the supply systems and the infrastructure necessary for the project. The goal of Tamera is to establish a healing biotope, in which a few hundred people live together according to the principles of non-violent cooperation with all co-creatures, and to establish a center for global peace work.

1. Seven Basic Tenets

1. Today we are approaching the greatest revolution since the Neolithic era. It is the transition from the patriarchal era to a new form of human civilization.

2. The global structures of violence and fear, war between the sexes and male dominance, racism and genocide, exploitation of the Third World, and exploitation of nature have historic origins and can therefore be changed historically.

3. The personal issues, for which today millions of people see therapists, also have historic origins and therefore require a societal and political answer in addition to an individual one.

4. The environmental crisis and the inner crisis are two aspects of the same overall disease. They can only be understood and overcome by being seen in their totality.

5. The love between the sexes has to a great degree been destroyed through the age-old war against woman and the historical repression of sexuality. A new, non-violent culture is rooted in a new relationship between the sexes.

6. The matriarchal and spiritual origins of human culture were lost through the imperialist expansion of male dominance through church, state, industry, and commerce. We must find them again at a new level to make a non-violent, global culture possible.

7. It is not enough to criticize the existing system. We need concrete places on earth where new life forms can be developed and tested. We call such places "healing biotopes".

2. There is Only One Existence

There is only one existence. All beings take part in the laws and forces of this one existence. All are in relationship with each other, and together they form the network of life.

The earth is a unified organism. All beings on earth together form a unified living body with a common underlying set of information (the genetic code), a common consciousness, and a common will to live.

When the network of life is disturbed through violence and fear, the entire life body becomes ill. The illness of nature and the inner illness of human beings are two sides of the same overall illness that has been caused by violence and fear.

To a large degree, modern human civilizations are based on the destruction of life (food, clothing, cosmetics, medicine, exploitation of resources, etc.). The victims are the plants, animals, and children, religious and ethnic minorities, peoples of the Third World, and we, ourselves.

The violence that we inflict upon others comes back to us in the form of illness, fear, and an inner weakening. The global civilization of our time (late capitalism) is a system of ill people, and it is connected with global violence. This type of illness cannot be healed through individual therapy.

The foundations of our current form of life can no longer be justified ethically. Either directly or indirectly they turn us into co-perpetrators of a global catastrophe and, if we continue in this direction, we ourselves will become its victims.

We cannot solve the problem through moral appeals or partial solutions. We need a new concept of human culture and society, a new concept of life, and a new concept for our existence on earth.

3. Charter of Human Rights and Rights for all Creatures

All beings – humans, animals, plants, tribes and peoples – have their special purpose and their special function in the structure of Creation. In the plan of Creation, they all have a right to their specific way of life and to their status of existence. They all have the right to grow and develop without fear.

All beings have a right to a healthy and free use of their bodies, their joy of life, their curiosity, their love relationships, their communities, their natural biotopes, and their special connection to Creation as a whole.

All beings come (as embryos and children) from a world of security and trust. They all have the lifelong right to grow and develop in this trust. They all have a right to a fundamental kind of inner health and freedom that comes from trust.

All beings that have skin and fur have a right to warmth and to those life conditions through which they stay warm.

All beings have a right to food and to the life conditions through which they get food.

All beings have a right to the freedom of movement necessary for their development, their joy, and for their bodily, emotional, mental, and spiritual health. They must not be tied up or kept imprisoned in small cages.

All beings have special organs that they use to discover life and to make contact with the world (limbs, genitalia, wings, horns, tails, claws, fins, etc.) They must not be stopped from doing this through clipping or mutilation.

All beings live together in a great cosmic brother- and sisterhood. The differences between human beings and animals are not ones of principle, they are gradual differences. All beings therefore have the same civil rights on earth.

4. The Global Chain of Violence and Fear

Today, we are experiencing the worldwide legacy of a bloody era of history. We can only endure what people do to each other, to their children, and to animals by rigorously turning our eyes away. Large areas on earth have already been given up by the international aid organizations, and the reason we do not hear anything in the news from many regions is that nothing more can be done. The only reason why we can still sleep peacefully is that we are not (yet) among the victims and that we cannot even imagine what reality lies behind such words as "holocaust", "genocide", "civil war", "arms trade", "secret police", "death squadrons", "torture", "female genital mutilation", etc. Today, all these things are a part of the everyday life of millions of people. The monstrous human rights violations in a country such as China are subordinated to financial considerations. The consequences of the international arms trade are measured in the size of bank accounts, not in terms of the indescribable human suffering that it is causing. What is happening here hits us mercilessly when we consider that the children, who are being burned and mutilated, could be our own. Ever since male imperialism raised itself against Creation, against life, and against the female principle, at the end of the Neolithic era, a network of violence has spread over the earth.

Ever since the patriarchal revolution, the meaning of power has consisted of perpetrating violence. All large political, economic, and ideological systems have since been systems of violence. Violence creates fear, and it is through fear that people can be ruled over. Fear is necessary to uphold the current systems of violence. It is the basic human illness in modern society, and it underlies all the psychosomatic epidemics of our time. Fear is the obstruction of our ability to love and engage in contact, and it is the block to contact between human being and animal. Fear is thus the central ecological bottleneck of our time. Fear and violence are twins, and they both create one another. Fear leads to a blockage and congestion of elementary life energies, resulting in latent violence in every fearful organism. The atrocities committed by German fascism also followed the cruel principle of this unleashing of energy. One must understand this process at a deep level in order to be able to solve and overcome it. Unleashing fearful organisms through slogans and images of an enemy leads to eruptions of collective violence, as we can currently see all over the world. We can only solve the problem if it becomes possible to break the global chain of fear and violence at a critical place.

It is not enough to appeal for peace or to present moral arguments, for fear and violence have become physiological processes that are deeply embedded into the structure of modern societies. Healing work and peace work is therefore not only individual work, it is always also political work. Today, to work for peace on earth means to create the life conditions, the economic structures, the methods of production, the social environments, the sexual environments, the ecological environments, and the mental and spiritual structures that can create structural peace and structural healing.

The key word for structural peace is trust. Fear and violence can only be overcome structurally by recreating the basic trust with which we all once began our lives. One of the most important tasks of modern peace work is therefore the creation of model environments of trust, in which this basic trust between all beings can arise again.

To work for peace also means to dedicate oneself with fearless pacifist militancy to the protection of life, no matter where one is. Life decisions of this kind require a high degree of revolutionary power. This power arises when we begin to understand what we have done to our fellow creatures through our habit of remaining silent.

5. Stop the Massacre of Animals

A special aspect of global violence is violence against animals. In terms of cruelty and frequency, the everyday atrocities that are carried out all over the world are beyond any possible description. What does a dog experience when it is dissected alive (vivisection) in the medical department of a university? What methods are used when raising and killing the animals that are the basis for our gastronomy, our cosmetic industry, our pharmaceutical industry, and our clothing industry? How much information of fear and cruelty is sent out thousands of times a day into the ether from an animal laboratory, a slaughter-house, or a fur farm? What journey of suffering does an animal have to go through before it ends up as a hamburger at McDonald's or as a hot dog? There can be no peace on earth as long as we, actively or passively, as perpetrators or co-perpetrators, allow the mass murder of animals.

Animals are beings just like us, only at another level of development. They are endowed with a soul, they are loving, playful, curious, contact-seeking beings, who need our support, in order to return to a meaningful development here on this planet. They are often like children. They belong to the life body of the earth and – each in its own way and with its own special abilities – play a role in the universal process of discovery through which life on earth gains its richness, its depth, and its completeness. They help us to understand life, see new possibilities and new directions, and learn new forms of communication. Some of them, especially whales and dolphins, have created, under water, a cosmic existence and an intelligence, which in many ways is superior to that of our modern culture. We need to learn from them, instead of killing them. Human beings and animals are a part of the same life body of the biosphere; they need and complement each other like the organs of a body. They are designed not only for co-existence, but for active communication with each other. Where this is possible again, we notice what the original peaceful cultures on earth have always known: that animals, just like we, are one aspect of existence and of one consciousness, and it is only together that we can realize the beauty of life on earth.

6. The Power of Concrete Utopia

If we want to overcome war, we need a concrete vision for peace. If we want to overcome the powerful global field of violence, we need a concrete vision for a powerful global field of peace. During the student revolution in the Sixties, we experienced how easily people are united to fight against something, yet at the same time find it difficult to live together. We were able to solve the problem of a police barricade, but we were unable to solve the problem of dishwashing in our communal households, the problem of hierarchy in our groups, and especially the problem of sexuality. Apart from the slogans for a life free from domination, we had no positive vision and no concrete utopia for a new lifestyle. Most struggles for liberation were fights against existing injustice and were not a fight for the realization of a clearly seen and realistic vision for peace and justice.

Tamera's task is to develop a concrete utopia for a new type of human civilization and society and a new way of connecting our life with the beings of Nature and the powers of Creation. Such a concrete utopia contains a relatively precise image and a complex informational totality for a real culture of peace. The difference between utopia and illusion is that utopia is compatible with the inner blueprint and the possibilities of reality, i.e. of the universe. All beings carry a concrete utopia (a so-called "entelechy" and a sought-for inner gestalt) inside of them that guides their development. The power of concrete utopia is immense. It turns a seed into a full-size tree, a caterpillar into a butterfly, and an embryo into an adult. Individuals do not have this power on their own, but through their connection with the whole. Concrete utopia is the matrix or blueprint through which the power of the whole can flow into the individual and bring it into being. If a caterpillar wanted to become a butterfly on its own, it would have an impossible task. Concrete utopia is the power in life that takes all beings beyond their present limitations.

The action of concrete utopia follows a principle of power, which is far superior to all mechanistic principles. A tiny sprout of grass is capable of pushing through a layer of asphalt that is five centimeters thick. Again, it is not its own power that empowers it; it is its connection to the whole, which is immanent in its inner blueprint. The power struggle between the sprout of grass and the layer of asphalt is thus determined on a completely different level. In a comparable manner, the forces for peace could succeed against the external superiority of the powers of destruction.

If we are able to find a suitable concrete utopia for us and our cultural development, there is no doubt that a fundamental turn toward a future without violence is possible. This would give us the matrix or blueprint through which the power of Creation could enter our work. It is the only power stronger than war. The main idea behind Tamera is to develop the concrete utopia that needs to emerge in the current entelechian development of history and to use the power of a utopia of peace to influence the struggles surrounding the major decisions of our time.

The inner "dream" of humanity is the still unfulfilled, but real vision of a global community of human beings and peoples, in solidarity with each other, linked together in mutual caring and love for all life on earth. What precisely does this dream mean for nutrition and production, the living together of the sexes, the political organization of new communities, global communication, and the collaboration between the beings of nature and the powers of Creation? What does this dream mean for our coexistence with wild animals, domestic animals, and snails in the garden? What precisely does it mean in relation to our daily life, our way of eating, working, loving, and praying? What kind of concentration of power and spirituality in our daily lives do we need, to be able to see and implement the concrete utopia immanent in us and in history? With these questions we are right on the threshold of the Archimedean fulcrum, where so many things are decided. There are no reasons to remain stuck in the constraints of the old life.

7. Places of Healing on Earth

The earth is surrounded and criss-crossed by a network of geomantic lines (lines of power). Our ancestors built their sacred sites and went on their pilgrimages along these lines. Still today we find many relics of ancient times along these lines, although they have often been altered during later eras. The Christian church, in particular, used the ancient "pagan" places of power for their own purposes. An impressive example of this is the cathedral of Chartres, whose immense Gothic structures rise over four layers of historical sites that all served ritualistic purposes. Wherever powerful energy lines come together or cross, there are natural healing points on earth. They can be compared to the acupuncture points in the meridian system of our bodies. Historically, powerful sacred centers of humanity were built on the strongest energy nodes. Here, long before our calendar began, the old stone circles were erected (many of them older than Stonehenge), as were the old oracle sites and temples, such as those on Malta.

Here, we also find the old initiation sites for those who were chosen to take on sacred duties. The priestesses as the caretakers of these centers had the special task of ensuring worldwide communication between these centers, thus maintaining and caring for the global healing field. Today, on all continents, we find the remains of these sacred centers of a primal global religion, for example in Peru, Portugal, Ireland, Eritrea, Malta, India, Tibet, Australia, and Polynesia. These places have not yet "died out"; their information and their spiritual life force is still active. Within the framework of global healing work it would be very meaningful to re-activate them and to re-establish their mental-spiritual connection with each other. The re-establishment of a healthy geomantic network over the entire earth is one of the healing tasks of the new era.

The second aspect of a global healing network has to do with the cultures of peace that still remain on earth. Despite their extermination during the patriarchal era, especially during Christian and colonial times, some of them still exist in a relatively original form, for example, some groups of Aborigines in Australia, native Tibetans, Eskimos, Native Americans, Indians, and Africans, some peoples of the Andes, etc. Here, ancient knowledge about a healthy earth and about the eternal connections within Creation is still alive. This knowledge must be reclaimed on a new level, so that we can reconnect with the power and the sacredness of Creation. Today, it is an absolute must that these peace tribes be protected from further destruction.

The modern spirit of the coming third millennium must reconnect with the timeless spiritual sources of ancient times, without thereby regressing to old cultural forms. For hundreds of thousands of years, humanity lived from these sources, before they were separated from them by the patriarchal revolution. The knowledge of these sources is stored in our cells. It is thus still in existence and can be reawakened today. The peace tribes that are still alive today are not tourist attractions; they are the last representatives of previously existing knowledge of peace on earth. We must engage with them, in order to connect the old "peace field" with the new one. They need our help and we need theirs.

8. The Gender Issue

There can be no peace on earth, as long as there is war in love. The five thousand year history of the patriarchal era is a history of a war between the sexes, and the war has not ended yet. The five thousand year long battle against the female world is the most cruel chapter in human history to date. None of us has yet recovered from that. We will not be able to develop fundamental peace concepts for the earth and human beings, until we understand this fight and its insane results in society and within ourselves. It is a primary task for all future projects to activate all energy to liberate the relationship between the sexes from the taboos, prejudices, and cruelties of a mad era. A new non-violent and loving culture is rooted substantially in a new loving and non-violent relation between the sexes. This is a point we cannot neglect in the new concepts for ecology, spirituality and healing, if we want to achieve realistic solutions. There can be no healthy ecology without healthy and fulfilled sexuality.

We all came into being through a sexual connection between man and woman. Sexuality is the biological source of our life, it is truly "issue #1", since we all exist in the body. A disruption of sexuality is a disruption of the entire organism. Almost all illnesses in Western society are at least partly caused by a disruption of the sexual energy balance, and most emotional and psychosomatic illnesses of our times are rooted in unresolved problems in the area of love between the sexes. Many more people die each year from unresolved love conflicts than from car accidents, and these, too, often have the same background. As long as the sexes do not find fulfillment in love, they must compensate this lack through tourism, consumerism, status, power, and war. These are the foundations of our current capitalist world society.

Some prerequisites for a future free of violence is that the war between the sexes be put to an end, that man be liberated from his secret sexual anxieties and feelings of inadequacy, that woman be reconnected with her original power sources and her central tasks in the human community, and finally that both be liberated from their delusion that jealousy is part of love. Man and woman are the two polar halves of the one human being. They must now come together in such a way that they "fit", so that they might find the permanent fulfillment that is an inherent part of the emotional and bodily love between the sexes. Here, we can no longer avoid confronting certain carefully thought-out concepts about free love. Love and sexuality are universal powers of life; in a universal society of peace they can no longer be bound to one single person, nor can they be surrounded by private fences. In a universal culture of peace, free love and committed partnerships do not exclude each other. Instead they are mutually dependent and complement each other. The old patterns of sexual "faithfulness" and jealousy are based on distrust between the sexes. The deepest freedom, which lies at the heart of all freedom, is the freedom of love between the sexes. This is the source of a new ethic and a new order, in which human beings no longer need to deny their own selves and hide from others. This freedom leads to a genuine, powerful, and nonviolent joy of life. This is of central importance in the concrete utopia that we now must bring to life.

Communities of the future and projects for a new way of life can only function in the long term if their members know and understand the principle of free love, if they know that it is not in opposition to an ethic of faithfulness and responsibility, and if they know that one is **allowed** to follow it. In order for this new force to develop, we need an encompassing environment of freedom and community. All forms of ideology or group pressure are counter-productive when it comes to such deep changes in our core areas. This is true for our erotic as well as for our mental and spiritual sources.

9. Global Field Creation through Selective Work

We can no longer meet worldwide violence through counter-violence; the era of violent revolutions is over. First, they are pointless in the face of the real balance of power; second, they never achieve the humane goal, for violence - including counter-violence - always produces fear and new violence. This is a psychological principle, which up to now could not be overcome by any revolution. For global peace work we therefore need a basically different concept. One central point in this new concept is that of global field creation through selective intervention, in short: the law of fields.

In order to relieve the body of an illness, one does not need to treat all its organs and cells individually. It suffices to introduce new information that acts as an impetus in the direction of healing, such as a medicine or a few acupuncture needles that are introduced at the right places. If the energy lines and energy centers of the body are impacted through this intervention, then the body takes care of the rest of the work by itself. This principle can be applied to the earth as an organism of its own. It suffices to input a concentrated impulse of peace at chosen "acupuncture points" or energy centers, in order to stimulate the earth as a whole. (I am here speaking about a theoretical principle. Concrete peace work in crisis areas of the world is absolutely necessary and it is a substantial part of the school for peace, which has been founded in Tamera - see point 11.)

The reason for this way of functioning lies in the fact that the earth and its biosphere constitute a **unified** organism, a **unified** life body, and a **unified** body of information. This can be seen, for example, in the genetic code, whose basic mathematical structure is the same for all living beings - for plants, animals, and humans. All beings therefore follow the same basic information of life. The mathematical similarity found in parallel universal formulas, such as the genetic code and the Chinese I Ching, attest to the similarity in the informational structure of both the molecular and mental-spiritual areas. Teilhard de Chardin called this informational body of the biosphere the "noosphere". If we introduce new information, compatible with the overall system, into the noosphere, the effect is the same as that of medication introduced into the overall system of our body. All beings are a part of the noosphere, and therefore - at least latently - the information that is introduced affects them all. It is through this information that a new "field" is born.

Every individual action can create a new field, if it is based on new information. When Reinhold Messner climbed Mount Everest without oxygen, he created new field-generating information. From then on it was also possible for others to climb Mount Everest without oxygen. There are many similar examples in the areas of sports and technology. The principle of "morphogenetic field creation" is present everywhere in evolution, for it is a direct consequence of the holographic functional logic of the global body of life, in which all beings are interconnected. If one succeeds in creating encompassing new information for the creation of a culture without fear and violence in a few new cultural centers on earth, then this information will not only affect these special places, but the entire noosphere of the earth. The result will be that, within a short period of time, other such models emerge at other places on earth.

We have been prepared for these kinds of possibilities, not only through medicine and the study of biological systems, but also through the models used in chaos research. Small changes, introduced at minute points on earth, can lead to enormous overall effects, due to the mathematical principle of self-amplification. The combination of such resonance and multiplication effects allows us to develop a political theory with a new logical structure. The system works "of itself" if its mechanism is given a new impulse in the right way.

Therefore, one of the most urgent tasks of global peace work is the development of such power points for concrete peace information. The more encompassing the new information is, the more areas of life are encompassed by it. The more complex it is, and the more deeply it addresses the basic connections of our mental-spiritual and biological existence, the more it becomes universally applicable and the more powerful is its global field effect. Here, we can understand the beautiful words by Victor Hugo: "Nothing is more powerful than an idea whose time has come."

10. The Establishment of Healing Biotopes

We call the power centers that are to be established "healing biotopes". A healing biotope is a life community of people, animals and plants, whose life forces complement each other and no longer block each other through violence or fear. The underlying healing paradigm is the result of the unity of all living beings.

There are no isolated structures. All beings live in relationship to others. All existence is communitarian. Healing is therefore not an isolated process, but a process that occurs in relationship to other beings. The healing of human beings occurs in their relationships to their fellow human beings as well as in their relationships to animals, plants, nature, and Creation. The deepest biological and mental-spiritual power of healing is trust. The hologram of fear must be replaced by the hologram of trust, all the way down to cellular processes. When this turning point has been reached, the new set of information necessary for the creation of a new force field will emerge in all relationships. This process is far-reaching. Some examples, based on experience: where there is trust, the fear of snakes disappears. Where there is trust, the courage emerges to jump into water from great heights. Where there is trust, the fear of abandonment disappears and so does jealousy. Also, no thoughts of hatred and violence arise. Trust is the energy of peace: trust between children and adults, between men and women, between different communities and people, between the human world and the world of animals, and between the human being and the Universe.

The creation of trust within a community requires great effort, for we tend to be more programmed to distrust in the crucial situations that deal with sex, love, power, or money. We need a very deep and well-founded concept of human community, in order to dissolve our traumatic conflicts and create trust. Trust is essentially a question of truth. How much truth can two lovers take, how much truth can a community take, and how does it deal with truth? Those, who no longer need to pretend or disguise themselves in front of others, do not need to fear that they will not be loved. Whoever does not have this fear, can develop true humaneness.

Building stable communities involves working on one's own character structures. For the forces of peace to be able to have an external effect, they must be firmly anchored within those who work for peace. Our personal defects are not our private issues; they are reflections of global defects, and the more we can heal them within ourselves, the more we can heal them in the outside world.

An interesting element of the healing biotope is the sanctuary. In earlier cultures, the sanctuary was a place where nobody could be punished. Criminals, who managed to reach this place, could not be hunted down and could start a new life there. For the healing of our own thoughts, it is important that we connect back to this tradition and that we fully understand the concept of forgiveness. Each of us has experienced hatred against certain people. Are we able and willing to forgive? Is our knowledge of peace and our desire for peace already strong enough for that? This is an issue that we have to deal with, if we truly want to break the chain of fear and violence. We are led uncompromisingly to those inner areas where the power and the sovereignty of our work for peace can prove themselves.In their structure and way of life, healing biotopes are connected to a new planetary way of thinking. Their energy supply, their use of water, diet, consumption, and recycling are oriented toward long term global healing. Their way of life is fairly simple, but energetic. Their focus and their power centers in life change, for they are integrated into the universal whole. In them, the ego principle gives way to a universal consciousness and a universal flow of energy. Reservoirs of power are thereby tapped, opening up new possibilities in the areas of healing, technology, and global field creation.

Healing biotopes are living seeds of the future, and they operate according to the principle of the "morphogenetic creation of fields". When the first model has been created, the probability for the creation of the next ones increases. The time is ripe for the establishment of such healing biotopes on all continents. The more healing biotopes are created - and we can expect this to occur within the next two decades - the more intense will be the global field effect. The coming global earth community will emerge from a network of healing biotopes, communities, and peoples, who have entered into a state of trust and cooperation with all fellow creatures.

11. The Tamera Project

Tamera is a 350 acre (140 hectares) property in Portugal, where for several years a growing group of peace workers has been working to create the life conditions needed to develop a healing biotope. The work is based on the thoughts and goals described above.

At Tamera, a school for peace (the Mirja School) is being created, in which the theoretical and practical foundations for global peace work are taught. This always includes the healing of one's own person. We cannot create a force for peace in the external world unless such a force exists within us. We need a concrete vision for peace, including our own peace, in order to be able to counteract war effectively. We need to re-cognize and overcome the worldwide chain of violence and fear in ourselves, if we plan to develop realistic concepts for their global dissolution. This permanent linkage between inner and outer structures constitutes a basic quality of holistic peace work. Consequently, the school teaches subjects related to our inner life, such as the following: the art of overcoming fear – sexuality and healing – the logic of love – building communities and facilitating groups – cosmology and the study of religion – evolution and early history – and the power of concrete utopia. All participants of the school go through a two-year physical and mental training program, through which they can free themselves from their own personal blocks. The goal of the training is for the participants to take on a professional task at Tamera, in another future-oriented community, or in international peace work.

The school for peace serves to train people who have committed themselves to their work and to their future profession in the service of healing and global peace work. Effective peace workers need a commitment and a professional energy that remains stable, even when, for example, their love life might be temporarily "on the rocks". But they also need a professional task and purpose which enable them to solve their personal conflicts and deepen their love life. Professional and "private" life, revolution and love, and political work and personal emancipation must come together if we want to create the power and the way of life that is necessary for the creation of peace on earth. This is an underlying premise for all training courses at the school for peace at Tamera. A non-violent culture requires new professions and new training courses, in order to make long-term productive work possible.

For younger people who want to acquaint themselves with this work, there is the "Youth School for Global Learning". For many young people, the thought of entering into the existing professional world has become meaningless. They need a different life perspective and the possibility to prepare themselves for their new professions in the framework of a global peace culture. For this reason, journeys will be undertaken from Tamera, during which young people will participate in peace work in other countries and thereby gain a "cosmopolitan" perception of the situation on earth. Qualified work leaders and jobs are available for technical and manual work training at Tamera. One aim of the youth school is also to develop a new relationship with nature and a real trusting relationship with animals. At Tamera, there is a horse farm with a riding school, which helps to serve this purpose.

12. Institute for Global Peace Work (German acronym: IGF)
The production and distribution of this manifesto coincides with the founding of the Institute for Global Peace Work at Tamera. The infrastructure has now been developed far enough to ensure the work of the Institute on a larger scale. The task of the Institute is to speed up global networking and to realize the goals of the healing biotopes in as many places on earth as possible. Once again, I would like to list the goals in key words:

- Cooperation with nature and all her beings;
- Re-integration of human biotopes into the overall holon of Creation;
- Fulfilled sexuality and ending the war between the sexes;
- Dissolving the global chain of violence and fear – also within one's own person;
- Establishment of future-oriented communities that introduce new overall information of peace into the world through their daily life practice;
- Collaboration and nurturing contacts with all groups and individuals, who are committed to building a global force for peace;
- Creation of a biosphere free of fear;
- Developing a concept for a global non-violent civilization on earth.

IGF cooperates with all individuals and institutions, who are interested in realizing the goals described above. In addition to the existing guest house and camping place, the construction of an international meeting place is planned to host our visitors.

Further Information:

The "Plan of the Healing Biotopes", as it is described in this book, is a complex vision based on over 25 years practiced research. An ever growing team of highly committed people are working all over the world to carry it out. What they work on are still prototypes. As with all cutting edge research these models are experi- ments and need time and resources for their development. Sustainable funding is urgently needed. Please support the Institute for Global Peacework. Go to www.tamera.org for recent information and activities.

Please contact us for donations from outside Europe.

Donations in Euro:

Raiffeisenbank Zürich
Account holder: Grace - Stiftung zur Humanisierung des Geldes, Zürich
Acct. No.: 92188.69
IBAN: CH9881487000009218869
BIC: RAIFCH22
Clearing 81487

(The bank's PC account: 87-71996-7)

Thank you very much!

Contact:
Tamera • Monte do Cerro • P-7630 Colos • Portugal
Tel: +351 283 635 484 • Fax: +351 283 635 374
email: igf@tamera.org • www.tamera.org

Biography of the Author

1942   Dieter Duhm is born in Berlin. After the war he experiences fear and violence as a refugee; these become important topics in his life. At an early age, he begins to paint, which occupies him until the age of 20. At 14 he participates in the protestant aid organization "Brot für die Welt" ["Bread for the World"]. Tries to live a life in accordance with the Sermon on the Mount and the 10 Commandments.

1959   Leaves the church.

1961   High school graduation. Thereafter voluntarily enters military service, where he attempts to establish a pacifist project together with friends.

1963   Stops painting for the time being, because "the other issues became more important". Initiates his philosophical and political work.

1964   Begins to study philosophy, sociology, and psychoanalysis. Diplomas: B.A. in Psychology (1969) and Doctorate in Sociology (1973). Studies biological cybernetics for a few semesters, thereby gaining an understanding of how biological circuits function and change.

1968   Works politically until 1994 within the Marxist Left in the Mannheim/Lud¬wigshafen area, where he takes on leadership roles in union youth work. "Ringleader" at demonstrations, school blockades, and anti-Springer events. Four legal proceedings for breach of the peace, which, however, were dropped by an amnesty decree by the Federal President Heinemann. Takes a stand against collectivistic and dogmatic tendencies in the New Left. Publishes the leftist bestseller *"Angst im Kapitalismus"* ["Fear in Capitalism"] in 1972 and becomes one of the main figures in the so-called "emancipation debate" concerning the connection between political work and personal liberation. Publishes the widely distributed *"Mannheimer Papier"* ["The Mannheim Paper"] and the brochure *"Revolution ohne Emanzipation ist Konterrevolution"* ["Revolution without Emancipation is Counter-revolution"].

1969   Begins his therapeutic work as a psychoanalyst, but gives this up after three years in order to focus exclusively on political work.

1970   Takes in and adopts a mortally ill three-year old child, whom he cares for until it is healthy again. Marries in an attempt to combine the concept of free love with the institution of marriage. This project fails in 1974.

1972   Intense studies of Teilhard de Chardin, Wilhelm Reich, and G.W.F. Hegel. Develops a dialectic worldview as a prelude to the holographic concept, which he developed later. Theoretical and practical work on various forms of living together, whereby socialist thinking was expanded and deepened by the vision of free love. Attempts to "overtake the communist idea on the left" by expanding it to the erotic area. Writes a book entitled *"Die Liebe und die Linke"* ("Love and the Left"), which is never published since his indignant wife throws the manuscript into the Neckar river.

1974   In spite of several offers to become a professor, Duhm leaves the university and his political work, explaining this decision in his book *"Der Mensch ist anders"* ["The Human Being is Different"]. Re-awakening of his religious interests: intense studies of the history of religion, spirituality, nature, ecology, and sexuality. Undertakes dangerous experiments with drugs, in order to systematically explore the spiritual spaces of extrasensory abilities and transcendental experiences. Without drugs, he then has revelations about the sacred and holistic structure of reality. Begins years of travel and learning, including visits to Friedrichshof, the notorious "sex commune" in the Austrian province of Burgenland, which was founded by Otto Mühl. Overcomes his initial antipathy against such collective projects and takes a public stand for the necessity of carrying out the kind of work that occurs there. Many leftist bookstores therefore refuse to carry his books.

1976   Experiences a spiritual crisis and is plagued by doubts and depression. 5 months' contemplative retreat in an isolated farmhouse in Niederbayern.

1978   Founds the "Bauhütte" Project, which was to lead to today's "Tamera" project in Portugal. Created the first functioning community. Met Sabine Lichtenfels with whom he soon guided the project.

1979   His book *"Synthese der Wissenschaft – der werdende Mensch"* ["Synthesis of Science – the Emerging Human Being"] is published.

1982   His book *"Aufbruch zur neuen Kultur"* ["Toward a New Culture"] is published. Takes up painting again after a break of twenty years.

1983   Leads the great community experiment in Schwand/Black Forest (until 1986). Beginning of the healing work. Surprising discoveries about the appearance and disappearance of bodily symptoms. Systematic exploration and use of "self-healing forces". Develops ideas about a larger project.

1985   Beginning of the cult campaign.

1986   Height of the cult campaign. First thoughts of emigrating.

1990   Lives in Lanzarote in preparation of the Healing Biotopes Project (until 1995).

1991   His book *"Der unerlöste Eros"* ["Eros Unredeemed"] is published.

1992   His book *"Politische Texte für eine gewaltfreie Erde"* ["Political Texts for a Non-violent Earth"] is published.

1995   Beginning of the creation of the first healing biotope "Tamera" in Portugal.

1999   Establishes the Institute for Global Peace Work (IGF).

2001   Works to prepare "Tamera Arts", a center for art and healing, in which the life-oriented basic principles underlying the healing work are to be developed within the medium of artistic creation, for the healing of the human being and nature.

Recommended Literature

Basic literature

Braunroth, Eike. In Harmonie mit den Naturwesen in Garten. Feld und Flur, Xanten, Organischer Landbau, 1997.

Dahl, Jürgen. Der unbegreifliche Garten und seine Verwüstung. Klett-Cotta, Stuttgart, 1995.

Deschner, Karlheinz. Das Kreuz mit der Kirche. Econ, Düsseldorf, 1986.

Duhm, Dieter. Towards a New Culture. Trans. Sten Linnander. Meiga, Belzig, 1993.

Duhm, Dieter. Eros Unredeemed. Berghoff & friends, Belzig, 1998.

Eisler, Riane. The Chalice and the Blade. Harper and Row, London, 1987.

Ghazal, Eluan. Schlangenkult und Tempelliebe. Heyne, Munich, 1999.

Lichtenfels, Sabine. Quellen der Liebe und des Friedens. Morgenandachten. SYNergie, Belzig, 2001.

Lichtenfels, Sabine. Tempel der Liebe. SYNergie, Belzig, 2001.

Lichtenfels, Sabine. Traumsteine. Hugendubel, Munich, 2000.

Lichtenfels, Sabine. Weiche Macht. Berghoff & friends, Belzig, 1996.

Lusseyran, Jacques. And there was light. Trans. Elizabeth R. Cameron. Floris, Edinburgh, 1985.

Lusseyran, Jacques. Ein neues Sehen der Welt. Freies Geistesleben, Stuttgart, 1996.

Talbot, Michael. The Holographic Universe, HarperCollins, New York, 1991.

Further recommended literature

Alexandersson, Olof. Living Water – Viktor Schauberger and the secrets of natural energy. Trans. K. and C. Zweigbergk. Gateway, 1994.

Alt, Franz. Jesus – der erste neue Mann. Piper, Munich, 1992.

Bach, Richard. Illusions – The Adventures of a Reluctant Messiah. Dell Publishing Company, 1991.

Bloch, Ernst. The Principle of Hope. Trans. Neville Plaice. Blackwell, Oxford, 1985

Boer, Hans de. Gesegnete Unruhe. Lamuv, Göttingen, 2000.

Boer, Hans de. Unterwegs erfahren. Peter Hammer, Wuppertal, 1989.

Bohm, David. Wholeness and the Implicated Order. Routledge, London, 1980.

Briggs, J. & Peat, F.D. Seven Life Lessons of Chaos – Spiritual Wisdom from the Science of Change. McGraw – Hill, New York, 1999.

Bumb, Birger & Möller, Beate (Eds.). Sommercamp im Wilden Westen. Meiga, Belzig, 1990.

Caddy, Peter. In Perfect Timing. Findhorn Press, Findhorn, 1997.

Chardin, Teilhard de. Der Mensch im Kosmos. Beck, München, 1994.

Coats, Callum. Living Energies - An Exposition of Concepts related to the Theories of Viktor Schauberger. Gateway, Bath, 1996.

Daimler, Renate. Verschwiegene Lust. Frauen über 60 erzählen von Liebe und Sexualität. Deuticke, Wien, 1999.

Delbée, Anne. Camille Claudel. Circe, 1995.

Deschner, Karlheinz. Für einen Bissen Fleisch. Aku-Presse, Bad Nauheim, 1998.

Deschner, Karlheinz. all other publications

Drewermann, Eugen. (All his books are intellectually fine and humane, making them readable in spite of their different orientation.)

Duhm, Dieter. Political Theory for a Non-Violent Earth. Meiga, Belzig, 1992.

Duhm, Dieter. Synthese der Wissenschaft. Kübler, Heidelberg, 1979.

Elworthy, Scilla. Power and Sex. Vega, London, 1996.

Estés, Clarissa. Women who run with the Wolves – Myths and Stories of the Wild Woman Archetype. Ballantine Books, 1997.

Fukuoka, Masanobu. The One Straw Revolution – An Introduction to Natural Farming, Rodale Press, 1978.

Geller, Uri. My Story. Robson Books, London, 1975.

Gogh, Vincent van. Worte wie Feuer. Herder, Freiburg, 1992.

Göttner-Abendroth, Heide. Das Matriarchat I. Geschichte seiner Erforschung. Kohlhammer, Stuttgart, 1995.

Göttner-Abendroth, Heide. Das Matriarchat II,1. Stammesgesellschaften in Ostasien, Indonesien, Ozeanien. Kohlhammer, Stuttgart, 1999.

Haetzel, Klaus. Wege auf Wasser und Feuer. Econ, Düsseldorf, 1990.

Helsing, Jan van. Secret Societies and their Power in the 20th Century - A Guide through the Entanglements of Lodges with High Finance and Politics. Ewertverlag, Gran Canaria, 1995.

Heufelder, Jeannette. Gloria Cuartas, Bürgermeisterin für den Frieden. Portrait der kolumbianischen Menschenrechtskämpferin. Lamuv, Göttingen, 1999.

Heyn, Dalma. The Erotic Silence of the Married Woman. Bloomsbury, London, 1992.

Hill, Julia Butterfly. The Legacy of Luna – the story of a tree, a woman, and the struggle to save the redwoods. Harper, San Francisco, 2000.

Horstmann, Ulrich. Das Untier. Suhrkamp, Frankfurt, 1985.

Jong, Erica. Fear of Flying. Panther, St.Albans, 1976.

Kelly, Petra; Bastian, Gert; Ludwig, Klemens. The Anguish of Tibet. Parallax Press, California, 1991.

Kleinhammes, Sabine (Ed.). Rettet den Sex. Ein Manifest von Frauen für einen neuen sexuellen Humanismus. Meiga, Belzig, 1988.

Langer, Felicia. Zorn und Hoffnung. Lamuv, Göttingen, 1996.

Leon, Donna. Latin Lover. Zürich, Diogenes, 1999.

Leonard, George. The Silent Pulse – A Search for the Perfect Rhythm that Exists in Each of Us. Dutton, 1978.

Lichtenfels, Sabine. Der Hunger hinter dem Schweigen. Annäherung an sexuelle und spirituelle Wirklichkeiten. Meiga, Belzig, 1992.

Long, Barry. Making Love – sexual love the divine way. Barry Long Books, London, 1998.

Manitonquat. The Circle Way. 2000.

Manitonquat. Return to Creation. Bear Tribe Publishing, WA, 1991.

Manning, Jeane; Begich, Nick. Angels don't play this HAARP – Advances in Tesla Technology. Earthpulse Press, Alaska, 1995.

McLean, Dorothy. To Hear the Angels Sing. Floris Books, Edinburgh, 1980.

Menschu, Rigoberta. An Indian Woman in Guatemala. Verso Books, London, 1987.

Messner, Reinhold. Free Spirit – A Climber's Life. Mountaineers Books, 1998.

Miller, Alice. Breaking the Wall of Silence. Virago, London, 1991.

Miller, Alice. Am Anfang war Erziehung. Suhrkamp, Frankfurt, 1980.

Miller, Henry. The Smile at the foot of the Ladder. Village Press, London, 1973.

Miller, Henry. Sexus. Olympia Press, Paris, 1960.

Moody, Raymond. Life after Life: the investigation of a phenomenon, survival of bodily death. Bantam, London, 1976.

Mühl, Otto. Aus dem Gefängnis. Ritter, Klagenfurt, 1997.

Mühl, Otto. Otto Mühl 7 (Exhibition catalog). Hatje Cantz, Stuttgart, 1998.

Muigg, Norbert. Sprache des Herzens. Begegnungen mit Weisen der Maya. Ibera, Wien, 1999.

Nicols, Preston B. & Moon, Peter. The Montauk Project. Sky Books, New York, 1992.

Nietzsche, Friedrich. The Genealogy of Morals. Dover Publishers, 2003.

Nigg, Walter. Das Buch der Ketzer. Diogenes, Zürich, 1998.

Osho. Meditation. Boxtree, London, 1995.

Pfau, Ruth. Das letzte Wort wird Liebe sein. Herder, Freiburg, 1998.

Pfau, Ruth. Verrückter kann man gar nicht leben. Herder, Freiburg, 1995.

Pogačnic, Marko. Die Erde heilen. Das Modell Türnich, München, Diederichs, 1996.

Reich, Wilhelm. The Mass psychology of Fascism. Trans. V.R. Carfagno. Penguin, Harmondsworth, 1975.

Reich, Wilhelm. The Discovery of the Orgone. Trans. Andrew White. Vision Press, London, 1974.

Reich, Wilhelm. The Murder of Christ. Souvenir Press, London, 1975.

Ritchie, George G. & Sherill, Elizabeth. Return from Tomorrow. U.S, 1978.

Risi, Armin. Machtwechsel auf der Erde. Govinda, Neuhausen, 1999.

Roger, Frère. Der Weg der Versöhnung. Gütersloher Verlagshaus, Gütersloh, 1985.

Schipflinger, Thomas. Sophia – Maria: a holistic vision of creation. Wieser, York Beach, 1997.

Schubart, Walter. Religion und Eros. Beck, München, 1989.

Schwepcke, Barbara. Aung San Suu Kyi – Heldin von Burma. Herder, Freiburg, 1999.

Schwenk, Theodor. Sensitive Chaos. Trans. Olive Whicher. Rudolf Steiner Press, London, 1965.

Temple, Robert. The Sirius Mystery. Sidgwick and Jackson, London, 1976.

Tompkins, Peter & Bird, Christopher. The Secret life of Plants. Allen Lane, London, 1973.

Ywahoo, Dhyani. Voices of our Ancestors. Shambhala, London, 1987.

Zillmer, Hans-Joachim. Darwins Mistake – Antediluvian Discoveries Prove Dinosaurs and Humans Co-Existed. Adventures Unlimited Press, 2003.

Zorn, Fritz. Mars. Trans. Robert Kimber. Knopf, New York, 1982.

VERLAG MEIGA
For a Future Without War

English Edition:

Sabine Lichtenfels: **Sources of Love and Peace. Morning Prayers** (2003)

Dieter Duhm: **Future without War. Theory of Global Healing** (2006)

Sabine Lichtenfels: **GRACE. Pilgrimage for a Future without War** (2006)

Dieter Duhm: **Eros Unredeemed. The World Power of Sexuality** (2010)

Leila Dregger: **Tamera. A Model for the Future** (2010)

Sabine Lichtenfels: **Temple of Love. A journey into the age of sexual fulfilment** (2012)

Dieter Duhm: **Towards a New Culture. From Refusal to Re-Creation. Outline of an Ecological and Humane Alternative** (2012)

Martin Winiecki: **Setting Foundations for a New Culture. Perspectives for the Global Revolution. Study Materials from the Terra Nova School** (2013)

Preview: Dieter Duhm, Sabine Lichtenfels: **The Erotic Manifesto**